D1603059

Sparta and Lakonia

States and Cities of Ancient Greece

Edited by
R. F. WILLETTS

Argos and the Argolid
R. A. Tomlinson

The Foundations of Palatial Crete
K. Branigan

Mycenaean Greece
J. T. Hooker

The Dorian Aegean
Elizabeth M. Craik

Sparta and Lakonia

A Regional History 1300–362 BC

Paul Cartledge

Lecturer in Ancient History
University of Cambridge

Routledge & Kegan Paul
London, Boston and Henley

First published in 1979
by Routledge & Kegan Paul Ltd
39 Store Street, London WC1E 7DD,
Broadway House, Newtown Road,
Henley-on-Thames, Oxon RG9 1EN and
9 Park Street, Boston, Mass. 02108, USA
Printed in Great Britain by
Redwood Burn Ltd, Trowbridge & Esher

British Library Cataloguing in Publication Data

Cartledge, Paul
Sparta and Lakonia – (States and cities of
ancient Greece)
1 Laconia – History
2 Sparta – History
I Title II Series
938'.9   DF261.L/   79–40977
ISBN 0 7100 0377 3

2249728

To Judith Portrait

Contents

Contents

Figures

Sparta and Lakonia

Preface

The basis of this book was laid in an unpublished doctoral
thesis Early Sparta c.950-650 BC: an Archaeological and
Historical Study (Oxford 1975). To my former supervisor,
Professor J. Boardman, and my examiners, Professors C.M.
Robertson and W.G. Forrest, I am principally indebted for
its conception and fruition. It could not, however, have
been completed without the unstinting assistance of many
archaeologists, historians and geographers, the staffs of
museums and libraries in Greece, Ireland and England, and
grants from research funds in the Universities of Dublin
and Oxford. The following scholars and friends are owed
especial thanks: R. Beckinsale, D. Bell, J.N. Coldstream,
K. Demakopoulou-Papantoniou, the late V. Desborough,
L. Marangou, G.E.M. de Ste. Croix, G. Steinhauer (Acting
Ephor of Lakonia), E. Touloupa, P.M. Warren, J.G. Younger.
The present book represents a considerable expansion,
conceptual as well as geographical and chronological, of
the thesis. It is not primarily a political history, but
an attempt, inevitably provisional, to map out a new kind
of history of ancient Sparta - one which does justice as
well to the area unified and exploited by the Spartans as
to the inhabitants of the central place. The inspiration
to write it was provided by the invitation of Professor
R.F. Willetts to contribute to the series of which he is
general editor. I wish to thank him and Mr N. Franklin
for their constant encouragement and helpful criticism.
Drafts of various chapters have also been read and greatly
improved by O.T.P.K. Dickinson, W.W. Phelps, J.B. Salmon
and G.E.M. de Ste. Croix. None of these of course should
be regarded as incriminated by the results, for which I
alone bear full responsibility.
I am also most grateful to the following for permission
to reproduce, sometimes in modified form, published maps
and illustrations: the Managing Committee of the British

xiii

School at Athens; the Swedish Institute in Athens;
J. Bintliff, J.N. Coldstream, R. Hope Simpson and W.A.
McDonald (Director of the Minnesota Messenia Expedition).

Trinity College, Dublin
June 1978   P.A.C.

Notes on the spelling
of Greek words and on dates

Consistency in the transliteration of Greek words is impossible of attainment. In general I have preferred to reproduce Greek letters by their nearest English equivalents
rather than Latinize them: thus Krokeai not Croceae, Lykourgos not Lycurgus. On the other hand, Lysandros for
Lysander, and similarly for other 'household' names, must
have seemed merely pedantic.

Unless otherwise specified, all dates are BC.

Part I
Introduction

2

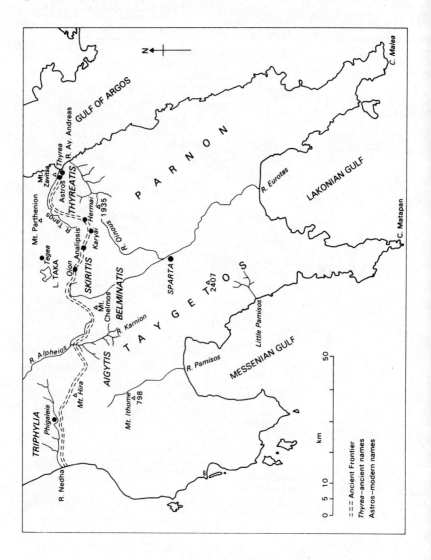

FIGURE 1 The frontiers of Sparta c.545

1 Boundaries

'Without a geographical basis the people, the makers of
history, seem to be walking on air.' So wrote Jules Mich-
elet in the 1869 Preface to his celebrated 'Histoire de
France' - but in vain, it seems, so far as most historians
of Sparta have been concerned. For it remains as true of
them today as it was of historians in general in the nineteenth century that, once the de rigueur introductory
sketch of geographical conditions is out of the way, the
substantive analysis or narrative proceeds 'as if these
complex influences ... had never varied in power or method
during the course of a people's history' (Febvre 1925, 12).
   There is, however, perhaps even less excuse for this
outmoded and harmful attitude in studying classical Sparta
than in studying some other ancient Greek states. For, as
is well known, the Spartans throughout the period of their
greatest territorial expansion and political supremacy
(c.550-370) rested their power and prosperity on the necessarily broad backs of the Helots, the unfree agricultural labourers who lived concentrated in the relatively
fertile riverine valleys of the Eurotas in Lakonia and the
Pamisos in Messenia. And besides the Helots there literally 'dwelt round about' the Perioikoi, who were free men
living in partially autonomous communities and providing
certain essential services for the Spartans but farming
more marginal land. Any serious account of Spartan history therefore is obliged to make more than a token ges-
at understanding the mutual relationships of these three
groups of population. Thus it is with the 'infrastructure
of land allotments, helots and perioeci, with everything
that includes with respect to labour, production and circulation" (Finley 1975, 162) that this study will be
primarily concerned, in a determined effort to bring the
Spartans firmly down to earth.
   In this connection it is encouraging to note the recent

upturn of interest in a more broadly geographical and materialist approach to Graeco-Roman antiquity - not to mention prehistoric Mediterranean studies, where, as we shall
see in more detail in Chapters 4 and 6, the lack of written texts necessitates an overriding concern with the
total recoverable human and natural environment. A leading
exponent of Roman agrarian history has recently defined a
major desideratum as 'close study, region by region, of
the changing patterns of land use and agricultural production, supported by analysis of demographic and other
socio-economic data provided by our sources' (White 1967,
78). This applies equally to Greece. Moreover, not only
does he state the objective clearly, but he conveys too
the limitation imposed by the available evidence.

However, before the nature, extent and quality of the
evidence can be explored, a prior question obtrudes itself. What is a 'region'? The answer is not as straightforward as might at first blush be supposed, for it implies a solution to the notorious problem of frontiers or
boundaries. 'Natural' frontiers may have been consigned
for good to the conceptual rubbish-heap, but should they
be replaced by a strictly geographical, a vaguely cultural
or a broadly political notion of regional demarcation? I
have little doubt that for the geographically minded historian like myself, as opposed to the historical geo-
rapher, the third course is the one to be adopted. To
quote Lucien Febvre (1925, 311) once more, 'all States
consist of an amalgam of fragments, a collection of mor-
sels detached from different natural regions, which complement one another and become cemented together, and make
of their associated diversities a genuine unity.' Our
task therefore will be to explain how the frontiers of
Lakonia came to be fixed where they were and why from
time to time they fluctuated.

There have been many Lakonias. That is to say, 'Lakonia' has experienced many incarnations and metamorphoses
between the earliest use of the name (in late Roman or
early mediaeval times) and its present application to one
of the provinces of contemporary Greece. The Lakonia of
my title, however, is none of these. Indeed, the name is
convenient and useful precisely because it has no exact
political denotation for the period chiefly under consideration in this book, c.1300 to 362. It should serve
therefore as a constant reminder that the size of Lakonia
in antiquity varied directly in proportion to the strength
and inclinations of the inhabitants of its central place,
which from about 1500 has been located in the vicinity of
modern Sparta.

Frontiers should not of course be viewed as it were

from the outside; but if 'Lakonia' is to be used for purposes of description and analysis, it requires spatial
definition. It has seemed most convenient, and on balance
historically least misleading, to fix upon the status quo
of c.545, a high-water mark from which the Spartan tide
was not compelled to recede for almost two centuries.
Hence my Lakonia, like the ancient terms 'Lakedaimon' and
'Lakonike' (sc. ge), will also encompass south-west Peloponnese, which will be referred to hereafter for convenience as Messenia. I shall not, however, use 'Lakonia' to
obliterate the separate identity of Messenia in the way
that 'Lakedaimon' and 'Lakonike' designedly did. For I
shall be principally concerned with Lakonia in a narrower
and more familiar sense, roughly the territory east of the
Taygetos mountain range (but including the whole of the
Mani). This is primarily because this smaller Lakonia was
the heartland and laboratory in which the Spartans first
experimented with the system whose essentials they later
transferred to Messenia, but also because the evidence for
Messenia has recently been collected, sifted and published
(admittedly with a primary emphasis on the Late Bronze Age)
in exemplary fashion by the University of Minnesota Messenia Expedition (MME; cf. now Meyer 1978).

Our sources for the frontier consist of scattered not-
ices in ancient authors, especially Strabo and Pausanias,
and those physiographical features that have undergone no
- or no significant - alteration since our period. (Epigraphical evidence, apart from some dubious cuttings in
the living rock at Arkadian Kryavrysi, is confined to the
western frontier of the reduced Lakonia after the liberation of Messenia from the Spartan yoke in c.370: Chapter
15.) Needless to say, no ancient literary source made a
consistent effort to define the extent of territory under
Spartan control at any given point in history, so all due
credit should go to Friedrich Boelte, the first scholar to
appreciate and exploit the potential of clear and detailed
geological maps (Boelte 1929, 1303-15).

On the east, south and west Lakonia is bounded by the
Mediterranean. Only in the north are the geographical
limits blurred, and even here the lack of clarity is merely in detail, for the main outline can be simply described. Once the Thyreatis (ancient Kynouria) had fallen permanently to Sparta as the prize for winning the 'Battle of
the Champions' in c.545, the frontier ran from a point on
the east coast some twenty kilometres north of modern
Astros (near ancient Thyrea) along a range of hills above
the River Tanos east of Mount Parthenion (1,093 m.).
Westwards the border was formed by the watershed of the Eurotas and the tributaries of the east Arkadian plain. To

the west of the Taygetos range the northern frontier of
Messenia skirts the southern edge of the plain of Megalo-
polis. West of the latter it loops round the ancient
Mount Hira (864 m.) to run out into the sea along the
Nedha valley, the southern boundary of the transitional
region of Triphylia.

The details are more complex, but the Thyreatis at
least poses few problems. It is bounded on the north by
Mount Zavitsa, on the west by the Parnon mountain range
and in the south by the river of Ay. Andreas. In the mid-
second century AD the frontiers of the Spartans, Argives
and Tegeans met on the ridges of Parnon (Paus. 2.38.7).
Thus if the Hermai have been correctly identified at modern Phonemenoi (Rhomaios 1905, 137f.; 1951, 235f.), the
frontier will have made the expected abrupt turn south of
Mount Parthenion and followed Parnon in a southerly direction for about ten kilometres.

Our next evidence consists in the identification of
Perioikic Karyai, which lay on the ancient frontier. It
almost certainly occupied the vicinity of modern Arachova
(now renamed Karyai) a short way south-east of Analipsis,
which remains a border-village to this day (Loring 1895,
54-8, 61;Rhomaios 1960, 376-8, 394). The statement of
Pausanias (8.54.1) that the River Alpheios marked the border between Spartan and Tegeate territory has caused difficulties, perhaps to be resolved by identifying Pausanias'
Alpheios with the river of Analipsis, the uppermost course
of the Sarandapotamos, which either did, or was believed
to, form part of the great Alpheios (Wade-Gery 1966, 297f.,
302).

Our next clue is the frequent mention in the sources of
the sub-region of Skiritis, whose control was vital to
Sparta since it lay athwart routes from Arkadia to Lakonia
and Messenia. Boelte identified Skiritis with the crys-
alline schist zone between the River Kelephina (ancient
Oinous) and the Eurotas to west of the 'saddle' of Lakonia. This is in harmony with the fact that the only ancient settlement in Skiritis accorded independent mention in
the sources is Oion, a frontier-village and guardpost
which was probably situated in a small ruined tract north
of modern Arvanito-Kerasia (Andrewes in Gomme 1970, 33).
In other words, at Analipsis the ancient frontier deviated
sharply from its modern counterpart and moved north-west
to make considerable inroads into the present-day province
of Arkadia.

West of the headwaters of the Eurotas Mount Chelmos
rises to 776 m. above sea-level. The region at its foot
has been securely identified with ancient Belmina or Belminatis (other variant spellings are found). This was a

frontier-zone hotly disputed between Sparta and Megalopolis after the foundation of the latter in 368 (Chapter 13)
as much for its abundant water-supply as for its strategic
position (Howell 1970, 101, no. 53). In the extreme
north-west angle of Lakonia lay Aigytis, a large trough
drained to the north-west by the River Xerillos (ancient
Karnion). Entering Messenia Mount Hira, like Andania further south (MME 94, no. 607?), is perhaps best known for
its role in the final stage of the Spartan conquest in the
seventh century. Further expansion to the north was bar-
red at this point by Phigaleia, but neither Phigaleia nor
Elis was able to prevent Sparta from exercising a fitful
de facto control over Triphylia, perhaps from as early as
the late eighth century. Messenia proper, however, was
bounded on the north by the Nedha valley, a 'natural no-
man's land' (Chadwick 1976a, 39).

Such was the area available to the Spartans from c.545,
some 'two-fifths of the Peloponnese' according to an ancient estimate (Thuc. 1.10.2) or about 8,500 km^2. No other
polis (city-state) could compete: Athens, for example,
Sparta's nearest rival, commanded only about 2,500. Mere
size, however, does not by itself account for the power
and influence wielded by Sparta for so long a period. The
question which the present work will attempt to answer is
how, and in particular how efficiently, did Sparta utilize
the possibilities afforded by this (in Greek terms) enormous land-mass.

We must conclude this first introductory chapter by
looking at a second, and in some ways the most important,
boundary, the one fixed by the available source-material.
Greek geography, broadly interpreted, developed alongside
history as a branch of Ionian 'historie' (enquiry) in the
sixth and fifth centuries. But whereas history (in something like the modern sense) was an invention of the fifth
century (Chapter 5), 'scientific' geography was a Hellenistic creation. At the threshold of the latter epoch
stood Theophrastos, the most distinguished pupil and successor of Aristotle at the Lyceum, to whom we owe the
first fumblings towards a systematic botany and geology.
Theophrastos by himself, however, despite his frequent
references to Lakonia, is totally inadequate for our purposes and must be supplemented by ancient literary evidence of the most disparate origins and of correspondingly
disparate value. We have already met Thucydides, Strabo
and Pausanias: in what follows I shall have occasion to
draw on - among many others - Alkman, Herodotus, Aristophanes, Plato, Vitruvius and Athenaios. By no means all
of these inform us directly of conditions in Lakonia, or
even of conditions in our special period; many have no

interest in the information for its own sake; all too
often they convey only the extremes experienced, precisely
because they were extreme.

There are, though, two main types of evidence by which
the unsatisfactory literary sources can be complemented or
corrected, archaeology and modern scientific data relating
to all aspects of the environment. Controlled excavation
in Lakonia has for a variety of reasons been lamentably
slight, a deficiency that for many historical purposes is
irremediable. There are, however, other methods of building up the archaeological record besides excavation, and
in the following chapters I shall be discussing, and utilizing the results of, all available archaeological techniques. Here, however, I propose to examine briefly what
I take to be the inherent limitations of archaeological
material as historical evidence, regardless of the quantity or quality of the available data (ideally of course
data susceptible of statistical analysis). For even
though the spade may be congenitally truthful, 'it owes
this merit at least in part to the fact that it cannot
speak' (Grierson 1959, 129). Material remains, in other
words, may be authentic testimony to the times they represent, but they are not self-explanatory, and a longstanding dispute concerns itself with the problem of precisely what kinds of inference it is possible or legitimate to draw from them. This dispute has of late received
a fresh injection of vitality from the so-called 'new'
archaeologists, who (in the words of a leading spokesman)
advocate a 'shift to a rigorous hypotheticodeductive
method with the goal of explanation' and believe 'there is
every reason to expect that the empirical properties of
artifacts and their arrangement in the archaeological record will exhibit attributes which can inform on different
phases of the artifact's life-history' (Binford 1972, 96,
94).

Now while I agree wholeheartedly with the stated aim of
the 'new' archaeologists of explaining whole societies in
systematic terms, I have to confess my profound disagreement on two counts. First, I do not believe that our categories of social analysis are yet sufficiently fine to be
capable of expression in the form of laws from which de-
ductions may automatically be made. Symptomatically, the
'new' archaeologists have been surprisingly happy to oper-
ate with models which resemble 'parables' and betoken
'creeping crypto-totalitarianism' (Andreski 1972, ch. 13).
Second, I remain firmly within the camp of such 'old'
archaeologists as Piggott (1959, ch. 1) on the question of
what kinds of inference one may legitimately draw from the
accidentally surviving durable remains of complex social

arrangements. I believe, in short, that there is a hierarchy or pyramid of levels at which material data may be
explained in economic, political and social terms. From
archaeological evidence alone we may infer (relatively)
much about material techniques, a considerable amount
about patterns of subsistence and utilization of the
environment, far less about social and political events
and institutions, and least of all about mental structures,
religious and other 'spiritual' ideas and beliefs. To
take a simple example, the fact that the art of Sparta's
colony Taras was largely in the Spartan tradition does not
by itself show that political relations with the mother-
city were cordial: the art of Kerkyra was wholly in the
Corinthian tradition, and yet we know from literary sources of political friction, even outright warfare, between
Kerkyra and Corinth from an early date (Boardman 1973,
219). This is not of course to deny that technique and
subsistence-patterns may themselves imply non-material
features of social existence. It is to deny that there
are assured criteria whereby one may automatically infer
the latter from the former. For 'there is sufficient
evidence that identical artifacts and arrangements of
artifacts can result from different socio-economic
arrangements of procurement, manufacture or distribution'
(Finley 1975, 90).

On the other hand, the 'new' archaeologists - apart
from those who adopt a non-historical or anti-historical
approach - have performed a signal service in asking questions which 'old' archaeologists, especially perhaps those
whose business is with the classical Graeco-Roman world,
had considered either outside their province or not worth
asking. To this extent 'social archaeology' (Renfrew
1973) represents a major step in the right direction, and
it is to be hoped that the questions, techniques and
methods it employs (minus the inappropriate 'systems' models) will consistently be directed to the material remains
of Graeco-Roman antiquity both in their excavation and in
their interpretation.

The rest of this chapter will consider how far the historian of ancient Lakonia can use modern scientific data
to eke out, modify or explain the notoriously unstatistic-
al ancient sources. Here we are brought hard up against
the recalcitrant problem of climatic change. For, since
climate influences human social behaviour primarily
through the medium of the plant, and since we are relatively well informed on the agricultural potentialities of
contemporary Lakonia, it is essential to assess first how
far the climate in our period resembled that known to have
prevailed in the last century or so and then whether it

had remained more or less constant in the interim.

Climate itself, however, is a complex concept. Its
basic conditions have been elucidated as follows (Lamb
1974, 197): the radiation balance; the heat and moisture
brought and carried away by the winds and ocean currents;
the local conditions of aspect towards the midday sun and
prevailing winds; the thermal characteristics of the soil
and vegetation cover; and the reflectivity of the surface.
Human influence on climate, though by no means negligible,
is problematic (Mason 1977). Thus the reconstruction of
past climate involves a variety of techniques, mainly
scientific. Progress in their application has brought the
realization that a rigorous distinction must be drawn between climatic fluctuations or oscillations, which are
regular and occur in cycles ranging from decades to centuries (intervals of 200 and 400 years appear to be quite
prominent), and climatic changes, which are relatively
infrequent.

However, it is also clear from the extent of disagreement among experts that there is, in the first place, room
for more than reasonable doubt as to which of the basic
conditions of climate are decisive for climatic change;
and, second, that for many periods of antiquity there is
insufficient evidence to decide for or against the inference of a climatic change as opposed to a fluctuation or
oscillation. These two points are well illustrated by a
controversy affecting the interpretation of the late prehistoric and early historical period in Greece. In 1966
Rhys Carpenter put forward the hypothesis that the downfall of Mycenaean civilization and the impoverishment of
the ensuing Dark Age were due in part to a shift in the
prevailing trade winds which brought on extended drought
lasting perhaps as late as 750. This hypothesis has received qualified approval on the climatological side from
Lamb and others, but another expert, H.E. Wright, whose
views pack the extra punch of first-hand experience in the
relevant area and period, has not only impugned the atmospheric mechanism invoked by Carpenter but adduced pollen
evidence which certainly does not confirm and may even re-
fute the hypothesis of extended drought (Wright 1968).
But in case anyone should be overawed by this seemingly
'hard' evidence, note should also be taken of the opinion
of a colleague of Wright, W.G. Loy (1970, 43), that, although drought may never be 'proven as the cause of the
Mycenaean downfall, it is even less likely that it will be
disproven as a major or at least contributing cause for
the apparent depopulation of the southwest Peloponnese
during the sub-Mycenaean period'.

The lay onlooker has every right to feel baffled in

face of such confusion and apparent contradictions. However, even if Carpenter's hypothesis should be proved correct, much of our period remains unaffected. More important still, an authoritative historical geographer has recently expressed what appears to be the more representative view that during this epoch 'in the Mediterranean region the climate was probably not perceptibly different from that of today' (Pounds 1973, 14). We may therefore cautiously adopt the working hypothesis that the climate of Lakonia in our period more or less closely resembled that of the present day (Chapter 3).

It still remains, however, to ask whether the climate in this region has remained substantially constant since the fourth century BC, and the answer is that it has not. That we may answer thus unequivocally is due to the intensive application to Greece by Bintliff (1977) of the findings of Vita-Finzi (1969) in the Mediterranean valleys generally. To summarize, the geomorphology of contemporary Greece differs radically from that of Greece in our period in that today's prime arable land, the 'Younger Fill', is ultimately the product of a climatic fluctuation occurring in the late Roman and mediaeval periods. The prime arable land of antiquity, on the other hand, was the 'Older Fill' laid down by at the latest 20,000. Both the 'Older' and 'Younger' Fills were generated, according to Bintliff, by cold and wet ('pluvial') climatic phases, between which there was sandwiched a warmer, dryer phase more akin to that obtaining today. It was this warmer, dryer climate which Lakonia enjoyed during our period. The most striking implications of Bintliff's research for our subject will be disclosed in Chapter 10, but it has of course a wider importance. For it bears on all matters relating to the utilization of the physical environment.

Not, to return to Febvre, that the physical environment is a narrowly determining factor in human history. Perhaps the chief merit of Febvre 1925 was to develop the insights of Vidal de la Blache, who rigorously distinguished between the possibilities and necessities offered or imposed by a given environment. On the other hand, Febvre perhaps did not go far enough. As I hope to show, it is the conditions of production, the economic basis of human society, which in the long run explain the nature and direction of social and political change.

NOTES ON FURTHER READING

The conception of 'human geography' developed by Gourou (1973) owes much to Febvre, to whose memory the book is dedicated.   The ideas of Vidal are conveniently brought together in the posthumous Vidal de la Blache 1926.

For a distinguished survey of the role of the environment in the Mediterranean, focused on the sixteenth century AD but with an enormously wider application, see Braudel 1972, I.   A start has been made in the study of Greece from a regional and ecological standpoint by Doxiadis and his 'ekistics' school, but this seems on the whole to be a false one: see Wagstaff 1975.   Bakhuizen 1975 is on the right lines.

A map of the contemporary provinces ('nomoi') of Greece is given in ESAG no. 107.

For the history of ancient geography see Aujac 1975; Pédech 1976.

For all my strictures on the 'new' archaeology, there is much of value in Renfrew 1972 (esp. the first four chapters) and 1973.

Rhys Carpenter's hypothesis of a prolonged drought from c.1200 is considered in context in Chapter 6.

2 The physical setting

The separation of the Peloponnese from the mainland and
its upheaval to its present altitudes can be shown to be
geologically recent from the strong resemblances in structure and relief between the mountains of the Peloponnese
and those of central Greece both east and west of the
Isthmus (of Corinth). At the end of the Pliocene (about
two million years ago) much of the peninsula was still
covered by a shallow sea or lakes, while the remainder
consisted of subdued mountains or hills. When the crust
eventually began to break irregularly, the bottoms of new
gulfs sank as bordering land was thrust up. This new land
around the margins ('Neogen') was composed of clays,
marls, sands and conglomerates, the old inland region being made up mainly of limestone.

Tectonically Lakonia, as we have defined it, falls into
six sections. (The geomorphology of Messenia is discussed
more briefly in Chapter 8.) From east to west they are:
the east Parnon foreland; Parnon; the west Parnon foreland, including the Malea peninsula; the Eurotas furrow;
Taygetos, including ancient Aigytis and Dentheliatis; and
the west Taygetos foreland. The principal features of
their relief and geology may now be described in this same
order.

The east Parnon foreland extends south from Mount Zavitsa to Cape Ieraka, where the Parnon range sheers off ob-
liquely and runs out into the sea. It takes the form of
an inverted triangle whose base is formed by the Parthenion mountains and their continuation eastwards as far as
the pass of Anigraia. The region subdivides naturally into a northern section, the ancient Thyreatis or Kynouria
(the ancient names were interchangeable: Meyer 1969), and
a southern section south of the river of Ay. Andreas.
These differ from each other especially in geological composition. The Thyreatis is a high upland plateau, made up

13

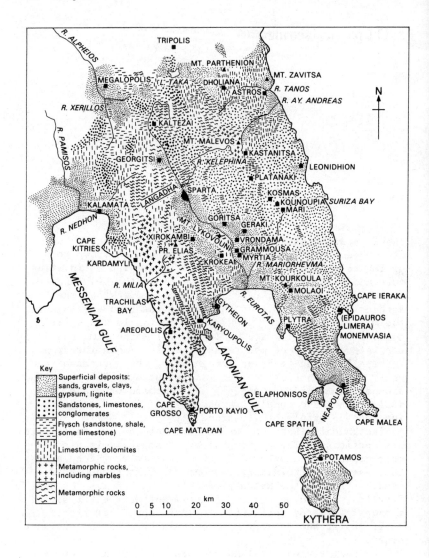

FIGURE 2   The geology of Lakonia

principally of Olonos limestone but overlain sporadically
by schist, whose imperviousness provides spring water and
so encourages settlement (Bintliff 1977, 100). The cultural centre in antiquity was the deltaic alluvial plain
of modern Astros formed by the action of the River Tanos
and that of Ay. Andreas which flow into the sea just six
kilometres apart. The southern section of the foreland by
contrast is mainly Tripolis limestone and, so far as is
known, schist occurs only on the margins of Parnon. The
coastline is the steep edge of a typical karstic plateau
broken by a fault. The area around Leonidhion (ancient
Prasiai) gives a good idea of the character of the area as
a whole. Inland the broad, high plateaux for the most
part reach 800 m. close to Parnon, fall away to 600 m.
further east, only to rise once more towards the coast,
this time to 1,200 m. The disappearance of the eastern
portion of the foreland through foundering has caused the
underground water of the remainder to flow steeply to the
sea and made the surface more waterless than ever.

Not unexpectedly, therefore, settlements are today few
and relatively large. Communications both within the
foreland and between it and the rest of Lakonia are poor.
True, the main route in antiquity from Sparta to Argos via
Tegea crossed the Thyreatis (Chapter 10). But north-
south travel by land was and is hindered by the deep, narrow and steep gulleys created by rivers flowing from Parnon, and there are no low passes over Parnon to link the
foreland to the Eurotas valley. Hence communication continues to be chiefly by sea from coastal settlement to
coastal settlement, although the exposure of the coast to
north-easterly winds must have made seafaring under ancient conditions perilous. These physiographical features
militated against the political unification of the area,
but this was nevertheless achieved by the Spartans, in the
teeth of Argive competition, after the middle of the sixth
century (Chapter 9).

The mountain range of Parnon (only once so called in an
ancient source, Paus. 2.38.7) is a residual ridge rising
quite gently from the plateau. Beginning in the hills
north of Dholiana it runs for ninety kilometres in a
south-easterly direction, the outermost spurs reaching the
sea north of Monemvasia (near ancient Epidauros Limera).
Its northern section, about thirty kilometres long, is on
average between 1,600 and 1,800 m. above sea-level. Here
the summit Mount Malevos (1,935 m.) is clad on both flanks
with fir and black pine. Despite the claim of Boelte
(1929, 1296) that the northernmost ridges are nowhere difficult to cross, although they are between 1,100 and
1,300 m., communication must always have been desultory.

Central Parnon occupies the twenty-two kilometres between
Platanaki Pass and Kounoupia ('mosquito-place' - ill-
omened name); like south Parnon, it is lower than the
northern section. Geographically and geologically Parnon
is but the continuation of the inner Arkadian chain, to
which it is joined by the broad threshold known in antiquity as Skiritis. The blue-grey, coarse-grained marble,
crystalline limestone and schist of the north give way to
Tripolis limestone south of Kosmas (ancient Glympeis/
Glyppia?). Above the fir woods, which grow in places at
1,750 m., 'alpine' grasses provide pasturage for the numerous sheep, which apart from sporadic charcoal- or lime-
burning today as in antiquity constitute the chief means
of livelihood in this inhospitable area.

The west foreland of Parnon may be subdivided into two.
The northern section to Goritsa expands southwards from
about six to fifteen kilometres in breadth. It is joined
to Skiritis, and thereby to the Eurotas furrow, on the
west and borders on the Spartan plain further south. Although it is predominantly a limestone plateau thinly
veiled by Kermes oak and phrygana (maquis-like scrub), im-
pervious mica-schists crop out to provide sites for fairly
large settlements. Skiritis geologically is a continuation of the central Arkadian highlands, but like Parnon
is distinguished from them by its substrate of schist.
The latter subdivides naturally at Kaltezai into a northern and southern section, the whole forming an inverted
triangle thirteen kilometres wide at the base and only
four at the apex where it disappears into the basin of
Sparta. South of the latitude of Sparta outcrops of mica-
schist become rarer, necessitating settlement on the limestone outliers of Parnon itself. Here the inhabitants are
forced to rely on cistern water, but this is not plentiful
since west Parnon falls in the rainshadow of Taygetos.

The southern section of the west Parnon foreland is for
the most part a mere three kilometres wide, but it broadens out to nine kilometres where it abuts on the north-
eastern perimeter of the Lakonian Gulf at Mount Kourkoula
(916 m.). Generally it does not rise above 500 m. and is
often hard to distinguish from Parnon itself. Worthy of
note is a series of basin plains ('Karstpolje') extending
south from Geraki (ancient Geronthrai) to the northern end
of the Molaoi plain and thence towards the bay of Monemvasia. Their surface is composed of relatively fertile
alluvial soil and contrasts with the surrounding area
where life-facilitating springs occur only on the impervi-
ous schist. The foreland with few exceptions has never
played any very important historical role and in recent
times has suffered severe depopulation.

The Malea peninsula continues the west foreland and not
Parnon. It is bounded on the north by a line running
N 55° W from Epidauros Limera to the northern end of the
plain of Molaoi and thence around Mount Kourkoula to the
Lakonian Gulf. From Molaoi to Cape Malea (of 'round Malea
and forget your home' notoriety) is a distance of fifty
kilometres; below Neapolis (ancient Boiai) the peninsula
is only five kilometres wide. Apart from a few depres-
sions filled with Pliocene deposit and alluvium, the upland is composed of strongly folded schists overlain by
massive black or grey Tripolis limestone. On the east the
highland descends abruptly to the sea, while on the west
groups of flat-topped hills fall steeply to the Lakonian
Gulf. Settlements today are located on the edges of
plains or at the junction of schist and limestone, as for
example the chain of villages near Neapolis. The area is
noted for its production of onions, part of which is exported. But in antiquity by far the most important natural resource it contained was iron (Chapter 7). Attempts
to re-open the workings in the last century failed for
lack of water, adequate transport and, it was said, enthusiasm on the part of the workers.
    Three offshore adjuncts of the Malea peninsula deserve
separate mention - Elaphonisos, Kythera and Antikythera.
In Pausanias' day, the second century AD, what is now the
island of Elaphonisos (ancient Onougnathos or 'Ass-jaw')
was still joined to the mainland (3.22.10). It had become
separated by at the latest AD 1677, and in the process of
separation at least one ancient settlement, the Bronze Age
site at Pavlopetri (Chapter 6), found its way underwater.
The cause of the separation is perhaps to be sought in a
eustatic rise in sea-level rather than in crustal movements due to earthquakes or in the compaction of sediments
(Bintliff 1977, 10-26, esp. 15, 25f.); but these are
troubled interpretative waters into which I need only dip
my toes. At any rate, the area has certainly been strongly affected by seismic activity during the period since
records have been kept (Galanopoulos 1964). Further up
the Lakonian Gulf at Plytra (ancient Asopos) submarine remains suggest a land-shift of at least two metres. Elaphonisos is now a roughly triangular slab of soft dark
limestone rising to 277 m. Its light and sandy topsoil is
liable to erosion and unsuitable for cultivation. For its
water-supply the population (a mere 673 in 1961) relies on
a few deep wells.
    Kythera belongs today to the province of Attiki. Prev-
iously it had been incorporated in the province of Argolis,
and it has often been somewhat distinct, historically,
from the rest of Lakonia - not least, as we shall see

(Chapter 4), in the Bronze Age. The separation of the island from the mainland is geologically recent: its structure is similar to that of the Malea peninsula, consisting
largely of Tripolis limestone. South of the limestone
hills around Cape Spathi a belt of schist stretches from
coast to coast as far south as Potamos, in whose vicinity
a fine-grained white marble is found. Despite the general
lack of fertile and cultivable land, the economy remains
primarily agricultural, supplemented by a plentiful supply
of seafood. The present-day pattern of settlement is dictated by considerations of security rather than accessib-
ility to natural resources, a reversal of the ancient
priorities.

Antikythera (variously named in antiquity) lies equidistant from Kythera and western Crete. It resembles an
oval with extended points, having a longitudinal axis of
ten kilometres and a maximum width of almost four. Its
plains and terraces rise to 364 m. and are composed of
marl up to 60 m. Although the island is poor in water and
mainly provides only fodder for goats (hence perhaps one
of its ancient names, Aigilia), it also yields barley in
the valleys and is self-supporting. However, population
density in 1961 was a paltry eight per km^2.

In the sharpest possible contrast the Eurotas furrow
is, and must always have been, the heartland of Lakonia:
population density in 1961 was sixty-eight per km^2. It
occupies an area of about 800 km^2. between the basin of
Megalopolis and the Lakonian Gulf. From a width of only
six kilometres in the north it broadens out to twenty-five
around the Gulf. Its relationship with the Megalopolis
basin is not clearly defined, for the upper reaches of the
latter spill over into the furrow at 500 m. without a
break, and the tributaries of the Alpheios and Eurotas are
linked by a valley watershed at 483 m. The furrow takes
its name from the Eurotas, the second largest river in the
Peloponnese, which flows mostly along its eastern margin
but is diverted below Goritsa to the western. Almost exactly in the centre of the furrow, on the Eurotas itself,
lies Sparta, the ancient and modern capital of Lakonia.
For convenience of exposition the furrow may be split into
four: a northern section stretching as far south as the
Langadha gorge on the west and the confluence of the Kelephina (ancient Oinous) and Eurotas on the east; the Spartan basin; a section comprising the hill-country of Vardhounia on the west and the Pliocene table of Vrondama on
the east; and finally the present Helos plain.

The northernmost section lies between north Taygetos
and Skiritis, whence flow the upper course and most important tributaries of the Eurotas. Geologically the upper

part of this section is Olonos limestone and flysch, the
lower schists. Population here has remained more or less
static since the end of the last century, but Georgitsi
(near ancient Pellana) has suffered appreciable depopulation, from 1,646 in 1928 to 984 in 1961.

The basin of Sparta lies between the sharply defined
central portion of Taygetos and Parnon. It is twenty-two
kilometres long, between eight and twelve kilometres wide,
and trends in a south-south-east direction. It was originally filled with Pliocene deposits of an inland sea, the
'Neogen' soil which formed the backbone of agriculture in
our period. But these have been partly removed by erosion
and partly overlain by the recent alluvium generated during the late Roman/mediaeval climatic oscillation mentioned at the end of Chapter 1. There are today three main
cultivated areas: the well-watered piedmont of Taygetos,
thickly forested with citrus (a post-classical import),
olive and mulberry (now fostered by artificial irrigation), and fertile in vegetables; the centre of the Spartan plain, which bears olives, wheat, barley and maize (an
import of the sixteenth or seventeenth century AD), the
peculiarity of its soil being that it can produce two cer-
eal harvests in a single year; third, the hills along the
Eurotas, which yield wheat or barley. Population in the
basin has unsurprisingly fluctuated little overall in recent times. Sparta itself has grown by well over a half
since 1928, despite the relatively primitive level of
industrialization.

In the south the basin of Sparta is blocked by the
Vardhounia hill-country, eighteen kilometres wide. Its
western portion merges with Taygetos and is composed
largely of schists; its eastern limit is marked by the
stream west of modern Krokeai, the Kourtaki. The area
rises to 516 m. at Mount Lykovouni and is geologically
very similar to south Taygetos. East of Vardhounia lies
the Vrondama plateau, composed of Pliocene conglomerates
and marls and named for its most important modern village.
The plateau is separated from the Spartan basin by a limestone ridge south-west of Goritsa. It declines gradually
from 300 m. in the north to 150 m. at Myrtia along a bed
of conglomerate overlying the marl. West of Grammousa the
Eurotas buries itself in the Tripolis limestone causing
routes of communication to deviate from the river and pass
either over the Vrondama plateau south-eastwards to the
Malea peninsula or through Vardhounia to Gytheion.

The Helos plain and adjoining land is bounded on the
west by the Vardhounia hills and on the east by Mount
Kourkoula, whose spurs in the form of a Pliocene table-
land reach down to the marshy coast. Apart from this

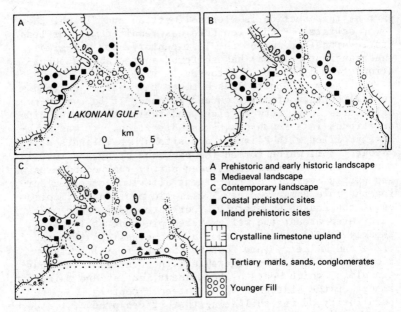

FIGURE 3   The Helos plain; geological change

narrow strip of marl on the east the soil is alluvium
brought down by the Eurotas and its tributary the Mario-
rhevma (which preserves the name of ancient Marios).   A
fact of inestimable significance, however, is that the
present form of the Helos plain differs markedly from that
of its ancient forerunner, which indeed was not strictly a
plain.   For the 'Younger Fill' around the head of the Lakonian Gulf is due to the climatic oscillation already
noted, in which cool and moist phases promoted alluviation
and coastal aggradation (Figure 3).   The ancient shore-
line, that is to say, lay appreciably further inland and,
as has recently been proved by a deep core, the ancient
landscape lies buried beneath in places five to fifteen
metres of recent alluvium.   Thus the agricultural character of the region today cannot simply be read back into
antiquity.   For example, the abundant irrigated crops of
citrus, cotton and rice grown on the 'Younger Fill' are

post-classical and indeed, in the case of the two last, twentieth-century imports.

The Taygetos range, known locally as Pendedaktylo ('five-fingered') or Makrynas ('far-off one'), runs for some 110 km. from the Megalopolis basin to Cape Matapan (ancient Cape Tainaron), the second most southerly point in continental Europe. In structure it is an upfold of several Peloponnesian rock-types. Crystalline schists and marble are overlain by various slates and limestones. With the last major upheaval great faults appeared along both sides of the range, the western marking the shore of the Messenian Gulf and the high eastern edge of the plains of Messenia. Transverse faulting split the range into three main sections, the central being elevated above the rest.

Northern Taygetos extends south as far as the Langadha gorge and the north-east angle of the Messenian Gulf. Its breadth (from twenty-one to twenty-four kilometres) falls into three longitudinal subdivisions. The eastern ridge is narrow and straight, rising gently southwards to 1,610 m. above the Langadha, and is made up of dark limestones, schists and shales. The western ridge is fairly broad but never exceeds 1,300 m.; it is uniformly composed of massive limestones. Between these two ridges lies much lower country worn out of the sandstones and fissured limestones by the southward flowing Nedhon (andient Nedon) and the northward draining Xerillos (ancient Karnion). The inhabitants of this intermediate zone, which embraces the ancient Aigytis and Dentheliatis, were the most backward of any encountered by Philippson.

Central Taygetos extends for thirty-six kilometres from the Langadha to the valleys of Xirokambi and Kardamyli (ancient Kardamyle) on the east and west respectively. This is the highest part of the range, the limestone peaks culminating in Proph. Elias at 2,407 m. The magnificence of the aspect on the east stems from the sharp contrast between the craggy walls of Taygetos and the flatness of the Spartan plain. To the west the lower crests are of marble and mica-schist; the eastern terrace is composed by bold limestone bluffs interrupted by deeply etched ravines. Central Taygetos seems to have been largely uninhabited in antiquity, when it was used by the Spartans as a hunting-ground (Chapter 10). Today the schist has been extensively planted to wheat, barley, rye and maize (the latter up to 1,300 m.).

Southern Taygetos comprises the block between the Xirokambi-Kardamyli pass and the gap between Karyoupolis and Areopolis, which carried the main ancient route to the southern Mani from Gytheion. This section is considerably

larger than the preceding and less sharply defined from
its surroundings. The eastern limestone chain sinks
abruptly from the summit to 1,500 m., but rises again to
1,700 m. at Mount Anina. On the west the marble is less
rigid and is dissected by valleys. The region as a whole
is more favourable to vegetation and habitation than those
to north and south. The whole eastern side is today rich
in small settlements, which often perch picturesquely on
ridges and slopes amid dense tree-growth; this may, however, have been largely virgin forest in our period.

South Mani is a continuation of Taygetos. Its main
summits, which are of marble, decline southwards from
1,100 to 310 m. three kilometres north of Cape Matapan.
In only a few places is the marble overlain by mica-schist,
where the mere four springs known to Philippson take their
rise. Unusually scanty amounts of soil result from the
weathering of the hard marble, and this is quickly swept
away in winter by rain-storms. Where it does stay put, it
is mixed with coarse blocks and small stones ('the Mani is
all stones' is a proverbial saying) - the farmer's bug-
bear. In such a context the annual migration of the quail
is of more than sporting interest; hence Porto Kayio (on
the site of ancient Psamathous) from the Venetians' Porto
Quaglio and the Frankish Port des Cailles. Depopulation
in this century has been drastic.

The final tectonic division of Lakonia, the western
foreland of Taygetos, runs from Kalamata (ancient Pharai)
to Cape Grosso not far north-west of Matapan. It is a
coastal terrace and a remarkable erosion-feature, originally cut level by the waves but unequally elevated thereafter by earth-movements. Later still, rivers incised
deep ravines, at whose mouths inlets have been produced by
sinking. The latter process has probably been furthered
by the solution of the marble through weathering. At Cape
Kitries in the north the terrace is eight kilometres wide;
it narrows to its smallest breadth at Trachilas Bay. From
400 m. at Kitries (ancient Gerenia?) it declines to 98 m.
at Cape Grosso. From Kardamyli to the estuary of the
river of Milia (Little Pamisos, an ancient frontier between Lakonia and Messenia: Chaper 15) the foreland is
chiefly composed of Tripolis limestone patchily overlain
by marl; in the Milia valley a zone of mica-schist gives
rise to the exceedingly rare spring water. Further south
marble is ever-present covered only by a shapeless mass of
loam produced by weathering. However, despite the forbidding nature of the terrain, Perioikic communities succeeded in maintaining themselves here - a suitable reminder
with which to close this chapter that man is never wholly
the slave of the physical environment.

NOTES ON FURTHER READING

The outstanding though somewhat outdated contribution to
our understanding of Greek geography has been made by
Philippson: Kirsten 1956 includes a bibliography of his
numerous works (by no means confined to Greece); for his
discussion of Lakonia and Messenia see Philippson 1959,
371-523. Also useful for many points is the Admiralty
Naval Intelligence Division Geographical Handbook of
Greece (3 vol, March 1944, October 1944, August 1945).
See now, however, Bintliff 1977, I, ch. 2; II, chs. 3-4.
The technical terminology can most easily be grasped
through Whitten and Brooks 1972 and Moore 1976. For the
relief of Lakonia and Messenia, and for the location of
modern place-names, the regional maps issued by the Greek
Statistical Service should be consulted. My Figure 2 is
modified from the map produced by the Institute of Geology
and Subsurface Research at Athens (1954). I have also
used the air photographs taken by the RAF in the last
world war, prints of which are housed in the British
School at Athens.

In general I have avoided citing modern population figures, partly because there are inherent dangers in interpreting census-returns (Cox 1970, 33-43), in part because
the most reliable modern census, that of 1961 (Kayser
1965), was taken well after Greece had been sucked into
the orbit of international finance capital. It is, however, perhaps worth noting that one third of the total
population was then living on less than 5 per cent of the
total surface area, almost one half on less than 15 per
cent.

The survival in the north Parnon region of a language
which retains certifiable traces of its ultimate Doric an-
cestor, Tsakonian, bears eloquent witness to the isolation
of the region.

Rogan 1973 is the work of an interested amateur; but
her maps clearly mark the extent and subdivisions of the
extraordinary Mani, and she traces settlement here from
prehistory to the present day site by site (with some bibliography).

3 Climate

The ancient Greeks' equivalent of our word climate was not
'klima' but something like 'krasis aëros' or simply
'horai' (seasons). By these terms they understood primarily changes in temperature, relative humidity and prevailing winds, but even for these they devised no instruments
to record their fluctuations. Our concept of climate is
immensely more complex, and modern instrumentation permits
it to be considerably more sophisticated (Chapter 1).

Climate rivals relief in its importance as a geographical factor. Since it determines which crops cannot be
grown in a particular region, it sets limits to the range
of ecological adaptations available to man. How far the
influence of climate extends into the spheres of personal
character or political organization were matters for debate even in antiquity, but its effects on health, patterns of settlement and life-styles are less obscure. In
this chapter only the climate recorded for Sparta will be
considered in detail, since it is not greatly different
from that recorded for Gytheion, Kythera and Leonidhion.
By contrast Messenia (represented by readings taken at
Kalamata) lies on the other side of the Taygetos weathershed, on the wetter, western side of the Greek mainland.

If the arguments of Chapter 1 are cogent, the Spartan
climate for most if not all of our special period will not
have been very different from that of today, although
within this period there will undoubtedly have been fluctuations. Our scanty literary sources tend to support
this assumption, apart from their suggestion of heavier
forestation, which can be more satisfactorily explained on
historical than on climatological grounds (Bintliff 1977,
I, chs 3-4). The overall picture of classical Greece they
present is of a generally rocky, infertile and poor country (esp. Hdt. 7.102.1), blessed with a few fertile
plains, notably those of Lakonia and Messenia (Eur. fr.

1083N). Nothing has changed here. The relative prosperity enjoyed by mainland Greece between c.700 and 300 was
due to a combination of historical variables, not to the
fact that its climate was in important respects better
than it is now.

Lakonia belongs to the climatic sub-group which embraces Attiki, Corinthia, Argolis and the Kyklades. This
does not of course mean that there are no divergences
within the sub-group: in temperature, for example, Sparta
is more continental, Athens more maritime. Indeed, there
are divergencies, though insignificant ones, within Lakonia itself. However, the sub-group as a whole is characterized by slight rainfall and marked, prolonged summer
drought, thereby possessing to the fullest degree the dif-
ferentiating qualities of the 'Mediterranean' climate and
landscape.

The most important climatic factor is warmth. The formula adopted in Greece for calculating mean daily temperature is to divide by four the sum of the temperatures
recorded at 0800 and 1400 hours plus twice the temperature
recorded at 2100. The mean temperature at Sparta in July
is 27° C, which when adjusted to allow for the height of
the meteorological station above sea-level (c.200 m.) is
the hottest in Greece. The (unadjusted) mean for January
is 8.8°, the range of 18.2° between January and July being
higher than that of Athens (17.8°). The absolute minimum
temperature recorded at Sparta is -6.3°, the absolute maximum a stifling 43.5°: again, there is an enormous range
here comparable to that recorded for Athens. As far as
the effect of temperature on crops is concerned, however,
mean monthly values are of little analytical significance
(Papadakis 1966, 16f.). What ought to be recorded are the
daily maxima and minima, from which the mean monthly maxima and minima may be computed. (The 0800 and 1400 hours
recordings are perhaps not far off the daily minimum and
maximum, but they are far enough astray to ensure systematic distortion.) Thus a freak reading like the -6.3° (or
the -11° at Athens) will lose much of its merely apparent
significance when it is thrown into the scales with all
the other daily minima for that month. In general temperatures do not begin to drop appreciably until December,
when the Spartan winter properly speaking starts, and even
then there are considerable day-to-day fluctuations. In
March the transition to spring is completed, the opening
of the ancient campaigning and sailing seasons and a time
of hunger (Alkman fr. 20.3-5 Page). By June summer has
come round again. The hottest days ('of the Dog') occur
towards the end of July and beginning of August, in other
words during the close season between the cereal-harvest

and planting.
    Next after warmth in order of importance is rainfall,
the 'key challenge' (Angel 1972, 88). Merely to state the
average annual rainfall at Sparta (81.66 cm.) is to disguise the essential characteristic of all Mediterranean
rainfall, its seasonal distribution. What we need to know
is how long and how much rain falls on the days it does
fall, on how many days it falls, and in which months. On
Kythera, for example, one fifth of the total annual rainfall recorded for one year fell within the space of a
few hours. Such rainfall causes severe flooding and extensive soil-removal: with good reason Theophrastos described Lakonia as 'liable to flooding, rainy and marshy'.
    The average annual number of rain-days at Sparta is
eighty-seven, about half that of southern England, which
receives a comparable quantity of rain per annum. The
annual drought at Sparta lasts two months: that is to say,
less than three centimetres of rain fall on average in
July and August together, compared to 1.25 at Gytheion,
1.5 at Leonidhion. As in most other places in Greece, the
mean monthly rainfall values show their sharpest rise between September and October, and one third of the total
annual rainfall is deposited in November and December.
The seasonal distribution does, however, have its compensations. For it makes a harvest of essential cereals possible everywhere in Greece - indeed, two harvests in
central Lakonia. But Sparta does not of course receive
the same amount of rainfall each year: the lowest annual
figure is less than half the annual mean, as it is for
Gytheion and Kythera too. What makes the average as high
as it is, bearing in mind how far south Sparta lies, is
its proximity to Taygetos, which increases the uplift
effect on moist airmasses in late autumn and winter.
    The key to understanding the Greek climate lies in the
study of atmospheric circulation and airflow. We lack
direct evidence for Sparta, but the picture obtained by
Lehmann (1937) for the plain of Argolis is said to hold
good for the east Greek mainland as a whole. From April
to June southerly winds prevail, but in all other months
winds are mainly northerly, reaching maximum frequency in
July and August. Sparta, exceptionally, receives northerly winds throughout the year - an important fact, because it confirms the view that it is not the prevailing
northerlies which cause the summer drought; besides, the
drought is shorter in Sparta than in many other places.
The cool north-easterly summer trade wind, the Meltemi,
which often reaches Force 7 or 8 on the Beaufort scale,
blows hard until 1700 hours and slows down the rise of
air-temperature. On summer evenings katabatic winds

gravitate down the slopes of Taygetos to Sparta and accelerate the cooling of the air, which begins in earnest when the sun disappears behind the mountain and suddenly swathes the town in shadow.   In winter stormy rain-bearing southerlies alternate with gusty northerlies which bring rain to the eastern side of the Peloponnese and cause snowfalls on the lowlands in December.

As far as thunderstorms are concerned, Parnon acts as a weathershed for the Eurotas valley.   One May Philippson observed repeated heavy storms on the west side of Parnon, while on the east there was either no rain or an insignificant amount.   His observations are confirmed by the meteorological data.   In May and June Sparta has on average twelve thunderstorm days per 1,000, few but over twice as many as Leonidhion.   The picture repeats itself in the mean annual figures: 3.5 per 100 at Sparta, only 1.3 at Leonidhion.   In July the frequency of thunderstorms declines to 2.3 per 1,000 at Sparta; they are virtually unknown in this month on Kythera.

Hail is not particularly common in Greece, and it was fortunate for the Spartans that the beginning of the growth period for cereals coincides with the lowest average number of hail-days (November).   The highest figure is recorded for May, before and during the harvest, but even this is insignificant.   In July it declines once more into non-existence.   The annual average compares favourably with that of Athens whose higher figure is accounted for by the amount it receives on average in October to December.

Snow is a climatic variable of considerable importance to the organization of daily life.   Brought by north-east winds, it falls especially in February on the north and east flanks of mountains.   Sparta itself receives snow very rarely: of the more important states of ancient Greece Athens and Sparta occupy opposite ends of the scale in this regard.   But the Spartans directly or indirectly experienced the effects of snowfalls.   For it remains on Taygetos, in appreciable quantity in some places, until the end of June, and so constituted a most effective obstacle to communication via mountain passes (Chapter 10). On the other hand, as was shown in midwinter 370-69 (Chapter 13), snow could act as a useful protection for Sparta by causing the Eurotas to run high; and in the summer the melting snow refills the mountain streams, which have a particularly beneficial influence on the piedmont at the western edge of the Spartan plain.

The harmful effect of frost on growing crops hardly needs special emphasis.   But in view of the undoubted hardiness of a Spartan upbringing it is perhaps significant that between November and April Sparta has on average twice as many frost-days per 100 as Athens. Although white frost is not uncommon in Greece, we have no inform-ation for Sparta.

Fog and cloud are negligible climatic factors in Greece and neither appears with sufficient frequency to detract from the famed blueness of the Greek sky, which is due to the dryness of the air. Attempts to classify visibility in terms of distance are of course ludicrous, and there is no better foundation for claims that there is a signifi-cant correlation between blueness of sky or clarity of air and traits of character. Sunshine, however, the inverse of cloud and fog, does have therapeutic qualities, and in-solation at Sparta is among the highest recorded in Greece. On average Sparta receives 329 sunshine-hours in June, 387 in July and 364 in August. As for relative hum-idity, another favoured candidate for the role of charac-ter-moulder, it reaches its peak at Sparta in December, then declines to its minimum in July, remaining throughout the year higher than that of Athens.

Finally, dew deserves a special mention, for a form of condensation which lies directly on vegetation is very important in a relatively rainless country. (Fog-drip from trees is negligible.) Figures for dew-nights are not available for Sparta, but the ancient evidence for the im-portance of dew in cult (mainly from Athens) suggests that they will not have been frequent.

To conclude, the climate of Sparta represents, what we might have expected from its location, a compromise bet-ween eastern and western Greece. In comparison to its nearest recorded neighbours, Sparta has a somewhat rougher winter climate, akin in some respects to that of Athens. In summer the differences are much slighter, Sparta being rather hotter, owing to its inland situation. In our brief survey the climates of Athens and Sparta have oc-casionally been compared. If such a comparison has any historical value, that of Sparta is harsher and more demanding.

NOTES ON FURTHER READING

The standard work of synthesis on the Greek climate is Philippson 1948; but see Lauffer 1950 for many supplements and some corrections. Useful companions are Livathinos and Mariolopoulos 1935 and ESAG. The figures I have cited are based on recordings made between 1900 and 1929. The relevant tables are reproduced in the Admiralty Handbook I, App. 9.

There is much of relevance in Papadakis 1966. He discusses in detail (39ff.) how he would set about making a
climatic classification and attacks attempts to base a
classification on figures like those used by Philippson.
The latter are, however, adequate for our purposes.

4 The Stone and Bronze Ages to c. 1300

'Revolution', like 'democracy', is a grossly overworked
term, one of the list of slogan-words which seems to justify the emotive theory of morals. But if ever a human
process merited the title, it is the one compendiously
dubbed the 'Neolithic Revolution'. For this was perhaps
'the greatest revolution ... in the history of Mankind'
(Theocharis 1973, 19). After maybe the better part of
three million years of hunting and gathering by various
species of homo, homo sapiens began instead to produce its
means of subsistence. Through the domestication of wild
grasses and animals there was unleashed the only kind of
progress of which it is any longer possible to speak without equivocation, progress in man's control over nature.
Not that the Neolithic Revolution was an inevitable process, nor did its onset mark a sudden complete break with
the past. Its advance, moreover, should not be likened to
that of a steamroller, especially if for any reason we
should be unwilling to accept that Neolithic techniques of
farming were diffused from the Fertile Crescent. It was
for its consequences, in other words, rather than the manner of its introduction, that its title is most fully
justified.

As recently as a generation back it would have been impossible to write a general survey of the Neolithic period
in Greece such as Theocharis 1973. Now, however, thanks
to the remarkable finds at the Franchthi cave in the Argolis, all the stages of the Revolution can be traced in
Greece from its immediate Mesolithic origins to the Final
or Epi-Neolithic threshold of our more immediate concern,
the Bronze Age. To specify, this cave has yielded a continuous stratigraphic sequence from the Late Palaeolithic
to the advanced Neolithic. Greece, however, may prove to
have yet greater surprises in store. For although Nean-
derthal skulls and Mousterian tools had signalled the

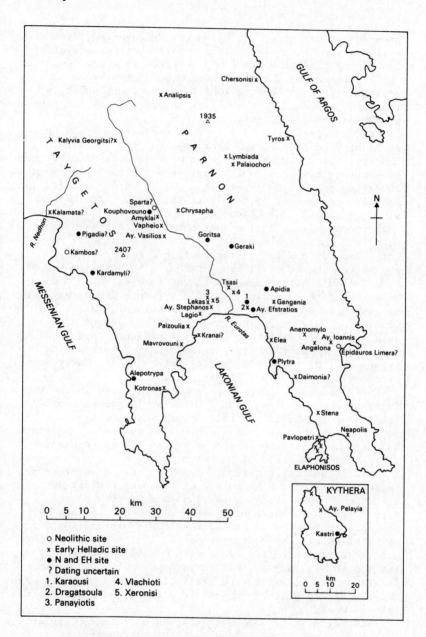

FIGURE 4   Neolithic and Early Helladic Lakonia

presence of man here, including the Peloponnese, from as
early as the Middle Palaeolithic period, it was reported
in 1976 that human bones found embedded in a stalagmite in
Chalkidiki had been dated some 700,000 years before the
present. If corroborated (which is, however, unlikely),
this find would upset prevailing theories about the geography of the evolution of man.

Fortunately we need not concern ourselves here with
such lofty heights of speculation about the progress of
man from ape to artist nor even with the ultimate origins
of plant-cultivation, which have recently been placed in
Palestine some 12,000 years ago. There is for a start no
Lakonian equivalent of the Franchthi cave. Its nearest
rival, however, is in Lakonia, the Alepotrypa ('Fox-hole')
cave in south Mani on the east coast of the Messenian
Gulf; but this does not seem to have come into its own
until towards the end of the Neolithic (Figure 4). Recent
excavations have, it is true, revealed doubtful craces of
Late Palaeolithic occupation in the form of tools and
bones. But the certainly datable evidence of pottery does
not make its appearance until the middle of the sixth millennium or late on in the Early Neolithic period. To
date, this pottery is the only sure evidence that Lakonia
was inhabited at this time, unless three remarkable marble
figurines (two certainly female) belong to the Early Neolithic (Theocharis 1973, figs 17, 200, 226).

These tiny sculptures were reportedly found in the vicinity of modern Sparta, but a more likely provenance is
Kouphovouno, a low mound site about two kilometres south-
south-west. This was, as it were, the Sparta of Neolithic
Lakonia, but settlement here cannot be firmly documented
before the last third of the sixth millennium, that is in
the Middle Neolithic period. By this time, however, attested settlement in Lakonia was attaining a wider distribution. Apart from Kouphovouno and (probably) the
Alepotrypa cave, there is evidence of occupation near modern Apidia in the west Parnon foreland south-east of Geraki. At Apidia, however, the pottery in question was not
unearthed in controlled excavation but picked up during
surface survey, and so this is perhaps an opportune moment
to stress how flimsy is the basis of evidence on which any
reconstruction of the prehistoric ('text-free') period in
Lakonia rests.

This may best be done by taking as our frame of reference the arguments of a leading prehistorian with experience of the problems of the Aegean (Renfrew 1972, 225-64).
Attempting to trace the pattern of settlement in Greece
from the Neolithic through the Bronze Age, Renfrew began
correctly by pointing out the inadequacy of the available

evidence, overwhelmingly assembled through surface exploration rather than scientific digging. Such evidence is
subject to a series of limitations as raw material for
'history' that can only be surmounted by - or at least not
without - excavation. For example, soil erosion, later
settlement, deep ploughing, alluviation and maquis-type
vegetation can singly or in combination obliterate or temporarily obscure traces of habitation. Different settlement patterns and cultural assemblages paint surface pictures of unequal perceptibility. Accidentally uncovered
worked stones can swiftly take on a new lease of life in
modern structures far perhaps from the site of their original discovery. Finally, and by no means least, the pre-
conceived notions of archaeologists can blinker their
field of vision.

Expressly recognizing these limitations, all of which
apply to the Lakonian evidence, Renfrew concluded that,
although inter-regional comparisons might be seriously
misleading, figures for developing intra-regional settlement patterns and population density could be statistically
significant. In fact, not even this more modest claim
will withstand scrutiny, at least not in the case of Lakonia; survey has been notably more thorough in, for example, Messenia. For a 50 per cent or less surface coverage
of the region leaves far too great a margin of error,
given the dearth of excavation; and the preconception that
prehistoric settlements of all periods were typically centred on 'akropolis' sites has been contradicted by more
recent surveys of other regions, which have restored the
low hillock and indeed the valley-floor to their rightful
place.

Renfrew's misapprehension of the number of sites occupied in the various prehistoric phases is compounded by un-
warranted assumptions about the character and size of
settlements, as we shall see in Chapter 6. However, to
return to the Neolithic, we have so far registered the occupation by 5000 of three sites, located in three of Lakonia's six main geological subdivisions. These three continued to be inhabited into the Late Neolithic (c.4500-
3500, according to Phelps 1975), when they were perhaps
joined by a fourth at Geraki. Although the quantity of
skeletons recovered from the Alepotrypa cave represents
the most impressive concentration in Greece, the situation
in Lakonia as a whole can hardly be described as one of
overpopulation. Something of a transformation, however,
seems to have been effected in the Final Neolithic period
(3500-3000/2500). Now the southern part of the Eurotas
furrow was settled at Asteri (Karaousi) and Ay. Efstratios,
while occupation continued to the north at Kouphovouno and

perhaps Palaiokastro (between Chrysapha and the Menelaion
site) and to the south at Alepotrypa. The presence of
silver jewellery in the latter suggests a measure of prosperity, but all good things must end and the collapse of
the roof crushed or trapped a veritable charnel-house of
corpses (Lambert 1972, 845-71). Traces of habitation
probably to be assigned to this same phase have been detected in a double cave at Goritsa in the west foreland of
Parnon west of Geraki (itself still occupied), at Goules
near Plytra in the Malea peninsula, and at Kardamyli,
Kambos and Kokkinochomata in north-west Mani.

Can we create a pattern out of these scanty and disparate materials? Given the apparent break in Lakonia between the Upper Palaeolithic and Early Neolithic (no Mesolithic), Neolithic techniques of farming must have been
imported rather than spontaneously developed here. At any
rate, the wild ancestors of the relevant domesticated
grasses and animals have only been found at Franchthi
(oats, barley). Whether the importation was through diffusion or immigration cannot be firmly decided without a
good deal more exploration and excavation, but 'the distribution of the known sites suggests that the neolithic
people first entered Lakonia by sea, via the Helos and
Molaoi plains' (Hope Simpson and Waterhouse 1961, 168).
On present evidence they did not venture far from the
coast but occupied roughly south-central Lakonia. Kouphovouno, however, is fairly far to the north and, to judge
by its houses, graves and stone artefacts, was perhaps the
single most important site. It would of course be rash to
speak of a hierarchy of settlements at this stage, but
Kouphovouno's central position in the Spartan basin is
noteworthy. For in view of the strong correlation between
the distribution of cornlands in Greece today and that of
the Neolithic tells, the chief crops must have been cereals, probably emmer wheat and barley (J. Renfrew in Theocharis 1973, 149).

Direct palaeobotanical evidence is lacking for Lakonia,
but three disc-shaped clay bread-ovens have been found in
the Alepotrypa cave. Here too were discovered the bones
of ovines or caprines and bovines, together with marine
shells. However, the chief evidence for the Lakonian Neolithic is its pottery, although this was a concomitant,
rather than a basic ingredient, of Neolithic culture. It
was hand-made (like all pottery in Greece before the Middle Bronze Age) and sometimes beautifully decorated, as
was for example the late polychrome ware at the Alepotrypa
cave and Apidia. By the Late Neolithic it is possible to
speak, with special reference to the pottery, of a cultural 'koine' stretching from Thessaly to the Mani.

More obvious evidence of cultural contact and communication is provided by the obsidian artefacts from Kouphovouno and Alepotrypa. The source of this volcanic rock
has been proved beyond doubt to be the island of Melos,
whence it was being obtained by the occupants of the
Franchthi cave as astonishingly early as 7000 or even earlier (C. Renfrew in Theocharis 1973, 180, 339-41). But
perhaps most exciting of all is the discovery of copper
tools in the Alepotrypa cave. The source of the ore and
the place where the metal was smelted are not yet established, but these implements provide a convenient transition to the Early Bronze Age, known in mainland Greece as
the Early Helladic (EH) era.

For 'man's discovery of copper ore and the means whereby it could be turned into metal was one of the major discoveries in history' (Branigan 1970, 1). Since there was
apparently no transitional ('Chalkolithic') phase in the
Peloponnese, the sharp break from the Neolithic to the
Bronze Age argues diffusion of the secrets of metallurgy,
possibly by immigrants, from the Near East via the Kyklades and perhaps the Troad (Branigan 1974, 97-102). At
first copper, beaten and hammered, was employed on its
own, then tin from Etruria, Sardinia or Spain was alloyed
with it to produce implements and weapons of bronze. However, EH and its tripartite subdivision are, like the
entire subdivision of the Aegean Bronze Age (Stubbings
1970, 241), based on the classification of pottery not the
typology of metal artefacts. So there is inevitably some
elasticity about the date at which a particular region or
site can be said to have entered the Bronze Age properly
speaking. For Lakonia, 2700 or thereabouts is a reasonable approximation.

The general features of EH Greece are fairly clear: a
dispersed 'farmstead' pattern of settlement on low hill-
sites preferentially near the sea; 'Urfinis' pottery and
the 'sauceboat' shape diagnostic of EH II; active trade
and communications, especially by sea; increasing use of
copper and silver. In short, this was a progressive and
on the whole prosperous era, although, as we shall see,
hardly one in which the 'way of life was urban and commercial rather than rural and agricultural' (Hooker 1977, 17).
As far as Lakonia is concerned, however, the dearth of
excavated evidence and especially of metal artefacts en-
forces a probably distorting reliance on the testimony of
pottery. On the other hand, the evidence from Kythera, to
which I shall return at the end of my discussion of EH
Lakonia, is unique in the Aegean world as a whole and potentially of great significance.

Surface surveys have revealed some thirty to forty

Lakonian sites, mostly dispersed farms or hamlets, occupied in EH times (Figure 4). The majority of these was attested by sherds alone, a handful by stone celts alone,
but it is at least clear that in this period all the main
geological sub-regions were settled, chiefly on or near
coasts. The main concentration was in the most fertile
area, the Eurotas valley, but the district around Vatika
bay in the Malea peninsula was also extensively settled.
No pottery of either the EH I or EH III sub-phases has
been picked up, but the quantity of the ware from the intervening sub-phase suggests that in Lakonia as elsewhere
EH II was a long and mainly peaceful epoch. Apart from
the pottery and celts, two fragmentary animal figurines
have been found, at Palaiopyrgi near Vapheio in the Spartan basin and at Laina near Goritsa. A special position
is occupied by the long since known but only recently published hoard of gold and silver jewellery allegedly from
the Thyreatis (Greifenhagen 1970, 17f.). This belongs to
the end of the EH period (c.2000) and includes filigree
work and other features betraying links with the Troad. I
suspect, though, that its original home was Lerna (below).
    Fortunately the surface surveys have been followed up
by excavation - but unfortunately at only one site, Ay.
Stephanos on the western edge of the present Helos plain.
EH pottery was unearthed in appreciable amounts associated
with burials (often in stone cists, perhaps an anticipation of Middle Helladic practice) as well as in settlement areas (Taylour 1972, 261). There was no EH III and
apparently no EH I either, a satisfying confirmation of
the picture derived from survey. So far as I can see, the
only published metal object from an EH context was a pair
of bronze tweezers (Branigan 1974, Cat. 1320). Indeed,
apart from the Thyreatis hoard, this is the only EH metal
object known so far from Lakonia. Finally, we must note
the now underwater necropolis of some sixty tombs, probably mostly EH, on the mainland side of the strait between
Pavlopetri islet and the Malea peninsula. Within the adjoining settlement (also submerged) many of the finds were
apparently of the end of the Bronze Age, and I shall return to them in various connections.
    In this present state of our knowledge of EH Lakonia we
cannot even begin to ask how the region may have compared
to the better known ones of the Peloponnese, Argolis and
Messenia. This is, to say the least, disappointing, because certainly two and possibly three major developments
occurred on the Greek mainland in the EH period. First,
social differentiation and societal complexity became such
that at Lerna in Argolis and at Akovitika on the north-
east shore of the Messenian Gulf (four kilometres west of

Kalamata) successive stages of building culminated in the
erection during EH II of structures suggesting the emer
gence of an individual or family-group as political over-
lord. The functions of such structures as centres for the
redistribution of goods and services has been admirably
explicated by Renfrew (1972, 52f.), although I cannot accept the 'systems' model of 'culture process' that he employs to explain them. Rather, the appearance of such
centres presupposes exploitation, that is the extraction
by a few rich people from the many primary producers of a
surplus of products thereby made available for redistribution.

   This surplus resulted from the second of our three
major EH developments, the establishment of the 'Mediterranean triad' of dietary staples (corn, olives and wine)
as the basis of subsistence. Again, the demonstration of
the occurrence and significance of this development is due
to Renfrew (1972, 265-307), and it is this development
which explains my earlier rejection of Hooker's character-
ization of the Early Bronze Age. I shall consider the
special qualities of the triad at the appropriate points
in later chapters.

   The third major EH development is far more controversial. Either towards the end of the period or, more rarely, actually terminating it, several destructions occurred
in mainland Greece. For reasons which it is outside the
scope of this book to explore, these destructions have
been attributed to Indo-European invaders from the north,
who spoke an early form of Greek, rode horses and used the
potter's wheel. Suffice it to say here that this neat
connection cannot be demonstrated on linguistic or archaeological grounds (Hooker 1976; 1977, 12-32). However,
what is more or less beyond dispute is that between c.2000
and 1900 the EH culture gave way to the Middle Helladic
(MH), that the foremost types of MH pottery were thrown on
the wheel and that some time before the inscription of the
earliest known Linear B tablets (Chapter 5) a form of
Greek was being spoken in mainland Greece.

   None of these three major developments, as I have said,
can be positively identified in Lakonia as yet. However,
some consolation for this lack of evidence may be gleaned
from Kythera. This island's destiny has often been a little distinct historically from that of mainland Lakonia,
but at no time was this distinctness more marked than in
the Bronze Age. Surface exploration had been conducted
since the nineteenth century, but it was only in 1963-5
that excavations were carried out in the most fertile
area, the Palaiopolis valley on the east coast. About
100 m. inland from the Kastri promontory a trial trench

on the spur Kastraki yielded sherds not only of EH II (and
nothing later) but also of EH I, the only sample of this
so far attested in Lakonia (it has Boiotian analogies).

Still more remarkable, however, were the finds from the
main dig on the Kastri promontory itself. For these represented the earliest known 'colony' of Cretan settlers,
who had emigrated to Kythera during the currency of Early
Minoan II pottery. The most economical explanation of
this succession of culturally distinct settlements is that
around 2500 'the Cretan newcomers ousted the mainlanders'
(Coldstream 1973, 35). Coldstream, indeed, goes further
and speculates that the Cretan occupation of the best land
on Kythera may have set up a kind of frontier between the
Minoan sphere of influence on the one hand and the Hel-
ladic/Cycladic on the other. I feel doubtful whether the
evidence (mainly pottery) will bear such a weighty super-
structure of hypothesis. Equally dubious is the suggestion that a small marble vase inscribed in hieroglyphs
(with the name of an Egyptian Fifth Dynasty solar temple
erected by Userkaf) is evidence of wide foreign relations.
For it was a sporadic find and could have made its way to
Kythera at a much later date.   •

Returning to rather firmer ground, evidence from survey
has revealed widespread settlement in MH Lakonia, but a
slightly altered settlement pattern (Figure 5). An appreciable number of EH sites is given up and some new ones
are selected, often on and around an 'akropolis'. The result is that, although fewer actual sites are known in MH
(between twenty and thirty) than in EH, these can sometimes be described as of 'village' type rather than isolated farmsteads and hamlets. The concentration of sites
in the Helos plain has provoked the suggestion that MH invaders entered Lakonia by sea (Hope Simpson and Waterhouse
1961, 170); but in the present state of our evidence it is
perhaps prudent not to fall back too readily on the invasion hypothesis. What is certain is that local versions
of the leading types of MH pottery - grey and yellow
'Minyan' and matt-painted - are present in Lakonia.

Three excavated sites call for special mention, two in
the Eurotas valley, the third in the west Parnon foreland.
The latter, Geraki, utilizing one of the basin plains mentioned in Chapter 2, had perhaps been occupied more or
less continuously from Neolithic times. But the trial excavation of 1905 suggested that it only grew to importance
in the MH period. Characteristically MH cist-graves (one
containing a fine bronze bird-pin) and matt-painted pottery were unearthed, the latter belonging especially to
the latest, MH III, phase. Potentially of most significance, perhaps, were the large blocks of walling on the

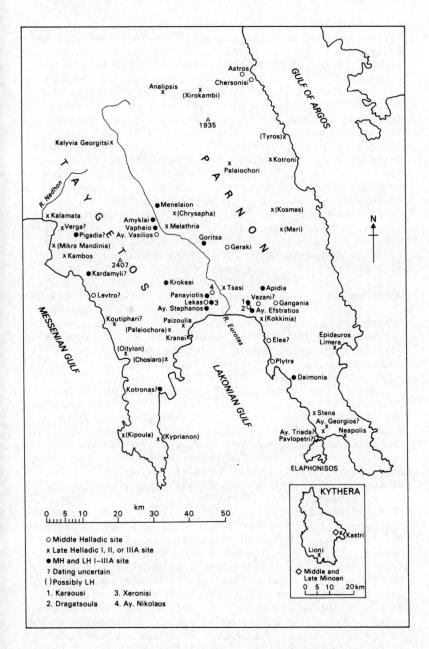

FIGURE 5   Middle Helladic and Late Helladic I-IIIA Lakonia

akropolis, but these are not certainly MH in date nor necessarily defensive in purpose. In the Spartan plain
Amyklai, later to form part of classical Sparta, had been
first settled in the EH period. Apart from an apparent
break at the end of MH (there is no LH I, at least), the
excavated site seems to have been occupied continuously
thereafter at any rate to the eleventh century (cf. Chapter 7). MH wares represented include grey and black
('Argive') Minyan, matt-painted and light-on-dark. The
latter may reflect contact with Minoan Crete, but it is
from our third and best known excavated site, Ay. Stephanos, that the Cretan connection is most clearly apparent.

Several burials and remains of houses have been found
at Ay. Stephanos, including a MH III house comprising one
long room communicating with a smaller one; along the long
side of the main room ran a low stone bench adjoining a
rectangular hearth composed of slabs and small stones.
Most significant of all, however, is the conclusion drawn
from a preliminary study of the pottery excavated in 1974,
which emphasizes the importance of the site in the transition from the Middle to the Late Bronze Age in Lakonia.
'There is a strong Minoan influence, and a very high percentage (over 50%) of the painted pottery finds persuasive
parallels for shape, range and decoration with the MM IIIB
and LM IA pottery of Kythera' (Taylour 1975, 17). In
other words, the cultural frontier postulated by Coldstream for the second half of the third millennium had been
trampled underfoot by the end of the seventeenth century.
Ay. Stephanos thus provides a perfect illustration of
Hooker's 'First Phase of Minoan Influence (Middle Helladic
and Late Helladic I pottery)', in which 'an imperfect
fusion between Helladic and Minoan leads to the beginning
of a distinctive Mycenaean culture' (Hooker 1977, 6; but
he is wrong in thinking that it was largely confined to
the Peloponnese).

A further note on terminology is appropriate here. The
Late Bronze Age in the Greek mainland is known conventionally as either the Late Helladic (LH) or the Mycenaean
period: Mycenae 'rich in gold' and the seat of Homer's
Agamemnon, sceptred 'lord of many islands and all Argos',
has yielded its treasures to the spade on a scale that
only an unbridled optimist like Schliemann could have envisaged. For many scholars the epithet 'Mycenaean' remains no more than a convention convenient to describe the
period of c.1550 to 1100/1050. By others, however, it is
given a precise political connotation, at least for the
thirteenth century. I am personally out of sympathy with
the latter, for reasons given in Chapter 6 and Appendix
2. But Mycenae none the less cannot be ousted from its

central position in the transition from the MH to the LH
period, despite the recent accessions of material from excavation which fill out and balance the picture.

Part of this balancing material comes from Lakonia, and
a recent attempt to define LH I pottery (Dickinson 1974;
1977, 25f.) has drawn extensively on the finds from Ay.
Stephanos and, especially, Kythera. Of far greater moment, however, are the finds from the two grave-circles at
Mycenae and their paler reflections at, for example, Peristeria in Messenia. The art of the Mycenae shaft-graves
and the raw materials of the artefacts entombed within
them display an enormously widened range of foreign relations, extending from Egypt perhaps to the Black Sea, from
Syria perhaps even to Britain. Hooker (1977, 36-58) has
convinced me that we should not regard the occupants of
the shaft-graves as barbarian intruders incarcerated with
the loot of their raids. Instead the evidence from Mycenae, where both grave-circles were inaugurated in the
late MH period, may be seen as a greatly enlarged and enlivened version of the humbler process of transition under
heavy Minoan influence apparent at Ay. Stephanos. Indeed,
Dickinson has suggested that the originators of the LH I
style of pottery could have been potters who emigrated to
Central Greece from Kythera, since mature Kytheran LM IA
seems to be the single most important influence on the
style.

However that may be, relatively little is known of LH I
in Lakonia, apart from Ay. Stephanos and perhaps Epidauros
Limera. Taking together therefore LH I and LH II, which
span roughly the sixteenth and fifteenth centuries, we
find occupation on only some fifteen to twenty sites, an
apparent decrease on the MH figure. The discrepancy, however, may simply be due to failure to find or distinguish
the relevant pottery, for by LH II at any rate there is
unambiguous evidence that a qualitative change has been
effected in Lakonian social, economic and political organization. In none of the preceding periods, as we have
seen, was it possible to establish with certainty the existence of a settlement hierarchy. But by the fifteenth
century three of the six main subdivisions of Lakonia can
boast a kind of monument which seems to presuppose economic prosperity, a high degree of social differentiation
and centralization of political control - the tholos (bee-
hive) tomb. From east to west early Mycenaean tholoi have
been excavated at Analipsis in the west Parnon foreland,
Vapheio in the Eurotas furrow and, if it may be dated so
early (cf. Dickinson 1977, 92), Kambos in the west Taygetos foreland.

Each has produced exotic and expensive grave-goods, but

far and away the most striking is the one at Vapheio,
which deserves closer attention for four main reasons:
first, the central place of Lakonia, whatever its precise
location, will henceforth always be found in the Spartan
basin; second, Lakonia is now seen to be marching in step
with the hitherto seemingly more progressive regions of
the Peloponnese; third, the quality of the artefacts from
the Vapheio tholos is strikingly high; finally, and perhaps most instructively, the promise of the fifteenth century is not apparently fulfilled in the thirteenth in Lakonia, as it is in the Argolis and Messenia.

The tholos itself is quite large (10.35 m. in diameter)
with a built approach (dromos) measuring 29.80 m. The
stones, however, are not well worked or laid, and the tomb
is somewhat unusual for being sited in the top of a hill
rather than cut out of the base of a slope. It was robbed
in antiquity for its contents (and more recently for its
worked stones), but the tombaroli overlooked an underground pit in the floor of the chamber. Herein lay the
'Vapheio Prince', his splendidly intact grave-goods offering a sharp contrast to his utterly disintegrated skeleton.
Rings, gems, beads, a mirror, an earpick, perfume vases,
cups, a sword, nine knives and daggers, a pair of hunting-
spears and axes - the range of artefacts is impressive
enough. Overwhelmingly impressive are their materials and
quality: 'Palace Style' pottery, two vases of alabaster,
an axe of Syrian type, a finger-ring of iron, beads of
amethyst and Baltic amber, scale-pans of bronze, lamps of
stone, two daggers inlaid with metal cut-outs and niello,
cups of silver. Finally, there are the most famous items
of all, the two gold cups now prominently displayed in the
National Museum at Athens; their bovine scenes have a
strongly Cretan flavour even if they were not necessarily
both executed by Cretan craftsmen. In short, the Vapheio
tholos and its contents seem to me neatly to encapsulate
the distinguishing features of Hooker's 'Second Phase of
Minoan Influence', namely 'the almost complete fusion between Helladic and Minoan and the adoption on the mainland
of Minoan art-forms and the external features of Minoan
cult' (Hooker 1977, 6).

Thus we may suppose that much of LH II Lakonia was divided into local 'princedoms'. But LH II was not only the
great age of the tholos tomb in the region. It also witnessed the inception or growth of the burial practice
which some prehistorians consider to be diagnostic of the
LH period as a whole, the entombment of generations of
families in chamber-tombs excavated from the softer rocks
rather than built in to them as most tholoi were. Chamber-
tombs of LH II date are known from Krokeai in Vardhounia

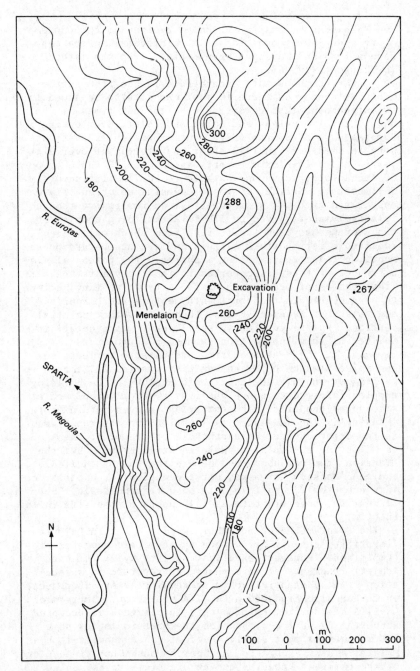

FIGURE 6   The Menelaion hill near Sparta

and Epidauros Limera in the Malea peninsula; the contemp-
orary stone-built oval tombs at Palaiochori in the east
Parnon foreland may have been derived from the latter
(Dickinson 1977, 63f.).

As far as the scanty excavated evidence from settlements is concerned there is just one site to be added to
Ay. Stephanos, that occupied in historical times by the
sanctuary of Menelaos and Helen on a bluff overlooking the
Eurotas east of Sparta (Figure 6). British excavations
were resumed here in 1973 after an interval of over sixty
years, and preliminary reports speak of a MH phase of occupation followed by one datable to LH IIA (including LM
IB imports). Neither of these deposits unfortunately was
associated with any structure, but an impressive though
relatively short-lived LH IIB-IIIA1 building complex of
two storeys has been identified, from which came a seal,
two female terracotta figurines and a contemporary house-
model, perhaps representing a shrine. The potential significance of these discoveries is that they mark the earliest phases of occupation of the site which many believe
to have become in the thirteenth century the Lakonian
equivalent of Mycenae, Pylos, Thebes and other palatial
centres. But as yet, as we shall see in more detail in
Chapter 6, this supposition cannot be corroborated.

However, the Menelaion site undoubtedly reflects the
general expansion of Mycenaean civilization in Lakonia in
LH IIIA or roughly the fourteenth century. The building
complex referred to above was itself quickly replaced at
the end of the fifteenth century by an even more elaborate
'Mansion'. The suggested explanation for the replacement
is the occurrence of an earthquake or tremor of the kind
to which the region as a whole is still prone. But the
'Mansion' too was abandoned before the end of LH IIIA1,
and the 'Mansion' area was not reoccupied for another century and a half, and then only on a reduced scale. Settlement is, however, attested elsewhere on the site in the
interim.

The twenty-five or so other LH IIIA sites in Lakonia
(identified chiefly by surface survey) pale somewhat by
comparison. However, excellent quality kylix (stemmed
goblet) fragments of this phase are reported in association with substantial building remains at Ay. Stephanos,
which has also produced a LH IIIA sealstone. There are
LH IIIA sherds from Palaiopyrgi, the large hill occupied
since the EH period with which the Vapheio tholos some
300 m. away is most easily associated. A chamber-tomb at
Melathria near Skoura in the Spartan basin has yielded one
of the earliest known Mycenaean pictorial vases, dated to
the end of the fifteenth century by Demacopoulou (1971).

A terracotta from Lekas in the Helos plain has been clas-
sed among the earliest ('naturalistic') Mycenaean figurines (French 1971, 110).   Finally, an amber seal with in-
decipherable design, one of the more ambitious Mycenaean
attempts at carving the material, was found with LH IIIA
pottery and other impressive grave-goods in a chamber-tomb
at Pellana in the northern Eurotas furrow (Strong 1966,
17f.).

I have left to the end of this final introductory chapter the early Late Bronze Age evidence from Kythera, which
yet again offers us a window on the wider Aegean world.
As we have seen, a Cretan 'colony' at Kastri probably ousted a settlement of mainland stamp around 2500.   The
Cretan character and connections of the 'colony' were
maintained unbroken until the LM IB phase; an eighteenth-
century inscription of Naram-Sin, King of Eshnunna, test-
ifies to continuing widespread foreign relations (unless
it too is a later immigrant like the Userkaf inscription).
Cretan influence on the mainland increased noticeably at
the transition between MH and LH, and the credit for the
change to LH I pottery was perhaps partly due to potters
from Kastri.   About 1500, however, a cataclysmic volcanic
eruption on the island of Thera destroyed a flourishing
'Minoanized' settlement there and perhaps much else: some
pumice was carried as far as Nichoria in Messenia during
the currency of LH IIA (Rapp and Cook 1973).   Thereafter,
perhaps in direct or indirect consequence of the Thera
eruption, Cretan influence in the Aegean waned.   Indeed,
it is widely believed that c.1450 the palace of Knossos
was taken over by mainlanders.   However, some seventy-five
years later Knossos too was reduced to political if not
physical insignificance.

This change in relations between Crete and the mainland
is nicely reflected in the way LM IB pottery (exported,
incidentally, to Palaiochori and Epidauros Limera as well
as to the Menelaion site) is increasingly jostled by LH
IIA at Kastri, until the settlement was actually abandoned
at the end of the currency of the style (c.1450).   Hardly
any LH IIB was found, but there was LH IIIA pottery in a
chamber-tomb further south at Lioni, and Kythera appears
to have attracted Egyptian attention in the first half of
the fourteenth century (Sergent 1977, 138).   In the succeeding LH IIIB phase (Chapter 6) the destiny of Kythera
was reunited with that of the mainland: both were firmly
Helladic.   Thus in the light of the Kytheran evidence
above all, but taking account also of the rest of the
finds from Lakonia, it seems to me misleading to describe
even the LH IIIA2 period, let alone LH IIIB, as the
'Third Phase of Minoan Influence' (Hooker 1977, 6).

NOTES ON FURTHER READING

For bibliography on the individual sites mentioned in this
and later chapters see Appendix 1.

With my remarks on the impossibility of giving figures
for population density in Lakonia compare and contrast
McDonald and Hope Simpson in MME 132: 'Of course, a solid
basis for even the most carefully hedged estimates of prehistoric population in Messenia does not yet exist. Some
of our colleagues have therefore pressed us to avoid absolute numbers entirely, since it is so easy for the most
cautious estimates to become accepted facts. Perhaps we
should have heeded their advice ...'

The 'Neolithic Revolution' is succinctly discussed by
Cole 1970. Hauptmann 1971 is an excellent review of recent research on the Stone Age, especially the Neolithic,
in the Aegean.

For the Early and Middle Bronze Ages in general see
Caskey 1971, 1973; Schachermeyr 1976. A good, though
dated, discussion of the transition between the two, as
indeed of all aspects of the Greek Bronze Age, is Vermeule 1964. The most recent discussion of the Mycenae
shaft graves is Dickinson 1977, 39-58. A pottery deposit
from Ay. Stephanos spanning the MH/LH transition (c.1700-
1450) has been fully published by Rutter and Rutter 1976.
Disagreeing with Dickinson 1974, J.B. Rutter suggests that
LH I was developed in the southern Peloponnese (perhaps
actually in Lakonia) earlier than in the northern Peloponnese and that the stimulus to the change was the immigration of potters from Kythera to Crete in MH III. Dickinson's most recent views may be studied in Dickinson 1977,
especially 24 and 108 (with its n. 2).

For the 'Cretan connection' from c.1525 to 1375 see
Hooker 1977, ch. 4. But his conclusions on the 'Mycenaean-
izing' of Knossos in the fifteenth century are vitiated by
his omission of the Warrior Graves and his unclear account
of Linear B.

Part II
Preclassical Lakonia c. 1300 – 500 BC

5 Greek oral tradition as history

A quarter of a century ago the Mycenaean period was fully prehistoric in the sense that it was 'text free'. (The Homeric poems, some aspects of whose historicity are considered in Appendix 2, are not of course contemporary texts.) But thanks to a combination of cryptographic detective work and linguistic scholarship it is now possible to read some of its documents. These are the accidentally baked clay tablets of varying shapes and sizes inscribed in 'Linear B', a syllabary devised to transcribe an early form of the Greek language. We cannot say certainly where or when the syllabary was invented, but the few findspots of the tablets are significant: Knossos, Pylos, Mycenae, Thebes and Tiryns. To these we may add the sites which have produced vases inscribed with Linear B symbols: Eleusis, Kreusis, Orchomenos, Chania and now the Menelaion site (Catling 1977, 34). The syllabary's total attested number of symbols (signs and ideograms) is about 200. To judge from the evidence of handwriting, the only available criterion, there were about 100 scribes working at any one time at Knossos, about fifty at Pylos. The contexts in which the tablets were found may be spread over a period of up to two centuries (c.1375 at Knossos to c.1200 at Pylos), but little or no stylistic development is discernible. The tablets reveal the existence of a basically agrarian economy with a developed division of labour and a multiplicity of social statuses and factors of production.

Such are the bare facts. The decipherment of the script - still contested by a few diehards - has undoubtedly made available an important new source of information and provoked a staggering volume of research. Yet in view of the tendency of some Mycenologists to rush to premature judgments it is necessary to state at the outset that the scope of the advance is restricted in terms both of geographical applicability and of the type of information the

49

tablets convey. Thus Lakonia is only one of the (archaeologically) important regions which have yet to produce
Linear B tablets, unless one of the two signs incised on a
schist tab found sporadically at Ay. Stephanos really is
Linear B (BCH 1974, 613). It is uncertain how far this
negative evidence should be pressed, although it is perhaps fair to comment that, if there had been a Lakonian
Pylos, it ought to have been discovered. Second, the tablets are in fact merely the everyday administrative mnem-
onics of centralized and bureaucratic monarchies, used for
the collection of raw facts primarily of a narrowly economic nature (accounts, lists, prices, assignments, requis-
itions and the like) and not for final digests or permanent records. They contain not a scrap of poetry, law, history or oratory. In short, although there is perhaps a
case for redefining the fourteenth and thirteenth centuries in the Mycenaean world as 'protohistoric', the Linear
B tablets do not mark the beginning of Greek history in
the strict, narrower sense in which that word is employed
in this chapter.
     Moreover, although it can never be demonstrated, it has
proved a highly fruitful working hypothesis that in c.1200
the Linear B script shared the fate of the palace-econom-
ies it had exclusively served (Chapter 6) and that subsequently there was felt neither the need nor the inclina-
tion to transmit the technique of writing to the rising
generation. In other words, in the 400 or so years before
the Greeks created an alphabet out of the Phoenician non-
vocalic sign-system they again communicated among themselves, as they had done before c.1500, solely through
oral discourse, whether in poetry or prose, and normally
in face-to-face contact. The fact of renewed illiteracy
is not perhaps in itself remarkable, since the Linear B
script was almost certainly a scribal preserve. But for
the historian of the period from 1300 to the eighth century or even later it raises the crucial problems of method
involved in handling Greek oral tradition.
     Before discussing these, however, I should point out
that, although 'historian', 'historiography' and kindred
expressions have a classical Greek etymology, their respective spheres of reference in ancient and modern (i.e.
'western') cultures do not wholly overlap either in the
activities they describe or in the aims to which the activities in question are directed. It is therefore at
first sight somewhat anomalous that Herodotus is now fêted
in the phrase of Cicero as the 'Father of History' and that
Thucydides is considered - admittedly with qualifications
and serious reservations - to be Klio's favourite son.
But it was long ago recognized that Herodotus was a very

different kind of historian from Thucydides and that both differed again from the ideal type of the modern historian. Where then do the differences lie? Not surely in the matter of objectives narrowly conceived - 'We have to discover not merely how it actually happened but why it happened that way and had to happen that way' (Beloch 1913, 7) - but rather in general outlook and technical methods, above all in the treatment of sources.

From the second half of the seventeenth century onwards the idea had become accepted that a modern scholar had as much justification in writing the history of antiquity as the ancients themselves, even if the methods adopted were strictly speaking as often those of the antiquarian as of the historian proper. The modern historiography of the ancient world began with Edward Gibbon, in the sense that it was he who fused the outlook and methods of the (antiquarian) 'érudits' with those of the enlightened but airy 'philosophes' (below). But the nineteenth century witnessed a remarkable development, sometimes dismissed unfairly as 'Hyperkritik', whose effect can be seen in a work like Bernheim 1894. The essence of the new approach, if it may be shortly summarized, was its canonical insistence that usable evidence must be securely dated, contemporary, documentary and of known provenance. When applied to the ancient world, this approach could lead to excesses, and Beloch himself was rightly castigated for confusing the methods of the historian with those of the various kinds of natural scientist. However, in what follows I hope to show that the reaction against the scepticism of Beloch has in some respects and in some quarters been too sharp.

A leading Homerist has written that 'the question how far tradition may be legitimately called in evidence is a living problem and a chief cause of irreconcilable disagreement among historians and critics' (D.H.F. Gray in Myres 1958, 228). The peculiar qualities of the Homeric epics may require, and they have been given (Appendix 2), somewhat specialized treatment. But this remark applies none the less to all the preserved literary evidence relating to the period from c.1300 to 480 or roughly the late Mycenaean, Dark and Archaic Ages. The discussion cannot be entirely confined to Sparta, but here the problems are seen in particularly sharp relief. For the state never produced a historian of its own, and the course of its eccentric development occasioned with time the phenomenon (by no means confined to the ancient world) aptly named 'the Spartan mirage', the distorted image of what both Spartans and non-Spartans for various and often mutually inconsistent reasons wanted Sparta to be, to stand for and to have accomplished. The reasons why Sparta

never produced a historian have repeatedly been canvassed,
and the conventional solutions are given in terms appropriate to differing views of Spartan abnormality. What is
really remarkable, however, is not that Sparta produced
none but that any Greek state ever produced one. If that
seems paradoxical, in view both of known historical traditions of long standing in other civilizations and the
fifth-century achievement in Greece, then a glance first
at the ways in which Greek writers from Homer to Herodotus
represented the past and then at the available means of
reconstructing it should render the paradox less impressive.

There is some dispute whether Greek historiography experienced a lengthy gestation or sprang fully formed from
the head of Herodotus. But there should be no doubt that
the earliest Greek literature, the Homeric poems, are not
history books. This fact can be established from several
different viewpoints - aetiology, chronology, geography,
delineation of character and motivation, overall intention
and so on - but it remains a fact, despite attempts at
interpretation which seem 'to make no distinction in principle between the tales of prehistoric wars and heroic
deeds retailed by the epic poets and, say, the account of
the Peloponnesian War by Thucydides' (Hampl 1962, 39).

Again, some (including even A.D. Momigliano) have seen
in Hesiod (c.700) the first stirrings of a historical consciousness. But the most immediately relevant passages,
the invocation of the Muses and their ambiguous response
in the preface to the 'Theogony' and the myth of the Five
Races in the 'Works and Days', seem to me to indicate the
contrary. A concept of truth which includes more (but not
much) than simply not-forgetting is outlined, but there is
no hint of methods of verification; truth is guaranteed by
memory, but memory is sacralized as the goddess Mnemosyne,
mother of the Muses, and thereby removed from the human,
empirical sphere; the time factor is taken into account,
but mutally incompatible ways of representing it are hopelessly confused; the aetiological perspective of history
is implicit in the attempt to account for present ills by
a description of the past, but the mortal races of Bronze
and Iron receive no connected narrative and are separated
by a notoriously inorganic interpolation (taken over from
Homer), the Race of semi-divine heroes. In short, the
historical achievement of Hesiod was no more - but from a
religious standpoint no less - than to provide the Greeks
with a mythical past from the Creation of the Gods to the
unexplained end of the Race of Heroes.

Lesser poets than Hesiod, both inside and outside the
'Epic Cycle', who were partly at least utilizing an inher-

ited stock of traditional oral poetical language, merely
'completed' the stories of the 'Iliad' and 'Odyssey' by
providing their events and characters with antecedents and
issue. A large portion of their work, however, consisted
in doing for contemporary humans, especially the blue-
blooded variety, what Hesiod had done for the immortal
gods: elaborating respectable but no less fictional
family-trees. The only Spartan poet in this genre - of
whom the name, a few lines and a handful of doubtfully attributed works are known - is Kinaithon (probably seventh
century). The suggestion that his subjects included the
deeds of Herakles and Orestes makes sense in the light of
the attempt of the Spartan royal families to connect themselves with these 'Achaeans' (Appendix 3) but it hardly
inspires confidence in Kinaithon's impartial striving
after veracity. Indeed, he may owe his rather dim remembrance to precisely this sort of religiose para-political
activity rather than to his skill as a poet.
    By about the mid-seventh century 'original' epic poetry
was beginning to lose its fascination for singers and aud-
iences alike and was being challenged by the more personal
genres of elegy and lyric, in which Sparta was excellently
represented by Tyrtaios (c.650) and Alkman (c.600) respectively. Apart from citing a few acceptable mythological
precedents, including the first surviving version of the
conflated myths of the 'Dorian invasion' and the 'Return
of the Herakleidai', Tyrtaios devoted himself to the present in a pragmatic fashion. Through a skilful fusion of
old and new, both in language and in ideas, he advocated a
moral and political ideal to which future generations of
military-minded Spartans paid more than lip-service.
Alkman was proud of his pedagogic inventiveness, but he
too was largely content to draw on an inherited mythological stock for his themes and may have had the same kind
of anti-historical outlook and effect as Tyrtaios and Kinaithon. His death meant also the death of the local poetic tradition. Half a century later around 550 the Sicilian Stesichoros visited Sparta. It is significant of
the prevailing Spartan intellectual climate that he lent
his voice to an interpretation of a myth-historical tradition (Orestes again) designed to validate the Spartan
claim to sovereignty over Arkadia and perhaps even the
Greek world as a whole.
    By 550, however, the intellectual epicentre had shifted
for good from the Peloponnese to east Greece, especially
Miletos. The prime movers in this inchoate Enlightenment
were natural philosophers (it is wrong to describe their
explanations of natural phenomena as 'scientific' or
'materialist'), and their advance was premissed on 'two

great mental transformations: a positive way of thinking,
excluding every form of the supernatural and rejecting the
implicit assimilation established by myth between physical
phenomena and divine agents; an abstract way of thinking,
depriving reality of that power of change with which myth
endowed it' (Vernant 1971, II, 106). These 'mental transformations' were accompanied by or presupposed corresponding changes in language, which perhaps is not merely 'a
reproducing instrument for voicing ideas, but rather is
itself the shaper of ideas, the program and guide for the
individual's mental activity' (Whorf 1956, 212). Together
they made possible history as we understand it.

Yet initially the spirit of critical secular enquiry
they expressed, including the new notion that men acquire
their knowledge through their own unaided efforts, led to
no search for new sources of information about the past
and no development of a historical consciousness beyond
the tendency, exemplified c.500 by Hekataios (not coincidentally from Miletos), to use personal experience as a
yardstick to measure the intrinsic plausibility of the
'many and ridiculous tales' about the past he picked up on
his travels. (The words in inverted commas are taken from
the Preface to Hekataios' 'Journey around the World',
which is quoted in full in Jeffery 1976, 34.) These
tales, whose content was often ultimately religious, were
thereby pruned of their fantastic accretions, but the
historicity of the residue was not questioned. Thus still
in the fifth century 'the atmosphere in which the Fathers
of History set to work was saturated with myth' (Finley
1975, 13).

Not all myths of course are narrowly speaking historical. But in one application of their general function -
myth 'anchors the present in the past' (Cohen 1969, 349) -
they can present themselves to the historian as evidence
about the past, and we must decide by what criteria they
are to be assessed. Clearly the strict application of
nineteenth-century 'hyper'-critical methods is inappropriate. But how far and in what direction can or should we
today improve on the rationalizing of a Hekataios or the
limited but devastating scepticism of an Eratosthenes, the
Voltaire of antiquity? There is no straightforward answer
to this question, but the best account of the problems involved I know is a now undeservedly little-read essay by
George Grote (1873), to which I shall return.

Any answer, however, must depend on the evaluation of
at least the following factors: the nature of oral tradition (defined as 'verbal testimony transmitted from one
generation to the next one or a later one' in Vansina
1973, xiii) in an illiterate or semi-literate society, or

in a society which did not keep records of a detailed, documentary kind; the distinction between accurate or exaggerated matter of fact on the one hand and variously plausible fiction on the other, and the psychological and sociological circumstances affecting the relationship between them, the ultimately religious content of much Greek legend; and the effects of political and social change on traditional material. It is only when the implications of all these factors taken together are squarely faced that the vastness of Herodotus' achievement - 'there was no Herodotus before Herodotus' (Momigliano 1966, 129) - can be viewed in correct perspective.

It will always be easier to say what Herodotus' achievement amounts to than how it was effected, because he was 'one of the great innovating geniuses of the fifth century' (Collingwood 1946, 28). The three aspects of his achievement which perhaps most commend him to modern scholars are these: his hierarchical ordering of types of evidence and the methods of obtaining it according to their intrinsic reliability; his unobtrusive creation of an acceptable though inevitably lacunose chronological framework; and his generally temperate exercise of that 'judgement' whose indispensability is primarily responsible for keeping the methods of the historian and those of the natural scientist conceptually distinct. We should not, however, exaggerate the discontinuity that Herodotus' work represents. Among his conscious influences must be counted Homer as well as Hekataios: the ancients hit the mark when they characterized Herodotus as 'most Homeric' ('Longinus' 13.3), for style is an essential ingredient of any historian's make-up. It is 'the image of character', as Gibbon put it in the first page of his autobiography. Besides, the critical principles of Herodotus fall short of the rigorousness of Thucydides, for whom 'getting the facts right was all-important' (Ste. Croix 1972, 6).

Thucydides, however, in striving for higher standards of veracity, set up a contradiction never resolved by his successors, even when altered conditions would have made its resolution possible. He believed that only contemporary, and above all political, history could be written adequately, but that the basis of historical documentation should remain oral testimony. That this was not unreasonable in his own day (and a fortiori at all earlier periods) may be judged from the fact that not before the end of the fifth century did his own democratic Athens, for all its energy in publishing documents involving the common weal, establish a central archive. This fact needs emphasis, since the historical methods described and practised by Bernheim and his fellow-thinkers paradigmatically

presuppose the existence of 'objective' documentary records, securely dated and incapable of distortion with the
passage of time. So powerful, however, was the example of
Thucydides that the habit of personal inspection of documents was but rarely acquired in antiquity, the supreme
irony being that from his day onwards the quantity and
quality of documentary material were steadily increased by
antiquarians like Hippias of Elis and Hellanikos of
Lesbos, both of whom, incidentally, visited Sparta and
wrote about Spartan institutions. The result was that, to
the detriment of the respective practitioners, 'political
history and learned research on the past tended to be kept
in two separate compartments' (Momigliano 1966, 4), a res-
trictive practice finally overcome by Edward Gibbon.

The intellectual development begun by the East Greek
philosophers in the mid-sixth century and embraced by all
leading Greek thinkers before Plato has been described as
'the emancipation of thought from myth' (Frankfort et al.
1946, ch. 8). However, even the most fervent admirers of
the 'rationalist' par excellence, Thucydides, are obliged
to admit that his acceptance as fact of certain beliefs
about the very distant (even pre-Trojan War) past sits un-
easily with his rigorous inspection of contemporary testimony and that in this respect he went further even than
the 'credulous' Herodotus. The fourth-century 'universal'
historian Ephorus, it is true, declined to treat of the
period before the 'Return of the Herakleidai'; but it is
not clear whether this reflects a sceptical outlook or the
view that the earlier period was irrelevant or had been
adequately treated already (e.g. by Homer). In any case,
neither he nor any other surviving author before Eratosthenes, head of the Library at Alexandria in the late
third century (and 'Beta', as he was known, was the exception to prove many rules), impugned the historicity not
merely of the variously fantastic accretions but also of
the supposedly true kernel of the traditional tales.

The proper question to ask then is not why it took so
long, but how far it would be possible - for historians in
antiquity from the fifth century on and for us alike - to
distinguish historical fact among the mass of traditional
material, which consisted partly of knowledge about the
past embedded in poetical or prose narratives handed down
through the generations, in part of sheer fiction handed
down in the same way, and partly of the learned specula-
tions of over-heated imaginations. For it seems probable,
as I have pointed out, that between c.1200 and c.800
Greece was illiterate and that between c.800 and c.450
there was no recitation or writing of history (as we understand that word) and precious little retrieval and

storage of the stuff from which history can be created. Indeed, in the case of Sparta an apocryphal 'rhetra' (ordinance) expressly forbade the inscribing of laws, and the only other records kept here were lists of names (victors at the great religious festivals, eponymous magistrates and kings) and oracles. The authenticity of the earliest sections of these lists and their properly historical value have both been questioned, with some justice.

Faced with this situation, Grote correctly asked (1873, 87): 'With what consistency can you require that a community which either does not command the means, or has not learned the necessity, of registering the phenomena of its present, should possess any knowledge of the phenomena of its past?' He himself, however, was too good a historian to deny outright that traditional material contained any factual element. He insisted only that belief should be withheld until the tradition itself could be independently verified.

The advantage we hold over Grote today is not so much a greater sophistication in methods as a vastly increased knowledge of the contemporary material remains, which are authentic, though not self-explanatory, records of the times they represent. These are the only sure basis on which to reconstruct the history of the period down to the eighth century, if not later; but they do not constitute a sufficient basis. In particular, archaeology rarely if ever warrants narrowly political inferences (see further Chapter 1). Certainly an explanation which takes account of both the traditional literary evidence and the material remains may be preferable to an explanation which ignores one or the other. But this by itself does not increase its likelihood of being correct. In short, I agree with Gibbon that 'ancient history' (properly so called) begins in the sixth century 'with the Persian Empire and the Republics of Rome and Athens'. I remain extremely doubtful that it will ever be possible to write a wholly convincing narrative or systematic account of Greek history before c.550, the starting-point of Herodotus, the 'Father of History'. In the remaining chapters of this Part, therefore, I can claim no more than to have based my account on all the available ancient evidence.

NOTES ON FURTHER READING

The fundamental publication of the Linear B syllabary is Ventris and Chadwick 1973. Most of the tablets are now fully published and transcribed. For the inscriptions on vases see Sacconi 1974. The controversy over the dating

of the Knossos tablets is briefly resumed by Hood (1971,
112-15); but Hood is one of the few who still reject the
decipherment. Perhaps the best general discussion of the
bearing of the tablets on the various aspects of Mycenaean
civilization is Hiller and Panagl 1976; a good short summary is Dow 1968.

An introductory work on the historical value of oral
tradition is Vansina 1973, but this is controversial even
among Africanists. Henige 1974 is in some ways superior,
but he too relies heavily on African evidence. This qualification is crucial, since the evaluation of oral tradition as historical evidence depends largely upon detailed
ethnographic knowledge of the features of oral history as
a system within the culture under study rather than as
isolated scraps of ideas.

I have briefly discussed the origins of the alphabet,
with special reference to Lakonia, in Cartledge 1978. The
basic account is still Jeffery 1961, 1-42; add now Coldstream 1977, ch. 11.

For the distinct activities of the historian and the
antiquarian, and a historical perspective on this restric-
tive practice, see Momigliano 1966, ch. 1. An excellent
discussion of Gibbon's contribution to historical method
is Momigliano 1966, ch. 2. But antiquarianism retains a
strong foothold in ancient history to this day.

For the essential distinctions between the methods of
the historian and those of the natural scientists see
Berlin 1960; Hexter 1971, ch. 1. But the gap may not be
quite as wide as they suppose.

The standard work on the 'Spartan mirage' in antiquity
is Ollier 1933, 1943. Tigerstedt 1965 and 1973 is more
complete, but belies its title; it is particularly useful
for its massive bibliographical footnotes. Far more en-
lightening is Rawson 1969, which brings the story down to
the Second World War. Starr 1965 is usefully succinct.

On post-Homeric epic poetry see Huxley 1969, esp. 86-9
(Kinaithon); but the assertion that 'a flourishing body of
local legends in Lakedaimon ... came down from the Mycenaean age, preserved and elaborated by the ... Achaean survivors from the ruin of the bronze age civilisations of
Peloponnese' (85) should be treated with caution.

Bibliography on Tyrtaios and Alkman may be found in the
notes to Chapters 8 and 9. For Stesichoros and Sparta see
West 1969, 148.

On Hekataios generally see Pearson 1939, ch. 2. His
possible contribution to the transmission of the Spartan
king-lists is considered in Appendix 3. For Herodotus'
place in the history of historiography see Momigliano
1966, ch. 8. On Thucydides see the notes to Chapter 12.

Eratosthenes' multifaceted intellectual achievement is assessed by Fraser (1970; 1972 passim).

An excellent recent restatement of what seems to me essentially Grote's position on mythical and legendary tradition is Finley 1975, ch. 1.

6 The last Mycenaens c. 1300-1050

The Linear B tablets, as we saw in the previous chapter,
do not enable us to write a history properly so called of
the late Mycenaean period. However, the use of tablets
made of clay does suggest at least a prima facie comparab-
ility with the contemporary civilizations of Egypt, Anatolia and the Levant and so provides a convenient transition to what I believe to be a proper context for studying late Mycenaean Greece. The documentary evidence for
contact or conflict between the Mycenaean Greeks and their
eastern neighbours in the political, diplomatic or military spheres may in many cases merely be the spurious outcome of 'a sort of philological game of hopscotch' (Carpenter 1966, 45). But the intercourse in articles of
trade (actual finds and inferences from the Linear B tablets), linguistic borrowings, artistic interconnections
and, I should say, the very use of the unsuitable medium
of clay for Linear B script - these are not so easily dismissed. I am of course far from believing that Mycenaean
Greece was just 'a peripheral culture of the Ancient East,
its westernmost extension' (Astour 1967, 357f.). But I
find it implausible that the contemporaneity of the Mycenaean 'time of troubles' with the series of destructive upheavals engulfing the whole eastern Mediterranean basin
was just a coincidence, even if the nature of the connection between them cannot be precisely demonstrated.
    Underlying tensions in the Middle East were given omin-
ously concrete expression in c.1300, when Egypt and Hatti
(the Hittites) fought a major but inconclusive battle at
Qadesh in Syria. Sixteen years later Rameses II and Hat-
tusilis III concluded peace on terms which included guar-
antees of mutual aid in case either power was attacked by
a third party. The treaty was then sealed in the accepted
manner by a marriage-alliance. The practical effect of
this elaborate diplomacy, however, was relatively short-

lived.   In c.1232 Merneptah was obliged to repulse an invasion of Egypt mounted by Libyans from Cyrenaica and
'northerners from all lands'; and in c.1191 and again in
c.1188 Rameses III defeated insurgents who came by land
and sea from the north-east to settle in the Nile delta.
In the interval between these onerous but successful exploits of the two Pharaohs the capital of the Hittites at
Hattusas in Anatolia was destroyed and their empire disintegrated.   The kingdoms of Ugarit, Alalakh and Alasia
(Cyprus?) met a similar fate, and there were further disasters elsewhere in the Levant.   In the space of about a
century the balance of power in the Middle East had been
forcibly and irretrievably altered.

In round numbers 1300 can therefore legitimately be regarded as a pivotal date in the history of the Bronze Age
civilizations abutting the east Mediterranean basin.   In
Greece it was approximately then that the Mycenaean civilization received its diagnostic expression in the construction of massive fortifications and palatial complexes
at Mycenae and elsewhere.   To be more exact, 1300 was the
date now most widely accepted for the transition from the
LH IIIA style of pottery to LH IIIB.   This may seem an improbable way of making a historical assertion, but history
is nothing without chronology, and the chronology of the
Aegean Bronze Age, as already remarked, is a matter of the
typology of its pottery.   The three main ceramic phases of
the Mycenaean period (LH I-III) are not incompatible with
the few available excavated stratigraphies (most recently
that from Nichoria in Messenia).   But the sub-divisions of
these phases - seven for the third alone and ten in all,
according to the still generally useful scheme of A. Furumark first proposed in 1941 - are based on somewhat subjective judgments of the direction and pace of stylistic
change and on arbitrary decisions as to where one sub-
phase ends and the next begins.   Absolute dates, moreover,
may be derived only from the association of Mycenaean pottery in datable Egyptian contexts or with objects that can
be cross-referenced with the Egyptian series.   Thus it is
hardly surprising that both the initial and the terminal
dates of LH IIIB pottery are disputed (1300 and 1200 are
strictly approximations and perhaps considerably too low)
and that the nature and pace of stylistic change are de-
tectable with assurance only at Mycenae.   These are not
trivial matters, since the 'historiography' of the late
Mycenaean period depends upon them.

It is not disputed though that pottery can and must be
used as evidence for chronology.   However, deeper problems
confront those who wish to draw other kinds of inference
from the various facets of pottery manufacture and dis-

tribution. These problems are particularly acute when
pottery, thanks to its fitness to survive, constitutes the
bulk of the artefactual or - as so often in prehistoric
contexts - the total evidence, and when the amount of controlled excavation has been comparatively slight. Such is
the situation in Mycenaean Lakonia. Take, for instance,
the question of population density. Of the inherent limitations of evidence from survey listed in Chapter 4 the
one particularly relevant here is that not all types of
pot have the same or even comparable potential for survival or for survival in an obvious or diagnostic way. For
the overwhelming proportion of Lakonian LH IIIB sites identified by surface survey alone made their presence known
through the medium of kylikes, deep bowls and stemmed
bowls, often by a combination of sherds from all three
shapes. Since the stems of the kylikes and stemmed bowls
are particularly durable and eye-catching, it is theoret-
ically possible that the apparently high relative density
of population in Lakonia in LH IIIB is a mirage arising
from an accident of cultural choice in the ceramic sphere.
Fortunately this inference can be checked against evidence
of other kinds and from other areas and is unlikely to be
correct. But it is not beyond a doubt incorrect, and the
possibility underlines the urgency of the need for more
excavation.

Mycenaean IIIB pottery was diffused very widely. 'Developed LH IIIB is the great period of the koine and mass
production' (Wace 1957, 222). On the mainland it enjoyed
common currency as far north as Thessaly, though it was
imported only desultorily into the mountainous interior of
Epirus. Overseas it was used in the east and the west
both by non-Greeks and by temporary or permanent Mycenaean
expatriates. The concentration of exports, which had
begun to gather momentum during LH IIIA, may be somehow
connected with the fall of Knossos c.1375 or more directly
with the establishment of Mycenaean traders in semi-perma-
nent overseas emporia, for example at Scoglio del Tonno in
the instep of Italy (near the later Spartan settlement of
Taras: Chapter 8), Ugarit in Syria and various places in
Cyprus. However, along with the increasing weight of production and breadth of distribution there developed a
striking homogeneity of fabric and style which makes it
difficult to discover the provenance of individual pots or
sherds. Thus the hope expressed by Wace and Blegen (1939)
that it would one day be possible to differentiate Lakonian and Corinthian LH IIIB pottery in the same routine way
as their Archaic successors has so far proved vain, although some progress has been made through optical emis-
sion spectroscopy and neutron-activation analysis. There

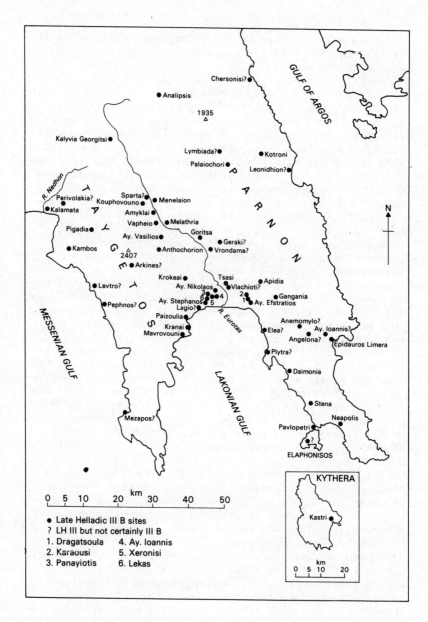

FIGURE 7   Late Helladic IIIB Lakonia

is, however, a certain amount of regional differentiation, visible to the naked eye and apparent to the touch, in both clay and paint.

So far thirty-five sites in Lakonia have certainly yielded LH IIIB pottery, and four more doubtfully so (Figure 7). Of the maximum of thirty-nine, however, only five are scientifically excavated habitation-sites. I shall return to these in due course, but first I want to dwell briefly on Pavlopetri in the Malea peninsula, the chief site in the Vatika plain and so the prehistoric forerunner of classical Boiai. This would have been the sixth excavated habitation-site were it not now underwater, where natural conditions prevented the recovery of more than a bare outline. But even this outline is instructive, in three main ways. First, the divers located only two chamber-tombs, which are usually considered the customary receptacles of dead Mycenaeans, as against thirty-seven cist-graves, which had been typical of the MH period. In view of this find (if the cists are indeed Mycenaean) and of recent discoveries of cist-grave cemeteries in Boiotia and Thessaly, it is perhaps prudent to suspend judgment on what was normal Mycenaean burial practice. Second, the settlement came to an end in LH IIIB and was not apparently reoccupied for many centuries. This experience is repeated throughout Lakonia. Finally, and uniquely, it was possible to get some idea of the total area of the settlement (at least 45,000 m.^{2}) and to rescue something of its plan, including rectilinear streets with their frontages of houses. These details bear directly and informatively on our discussion of Renfrew's estimate of the population of prehistoric Greece which we left hanging in the air in Chapter 4.

For Renfrew assumed that Late Bronze Age settlements in the Aegean were typically 'of urban or proto-urban nature'. This assumption may perhaps not be contradicted by Pavlopetri; but his second assumption, that the average size of a Mycenaean settlement was 20,000 m.^{2}, certainly seems to be. The difficulty of course is to decide whether Pavlopetri was of 'average' size, since what Renfrew keeps well hidden is that in the absence of total excavation or survey there is no scientific way of estimating the size of an ancient settlement with any precision. True, Hope Simpson (in Loy 1970, 149-55) has attempted a self-confessedly subjective classification of some ninety Mycenaean sites in Messenia as Small, Small-Medium, Medium, Medium-Large or Large on the basis of the scatter of surface sherds. But the sherd-scatter is a wildly unreliable criterion: for example, the area of some 200,000 m.^{2} assigned on this basis to the Palaiopyrgi hill near Vapheio,

which thus becomes the largest known site in prehistoric
Lakonia, seems utterly disproportionate. However, to be
fair to Hope Simpson, a cursory comparison of his individual classifications with the evidence of the sherd-scatter
ostensibly supporting them reveals no strict correlation.
In other words, factors besides sherd-scatter - such as
extent of arable land (by far the most important), strat-
egic/commercial position and available water supply - were
equally and rightly taken into account. Thus, to sum up
our long discussion, Renfrew's estimate of 50,000 inhabitants for Mycenaean Lakonia may or may not correspond to
reality. We just cannot say for certain. However, since
this is the figure attributed by McDonald and Hope Simpson
to the larger and far more intensively surveyed region of
Messenia in LH IIIB, I should suppose it to be a considerable overestimate, at least on present evidence.

The five excavated LH IIIB habitation-sites in Lakonia
are Amyklai and the Menelaion complex in the Spartan
basin, Karaousi and Ay. Stephanos on either side of the
Helos plain, and Anthochorion in west Vardhounia. The results from Karaousi and Anthochorion were relatively disappointing, but the other three were interesting in their
different ways. Amyklai's chief significance lies in its
evidence of late Mycenaean cult (below). The akropolis of
Ay. Stephanos was fortified, perhaps more than once, during LH IIIB (to judge from the associated pottery). It
thereby takes its place with Mouriatadha in northern Messenia among fortified settlements in the southern Peloponnese, and its identification with the Helos of the Homeric 'Catalogue of Ships' (Appendix 2) is a definite possibility. Certainly the site was strategically placed to
guard both the western side of the lower Eurotas valley
and the approach to Lakonia via the Lakonian Gulf and was
advantageously situated to exploit marine resources. On
the other hand, the surrounding arable land is extremely
poor, a deficiency which was remedied maybe through sym-
biosis with 'the land-locked Panayiotis community around
the extensive Neogen soils on the north-east corner of the
plain' (Bintliff 1977, 476). Thus the main focus of interest must be the apparently unfortified settlement on
the site of the historical sanctuary dedicated to Menelaos
and Helen.

As we have seen, the archaeological picture for the
Mycenaean occupation has been clarified by the recent (and
not yet finally published) British excavations, but there
is still no conclusive corroboration of the widespread
view that this was the palatial seat of a Mycenaean Menelaos. The settlement was undoubtedly the central place of
Mycenaean Lakonia, but archaeologically all we have is a

well-appointed 'mansion' reoccupied partially, after a gap
of more than a century, during LH IIIB ('Dawkins House')
and then destroyed by fire, together with its store of
sealed wine-jars, towards the end of the same phase. The
agents and motive of the destruction are alike unknown,
and it would be incautious as yet to link this destruction
of a single building with those attested on a number of
the major Mycenaean centres elsewhere on the mainland in
LH IIIB or C, let alone to think of the settlement as a
whole in terms of Mycenae, Tiryns or Pylos. An isolated
find complicates the picture further. This is a fibula
(safety-pin) of the 'violin-bow' type which Blinkenberg in
his classic synoptic study (1926, 50) deemed to be the
earliest of the class and of LH IIIB/C origin. Our example could have come from a late Mycenaean tomb. Alternatively, like a handful found in the Orthia sanctuary at
Sparta itself, it was dedicated in the eighth century or
later and had survived the interval perhaps as an 'antique'
heirloom.

The evidence for cult in LH IIIB Lakonia is even less
extensive than that for habitation, being practically confined to the site at the historical sanctuary of Apollo at
Amyklai four to five kilometres south of classical Sparta.
There was a Bronze Age settlement here from EH times but
this seems to have been temporarily interrupted at the
close of the MH period. In LH IIIB a sanctuary was established, as is shown by the large number of terracotta figurines of stylized 'goddesses' and animals found, together
with two fragments of almost life-sized human figures in
clay. The motive for setting up the cult is of course unknown, and, given the nature of our evidence for Mycenaean
religion - inferences from archaeological material, later
literary testimony and in some cases Linear B tablets - it
is always hazardous to conjecture the identity of Mycenaean deities, let alone their possible powers and attributes. But Amyklai is one of the places where the evidence
has seemed to justify bolder hypotheses. Since this has a
more immediate bearing on the 'Dorianizing' of Lakonia,
discussion has been deferred to the next chapter.

The remainder of the excavated LH IIIB evidence comes
from tombs distributed throughout Lakonia, nearly all of
the chamber-type (Melathria, Krokeai, Tsasi, Mavrovouni,
Pellana, Kotroni, Epidauros Limera and Kythera). Krokeai,
however, in east Vardhounia has also produced a slab-
covered shaft-grave in use from LH II onwards. The associated settlement was probably connected with the 'antico
verde' or 'lapis Lacedaemonius' (i.e. labrador porphyrite)
quarries at the appropriately named Psephi. The stone was
widely used in Mycenaean Lakonia; worked cores have been

found, for example, at Ay. Stephanos. Indeed, it was certainly being used in Crete by LM I for both vases and
sealstones (Warren 1969, 132f.). Like the 'antico rosso'
from Kyprianon in south Mani, it was employed to face the
thirteenth-century tholos tomb known as the Treasury of
Atreus at Mycenae. Neither stone, however, appears to
have been used in Lakonia between the thirteenth century
BC and the Roman period, although there may be a reference
to 'verde antico' in Theophrastos ('De Lapidibus' 4.25, if
the emendation 'Lakainon' is adopted). The tholoi at Analipsis and Kambos may just have remained in use until LH
IIIB, suggesting the continued existence of local nobilit-
ies. The other side of the social coin may be represented
by the above-mentioned cists from Pavlopetri and some single inhumations from Ay. Stephanos.

This leaves twenty-one sites where occupation is attested by surface finds alone and one, classical Sparta,
where LH IIIB has indeed turned up in excavation on the
akropolis hill but (despite the intensity of exploration)
in such minute quantity as to suggest a minor and perhaps
not even a permanent settlement. This is of considerable
significance, as we shall see in the next chapter.

The resulting settlement-pattern suggests a relatively
high density of population in thirteenth-century Lakonia,
concentrated unsurprisingly in the Eurotas valley but extending suggestively into upland and sometimes mountainous
country too. As Bintliff (1977, 699) has noticed, the
major settlements in the Sparta plain are regularly spaced
at intervals of five kilometres so as to exploit the adjacent terrain with maximum efficiency. If we include
those sites whose surface pottery cannot be more precisely
classified than LH III, the total of sixty-three does not
lag so conspicuously behind that obtained for south-west
Peloponnese after several seasons of intensive and co-
ordinated survey work. The latter region too shows a maximum density of settlement in the LH IIIB period, as one
might have inferred from the plentiful archaeological and
documentary evidence from the 'Palace of Nestor' not far
north of classical Pylos. However, the Messenian evidence
is perhaps significantly richer and more variegated: the
palace has its mortuary correlates in a finely constructed
and lavishly endowed tholos and impressive chamber-tombs
for which the only real Lakonian parallel, Vapheio, belongs
to an earlier epoch. The correspondence, in short, is
only of a very general nature.

Nevertheless, one aspect of this generally weak correspondence has been heavily stressed in some recent 'historical' accounts of the Mycenaean period, perhaps with good
reason, namely the exponential decline in the number of

Lakonian sites attested for the LH IIIC period (seven certain, another eight possible) in contrast to the LH IIIB
peak of thirty-nine (max.). The corresponding figures for
Messenia are thirteen certain and another three possible
LH IIIC sites as against sixty-seven (min.) LH IIIB. It
therefore seems a fair inference that 'in the twelfth and
eleventh centuries this fertile and well-watered area was
occupied by scarcely more than 10 per cent of the people
who had lived there in the thirteenth century B.C.' (MME
143). The rest of this chapter will be addressed to an
attempted explanation of this massive problem.

First, though, the evidence for LH IIIC occupation of
Lakonia (Figure 8). At Amyklai there is actually an ob-
servable increase either in population or perhaps just in
cultic activity; continuing external contact is shown by
one sherd and a fragment of a wheel-made terracotta statuette, both decorated in the 'Close Style' of the Argolis.
Occupation may have continued in the area into the eleventh century, but thereafter, archaeologically at any rate,
there is a break in continuity - to whose significance I
return in Chapter 7. Geraki yielded three 'goddess' figurines apparently of the 'psi' type, but these may not
even be Mycenaean (French 1971, 139). A little LH IIIC
pottery has been excavated at Karaousi and Anthochorion
and found on the surface at Apidia. The excavated tomb-
sites are slightly more promising. A kernos of unique
form from a chamber-tomb at Krokeai shows that life was
still supportable in eastern Vardhounia. Seven LH IIIC
vases from two chamber-tombs at Pellana and one whole pot
and some sherds from Ay. Stephanos indicate the same for
the northern and southern ends respectively of the Eurotas
furrow.

But most impressive and revealing of all in their richness and chronological range, together with their evidence
of external contacts, are the finds from chamber-tombs at
Epidauros Limera. These may be thought to represent some
general trends of the period in Greece as a whole. The
area undoubtedly received an influx of settlers during LH
IIIC. We cannot be sure whether their Aegean connections
(below) were established before or after their arrival,
but in view of the evidence for depopulation elsewhere in
Lakonia it is reasonable to suggest that the newcomers
were displaced Lakonians. The most obvious point of origin is the Spartan basin, which has easy routes of communication with Epidauros Limera (Chapter 10) and suffered
apparently the greatest depopulation. It is at least
highly suggestive that this area was precisely the place
of refuge selected by the inhabitants of the Sparta area
in face of the Slav invasions of the late sixth century

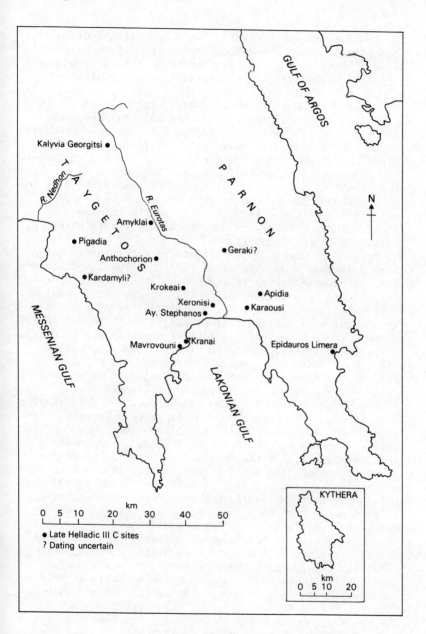

FIGURE 8 Late Helladic IIIC Lakonia

AD (Pavlopetri was another). Once established at Epidauros Limera, these Mycenaeans formed part of an Aegean
'koine' embracing sites like Perati in Attika (probably
another refugee-settlement), Asine in the Argolis and
Naxos in the Kyklades. Indeed, their pottery in the earlier stages of LH IIIC shows contact even with Crete. The
cemetery, moreover, remained in use into sub-Mycenaean
times, perhaps as late as c.1050. When the other members
of the 'koine' dropped away, the potters of Epidauros
Limera may have turned for their continuing inspiration to
the communities of central Greece. The latest finds, however, fail to bridge the all-important transition from the
sub-Mycenaean to the Protogeometric period, and the subsequent fate of the erstwhile refugees is unknown. In
fact, Epidauros Limera ceases to exist, archaeologically,
until the seventh century.

To sum up, the LH IIIC settlement-pattern marks a radical departure from that of LH IIIB in Lakonia. The number of inhabited sites is reduced by about 62.5 per cent
overall and by a greater percentage in the Eurotas valley.
Some habitation, it is true, is apparent in all the main
geological areas of the region, but it is on an enormously
reduced scale. Conversely, Amyklai possibly and Epidauros
Limera certainly increased in size. After c.1100, however, Lakonia to all outward appearances was uninhabited
for the first time since Middle Palaeolithic times, but
that is a problem to be considered in Chapter 7.

The phenomenon of late Mycenaean decline, if correctly
identified, is by no means peculiar to Lakonia. The parallel situation in Messenia has already been noted and in
fact it extends to all the major regions of Mycenaean
settlement. Equally the internal redistribution of population inferred from the Epidauros Limera evidence is
written large in the influx of settlers during LH IIIC to
previously marginal areas such as Achaia and the Ionian
islands of Ithaka and Kephallenia, not to mention those
who went as far afield as Cyprus and Crete. Indeed, there
is later literary evidence which suggests that Lakonians
figured prominently among the emigrants. However, these
parallels should not perhaps be pressed. The Lakonian
evidence is provisional and in particular there is only
the destruction of the 'Dawkins House' at the Menelaion
site to compare to the disasters which overtook Thebes,
Gla, Iolkos, Mycenae, Tiryns and Pylos (to name only the
more prominent centres) during LH IIIB and C. None the
less, the mainland Greek disequilibrium coincides broadly
with the upheavals that engulfed the entire east Mediterranean basin at about the same time, and it would be anomalous, I think, if the Lakonian development were wholly

independent of them.

At first blush a hypothesis which accounted for all these geographically disparate yet superficially similar and roughly contemporary phenomena would appear to have the merits of simplicity and economy. But in the present state of our knowledge no such hypothesis can be convincingly advanced. That of Rhys Carpenter, for example, which postulates a shift in the trade winds bringing on an extended drought and consequential famine, disease and possibly riots, seems unsupported and possibly falsified by what relevant evidence there is from Greece (Chapter 1). Nor does the documentary evidence of famine at Hattusas and Ugarit c.1200 prove that there was a climatic change then either in the central Anatolian plateau or anywhere else in the Near East, let alone Greece. Conversely, the theory of a widespread epidemic of bubonic plague cannot be evaluated for lack of evidence. Nor can it be shown that the peoples who confronted the Egyptian Pharaohs were directly responsible for the downfall of the Hittite empire or the destructions of Ugarit and other sites in the Levant and Greece.

It is therefore permissible to look for more localized and specifically Greek explanations. Using the evidence of archaeology and the Linear B inscriptions, it could be argued that the intensification of settlement, large-scale pasturage and expansion of overseas trade during LH IIIB had led to extensive forest-clearance and the exhaustion of marginal land, and that the resulting deforestation and erosion had had a critically deleterious effect on the vegetational climax. Thus the depopulation in LH IIIC could have been the consequence both of flight to less heavily settled areas in search of food and of the death by famine and disease of many of those who remained behind.

Deforestation and soil-erosion, however, are not a sufficient explanation of the material record: they leave out of account the destructions. Since these were inflicted by people who have left no other distinguishing mark of their presence, and since the Mycenaean way of life continued thereafter, albeit on a reduced scale, it follows that the attackers either were themselves Mycenaeans or were outsiders whose material accoutrements were either Mycenaean or perishable or hitherto unrecognized or not left behind. Unfortunately, the Linear B tablets - despite the ingenuity of those who regard a possibly extraordinary requisition of bronze, the dispostion of a coastal watch and possible human sacrifice as signs of a military and social crisis in the Pylos kingdom - cannot shed further light on the nature of the crisis or the identity of the destroyers. The wall across the Isthmus of Corinth (if, as it surely is, it is a fortification-wall and spanned the entire Isthmus) is ambiguous too: it was built in the LH IIIB/C transition by users of Mycenaean pottery and, like the attempts to safeguard water-supply at Athens, Mycenae and Tiryns, seems to betoken exceptional concern for defence; but the dispute over relative pottery chronology at this critical point leaves open the possibilities that it was constructed after some, most or even all of the LH IIIB destructions in the Peloponnese.

Two competing hypotheses, which are not in fact mutually exclusive, have therefore been proposed to explain the archaeological 'facts' of destruction followed by dispersal and reduction of population. The first, which brings invaders by land from north of the Isthmus and indeed of Greece, suits the LH IIIC picture of relative prosperity in the Aegean and influxes of population into Achaia, the Ionian islands and further afield to south and east. It might also account for a number of intrusive artefacts of vaguely 'northern' type, especially hand-made pottery, which made an appearance in southern Greece around the LH IIIB/C transition. On the other hand, the marked increase in cist-burials after c.1150, which has been claimed as another indication of northern intruders, could be a purely endogenous phenomenon. More important still, though, this hypothesis fails to explain satisfactorily why the postulated invaders confined their attention in western Peloponnese to the 'Palace of Nestor' and why they did not settle in Greece - unless, that is, they were in fact Mycenaeans and so archaeologically indistinguishable.

It is this latter possibility which has given rise to the second main explanatory hypothesis, embraced for example by Hooker (1977), namely civil war. For if the destroyers were Mycenaeans, then they could be either the common people in opposition to the palace-bound ruling class in each region, or disaffected members of the ruling stratum and their supporters, or rulers (or coalition of rulers) of other regions. Further speculation could be, and usually is, conducted on the basis of the material remains alone. But as a rule it is not long before recourse is had to the very much later literary sources to eke out the archaeological evidence. For the reasons set out in Chapter 5 and Appendix 2 I do not believe such recourse is legitimate.

However, if pressed to provide an explanation I would adopt elements of the two main hypotheses outlined above and combine them with my starting-point in this chapter, the wider upheavals in the east Mediterranean basin. Thus a domestic economic slump aggravated by the disruption of

overseas trade could have weakened the authority of the
Mycenaean rulers and impelled them to solve their problems, in a manner familiar to students of the eighth century (Chapter 8), at the expense of the cultivable land of
their neighbours. The resulting warfare, perhaps accompanied by civil strife and influxes of barbarian intruders, might have destroyed the finely balanced economic and
social system which the palace-bureaucracies administered,
together with the palaces themselves. Once their centri-
petal force was gone the unified regions of the Mycenaean
cosmos will have dissolved once more into isolated islands
of population adrift in an uncharted political sea and
forced back on their own immediate resources much as at
the beginning of the MH period.

NOTES ON FURTHER READING

The problem of correctly characterizing the political and
economic structure of the (tablet-using) Mycenaean state
can only be complicated by the use of misleading analogies
or loose teminology, above all that of feudalism: Finley
1957. On the other hand, that mediaeval analogies can
elucidate Mycenaean economic development is shown in Hutchinson 1977, even if many of his historical conclusions
are unconvincing.
      The 'philological game of hopscotch' referred to by
Rhys Carpenter is best exemplified in Astour 1967, ch. 1.
Like hopscotch, this sort of approach explains nothing and
gets you nowhere. For artistic interrelations between
Greece and the Orient see Kantor 1947 and Smith 1965. The
mechanisms of foreign trade, however, are opaque: it could
perhaps be argued that the need for metals impelled the
Mycenaeans to take to the sea, but the equally crucial
Athenian corn-supply in the Classical period was by no
means in Athenian hands exclusively; and the only excavated wreck of the period, really a travelling bazaar, is
probably Syrian or Palestinian (Bass 1967).
      For the absolute chronology of the Late Bronze Age I
have followed Thomas 1967 and Rowton 1970. The destructions and upheaval in the east Mediterranean basin are
discussed by Hooker (1977, 156-60). I agree with his rejection of 'the picture of the Sea Peoples as a powerful
army, moving irresistibly and of set purpose, until their
final defeat at the hand of the Egyptians' and with his
explanation of the ferment as stemming from the collapse
of the Hittite empire; on the 'Sea Peoples' see now the
intelligent synthesis of Sandars (1978).
      The standard textbook of Mycenaean pottery is still

Furumark 1941. For the LH IIIA and B phases at Mycenae a
stream of articles by E. French is indispensable reading,
but the details of the sequence elsewhere are still controversial: 'when we say Mycenaean IIIB pottery, what
exactly do we mean?' (Mylonas 1964, 373). For recent
developments in scientific analyses of Mycenaean pottery
see Bieber et al. 1976.

The most convenient reference work on Mycenaean sites
is Hope Simpson 1965; a second edition by Hope Simpson and
O. Dickinson is in preparation.

For the stoppered wine-jars from the Menelaion see
Vickery 1936, 32, 59. Pace Oliva (1971, 16), there is no
evidence that they were 'clearly ready for despatch'.

Mycenaean cult-places are conveniently listed in Haegg
1968. For some sensible remarks on the difficulties of
discussing Mycenaean religion see Hooker 1977, 192ff. (but
even he succumbs to the desire to know).

The evidence of destructions in LH IIIB is given in
Buck 1969. For the decline in population in LH IIIC in
Greece generally see the table in Aalin 1962, 148 (now
considerably out of date).

7 The first Dorians c. 1050-775

The middle word of this chapter's title, like my agnostic discussion of the destructions and depopulation in southern Greece during the latest Mycenaean period, conceals a parti pris. For although an impressive roll-call of scholars have attempted to explain the archaeological facts (if they are facts) set out in Chapter 6 in terms of the 'tradition' concerning the Dorians and their movements (Buck 1969, 280 n. 31; Rubinsohn 1975), most of these have not perceived that the 'tradition' must itself first be evaluated on its own merits before it is appropriate to apply external tests. When the 'tradition' is thus evaluated, it is seen that the literary evidence is so far removed from the 'Dorian invasion' in time and so distorted according to the bias or ignorance of the speaker or writer that an extreme sceptic like Beloch (1913, 76-96) could even legitimately deny its very occurrence. I shall argue that scepticism need not be carried so far, but a glance at the main items of literary evidence (Hooker 1977, 213-22) will help to explain Beloch's stance: the deceptively coherent narrative of the Dorian migration and occupation of the Peloponnese produced by a rationalizing mythographer like Apollodoros in the second century represents 'only the main element in the tradition'; and there are other elements recorded by various authors at sundry times and places which are 'conflicting and even contradictory' (Tomlinson 1972, 59-61).

   The history of Sparta was particularly badly mauled in this regard, not at all without Spartan connivance, in a manner made possible by the attitudes to preservation of knowledge about the past described in Chapter 5. We may perhaps distinguish four main levels in the process of systematic distortion. In the first place, as Edward Gibbon put it, 'some decent mixture of prodigy and fable has, in every age, been supposed to reflect a becoming

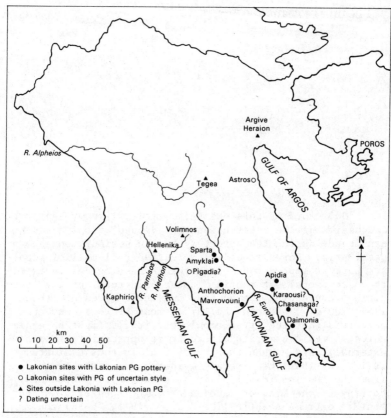

FIGURE 9   Protogeometric Lakonia

majesty on the origin of great cities'. Since the real
Dorian Sparta could hardly be called a 'great city' before
the eighth century, it was presumably then that 'prodigy
and fable' in the guise of the myth of the 'Return of the
Herakleidai' (Tigerstedt 1965, 28-36) were first laid
under contribution to shed their retrospective glory.
Next, the power and territory acquired by force of arms
was justified, again in the language of myth but also with
the aid of Delphic Apollo, as merely the taking of what
anyway belonged to the Spartans by right of their rulers'
'Achaean' descent. Third, and by a less obvious process,
the king-lists of the two Spartan royal houses transcended
their local significance to secure a cardinal position in
the chronography and historiography of the post-heroic age
of Greece as a whole (Appendix 3). The surviving narrative accounts of the 'Return', the earliest of which is
that of Ephorus (70F117), all show signs of contamination

from this source. Finally, the Sparta which emerged into
the light of history as the most powerful state in Greece
possessed customs and institutions that seemed alien and
antiquated to those interested in recording them. Reviv-
alist movements in the third century and again during the
early Roman Empire naturally served to reinforce this conservative image (Bourguet 1927, 21), and Sparta came to be
regarded as archetypally 'Dorian'. This aspect of the
'Spartan mirage', as we shall see, is perhaps the hardest
of all to penetrate with assurance.

The most hopeful method of demolishing the more extrav-
agant claims of 'tradition' is a sober statement of the
archaeological record, fragmentary and one-sided though
this undoubtedly is. Before examining it closely, however, it is necessary to reiterate that, as with the
Trojan War (Appendix 2), disbelief in the elaborated details and alleged attendant circumstances of an event does
not entail disbelief in the event itself. For by one of
those quirks of scholarly fashion Beloch's formerly generally discredited denial of a 'Dorian invasion' has recently received seemingly powerful and independent support
from philology, archaeology and the history of religion.

First, then, philology. In the last chapter I asserted
dogmatically that the Linear B tablets were unable to shed
light directly on the destructions which accidentally en-
sured their preservation. In fact, though, Chadwick
(1976b) has now argued that the presence of Dorians in the
Peloponnese already in the Mycenaean period may be inferred from certain linguistic features of the tablets. To
be more precise, Chadwick is even prepared to argue on
this dialectological basis that the oppressed majority in
each of the Mycenaean kingdoms spoke Doric (or rather
proto-Doric) and that it was these proto-Doric speakers who
overthrew their 'Mycenaean'-speaking masters, burned their
palaces and emerged later as the historical Dorians.

I am no philologist, let alone Mycenologist, and we
must wait and see what considered reactions this startling
theory provokes from the experts in the field (initial
reaction, I understand, has been far from unanimously favourable). It is, however, fair for me to point out that
it is extremely dangerous to draw far-reaching inferences
of a dialectological nature from the Linear B tablets.
This should be obvious simply from their fragmentary preservation and the character of the information they convey,
but it is worth stressing that current philological views
of their dialectal significance are highly heterogeneous,
leaving aside those which do not even accept the decipherment as Greek. At one end of the spectrum there is the
view that Linear B is merely a 'common trading language,

... some kind of lingua franca, or commercial "jargon"'
(Hooker 1977, 77), which may bear little or no relation
to the language or languages actually spoken in the Mycenaean kingdoms or elsewhere in Greece. At the other end
scholars like Bartonek (1973) hold that the language of
the tablets is the dialect common to all areas of Mycenaean
culture (apart perhaps from Thessaly and Boiotia, where
proto-Aeolic may have been spoken) but distinct from the
dialect of north-west Greece, which was early Doric.
(The hypothesis that of the historical dialects Ionic and
Aeolic but not Doric are post-Mycenaean formations was
first proposed by Ernst Risch and is now commonly accepted.) It will become clear later on why I incline to
place myself at Bartonek's end of the spectrum. Here I
shall confine myself to what seem to be the fatal historical and archaeological objections to Chadwick's new
theory.
    First, and most obviously, although the Dorians could
have invented the idea of an immigration into the Peloponnese to hide their subjection to Mycenaean overlords, the
theory does not explain why they invented the myth of the
'Return of the Herakleidai' if in fact the Heraklid rulers
of the Dorian states could have claimed hegemony in their
respective areas of the Peloponnese as the just reward of
their revolutionary efforts. Nor does it account for the
fact that the 'Return' myth applied only to those Dorians
who could claim descent from Herakles. For Thucydides
(1.12.3) does not, pace Chadwick (1976b, 105), call the
Dorians Herakleidai but, like Tyrtaios (fr. 2.13-15), our
earliest surviving source, expressly distinguishes between
the Dorians and the returning Herakleidai. In other
words, both of these ancient sources clearly believed that
there were no Dorians at least in the Peloponnese before
the fall of Troy, a belief which is consonant both with
the claim of the Arkadians to be the only 'autochthonous'
population in the Peloponnese (Xen. 'Hell.' 7.1.23; cf.
Hdt. 2.171.3; 8.73.1) and with the clear affinity between
Linear B and the historical Arkado-Cypriot dialect.
Third, the theory presupposes not merely continuity of
settlement but identity of culture between the Mycenaean
and historical Peloponnese. This may be demonstrable in
some sense for the Argolis (Tomlinson 1972, 64), but the
archaeological evidence for the other Dorian areas of the
Peloponnese indicates a sharp, though not of course a complete, cultural break after c.1050. For example, Lakonian
Protogeometric pottery, as we shall see, notoriously does
not 'grow out of Submycenaean' (Chadwick 1976b, 104);
strictly speaking not even continuity of settlement can be
proved archaeologically for Lakonia; and the central place

of Dorian Lakonia was significantly different from its
Mycenaean predecessor.

Bearing this in mind, let us turn to the specifically
archaeological arguments of the neo-Belochians. It has of
late become an acknowledged scandal that the Dorians,
archaeologically speaking, do not exist. That is, there
is no cultural trait surviving in the material record for
the two centuries or so after 1200 which can be regarded
as a peculiarly Dorian hallmark. Robbed of their patents
for Geometric pottery, cremation burial, iron-working and,
unkindest prick of all, the humble straight pin, the hap-
less Dorians stand naked before their creator - or, some
would say, inventor. For, it is argued, if they cannot be
identified archaeologically, this is because they had been
in the Peloponnese all the time - or at least for a considerable time before 1200. How then did they obtain
their political and linguistic dominance in the Peloponnese? It was, according to Hooker (1977, 179), the
'Doric-speaking subjects' who were 'responsible for the
overthrow of the palatial system (and perhaps for the destruction of the palaces themselves)'; and 'it is these
insurrectionists who are commemorated in the traditions
about the Return of the Heraclids'.

This hypothesis is clearly vulnerable to the same objections as Chadwick's philologically based theory; indeed, it is more obviously vulnerable inasmuch as it was
not the mass of the insurrectionists but primarily their
later rulers who are commemorated in the 'Return' myth.
It should, however, also be noted that invasions do not
necessarily leave recognizable material traces, often because the conquerors have taken over the culture of the
conquered when the latter stood on a higher level. We
might cite the Slav invasions of Greece in the early Byzantine period as an instance. Thus continuity of material
culture despite a series of man-made destructions such as
is attested for the Argolis during LH IIIB and C does not
by itself exclude the possibility of an invasion by non-
Mycenaeans. But such an argumentum ex silentio is no
more susceptible of proof and no less hazardous than the
one on the other side drawn by Hooker from the non-intru-
sion of 'Dorian' cultural traits into the Peloponnese at
this or a later time. Again, the crucial point is the
fact of cultural discontinuity after the Mycenaean period,
at least in Lakonia.

The argument from the history of religion is even more
complex in its ramifications and is based explicitly on
Lakonian evidence. As stated in Chapter 6, it is impossible to be too precise about the identity, powers and
attributes of Mycenaean deities. None the less, evidence

from Amyklai has been used to support confident hypotheses. In the historical period, after Amyklai had become the fifth constituent village of Dorian Sparta (Chapter 8), the chief deity here was Apollo, worshipped in martial guise. His cult, however, coexisted happily, if to us rather obscurely, with that of Hyakinthos: the three days of the annual Hyakinthia festival, whose importance will emerge in later chapters, were divided between them, the first being consecrated to Hyakinthos, the last two to Apollo. Now Apollo was of course a key member of the celestial Olympian pantheon. But Hyakinthos, a more shadowy figure, may originally have been a vegetation deity, and his worship was clearly chthonic (earth-bound) in character. How, then, when and why did the cult of these disparate immortals become associated in this way?

According to the mythical account, Apollo killed his favourite Hyakinthos with an accidentally misdirected discus-cast. This type of myth 'may reflect dimly Apollo's increasing popularity during the Dark ages' (Starr 1961, 182), and that may be thought to answer the why of the question posed above. It does not, however, tell us how and when the two cults first came into contact or collision. The pooled resources of philology, archaeology and the history of religion produced a solution along these lines (e.g. Desborough 1972, 280). The name Hyakinthos contains the -nth- suffix which is not merely pre-Dorian but pre-Greek; the name itself perhaps referred to a natural topographical feature. Thus Hyakinthos was the aboriginal deity of Amyklai taken over by the Indo-European speakers when they arrived in Lakonia around the turn of the third millennium. It was to Hyakinthos that the archaeologically attested cult was being paid at Amyklai late in LH IIIB and/or in IIIC. The date of Apollo's entry upon the Greek scene and his place of entry cannot be firmly ascertained, but his close association with Dorian communities in the historical period suggests that it was the incoming Dorians who amalgamated the Bronze Age cult of Hyakinthos with that of Apollo some time after the inauguration of a non-Mycenaean, Dorian culture in Lakonia.

This looks a plausible and economical hypothesis. It is not in fact so secure as it seems. For a start, the date and manner of the 'coming of the Greeks' are controversial (Chapter 4), and the exclusively Dorian affiliation of Apollo has been exaggerated, most conspicuously by Mueller (1839). More specifically, there are two major obstacles to accepting the hypothesis as it stands. First, the historical Hyakinthia remained pre-eminently a local Amyklaian rather than a generally Spartan festival,

which suggests that the Dorian/Mycenaean and Apollo/Hya-
kinthos antitheses have been misconceived or are irrelevant in this context. Second, the distribution of the
month Hyakinthios in historical times (Samuel 1972, 93,
291) indicates an exclusively Dorian rather than a broadly
Mycenaean Greek attachment: Hyakinthos, in other words, is
more likely to be 'Dorian' par excellence than Apollo, and
if any elements in the Hyakinthia may be considered intrusive they are those associated with Apollo. For these
reasons therefore (and others which could be adduced by
advocates of either hypothesis) Dietrich (1975) has now
argued that Hyakinthos was already a Dorian cult-figure in
the Late Bronze Age and that his cult, which began at Amyklai, was diffused thence by Dorians. In other words,
there was no 'Dorian invasion' of Lakonia as usually conceived, either at the end of the Bronze Age or in the immediate post-Bronze Age period.

There is much of value in Dietrich's article. In particular, he has attacked the 'traditional' picture of an
ethnically distinct and mutually antagonistic 'Dorian'
Sparta and 'Achaean' Amyklai at its weakest spot, religious practice, and his attack has struck home. On the other
hand, neither he nor Chadwick nor Hooker has yet persuaded
me to stop flogging the old warhorse of a Dorian invasion
of some kind. For all three are obliged to appeal to
archaeological evidence, and this is really their Achilles
heel. It may be true, as Dietrich argues, that archaeology need not signify an actual break in cult for a century
or more at Amyklai, though formally, as we shall see, it
does just that. But archaeology undeniably does signify a
break in cultural continuity at the site, and the picture
is repeated throughout Lakonia. It is time therefore to
examine the archaeological evidence more closely, and in
particular the stratification and pottery-sequence of
Amyklai, which happens also to be the type-site for Protogeometric (PG) and Dark Age Lakonia as a whole. (The significance of these labels will emerge in due course.)

The hill of Ay. Kyriaki, one of the central chain running down the Spartan plain on the right bank of the Eurotas, was occupied, though not perhaps continuously, from
the early Bronze Age. What concerns us particularly here
is a small layered deposit uncovered in the German excavations of 1925 at one point immediately outside and below
the terrace-wall which wholly or partly enclosed the historical sanctuary (Figure 10). The uppermost layer contained a little Byzantine and other material. Below came
the 'Aschenschicht' permeated by charred earth with objects ranging in date from Hellenistic back to Archaic.
Under this was the layer of clay, one metre deep, which is

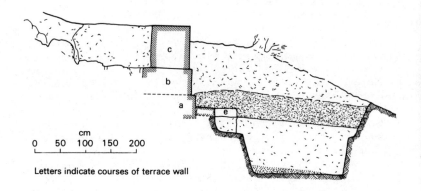

FIGURE 10   Stratification at the Amyklaion sanctuary

the crucial one for our purposes. The top twelve or so
centimetres contained 'Geometric' pottery, the bottom few
some pre-fourteenth-century ware; in between fell the
'Protogeometrische Schicht' characterized by PG pottery
but contaminated at varying levels by three small Mycenaean sherds, one Mycenaean terracotta 'goddess' figurine
and a fragment of a large Mycenaean terracotta animal
statuette. The layer also held several artefacts of
bronze of post-Mycenaean manufacture.

The problem of interpretation results from the fact
that this is not the stratification of a settlement, with
recognizable and continuous floors of occupation, but an
isolated votive deposit (no sanctuary building was recovered) formed by the discarding of accumulated votives.
The question is whether we are to suppose that votives
were continuously washed or thrown down this same part of
the hill. Discontinuity seems inevitable as between the
Byzantine layer and the 'Aschenschicht', but how does the
PG layer relate to those immediately below and above?

There are a couple of footholds in this slippery mor-
aine. First, the 'Geometric' pottery above the PG layer
is in fact what we now call Late Geometric in style. Thus
the supposition of continuous deposition would entail the
view that Lakonian PG pottery continued to be made or dedicated until roughly the mid-eighth century. Second, although there was no purely Mycenaean stratum below the PG
layer, the Mycenaean material found in the latter or
closely associated with PG pottery on the surface included
sherds, animal statuettes and 'goddess' figurines of the
latest (LH IIIC) phase. Thus if the 'stratigraphical' and

surface associations imply direct continuity between LH
IIIC and PG, then Lakonian PG pottery should have begun
not later than 1050, giving a timespan for the fabric of
some three centuries. However, detailed stylistic analysis, of which a highly condensed summary follows here,
does not bear out the truth of either the protasis or the
apodosis of the preceding sentence.

The fundamental study of the PG style of pottery in
Greek lands is still Desborough 1952. Thanks to this, we
are able to say that the style is not merely an amalgam
of shapes and decorative motifs antedating and perhaps
prefiguring the full Geometric style but comprises shapes
and decoration that would have been impossible but for
two, possibly Athenian, technical innovations of the eleventh century, the faster wheel and the use in conjunction
of a multiple brush and dividers. It is not possible to
say much about Lakonian PG shapes for lack of complete
profiles, and the multiple brush and dividers were used
here in a highly individualistic fashion. Nevertheless
the substantive point remains that Lakonian PG shares
after its own manner the two fundamental technical ideas
of the style.

I have spoken of 'Lakonian' PG. This is meant to convey that the conclusions of Desborough - namely that there
existed a local pre-Geometric PG style at Amyklai and 'related' or comparably early wares at the sanctuaries of
Athena and Orthia in Sparta - may now be expanded into the
assertion that a PG style was common to much if not most
of Lakonia (Figure 9).   Surface finds have been made at
Stena near Gytheion, Apidia in the west Parnon foreland,
Daimonia (ancient Kotyrta) in the Malea peninsula, Volimnos (sanctuary of Artemis Limnatis) in the west Taygetos
foreland (ancient Dentheliatis) and perhaps also Phoiniki
(temple of Apollo Hyperteleatas) in the Malea peninsula.
Indeed, Lakonian PG found its way outside Lakonia to Tegea
and perhaps the Argive Heraion, and sherds of Lakonian PG
type have been picked up at Kaphirio and Hellenika (ancient Thouria) in south-east Messenia. The possible historical significance of this distribution will be considered
at the end of this chapter. Here we must first discuss
the origins, development and chronology of the style.

It should be stressed straightaway that any discussion
is necessarily provisional and tentative, since no stratified occupation levels have yet been excavated in an
early post-Mycenaean Lakonian settlement. So far only
three sites have produced both LH IIIC and PG material:
Amyklai, Anthochorion in west Vardhounia and Apidia. The
latter can safely be discounted, since there is only a
handful of relevant sherds and the finds are sporadic.

The other two have at least revealed some form of stratification in controlled excavation, but at Amyklai certainly
and at Anthochorion possibly the stratification is that of
votive accumulations, and both sites show disturbance in
the levels that concern us here. The test of continuity
therefore resolves itself into the question of the stylistic relationship between the latest Mycenaean and the PG
pottery. Can the latter be said to grow out of, be derived from or throw back to the former?

Since we are dealing with levels in which indubitably
Mycenaean and indubitably PG ware was found in association, we cannot without begging the question answer it
with reference to artefacts whose stylistic attribution is
uncertain. A special problem, however, is posed by the
wheel-made animal statuettes from Amyklai. These bulls,
horses and so on were first made some time in the late
thirteenth century, but they certainly continued into the
twelfth, and one Mycenaean example may be from the early
eleventh. In a masterly survey of Greek terracotta votive
statuettes between c.1200 and 700 Nicholls (1970, 10) has
stated that there are fragments of this type with PG ornament from the PG level. In fact, though, the only example
he cites is not beyond a doubt PG, and there are no others
so decorated from the PG level. I do not therefore think
it justified to use this one piece as evidence of continuity except to corroborate such a finding based on other
evidence. To this we must now turn.

The criterion of shape is barely considerable, since we
have only two wholly preserved profiles: the hydria
(water-jar) and the trefoil-lipped oinochoe (wine-jug).
The former was developed during the sub-Mycenaean, not the
full Mycenaean, period. The latter makes its first appearance in early LH IIIC (an example has been excavated
at Epidauros Limera), but the developed conical foot of
the example from the Heroon sanctuary in Sparta is apparently a PG innovation. For the rest, the fairly common
deep skyphos (drinking cup) is probably derived from the
'Granary Class' LH IIIC deep bowl of the Argolis, but the
decoration of the best preserved Lakonian PG example,
again from the Heroon, isolates it somewhat from the main
Lakonian series. The neck-handled amphora, a good example
of which was found at Stena (Figure 11c), is 'plainly an
adaptation of a Mycenaean type' (Desborough 1952, 6), but
the adaptation took place in Attika.

If we move from shape to decoration, the signals are
equally muted. The use of horizontal grooving, whether
tectonic or decorative in function, is one of the two most
distinctive Lakonian PG traits and is unambiguously not of
Mycenaean ancestry. On the other hand, the system of

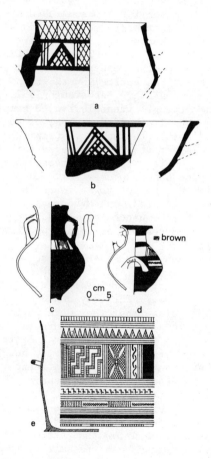

FIGURE 11   Lakonian Protogeometric and Geometric Pottery
a-d PG (a-b Amyklaion; c-d Stena, near Gytheion)
e LG (Orthia)

panelling and the use of cross-hatched triangles (Figure
11a,b) do have forbears in the latest local variants of
the Mycenaean style. Formal similarity, however, is not a
guarantee of derivation, and the Lakonian way with these
was substantively different. Thus the treatment of the
panelling in a rigidly compacted manner contrasts with the
more relaxed Mycenaean approach; the triangle is greatly
outnumbered by the un-Mycenaean horizontal or vertical
lattice as a configuration for cross-hatched ornament; and
the overwhelming predilection for cross-hatching per se,
the other peculiarly Lakonian PG characteristic, is foreign to Mycenaean. Lastly, but perhaps most important,
there is the question of the conception of the pot as a
whole. Lakonian PG is 'an entirely dark-ground system ...
not to be found in Mycenaean' (Desborough 1952, 287). If
these arguments are thought inconclusive, a comparison between the Lakonian and Ithakan PG styles, as suggested by
Desborough, should settle the matter. Despite significant
points of mutual contact (to be considered further below),
the Ithakan relates to its Mycenaean predecessor in a discernible way that the Lakonian does not. In sum, the
origins of Lakonian PG are not to be found in the local LH
IIIC or the (barely attested) sub-Mycenaean styles. The
significance of this is enhanced by the absence of anything later than sub-Mycenaean at Epidauros Limera (cf.
previous chapter).

Are its origins then to be sought in the leading PG
regional styles of Thessaly, Attika or the Argolis, for
each of which an originating or inspirationally independent role has been claimed? Thessaly could be ruled out on
grounds of geography alone, but there are in fact no
grounds for suggesting a link with Lakonia in any case.
The influence and often the inspiration of Attic PG have
been demonstrated for many areas of Greece, but for Lakonia neither can even be argued with confidence. As for
the Argolis, the shape and decorative scheme of the Heroon
skyphos, together with its conical foot, may well be derived from here, but otherwise evidence of such contact, so
rich in the succeeding period (Chapter 8), is conspicuous
by its absence, even if we allow that Attic influences
(such as they are) may have been transmitted indirectly
through the Argolis. We must therefore answer the above
question in the negative. Nor ought this to surprise us.
For in each of these areas continuity or virtual continuity of settlement from the Mycenaean into the historical
period is assured, and there is a corresponding congruence
between the relevant pottery styles. Lack of such congruence in Lakonia suggests the possibility of a break in
occupation or at least external communications.

If this possibility is admitted, whatever form the
break may have taken, then we have grounds for looking
away from the three 'mainstream' styles to discover the
source or sources of the PG elements in the Lakonian style.
In practice this means either to those styles which stand
in some demonstrable relation to the mainstream (the 'related' group) or to those whose individuality argues some
degree of independence from it (the 'independent' group).
Crete apart, geography alone tends to exclude the members
of the 'related' group as potential inspirers or influences; and Cretan artistic development appears somewhat
esoteric after the Mycenaean/Minoan period. Let us therefore direct our attention to the 'independent' group,
which embraces Ithaka, Aitolia, Achaia and Messenia
besides Lakonia itself.

Gratifyingly we find immediately satisfied here two a
priori criteria of inspiration, geographical proximity and
stylistic affinity. The latter is worth dissolving into
its constituent parts: the mug shape, especially common in
Achaia but also frequent on Ithaka and in Aitolia; the
shape and decoration of a skyphos from Tragana just north
of Navarino Bay; grooving and cross-hatching at Nichoria
in south-east Messenia; a special fondness for cross-
hatched ornament in Achaia, Ithaka and perhaps Aitolia; a
singular triangular motif from Derveni in Achaia, parall-
eled at Medeon in Phokis and perhaps Aetos on Ithaka; the
enclosing of cross-hatched triangles in metopes in Achaia;
concentric circles with few arcs and a suggestively similar total decorative approach at Aetos. The exports, if
they are exports, to Thouria and Kaphirio are perhaps also
relevant. However, and this is the salient fact, for all
these points of resemblance Lakonian PG still remains a
law unto itself. Admittedly we still have scanty evidence
of PG from the western Peloponnese or Ionian islands (see
Desborough 1972, 243-57); but there is perhaps enough to
justify their classification stylistically as a 'West
Greek' group and enough to see that Lakonia cannot be
neatly slotted into it.

So the outcome of this extended discussion is that Lakonian PG cannot be simply derived either from an antecedent
Mycenaean style in Lakonia or from a contemporary PG style
elsewhere. Contact with the 'West Greek' group may have
been a necessary, but it was not a sufficient, condition
of its origin. Some further factor or factors must be
postulated, and it is not wholly frivolous nor (pace
Hooker 1977, 173) merely reactionary to suggest that, had
we not been told that newcomers made their way to Lakonia
some time after c.1200, we would have had to invent them
to explain their pottery. Since the style could not have

originated within Lakonia in total isolation, the most
economical hypothesis from the archaeological side would
so link the newcomers with the new style of pottery as to
explain both the PG and 'West Greek' elements. This is
done most easily by postulating that the 'West Greek' area
was where they became acquainted both with the techniques
of the PG style in general and with particular local
shapes and decorative motifs.

I am of course keenly aware that it can be 'highly sim-
plistic and misleading' to explain ceramic change in terms
of a movement of population, 'in view of the range of factors (excluding invasion) which are known to precipitate
it' (Nicklin 1971, 47) - for example, the quality of the
craftsmen, local fashion or utilitarian considerations.
Moreover, I appreciate that the stylistic range of a ware
is more likely to have a geographical than a tribal or
ethnic significance, and that I must seem to be imposing
an intolerable burden of inference on ceramic evidence.
Above all, I am only too conscious of the irony in my holding the views expressed in Chapter 5 and yet also in some
sense defending 'tradition' against Beloch, with whose
sceptical outlook I am in general sympathy. Still, the
hypothesis outlined above seems to me to account best for
the stylistic anomalies of Lakonian PG and in particular
to explain how the craft of pottery-making, which is highly traditional and resistant to political disturbance, was
apparently interrupted and restarted in Lakonia. Furthermore, this hypothesis may be accommodated within a larger
historical scheme. However, before pottery can become
fodder for the historian a further ingredient, chronology,
must be added to the farrago.

In this connection the student of early post-Mycenaean
Lakonia is confronted by one of those dispiriting paradox-
es with which all students of Sparta must make their
peace. The archaeological contexts which have produced
apparent links with the more securely dated mainstream
styles, the Heroon and Stena, are unstratified and without
chronological anchors, whereas the 'stratified' Amyklai
and Anthochorion deposits betray no chronologically significant external relations.

To take the unstratified material first, it seems on
balance unlikely that such knowledge of Aegean styles
could have been displayed in quite this way very long
after PG in Attika and the Argolis had given way to Early
Geometric c.900. It is, however, worth emphasizing that
these vases stand apart from the main Lakonian PG series
both in technique and in decoration. For example, they
lack the metallic gleam of the paint produced both at
Amyklai and (on a lesser scale) in Sparta by firing at

high temperatures. The Heroon vases, seemingly the earliest of any, perhaps represent an unrepeated attempt to
translate mainstream styles into a Lakonian idiom. The
Stena group (Figure 11c and d) may show the fruits of maritime contact with the Aegean through nearby Gytheion,
but, if so, this would be the earliest evidence for the
occupation of Gytheion since the thirteenth century and
there is none thereafter until the sixth.

For the main series we must rely on the stratification
at Amyklai, and it is salutary to reflect that we do not
know either if this isolated votive deposit contains the
earliest PG material or what proportion of the total PG
dedications it represents. Our only control lies in the
overlying stratum with Late Geometric pottery. This,
taken with the absence of a settled Early or Middle Geometric phase in Lakonia, allows us to be fairly sure that
the PG and Geometric layers are immediately successive.
We thereby arrive at a terminal date for Lakonian PG of
c.750, which is perhaps confirmed by the indiscriminate
mixture of PG and Late Geometric in the 'Geometric' levels
at the Orthia sanctuary (cf. Chapter 8 and Appendix 5).
For the upper terminus we have a date of c.950-900 to
allow for the non-derivation from Mycenaean and the pre-
sumed imitations of Attic or Argive PG.

The question then arises whether we can conceive the
style lasting upwards of a century and perhaps as much as
two. There are a number of arguments, individually weak
but reasonably cogent in conjunction, to suggest that we
can. Droop (in AO 66 n. 16) thought he could detect a
chronological development from Amyklai (no slip, few concentric circles) through the sanctuary of Athena on the
Spartan akropolis (some slip, more concentric circles) to
the Orthia sanctuary (mainly slip, many concentric circles). He was writing before PG had been distinguished
from 'Geometric', and he may have been wrong to explain
the development in terms of the order in which the cults
were founded, but there is still something to be said for
the developmental scheme itself. A second argument is
based on the natural inference from the character of Lakonian PG that the potters and painters were considerably
isolated from their counterparts in other regions, an inference corroborated by the metallic dedications at Amyklai (below). In conditions of cultural isolation or deprivation there is a tendency towards conservatism or at
least an absence of stimulation to innovate. Finally, we
may argue from the simplicity and monotony of the decorative repertoire that the style could have lasted a relatively long time, since as a rule it is where decoration is
complex that there is a propensity to variation and style

changes relatively fast. Thus, I suggest that Lakonian PG
began in the later tenth century, at least at Amyklai, and
ended around the middle of the eighth, thereby spanning
between one and two centuries.

Let me correct any misapprehensions created by my concentration on pottery by examining the metal artefacts
'stratified' with PG pottery or typologically similar to
independently datable contemporaries from other areas.
The immediate post-Mycenaean era in Lakonia is often described as the 'Early Iron Age', but it must be realized
how far this equation is merely conventional. For, whatever the cause, the quantity of known iron artefacts from
Lakonia only becomes considerable in the seventh century
and even thereafter remains slight. This is surprising,
for two main reasons. First, as the later literary sources such as the third-century Daimachos (65F4) stress,
Sparta was fortunate in possessing extensive amounts of
workable iron ore within its own territory. This testimony is corroborated by geological and archaeological
study: ores are widely distributed, and the chief ancient
workings were situated near Neapolis (ancient Boiai),
whose ores show the highest percentage of iron content in
Greece. Second, by c.700 Sparta controlled not only Lakonia but a sizable chunk of trans-Taygetan Messenia, and
the latter was, to use the Greeks' expression, 'obtained
by the spear'; by that date spearheads, like swords, daggers, knives and axeheads, had for some time typically
been made of iron. In short, the apparent dearth of iron
artefacts in 'Early Iron Age' Lakonia must surely be put
down to the chances of survival and discovery.

However, the supersession of bronze by iron for cutting
implements is not in any case a straightforward process.
It is true that iron in its various natural states is distributed more plentifully than copper and tin in Greece as
elsewhere (Muhly 1973); in fact, both copper and tin had
to be imported. On the other hand, the techniques of
iron-working are more intricate and differ in kind from
those relevant to the production of serviceable bronze.
Thus while the ideal superiorities of iron artefacts are
easy to state - larger and local supplies potentially
cheapened production; greater rigidity, lightness and ability to take an edge increased efficiency and working
life - it is more difficult to say by what steps and over
what period these superiorities were realized in finished
Greek goods. The case of Lakonia must be dismissed for
lack of evidence, but there is enough to attempt to interpret the overall Greek experience.

This has been done, to put it schematically, according
to two mutually incompatible hypotheses, which envisage

respectively a long, drawn out, piecemeal process extending over several centuries (Pleiner 1969) and a relatively
sudden and great leap forward c.1000 (Snodgrass 1971, ch.
5). The divergence stems partly from disagreement over
the definition of an Iron Age, in part from the uneven
character of the evidence; and neither hypothesis perhaps
is wholly persuasive. That of Pleiner goes beyond the
archaeological evidence and rests on a false distinguishing criterion of diversity in usage. In fact, Greek
blacksmiths (significantly called bronzesmiths, chalkeis)
never learned to cast iron; and bronze was retained for
almost all large objects of beaten metal even after the
beginning of the Iron Age (on any definition). Snodgrass's hypothesis, on the other hand, has limited conceptual and geographical applicability. The evidence forbids
us to judge whether the known sample of his 'fundamental
classes' of edged implements is statistically significant;
above all, there are insufficient agricultural implements
for comparative purposes. However, if an approximate date
for the beginning of the Iron Age in Greece should still
be sought, then perhaps Hesiod's iron-shod plough of c.700
(Kothe 1975) provides a feasible terminus ante quem.

To return to Lakonia and darkness from the confused
light of the outside world, we find just one iron artefact
securely dated to the PG period. Its preserved length is
32 cm., but it is so poorly preserved that its identification as a spearhead is no more than plausible. It was
found at Stena with the two PG pots already discussed, so
we should probably infer that we have here a male burial.
In fact, this is the only burial of the period known from
Lakonia, but both the burial rite and the form of grave
are unrecorded. The only other possibly PG iron artefact
from Lakonia is a sword from Amyklai assigned to this period on typological grounds. The material at least conforms
to that of the majority of PG swords.

The bronze artefacts from the PG stratum at Amyklai are
perhaps marginally more informative. There were two small
spearheads, but their material and size suggest they never
saw the front line. Certainly too they are remarkably
primitive in technique, and Snodgrass's date of c.800
(1971, 245 and fig. 88) may be appreciably too low. There
were also several ringlets of rolled sheet bronze, some
with a midrib, others decorated with repoussé dots. A few
at least may have been used to hold locks of hair dedicated on the occasion of a perilous undertaking such as a
long journey, war or a 'rite de passage'. The magical significance of hair is well attested in ancient as in modern
Greece (and elsewhere), and the Spartans' interest in cap-
illary matters was notorious. Finally, some strips of

sheet bronze have been interpreted as the legs of simple
tripod-cauldrons which, as we know from Homer and archaeology, served as a symbol and store of wealth and were
regarded as particularly acceptable dedications to Zeus
and his son Apollo.

The impression of isolation and relative cultural deprivation conveyed by the pottery is thus amply corroborated by the metal-work. Referring to the spearheads,
Snodgrass (1971, 246) has remarked that 'the bronzes would
have looked very old-fashioned even at the earliest possible date suggested by their associations; and this ...
suggests such a period of restricted and somewhat primitive metallurgy, with partial dependence on Bronze Age
heirlooms, as we have inferred elsewhere.' It is, I
think, not irrelevant that the areas with comparably backward metallurgy include Achaia and Kephallenia, both
within the ambit of the 'West Greek' PG pottery group.

We may sum up the historical implications of the archaeological evidence as follows. First, the Amyklai
'stratigraphy' and the stylistic analysis of Lakonian PG
pottery demonstrate a sharp cultural break between Mycenaean and PG Lakonia and strongly suggest an influx of newcomers, immediately from 'West Greece', some time in the
tenth century. On the other hand, if taken at face value
the pottery evidence would also indicate that, following
the apogee of prosperity in the thirteenth century and the
exponential decline of population in the twelfth and early
eleventh, Lakonia was actually uninhabited between c.1050
and 950. For reasons to be given below I do not believe
that the pottery should be so taken in this regard. Undoubtedly, though, the small number of sites known to have
been occupied in PG times (nine) and the backward character of the pottery and metal-work do suggest that the
label 'Dark Age', which has been vindicated by Snodgrass
(1971) for Greece as a whole at least between c.1100 and
850, is nowhere more appropriate than in Lakonia.

Too much retrospective doomwatching, however, would not
be appropriate. For the years from c.950 to 775 were
also, as we can say with hindsight, the formative period
of historical Lakonia and specifically of Dorian Sparta.
We are bound therefore to make what we can of the literary
evidence and attempt to spin some 'gossamer ... out of
legend and the weakest of tradition' (Starr 1968, 19),
using the archaeological evidence as a kind of quality
control on the flimsy product. The following summary account is necessarily provisional and highly speculative,
but it may claim to have used all the available evidence.
In accordance with the aim of the book as a whole I shall
be less concerned with internal political developments in

Sparta itself than with the relationship between Sparta
and the rest of Lakonia.

The three Dorian tribes of the Hylleis, Dymanes and
Pamphyloi, whose existence in Sparta is directly attested
for the first and only time by Tyrtaios (fr. 19.8), almost
certainly joined forces before the long march south.
Their most likely point of immediate origin is the Illyr-
ian-Epirote region of north-west Greece, which had been
for the most part untouched by Mycenaean civilization;
some have seen an etymological link between the names
Hylleis and Illyria. But the Dorians may have been impelled and even joined by peoples from still further north.
(One thinks of the hand-made pottery mentioned in Chapter
6.) The etymology of 'Dorians' is unclear, but their alleged connection with Doris in central Greece was probably
invented or at least enhanced by later propaganda from as
early as the seventh century (Tyrtaios fr. 2.14).

The route or routes the Dorians took are not certainly
ascertainable, but the suggestion that those who became
Spartans or Lakonians followed a westerly course may, I
believe, be supported by reference to the ceramic evidence
discussed earlier. If this suggestion is correct, they
will have proceeded southwards through Aitolia, crossed
the Corinthian Gulf from Antirhion to Rhion (a crossing
supposedly commemorated by the carrying of model rafts at
the annual Karneia festival in Sparta: Huxley 1962, 99 n.
34), then continued down the western Peloponnese to the
Alpheios valley, across to the headwaters of the Eurotas
and finally along the Eurotas furrow to Sparta.

The very choice of this low hill site may be thought to
corroborate the inference of a dramatic change in political and economic conditions, if not of population, in Lakonia. For under the Mycenaean régime the site of classical Sparta had not been important, if indeed it had been
permanently settled; and the central place of Lakonia had
been situated on and around the Menelaion hill to the
south-east on the other, left, bank of the Eurotas. The
considerations governing the Dorians' choice will have included at least the following factors, apart from the absence of an existing settlement: first and foremost the
availability of adequate arable and pasturage; then a constant supply of fresh water; third, good communications
north and south; fourth, distance from potentially hostile
mountain-dwellers; and finally the settlement a few kilometres south at Amyklai, to whose political relationship
with Sparta I shall return in the next chapter.

The date of the Dorian settlement of Sparta is an open
question, but archaeology, that is pottery, indicates a
terminus post quem of c.950. This flatly contradicts the

central article of the much later 'tradition' embodied in
the 'Return of the Herakleidai' myth and the Spartan king-
lists, namely that Dorians occupied Lakonia under Heraklid
leadership a couple of generations after the Fall of Troy
or, in our terms, within the twelfth century. 'Tradition'
should in this case be rejected, but it is harder to say
how far excision and oblivion should be carried. Indeed,
it is almost impossible to conjure up any sort of picture
of what was happening in Sparta and Lakonia between the
Dorian settlement and what I take to be the next certifiable event in Spartan history, the conquest or rather assimilation of Amyklai in the first half of the eighth
century.

Certainly there can be no question of describing personalities, even though the literary sources generally put
the wondrous reformer Lykourgos somewhere in the ninth
century in our terms (Kiechle 1963, 183). But our ignorance of fundamentals is more difficult to have to admit.
For instance, we do not know the size and nature of the
original settlement or the number of settlers; the 2,000
suggested by Isokrates (12.255) in the fourth century is
merely a guess (cf. Chapter 14). We do not know the extent of surrounding land utilized directly or indirectly
by the Spartans nor, despite the ingenuity of those scholars who have tried to salvage something from the mess left
by the 'Spartan mirage', on what conditions it was originally distributed and held. Nor do we know whether the settlers were predominantly agriculturists or pastoralists.
And so the basic problems continue. Not that our ignorance is greatly diminished for the period after 775, but
here it is well-nigh total. However, despite the correct
warning that, in regard to early Spartan history, 'we are,
I fear, sometimes in danger of becoming Hellenistic rumor-
mongering historians' (Starr 1965, 258), I shall tentatively offer some suggestions on the process of the Dorian
settlement and on the origins and status of the Helots and
Perioikoi.

At the risk of being dismissed as a reactionary trad-
itionalist by Hooker, I suggest that the old picture of
the Dorians as Vlach-type transhumance pastoralists (e.g.
Myres 1943, 41) still has something to commend it. At any
rate in Byzantine times the Koutsovlachs from the eleventh
century regularly travelled from the Pindus to Cape Matapan (ancient Tainaron); and the Dorians' suggested place
of origin, north-west Greece, together with the apparent
gap in time between the Dorian settlement of Argos (eleventh century) and Sparta, may be indications of a primarily pastoral orientation. Possibly relevant is the name
'bouai' meaning 'herds' given by the Spartans to the age-

classes into which the youth was divided for educational
purposes. If a more recent parallel be sought, the case
of the Bahima or Bahuma in Uganda comes to mind: these invading pastoralists enslaved the resident agricultural
population (Oberg 1940).

If this suggestion is cogent, then the political vacuum
ensuing after the Mycenaean débâcle would certainly have
provided a perfect opportunity for such an infiltration of
pastoralists into the Peloponnese. What was it, then,
that chiefly encouraged the Dorians to settle permanently
in Lakonia? The answer, I suggest, is 'the cultivation of
useful trees - a culture long in maturing, which requires
great care both against the crafty hands of men and the
voracious teeth of animals' (Febvre 1925, 294). In particular, it was perhaps the cultivation of the useful
olive which played the decisive role. There is no direct
evidence from Lakonia to support this suggestion, but it
is at least not contradicted by pollen evidence from the
Osmanaga lagoon near Pylos (Wright 1968, 123-7; but see
Bintliff 1977, 70) nor by the olive-press of c.700 found
above the ruins of the Mycenaean palace nearby (Coldstream
1977, 162). It is therefore worth digressing briefly to
consider the merits of the olive and the history of its
cultivation in Greek lands, especially as the olive without doubt occupied an important position in Spartan life
subsequently (Chapter 10).

Seeds of the less productive wild olive (oleaster) have
been found in the Mesolithic levels of the Franchthi cave
(cf. Chapter 4), but it was not apparently firmly established in its domesticated form before the Early Bronze
Age. Indeed, production may not have become significant,
at least in the Peloponnese, until Mycenaean times, when
the role of olive oil as lighting fuel may be inferred
from lamps found, for example, in the Vapheio tholos.
However, between c.1100 and 700, according to the palyno-
logical evidence just mentioned, the olive became not
merely important but actually the single most important
agricultural product in western Messenia, taking the place
held previously by cereals. The radiocarbon date should
perhaps be calibrated and so raised somewhat, but the evidence is still, I feel, highly suggestive of changed agricultural conditions in the Dark Age. However that may be,
the calcareous soils and climatic conditions of south-
eastern Greece in particular are ideally suited to olive-
production. Today some 95 per cent of all olives are
crushed for oil. The percentage will have been even higher in antiquity, when olive oil provided not only food but
light and unguent. Besides, olive wood is a suitable material for building and fuel, and cereals can be grown in

among olive trees ('cultura promiscua') to maximize the
use of Greece's restricted arable soil.

My second set of tentative suggestions concerns the
human aspect of the economic basis of Sparta's future
power, the Helots. Archaeologically, as we saw, it is not
possible to demonstrate that Lakonia was inhabited between
c.1050 and 950. There are, however, several reasons why I
am unwilling to reject out of hand the literary evidence
for continuity of settlement between the 'Achaean' and
'Dorian' periods. First, Hyakinthos, whatever his ethnic
affiliation, was probably worshipped continuously from the
Bronze Age at Amyklai. In the archaeological intermission
of a century or so his cult must have been perpetuated
with perishable offerings or in media we have not yet
found or recognized. Second, the evidence of dialect
(Solmsen 1907) and religion (Kiechle 1963, 95-115) in historical Lakonia indicates a thorough interpenetration of
Dorian and non-Dorian elements. For example, a bronze
fish found near Amyklai was dedicated in the sixth century
to Pohoidan (Jeffery 1961, 200, no. 34). This Lakonian
form of the Earthshaker Poseidon's name is clearly related
to Arkadian Posoidan and so to the language of the Linear
B tablets, whereas the normal Doric form is Poteidan.
Other cults of Pohoidan are attested epigraphically, from
the sixth century (restored) at Akovitika in south-east
Messenia, from the fifth at Tainaron (a recognized asylum
for Helots) and Helos. These last two are especially suggestive. For my chief reason for believing in the survival of a remnant of the Mycenaean population is that this
seems to explain most plausibly the origin of the Lakonian
Helots.

The ancients were no less fascinated by this problem
than the moderns, and the variety and mutual incompatibil-
ity of their views are displayed in Appendix 4. As usual,
however, it is the modern tools of geoarchaeology and
philology which have made the decisive contributions to
our still incomplete understanding. In the time of Thucydides (1.101.2) most of Sparta's Helots were descendants
of the Messenians enslaved in the eighth and seventh centuries; indeed, the terms 'Helots' and 'Messenians' were
by the late fifth century more or less interchangeable.
Consideration of the geomorphology of Lakonia, as recently
explicated by Bintliff (1977), confirms that the numerical
balance will always have been tipped in favour of the Messenians. There just was not enough arable land in the
lower Eurotas furrow in our period to accommodate as many
Helots in Lakonia as could the Pamisos valley in Messenia.
Presumably, though, it was in the Helos plain, as this
stood in antiquity, that most of the Lakonian Helots were

always concentrated. The Heleia was the most fertile
region of Lakonia (Polyb. 5.19.7), and a recurrent ancient
aetiology derived the name 'Helots' from a place called
Helos.

    In reality, however, the name was almost certainly der-
ived from a root meaning 'capture', and this is a powerful
hint that the status of the Lakonian Helots, like that of
the Messenians and indeed of the other serf-like populations of the classical Greek world, was acquired through
conquest. At all events, there is nothing in the ancient
literary sources to suggest that the status of the Lakonian Helots differed from that of the Messenians, whose
origins are not in this respect controversial. The transformation of the inhabitants of the lower Eurotas furrow
into Helots occurred, I believe, not only long before the
full development of chattel slavery (the characteristic
form of forced labour in Greece down to the later Roman
Empire) but early enough for them, unlike their Messenian
fellows, to have forgotten their 'nationality' by (at latest) the fifth century. In other words, I am prepared to
suggest that the relatively few Lakonian Helots acquired
their status soon after the Dorian settlement of Sparta,
perhaps as early as the tenth century. Again, the Bahima
analogy may be worth recalling or, closer to home, the
fate of the Thessalian Penestai. Thus the 'narrative' of
Pausanias' third book may be nowhere more seriously misleading than in its suggestion that Sparta did not secure
its Lakonian Helots until the eve of the invasion of Messenia c.735 (cf. Chapter 8). On the other hand, for the
reasons given in Chapter 5, I would not wish to adduce as
'proof' of my dating the 'traditions' ascribing the conquest of the Lakonian Helots to either Agis I or Soos (who
was in fact fictitious: Appendix 3).

    We shall return to the status and functions of the
Helots, Messenian as well as Lakonian, in later chapters.
To conclude the present chapter on the formative period of
Lakonia, some suggestions will be made concerning the
'third force' in Lakonian political and economic development, the Perioikoi. Whereas the ancients agreed that the
institution of Helotage was a once-for-all affair (though
they disagreed over the modalities), they offered no such
unitarian solutions to the problem of the origin of the
Perioikoi. Indeed, with rare and axe-grinding exceptions,
they can hardly be said even to have addressed themselves
to it systematically. We are therefore mostly reduced yet
again to speculation, constrained only by our suggested
view of the origin of the Lakonian Helots and by the archaeological evidence.

    Of one thing, however, we may be sure: the Perioikoi of

the classical period had not all arrived at their shared
half-way political status (Chapter 10) by the same route.
Of the supposedly 100 Perioikic communities in Lakonia and
Messenia (Androtion 324F49, with Jacoby's commentary) at
least two were the outcome of Sparta's resettlement of
refugee populations. The earlier of these, Asine (modern
Koroni), suggests that already by the end of the eighth
century Spartan writ ran as far as the southern tip of
Messenia. But what was the situation in Lakonia prior to
Spartan intervention in Messenia, which was said to have
occurred first in the reign of Teleklos (perhaps 760-740)?
Given that the Lakonian Perioikoi of the classical period
were indistinguishable ethnically, linguistically and culturally from the Spartans, there are three main ways
whereby a Perioikic community could have been created.
First, a formerly independent pre-Dorian or Dorian community could have been conquered or otherwise politically
subjected by Sparta or even perhaps have submitted to
Spartan suzerainty voluntarily. Second, a settlement
could have been established ex nihilo by Sparta with Perioikic or perhaps rather proto-Perioikic status. Third, a
pre-Dorian community could have received an influx of
Dorian settlers, the latter perhaps constituting themselves a ruling stratum.

Each of these three possibilities has received vigorous
support in the modern scholarly literature, and parallels
of varying degrees of plausibility from both Greek and
Roman history have been produced. In the present state of
our evidence, however, it is illegitimate to come down
heavily in favour of any one of them. For example, if we
were to take the archaeological record of total depopulation at face value, we might argue that all the Perioikic
communities in Lakonia were new foundations sponsored or
adopted by Sparta on the lines of the Roman colonization
of Italy. However, as already suggested, the archaeological evidence should not be so taken. On the other hand,
the apparently circumstantial accounts of the fate of such
'Achaean' communities as Helos cannot in my view form the
basis of a historical reconstruction either. On balance
therefore I would tentatively accept the third of the possible solutions outlined above, but I would lay less emphasis on such speculation than on the distribution of PG
pottery in Lakonia outside Sparta and Amyklai.

The number of sites involved is admittedly very small,
but their geographical range may none the less be significant. For it suggests, what we might have suspected on
other grounds, that 'Lakedaimon' or 'Lakonike' did not yet
encompass the east Parnon foreland by c.775. True, a 'PG
necropolis' was reported in the 1920s from Astros in the

Thyreatis (Wrede 1927), but this report has never been
corroborated by published finds and the pottery is anyway
more likely to have been in the Argive than in the Lakonian style. Moreover, despite the migration of a few Lakonian PG pieces to Tegea and possibly one to the Argive
Heraion, I cannot accept the 'tradition' that Sparta was
in contention for the Thyreatis as early as the reign of
Labotas (c.850?: Paus. 3.2.3). As Kelly (1976) has forcefully, perhaps even too forcefully, argued, much of early
Argive history was distorted retrospectively by the idea
that the mainspring of the foreign policy of Dorian Argos
was from the start rivalry with Dorian Sparta for leadership of the Peloponnese. Whether Spartan influence or
control had been extended as far south as the Mani by 775
cannot be tested archaeologically, but the inclusion in
the 'Catalogue of Ships' (Appendix 3) of Oitylos and Messe
(if it is to be located at modern Mezapos) may indicate at
least a Spartan claim to control them during the Dark Age.
    What we are left with, then, is the core of historical
Lakedaimon between the Taygetos and Parnon ranges, together with one site in the west Taygetos foreland whose
marginal situation was pregnant with future developments.
Anthochorion, just south of the Spartan plain and somewhat
off the beaten track from Sparta to Gytheion (Chapter 10).
has not been securely identified with an ancient site.
Stena, however, is near Gytheion, which, thanks to its
role as Sparta's port, became the single most important
Perioikic community at latest by the sixth century.
(Toynbee 1969, 192f., has not convinced me that Gytheion
was a Spartan town between c.750 and 195.) Apidia is
generally, and probably rightly, identified with Palaia
(Paus. 3.22.6) or Pleiai (Livy 35.27.3), but its political
status, presumably Perioikic at least by the seventh century, is not known for certain. In the Malea peninsula the
PG (or LG?) pottery reported from the Hyperteleaton (Skeat
1934, 34 n.4) is of uncertain style; I failed to locate
the sherds in the Sparta Museum. In Roman times, following the liberation of the Perioikoi from Sparta in 195,
the sanctuary became the centre of the Eleutherolakonian
League (Chapter 15); under the Spartan domination there
may have been a Perioikic community called Leukai here.
Daimonia further south is Perioikic Kotyrta, presumably
linked to the Eurotas valley chiefly by sea at this time.
Finally, the Volimnos site is that of the sanctuary of
Artemis Limnatis on the ancient border with Messenia. The
alleged assassination of king Teleklos here c.740 provided
the Spartans with a casus belli for their invasion of
Messenia.
    In conclusion we may, I think, fairly infer from the

conquest of Aigys (to which I return at the beginning of
the next chapter) that by c.775 the northern end of the
Eurotas furrow, including the Skiritis and the important
Perioikic communities of Sellasia and Pellana, was also
under Spartan control. Thus by the second quarter of the
eighth century the disunion of LH IIIC and sub-Mycenaean
Lakonia had been healed by the military and diplomatic
physic of the Spartans. Economically speaking, however,
we can do little more than apply to Sparta and the Eurotas
valley, mutatis mutandis, the words of Braudel (1972, 101):
'while a plain is coming to life, overcoming its dangerous
waters, organizing its roads and canals, one or two hundred years may pass by.' Clearly, though, by about the
middle of the eighth century the stage was set for perhaps
the most remarkable century or so in all of Sparta's long
and chequered history.

NOTES ON FURTHER READING

'Dorian' probably did not acquire its adulatory or pejor-
ative connotations until after the Persian Wars of the
early fifth century, and the reason for this semantic development was a political, not a cultural, dichotomy: Will
1956; Rawson 1969, esp. 57-9, 318-20; Oliva 1971, 9-11.
Will and Rawson note how comparatively recent racist 'the-
orizing' has further distorted perspective.
    Vitalis 1930 and Kiechle 1966 are notable exceptions to
the rule that the 'tradition' about the 'Dorian invasion'
is not evaluated on its own merits. I cannot, however,
accept many of their substantive conclusions.
    Chadwick's new hypothesis concerning Dorian origins
(1976b) has already made at least two other appearances.
It is incorporated in his résumé of the contribution of
philology to the reconstruction of early Greek history
(1976c); the responses of Schachermeyr, Pittioni and Kirsten, which are printed after Chadwick's paper, are uniformly unfavourable. I am in general sympathy with Kirsten's position, especially his picture of the Dorian newcomers as shepherds; cf. Sarkady 1975, esp. 121. Second,
the new hypothesis is hinted at in Chadwick's survey of
the Mycenaean world (1976a). Here the historical Helots
are explained as 'presumably the subject class of Mycenaean times, a people of non-Greek origin' (62: but where
then are the Late Bronze Age Dorians? or were there two
'subject classes' in Mycenaean Lakonia?); the Perioikoi
are regarded as being 'very likely the pre-Dorian Greeks
of Lakonia, the descendants of the Mycenaean population'
(62: but if, as Chadwick argued in 1976b, there was not

room in north-west Greece to accommodate the number of
Dorians required to complete the 'Dorian invasion' of
'tradition', then it seems to me even less likely that
there were enough ex-Mycenaeans to go round the numerous
Perioikic communities of historical Lakonia).

Burkert (1977, 228) has suggested that the form in
which Apollo was represented at Amyklai may have been borrowed in the twelfth century from the Syro-Hittites via
Cyprus, but that Apollo as such originated in the Peloponnese.

The most recent published study of Lakonian PG pottery
is Desborough 1972, 241-3; I have added some details in my
unpublished doctoral dissertation (1975, 87-99). On the
problems of method involved in interpreting pottery evidence see Desborough 1972, ch. 19. Nicklin 1971 is a stimulating review article discussing the sociological approach to the potter's craft.

For the geological properties of Lakonian iron see
ESAG, no. 401.

Snodgrass 1971 is probably the finest historical discussion of the Greek Dark Age, although his chronological
limits (c.1100-700) are too wide at the lower end. Desborough 1972 ends the Dark Age too soon (c.900). For an
intermediate position see Coldstream 1977. Also useful is
Bouzek 1969, but this somewhat exaggerates the undoubted
connections between Greece and central Europe.

On the 'Dorian invasion' see Starr 1961, ch. 4; Bengtson 1977, 50-66; and with special reference to Sparta
Oliva 1971, 15-23. Of the older accounts Busolt 1893,
201-62, is perhaps the most valuable.

For the cultivation of the olive see ESAG, no. 316. In
1961 the eparchy of Gytheion came ninth in the whole of
Greece with 9.58 per cent of its cultivated area being
devoted to the fruit, that of Lakedaimon (roughly the Eurotas valley) nineteenth with 6.78 per cent.

On Pohoidan see Solmsen 1907, 332f.; Gschnitzer 1962;
the recent discoveries at Akovitika are published in Themelis 1970. The case for continuity of occupation in
southern Lakonia, especially the Mani, has been stated
forcefully, if somewhat uncritically, by Kiechle (1963,
95-115). For reasons given in Chapter 8, I cannot accept
his picture of Amyklai (49-67) as the bulwark of 'Achaean'
Lakonia resisting the Dorian intruders.

Modern views on the Helots are cited in the notes to
Chapter 10; so too for the Perioikoi.

8 The Lakonian Renascence c. 775-650

George Grote, taking his cue from Eratosthenes, sub-divided the ancient Greek past into a 'mythical'and a 'historical' portion. The dividing-line he put at 776, the traditional date established by the Sophist Hippias of Elis
(c.400) for the foundation of the Olympic Games, which
were a truly panhellenic festival open to all and only
Greeks. I should myself put the dividing-line rather
later, but recent scholarship has in a sense vindicated
Grote by demonstrating that the years around 775 did indeed mark the beginning of a new epoch in Greek history.
First, 'after centuries of illiteracy ... the country got
a script once more: the simple, practical, easily-taught
alphabet from which all our western scripts descend' (Jeffery 1976, 25). Second, the movement of western 'colonization' began about this time, with the settlement of Euboian islanders on the island of Pithekoussai (modern
Ischia) off the bay of Naples. Third, a great advance in
metal-working was made, visible initially in the production of solid bronze figurines but culminating within a
couple of generations in the manufacture of sophisticated
armour of hammered bronze and such agricultural implements
as Hesiod's iron-shod plough. Finally, the Homeric epics,
with all their ethical, religious and national significance, were being shaped into their monumental form.

Lakonia in fact did not play a leading role in any of
these four developments, despite some unreliable ancient
testimony to the contrary. The Lakonian Doric dialect had
presumably evolved into its historical form by the eighth
century, but the earliest known example of the Lakonian
local script is of mid-seventh-century date (below). L.H.
Jeffery (1961, 185) has suggested that the alphabet was
transmitted to Olympia from Sparta, but, if true, this
would merely serve to confirm doubts held on other grounds
that a contemporary written record of victors was kept at

Olympia from 776. Still more dubious is the role of co-
founder of the Olympic Games assigned to the Spartan lawgiver Lykourgos by Aristotle (fr. 533 Rose) on the basis
of an inscribed discus he had seen at Olympia. Regrettably too the story that Lykourgos was responsible for bringing the Homeric poems from Ionia to the Greek mainland
(Plut. 'Lyk.' 4.4) must be dismissed as a fable of the
kind which tended to accrete around such legendary figures. However, the establishment of the Menelaion sanctuary c.700 (below) suggests that the Homeric poems had by
then reached Sparta, and the language of Tyrtaios is heavily influenced by the epic. As far as metal-work goes,
worked iron is conspicuous by its dearth in Lakonia before
the seventh century. On the other hand, it was perhaps as
early as c.775 that the first bronze animal figurines made
by Lakonian craftsmen were being dedicated at Olympia.
Finally, Sparta barely participated in the colonization
of the west (or indeed elsewhere) for reasons to be explored in the present chapter. It is possible though that
the settlement of Lakonians on Thera c.800 or shortly
after reflects economic pressures similar to those which
stimulated the Euboian pioneers.

From what has been said so far it would be justified to
infer that in c.775 Lakonian horizons did not extend beyond Olympia in north-west Peloponnese at the very furth-
est. On the whole, I think, this fairly reflects the
continuing isolation of Lakonia from the wider Greek or
even Peloponnesian world down to the middle of the eighth
century. There is, however, one piece of evidence suggesting this was not the whole story. For in the joint
reign of Archelaos and Charillos the Delphic Oracle is
said to have given its blessing to the Spartan conquest
and annihilation of Aigys in the north-west angle of Lakonia (Parke and Wormell 1956, I, 93; II, no. 539).
Chronologically, this is just possible. The joint reign
may be dated c.775-760, and this seems to have been about
the time the Oracle began to attract 'international' attention on the political plane. Moreover, as with Olympia, the Spartans undoubtedly established an early and
continuing 'special relationship' with Delphi of a religi-
ous-cum-political nature. My chief reason, however, for
believing in the authenticity of this oracle is that it
was delivered to both the Spartan kings jointly. Indeed,
the conquest of Aigys is the first enterprise of the Spartan state recorded to have been undertaken by both kings,
a circumstance which has prompted the suggestion (most
recently Jeffery 1976, 114) that Archelaos and Charillos
were in fact the first joint kings of Sparta.

It is outside the scope of the present book to discuss

internal political developments at Sparta in any detail,
but a brief comment on the dual monarchy may help to bring
the political background of the Lakonian renascence into
sharper focus. In the long view the Spartan monarchy was
remarkable on two main counts: first, it was a collegiate
kingship with hereditary succession to the thrones through
two distinct royal houses, the supposed descendants of
Agis I (Agiads) and Euryp(h)on (Eurypontids); second, it
was a by no means titular monarchy, which lasted in something like its traditional form (at least as we know it
from the sixth century) until the second half of the second century, thereby surviving the general extinction of
hereditary monarchy in Greece in the early Archaic period
as well as the establishment of extra-constitutional personal rules known as tyrannies. The fact of monarchy in
Dark Age Sparta calls for no special comment: the process
of the Dorian settlement and subsequent survival of Sparta
in an alien and potentially hostile environment will have
called for strong, centralized leadership. But the origin
of the dual kingship, thanks to its uniqueness (Molossian
and still less Iroquois parallels are not really convincing) and the poverty of the evidence, is and will remain a
vexed question. From the welter of speculation both ancient and modern I would distinguish only two hypotheses as
more than merely plausible, namely that the founders of
the royal lines were the eponymous Agis and Euryp(h)on,
not (as the 'Return of the Heraklids' myth demanded) Eurysthenes and Prokles or even, as the Spartans uniquely believed, Aristodamos (Hdt. 6.52.1); and that succession was
from the start hereditary within each family or clan.
    There are, however, good reasons for thinking that the
two royal houses did not rule jointly as early as the
lifetimes of the eponyms. The Eurypontid Soos is almost
certainly a 'spurinym' and is omitted from the most reliable Eurypontid king-list (Appendix 3). No less unreal,
to judge from their names and association with Lykourgos,
are Prytanis and Eunomos, supposedly the son and grandson
respectively of Euryp(h)on himself. Thus, if we strike
out these three and the eponym, there is just one Eurypontid predecessor for Charillos compared with four or five
for the Agiad Archelaos. The source of the discrepancy
should be sought in reality: the fact that the Agiads were
reckoned, apparently with Delphic approval (Hdt. 6.52.5),
to be the senior of the two royal houses (Hdt. 6.51) suggests that they had been in some sense royal before the
Eurypontids, perhaps indeed as early as the second half of
the tenth century, when Sparta may have been settled by
Dorians (Chapter 7). This at any rate corresponds to a
genealogically plausible modern dating of Agis I (930-900).

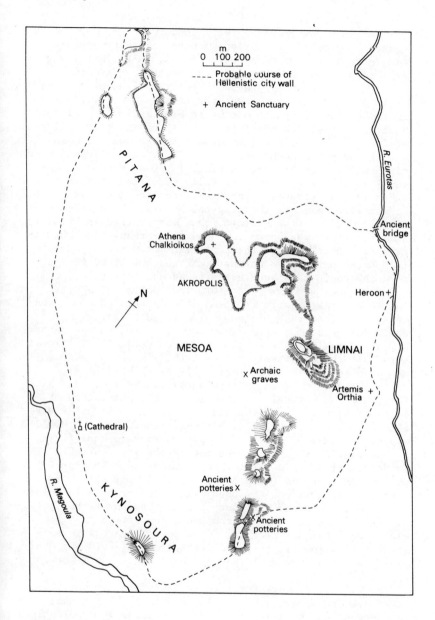

FIGURE 12   The villages of Sparta

The questions therefore arise how, when and why the two
houses came to rule jointly. I have no new hypothesis to
add to those collected by Oliva (1971, 23-8), but I suggest than an explanation in terms of the amalgamation of
two communities makes the best historical sense.   In the
fifth century it was a cause for remark (Thuc. 1.10.2)
that the town of Sparta had never been fully 'synoecized'.
That is to say, the separate identity of the four villages
of Sparta town - Limnai, Kynosoura (or Konooura), Mesoa
and Pitana - had never been entirely reduced. Indeed, the
fifth village of Sparta, Amyklai, to whose incorporation I
shall shortly turn, was physically separated from the
other four by several kilometres. Now the two royal
houses were based in the original Sparta, the Agiads in
Pitana, the smartest village, the Eurypontids in Limnai.
At least, this was where they had their respective burial-
grounds, burial within the settlement area being permitted
in Sparta contrary to normal Greek custom. Thus the joint
monarchy could have been established when Pitana and Limnai coalesced politically to form the 'polis' of Sparta,
the former taking with it Mesoa, the latter Kynosoura/Kon-
ooura - if topography is any guide (Figure 12).   That the
amalgamation of these four was completed before the absorption of Amyklai is strongly suggested by an institutional
survival; the important cult of Orthia in Limnai was common only to the original four villages (Paus. 3.16.9),
whereas the cult of the patron deity of the state Athena
Poliachos was naturally shared (after the absorption of
Amyklai) by all five. The dates at which these cults were
established cannot be precisely determined, but one would
expect the cult of the state's patron to have come first,
an expectation that is not belied by the archaeological
evidence, if Droop's relative chronology of Lakonian PG
pottery is accepted (Chapter 7). Both at any rate were
certainly in existence by the joint reign of Archelaos and
Charillos. Thus, to conclude this discussion of the early
history of the Spartan monarchy, the suggestion that Archelaos and Charillos were the first joint monarchs is consistent with the literary and archaeological evidence deployed above and so should perhaps be accepted as a working
hypothesis.
   Let us make it work first to help explain the political
status of Classical Amyklai. According to the dominant
tendency of the much later literary evidence, conveniently
represented by the 'narrative' in Pausanias' third book,
'Achaean' Amyklai and 'Dorian' Sparta were locked for centuries in an eyeball-to-eyeball confrontation in the Spartan basin. Their route to the south thus effectively
blocked, the Spartans eventually turned their aggressive

attention to the north and, as we have seen, under Archelaos and Charillos destroyed Aigys. In the reign of Teleklos, son of Archelaos, Amyklai at last fell to Sparta
through treachery and armed attack. The way now lay open
to the rest of Lakonia - and even Messenia, on whose borders Teleklos met his end. Pharis and Geronthrai were also
taken by Teleklos, Helos by his son Alkamenes despite
Argive intervention.

Thus far 'tradition' - geographically not impossible
perhaps, but historically worthless, notwithstanding the
claims of Pausanias' modern supporters. For, leaving
aside the question of Pausanias'sources, it is unlikely
that Teleklos would have been dabbling in Messenia before
getting Helos (or the Helos region) under his belt. Moreover, as argued in Chapter 7, the conquest of the area of
which Helos was the chief place is more likely to have occurred in the tenth or ninth century. Second, the notion
of Amyklai blocking Sparta's progress southwards is anachronistic for the eighth or any earlier century. Third,
the alleged captures of Pharis (site unknown) and Geronthrai are probably no more than a clumsy attempt to accommodate the data of the Homeric 'Catalogue' (Appendix 2)
in a coherent historical picture. Finally, and most seriously, the 'Dorian'/'Achaean' antithesis is greatly over-
done. This point has already been made in connection with
the Hyakinthia (Chapter 7); we may add here that, so far
as the evidence of archaeology goes, there is nothing to
justify the idea that Sparta and Amyklai were after c.900
culturally distinct. How then should we interpret the
'tradition' of conquest by Teleklos?

An inscription of Roman date (IG V.1.27) proves that
Amyklai became one of the 'obes' of Sparta, but there is
considerable controversy both over the number of the 'obes'
and over their relationship to the 'villages' of Thucydides and the 'tribes' referred to in the Archaic document
known as the 'Great Rhetra' (Plut. 'Lyk.' 6). To cut a
very long story short, I follow the line of argument proposed by Wade-Gery (1958, 37-85), to the effect that there
were in all five 'obes', namely the four 'villages' of
Sparta plus Amyklai. The most economical hypothesis to
explain the 'traditional', archaeological and epigraphical
evidence is to suppose that Amyklai, already considerably
'Dorianized' and perhaps politically subordinated, was incorporated as the fifth 'obe' of the enlarged Sparta by
Teleklos c.750. The precise location of the 'obe', however, is still unclear. Several pieces of evidence, including the Roman inscription, suggest that it lay at
Sklavochori (now, typically, officially renamed Amyklai);
but this location tallies neither with the distance of

Amyklai from Sparta given by Polybius (5.19.2) nor with
the historian's description of the sanctuary of Apollo as
lying on the seaward side of the settlement. One solution
might be that Amyklai extended in an arc from the range of
hills north and north-west of the sanctuary to the site of
modern Amyklai.

We need not of course believe the story of an actual
military conquest involving the pitched battle and fifth-
columnry characteristic of the fifth and subsequent centuries rather than the eighth. In particular, the leading
military role assigned to Timomachos may owe more to mid-
fourth-century Theban propaganda than to mid-eighth-cent-
ury Spartan reality (cf. Toynbee 1913, 251-4). On the
other hand, there is no good reason to reject the 'traditional' view that the incorporation was far from being a
painless and smooth operation. The cult of Apollo/Hyakin-
thos remained a pre-eminently Amyklaian affair, in contrast to the Spartan cult of Orthia. This may have been
part of the price Sparta had to pay to persuade Amyklai,
or rather its leading aristocrats, to come over quietly.
Above all, the king of Amyklai, if such there was, may not
have taken too kindly to losing his throne.

The other main group of dissidents in Amyklai seems to
have been the so-called Minyans, whose story is told so
picturesquely by Herodotus (4.145ff.) in connection with
the settlement of Thera, the island whose massive eruption
in c.1500 we noticed in Chapter 4. It is hard to disembed
fact from fiction in Herodotus' account, but the Minyans
were presumably survivors of the Bronze Age population of
Lakonia, who had taken to the hills (Taygetos) during the
Mycenaean 'time of troubles' and returned to the plain
when the dust had settled. Archaeology may provide a clue
to the date of their migration to Thera, led by the suspiciously eponymous Theras; for the earliest evidence of
post-Mycenaean habitation on the island belongs around
800. It is therefore tempting to see the settlement as a
consequence of increasing political disagreement between
Sparta and Amyklai which ended in the latter's partial
loss of its separate identity or formal independence.

There may, however, have been more narrowly economic
factors involved too. In the fifth century Thera regarded
itself as a colony of Sparta, a claim backed by its Doric
dialect and perhaps also by its possession of Ephors (cf.
Kiechle 1963, 83-95). The same claim was advanced by the
nearby Melos (Thuc. 5.84.2, 89, 112.2), by Knidos in southern Asia Minor (Hdt. 1.174.2) and by Kythera (Thuc. 7.57.
6). Not all of these can have borne the same relationship
to the alleged mother-city, and Kythera at least, as we
shall see later in this chapter, shows no organic connec-

tion with Sparta in the eighth century. But it is at
least possible that the settlement of Melos (traditional
date 1116) like those of Amyklaion near Gortyn and Amyklai
on Cyprus, is to be associated with a ninth- or eighth-
century rather than a twelfth-century emigration from Lakonia and so to be regarded as an anticipation of the full-
blown colonization movement of the 730s onwards, from
which the enlarged Sparta preferred to abstain.

However that may be, the reign of Teleklos (c.760-740)
was clearly a time of movement in other respects. In
archaeological, specifically ceramic, terms it witnessed
the transition from PG to Late Geometric (LG) pottery in
Lakonia - or rather the abrupt break between them. For
after some two centuries of what looks for the most part
like conservative stagnation the native pottery tradition
was transformed by a deluge of external influences emanat-
ing above all from the Argolis and the Corinthia. Only a
few items from the old stock managed to keep their heads
above water and that at the cost of varying degrees of
metamorphosis. The new synthesis, the local Lakonian LG
style, was generally colourless and insipid, enlivened by
few sparks of native ingenuity (Figure 11e). But at least
it was new, it was in line with changes elsewhere in
Greece, and the fabric achieved a far wider distribution
than its PG predecessor both inside and outside Lakonia,
particularly within Sparta itself (Figure 13).

The causes of change in ceramic style are complex and
hard to discover, even where both the literary and the
archaeological evidence are rich, but broadly speaking
they are social. No artist is an island. His (one assumes that specialist potters and painters were male)
thought-patterns, potentialities and techniques alike reflect and reveal the level of development attained by the
society of which he is a part. Indeed, we are entitled to
assume that the Greek Geometric artist, no matter what his
medium, was more firmly affixed to his cultural matrix
than his modern counterpart through direct social, economic and psychological ties. Thus a change in style so profound as that from PG to LG pottery in Lakonia (and elsewhere) presupposes equally radical changes in Lakonian
society affecting the relationship between Lakonia and the
wider world outside. If the stagnation of PG was fostered
by geographical isolation, insecurity and a low level of
technology, then the re-establishment of communication by
land and sea and the rising standard of technique should
be at least part of the explanation of the change from PG
to LG. Certainly, the Spartan ruling aristocracy, as we
have seen, had begun to display an interest in the world
beyond their immediate purview during the first half of

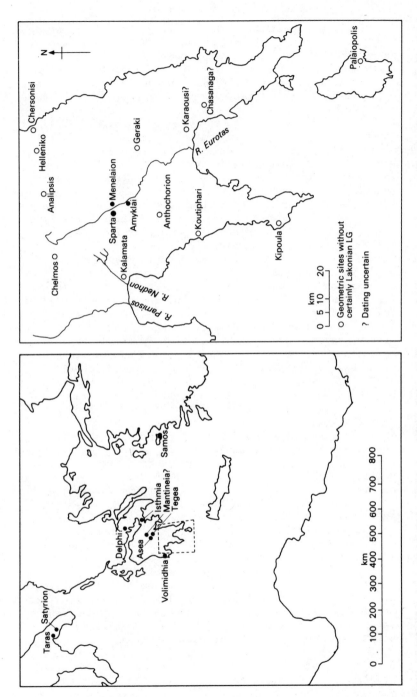

FIGURE 13   The distribution of Lakonian Late Geometric
            pottery

the eighth century. 'Governmental' action, however, is
unlikely to have preceded the activities of individuals
and small groups who, in transacting their daily business,
established peaceful, stable and routine channels of intercourse, at first within Lakonia (witness the distribution of Lakonian PG) and then between Lakonia and other
regions of the Peloponnese.

The decisive contacts, artistically speaking, were with
the Argolis, another major area of Dorian settlement entering an expansionist phase. On present evidence the
medium of Argive influence was not imported pottery, although a few Argive MG pieces did make their way to the
Orthia sanctuary. So, if pots were not travelling, people
must have been; and I see no difficulty in visualizing
Lakonian potters and painters visiting Argive workshops
and sanctuaries or, if the Argolis is thought to be too
distant, at least Tegea, where Argive pottery was imported
for dedication in some quantity. (I cannot support the
political explanation of Argive ceramic influence proposed
by Coldstream 1977, 156, 163.) From the Argives the Lakonians borrowed the essential LG motifs like the meander
(including the characteristically Argive step-meander),
the lozenge or diamond, and the zigzag. These and the
'metopal' scheme of composition they applied to the larger, cruder shapes such as the krater (mixing-bowl) and
amphora. It was also under Argive inspiration that the
Lakonians inaugurated a somewhat clumsy and inchoate
figure-style, depicting chiefly horses, the aristocratic
hallmark, and rows of dancing men and women.

Corinthian influence was less marked to begin with. For
whatever reason, the Corinthians did not follow the Argives
in developing a Geometric figure-style, but their LG was
exceedingly competent and may well have influenced Lakonian
at least by its characteristic system of fine banding. It
was, however, the revolution implied by the Early Proto-
corinthian (EPC) linear and orientalizing styles that was
most keenly felt in Lakonia from c.720. A few bolder
spirits flirted with the new black-figure technique in
blatant imitation of Corinthian work, but the majority
sensibly decided that the time was not yet ripe for moving
into a full-blown black-figure style. Instead, they turned to Corinth for the fine 'half-tone' ornament which they
applied to the smaller, thin-walled shapes like the skyphos and lakaina (both drinking-vessels). New shapes like
the globular aryballos (scent-bottle) and lekythos (oil-
flask) were also borrowed from the same source. Utilizing
our understanding of the relationship between, on the one
hand, Lakonian LG and, on the other, Argive LG and Corinthian LG and EPC, we may justifiably argue that Lakonian

LG began c.750 and ended c.690. Neither date unfortunately receives independent corroboration from the stratigraphy of the Orthia sanctuary in Sparta, the site which,
for the reasons summarized in Appendix 5, provides the
basis of our knowledge of all Lakonian archaeology from
the mid-eighth century onwards.

Lakonian LG pottery was, as I remarked earlier, far
more widely distributed than PG, though this need not of
course mean in each case that the site in question had
previously been unoccupied. Outside the two main Spartan
sanctuaries of Athena and Orthia, it has been excavated in
a 'domestic and commercial' area of the village of Pitana,
at several sites in Limnai (including the Heroon sanctuary) and a couple of places in Mesoa. Across the Eurotas
LG pottery dates the inauguration of the important cult of
Menelaos and Helen, whose significance will be considered
further below. At Amyklai in addition to the continued
worship of Apollo/Hyakinthos another new LG cult was established near the modern chapel of Ay. Paraskevi. The
recipient deity was probably Alexandra, whom the Amyklaians identified with Trojan Kassandra in Pausanias' day
(3.19.6); but her worship may only have been associated
with that of the heroized Agamemnon from the sixth century, when such 'Achaean' connections were found politically expedient (Chapter 9). 'Geometric' pottery is reported
confidently from Analipsis (perhaps ancient Iasos) on the
northern frontier, and from Helleniko (ancient Eua) and
Chersonisi in Kynouria, more doubtfully from Geraki (ancient Geronthrai). Since I have not seen these pieces, I
cannot say whether they are to be assigned to the Lakonian
LG style properly so called; perhaps, like those from
Kastri/Palaiopolis on Kythera, they are strictly local
products. Outside Lakonia, though, certainly Lakonian LG
ware has been excavated at Volimidhia in Messenia, at
Tegea and Asea in Arkadia, and at the sanctuary of Poseidon north of the Isthmus of Corinth; the suggested pieces
from Nichoria, Mantineia and Delphi, however, are doubtfully Lakonian.

Of all these finds the most directly relevant in the
immediate context is the two-handled cup or tankard from
Volimidhia. It was found, together with two local Messenian pots and seven Corinthian LG I imports, in the dromos
of a Mycenaean chamber-tomb, part of an offering to a by-
gone hero. This humble tankard is thus proof positive of
relations between Sparta and Messenia c.740-730 (Coldstream 1977, 162, 182), although we cannot of course say
precisely how or why it made the journey to its place of
discovery. It may not, however, have been the first Lakonian pottery to make the trip. In Chapter 7 we noticed

the certainly Lakonian PG from the border sanctuary of
Artemis Limnatis at Volimnos and the sherds of Lakonian PG
type at Kaphirio and perhaps Hellenika (ancient Thouria).
These, together with some suggestive stylistic analogies
at Nichoria, also in the same general area of south-east
Messenia, may indicate that contact between Messenia and
Sparta had been firmly established before 750.

This indication receives apparently powerful support
from a notice in Strabo (8.4.4,C360) that Teleklos established colonies in south-east Messenia at Poieessa,
Echeiai and Tragion (none of these has been identified
archaeologically). Indeed, the sober Busolt (1893, 229-
32) was prepared to argue that south-east Messenia, or the
part of it probably to be identified with the ancient Dentheliatis, was actually in Spartan control in the time of
Teleklos before the full-scale invasion of Messenia from
the north-east c.735. If so, then the three towns will
presumably have been of Perioikic status, and their foundation will have had a direct bearing on the outbreak of
Spartano-Messenian hostilities.

The route taken by Teleklos into Messenia is not recorded, but, if Kiechle (1963, 100) is right, he did not take
the short cut over Taygetos from Xirokambi to Kardamyli,
which would have been hazardous for an army. Instead perhaps he will have marched down the Eurotas valley, across
Vardhounia to Gytheion, then along the 246 m.-high Karyoupolis divide to the site of modern Areopolis before continuing up the coast via Oitylos and Kardamyle to Pharai
(modern Kalamata). The latter Teleklos may have brought
into the Spartan sphere, again as a Perioikic dependency;
at any rate, it was later regarded as a Spartan colony.
In the end, however, Teleklos appears to have overreached
himself and was assassinated by dissident Messenians - or
so the Spartans claimed - at the border sanctuary of Artemis Limnatis.

It is now time to consider what may have prompted this
first intervention of the Spartans in Messenia in the
light of their full-scale invasion a generation or so
later. First it must be made abundantly clear how poor is
the available literary evidence for this crucial moment in
Lakonian history. Apart from a few scraps of the fourth-
century Ephorus, we are chiefly dependent on the fourth
book of Pausanias, who utilized, directly or indirectly,
the prose 'Messeniaka' of Myron of Priene and the verse
epic of Rhianos of Bene, both third-century writers, cor-
recting or supplementing them from the poems of Tyrtaios.
This is a dispiriting reversal of the proper historical
procedure, but then Pausanias was of course no more a historian than the writers upon whom he chiefly drew. There

is, however, also a wider problem of evidence. For the
Spartan conquest and annexation of Messenia introduced a
new and enduring facet of the Spartan 'mirage' (Chapter 5),
what we might more properly call the 'Messenian mirage'.
   The chief causes of the distortion of early Messenian
history were threefold (apart from those applicable to all
early Greek history). First, as the Greek expression
'Messenian War (or Wars)' implies, the conflict has usually been viewed from the Spartan side of the barricades,
like, for example, the struggle between Rome and the
Etruscans; and the main - some would say the only - reliable literary source is the Spartan Tyrtaios. Second, as
with the 'Tourkokratia' from AD 1453, the harshness of the
Spartan occupation stimulated among the vanquished Messenians (including those of the Diaspora) a flourishing folk-
lore of resistance, of which the exploits of Aristomenes
are but the most conspicuous products. Third, the liberation of Messenia from the Spartan yoke and the (re-)foun-
dation of the 'polis' of Messene in 370-369 (Chapter 13)
transferred the war from the physical to the verbal plane.
Every aspect of the post-Mycenaean past of Messenia became
raw material for political propaganda and 'creative' historiography in a fiery debate whose strength can be gauged
from the embers raked over for us in Pausanias' travelogue.
In short, while our sources give us a variety of unconvincing and mutually inconsistent 'aitiai kai diaphorai'
(causes of complaint and clashes of interest) before the
outbreak of hostilities, they provide us with no cogent
'alethestate prophasis' (truest explanation).
   We are forced, therefore, to look elsewhere, and the
most fruitful line of approach is undoubtedly to view the
Spartan initiative in the context of Greek, and especially
Peloponnesian, development as a whole. The sudden increase in direct and indirect external contacts around 750
suggests that at this stage Sparta was in some sense becoming one of the more advanced mainland Greek communities. Some fifteen years later Corinth, another Dorian
city and then perhaps the most advanced of all, followed
the lead given by the Euboians, though perhaps for different purposes, and despatched settlers to the west (Kerkyra
and Sicily). Since this was just about the time, according to a plausible chronology inferred from the Olympic
victor-lists, that the Spartans invaded Messenia, there is
a case for asking whether these events had anything in
common. Despite large differences of geographical situation and political organization, the answer, I believe,
is that the common factor was overpopulation - or, to be
precise, relative overpopulation. Hypothetically, the
causal nexus was roughly as follows. The fertile Eurotas

valley had been somehow distributed among the Spartans,
but inequality of ownership allied to an increase in population had created an unacceptable level of social discontent and physical hardship. The settlement of more
marginal areas of Lakonia and of the fertile (but politically far more sensitive) south-east Messenia had proved
ephemeral palliatives. A more drastic solution was required, and the conquest of Messenia or rather the Pamisos
valley filled the bill.

Several theoretical objections might be raised to this
hypothesis, but they can all be met so long as it is remembered that the overpopulation in Lakonia was relative
and that it was in any case a necessary not a sufficient
condition of such a giant undertaking. The ancient sources, needless to say, are more interested in personalities
than in what we might call social pressures, but an eccentric apophthegm attributed to the Agiad king Polydoros
(Plut. 'Mor.' 231E) provides a whisper of support for the
view that land-hunger was the primary motivation. If we
were to treat seriously the story of the quarrel between
the Messenian Olympic victor Polychares and the Spartan
Euaiphnos (Paus. 4.4.5-5.7), which was the Messenians'
reply to the Spartan claim to be avenging the death of
Teleklos, we might perhaps infer that a dispute over
transhumance rights was a contributory factor. It remains
true, however, that the case in favour of the hypothesis
outlined above must be argued in terms of probabilities.

Let us first approach the question negatively. If for
the sake of argument it is granted that there was critical
overpopulation in the Eurotas valley, what other remedies
besides the conquest of the Pamisos valley were open to the
Spartans? 'Internal colonization', of the kind successfully practised in comparably spacious Attika, Boiotia and
the Argolis in this period, had already been tried in Lakonia and found wanting. Moreover, it was ruled out for
the future by political considerations, since the bait of
land in exchange for the loss of citizen rights (however
ill-defined at this primitive stage) was not so attractive
to the poor Spartan as it later proved to be for the poor
Roman of the early Republic, for two main reasons: first,
the land available was less desirable agriculturally; and,
second, the divide between Spartan and Perioikic political
status was in decisive respects absolute, unlike that between Latin and Roman status. On the other hand, overseas
colonization was not a natural choice for an inland state
like Sparta (compare, for example, Thebes), as is amply
demonstrated by the circumstances in which Sparta's only
true colony, Taras, was later established (below). Third,
the importation of essential foodstuffs to offset any

shortfall there may have been in domestic production was
not a practical proposition in the second half of the
eighth century, for both economic and political reasons.
   Negatively, therefore, the acquisition of new land was
the only feasible solution. There were strong positive
arguments in its favour too. The Spartans had already
demonstrated skill both in war and in the control of dependent populations. They had proved in Lakonia that they
could compel their subjects to yield up a surplus of agricultural production which they were unable or perhaps unwilling (Hesiod apparently attests the regular employment
of slaves in Boiotia by 700) to extract by other means.
Furthermore, the potential source of new land was one of
the most fertile areas of all mainland Greece, Messenia
'good for ploughing, good for growing', as Tyrtaios (fr.5.
3) succinctly put it. However, the final and, for me at
least, incontrovertible proof of the kind of pressing need
created by overpopulation lies in two further considerations. First, between Sparta and Messenia runs the Taygetos massif, a formidable deterrent to communication, let
alone conquest and permanent subjugation, even if such
strategic advantage as it offers does lie on Sparta's
side. Second, the treatment meted out to the unfortunate
Messenians was unparalleled in the whole of Greek antiquity, being comparable perhaps only to the treatment of the
Irish by England in more recent times. I conclude, therefore, that the so-called First Messenian War (c.735-715)
was triggered by relative overpopulation in the Eurotas
valley.
   Before we look briefly at the course of the war it is
necessary to consider the physical setting and post-Mycenaean history of Messenia (Figure 14). The northern boundary is marked by the valley of the River Nedha (Chapter 1),
the eastern by Taygetos. The area thus delimited may be
sub-divided in the following manner. On the north-west
south of the River Kyparissia there begin the Kyparissia
mountains, which extend southwards in the Aigaleon and
other ridges, Mount Ithome being the easternmost. Southwards again lies the plateau east of Pylos, which continues to the foot of the Messenian peninsula. East of the
Kyparissia mountains is the central valley of Messenia,
essentially a northward projection of the Messenian Gulf,
whose geomorphology appears not to have been so drastically altered by late Roman and mediaeval alluviation as
its counterpart in Lakonia. It is this valley which occasioned the eulogies of Tyrtaios and later writers such
as Euripides (fr. 1083 N). The valley itself is further
sub-divided by the Skala ridge east of Ithome into a lower
portion, known in antiquity as Makaria (Blessedness), and

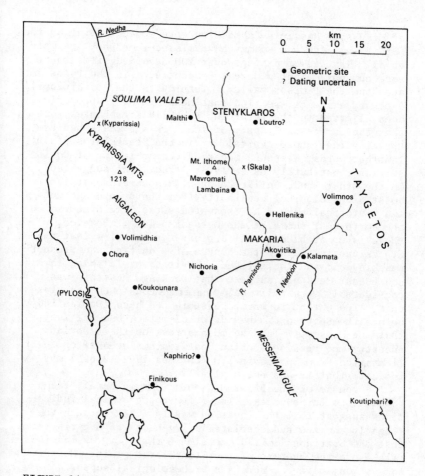

FIGURE 14 Messenia in the eighth century BC

an upper, the plain of Stenyklaros. To west of the latter
extends the Soulima valley, while the east of the central
plain as a whole is blocked by Taygetos.

This region had been among the most populous and important of all Greece during the Mycenaean heyday of the thirteenth century (Chapter 6). By the tenth century, however, the dismal picture we have painted for the region on
the other side of Taygetos was mirrored here, although it
should be stressed that the participants in the University

of Minnesota Messenia Expedition were concentrating on the
Late Bronze Age and so may have missed some Dark Age material. Instead of perhaps over 200 occupied sites there
were now only about a dozen, concentrated in the Pylos
area and the Pamisos valley. Turning to the 'traditional'
literary evidence, we find that Messenia had supposedly
been allotted to the returning Heraklid Kresphontes, but
that the successor dynasty of the Dark Age was known as
the Aipytids, whose capital lay in the Stenyklaros plain.
In other words, Messenia too received an influx of Dorian
settlers, but hardly as early as 'tradition' suggested.
On the other hand, unlike Lakonia, Messenia can at least
boast archaeological continuity from the Bronze Age into
the historical period at excavated sites like Nichoria on
the north-west shore of the Messenian Gulf. However,
there is no archaeological support for the view that the
Stenyklaros plain was the centre of a unified and prosperous kingdom; and the alleged activities of Teleklos in
south-east Messenia suggest that Dark Age Messenia was
considerably more politically heterogeneous even than Lakonia. The extent to which Messenia had been 'Dorianized'
before the Spartan takeover is problematic, but the fact
that the Messenians laid so much stress on their Dorian
ancestry and retained Dorian institutions even after their
liberation from Sparta in 370 (Chrimes 1949, 276f.) may
indicate that it was not negligible.
     The course of the First Messenian War is barely recov-
erable from our sources. Their few topographical indications suggest that the invasion was launched through the
recently annexed and desolate 'bridgehead' of Aigytis and
that the Spartans limited the aim of their aggression initially to the capture of the Stenyklaros plain. Neither
suggestion, however, receives archaeological support.
Moreover, the precise route followed by the Spartan army
to Aigytis is controversial. Most scholars prefer to
think of it as proceeding up the Eurotas valley to the
southern edge of the Megalopolis plain and so skirting the
northern extremity of Taygetos. Boelte (1929, 1343f.),
however, argued cogently for a shorter, more southerly
route actually crossing Taygetos from modern Georgitsi to
Neochori and Dyrrhachi. According to Tyrtaios (fr. 5.7),
the fighting was spread over twenty years, but this figure
is suspect as being twice the length of the Trojan War.
There is no reason, however, for doubting that the war was
a long drawn out affair nor that (not for the last time)
the final resistance centred on the low mountain bastion
of Ithome. The generalship of the victorious Eurypontid
king Theopompos (Tyrtaios fr. 5.1f.) is an unknown quantity, but his employment of Cretan mercenary archers (Paus.

4.8.3, 12; 4.10.1) is perhaps supported by the find of an
as yet unpublished bronze helmet of Cretan type. The only
other pieces of archaeological evidence which may be directly connected with the war are a warrior's pithos burial
of c.725 recently excavated at Nichoria (Coldstream 1977,
162, 163f.) and two rather earlier inhumations in a possibly Mycenaean chamber-tomb from the same site (Coldstream 1977, 161). Unfortunately, though, we cannot tell
which side our heroes had fought on.

For the moment, then, the Spartan snake had triumphed
over the Messenian fox. The consequences were dramatic.
The Stenyklaros plain and perhaps also the western half of
the Makaria were seized by Sparta, and some of the former
owners, it seems, were compelled 'like asses exhausted
under great loads to bring their masters full half the
fruit their ploughed land produced' (Tyrtaios fr. 6).
Other Messenians were more fortunate and escaped either to
other parts of Greece (Arkadia was a natural haven) or
perhaps overseas (to Sicily and south Italy). Yet others,
outside the Pamisos valley, acquired or had confirmed the
then status of Perioikoi. We should not perhaps envisage
Sparta as controlling all Messenia as early as 700, but
the founding of a New Asine at modern Koroni about the
same time (in the circumstances described below) implies
that Sparta was at liberty to intervene at least in the
foot of the Messenian peninsula. This Asine, together
with Mothone (Chapter 9), were illuminatingly described by
Professor Wade-Gery in a marginal note to his copy of
Pareti 1917 as 'the Ulster of the Messenian Ireland'.

The conquest made the Spartan state - or rather certain
Spartans - the wealthiest in Greece, and we could ask for
no clearer indication of the influx of riches to Sparta
than the finds from the sanctuary of Orthia. G. Dickins
(in AO 163) convincingly linked the building of the second, all-stone temple of Orthia to a notice in Herodotus
(1.65.1) concerning Spartan military success in the joint
reign of Leon and Agasikles (c.575-560), a link reinforced
by the revised dating (Boardman 1963, 7) of the second
temple to c.570-560. Precisely the same connection can
be posited for the construction of the first temple on the
site, correctly downdated by Boardman to c.700. For, as
Pritchett (1974, I, 100) has aptly remarked, 'without
wars, few of the temples and other sacred buildings of
Greece would have been built.'

Like warfare, the construction of a temple was always a
public enterprise in Greece, but in the Archaic period it
was regarded pre-eminently as an opportunity for the rich
to display their wealth in a gesture of apparent piety towards the gods and goodwill towards the community as a

whole. The early temples, in fact, were among the first
known examples of that system of liturgies or 'giving for
a return' which was to be politically institutionalized in
the Athenian democracy and later throughout the Roman Empire. They also had important side-effects. The existence of a permanent roofed structure was an inducement to
dedicate objects in precious perishable materials. The
desire to make such dedications created a demand for skil-
led labour which could not always be satisfied by local
resources. The introduction of foreign artisans to carry
out specific commissions provided a tremendous stimulus in
ideas and expertise to the native tradition. This, I suggest, explains how in the last quarter of the eighth century Lakonia was for the first time brought within the
orbit of trade in luxury goods and raw materials and introduced to the most progressive ('orientalizing') artistic currents of the day.

In other words, it is the conquest of Messenia, or at
least the upper Pamisos valley, which accounts for the
presence at the Orthia sanctuary from c.700 of expensive
and exotic ex-votos in imported materials like gold, silver, ivory, glass, faience and amber, as well as a variety
of bronze manufactures from within and outside the Greek
world. The certain or probable provenances of the bronzes
alone include Macedonia, central Greece, the Aegean islands, East Greece, Phrygia, the Near East and Cyprus,
together with other regions of the Peloponnese. Of the
local schools of craftsmen thus stimulated we might single
out the workers in ivory and bronze for the quantity and
quality of their production. For example, bronze horse
figurines of Lakonian style datable c.750 to 700 have been
found not only in Messenia (at Akovitika) but in Attika,
Boiotia, Achaia, Phokis, Arkadia and perhaps even Egypt.
Indeed, by 750 the makers of such figurines were established in workshops in the Altis at Olympia, a sign of
fairly advanced organization of the craft; their products
were no doubt dedicated principally by the outstandingly
successful Spartan aristocratic competitors in the Games.
Taken as a whole, the finds from Orthia will stand comparison with the contemporary votive assemblages to Hera at
Corinthian Perachora and the Argive Heraion. The sanctuaries of Athena on the Spartan akropolis and Apollo/Hya-
kinthos at Amyklai are admittedly less well appointed, but
this may be simply because there was no protective layer
of sand at these sites to seal in the earliest finds. For
the bronze cauldron-attachments found here do suggest
wealth comparable to that displayed at the Orthia sanctuary.

Moreover, about the same time as the building of the

first temple of Orthia the Spartans established a new
sanctuary with interesting implications. This was the Menelaion, dedicated to Menelaos and Helen on the site of the
most important Late Bronze Age settlement in Lakonia. The
sanctuary had been excavated on and off since the 1830s
and long since identified from the fairly abundant literary sources. But it was not until 1975 that incontrovertible proof of the identification was discovered in the
shape of bronze artefacts inscribed with dedications to
Helen (Catling and Cavanagh 1976). The earlier of the
two, a pointed aryballos of c.650, provides the earliest
evidence of Lakonian alphabetic writing.

Helen is arguably a faded version of the 'Great Mother'
or, less grandly, a tree-goddess; her brothers, the Dioskouroi, who were supposed to live underground at Therapne
(Alkman fr. 7) and generally played a major role in Lakonian cult and politics, may have been house-spirits before
they became heroes. But Menelaos' only previous existence
had been in the world of Homer (Appendix 2). On one level,
therefore, the establishment of a sanctuary of the Homeric
king of Lakedaimon, brother of Agamemnon and alleged oc-
cupant of a fine palace, was a matter of political convenience for Dorians seeking to bolster their claim to rule
the south-east Peloponnese by right. On another level,
though, this was simply a variation on a theme being played in widely separated parts of the Greek world at this
time, the veneration of the heroes of the past.

There is, however, no other archaeologically attested
Lakonian site of the late eighth century which remotely
rivals the Menelaion in its apparent display of wealth and
prosperity. This dearth of evidence is especially disappointing in the case of Perioikic communities like Pellana, Geronthrai, Boiai and Prasiai, whose early importance is strongly suggested by literary evidence. Pellana
disputed with little Pephnos in north-west Mani the privilege of being the birthplace of the Dioskouroi (Chapter
10). Geronthrai, as we have seen, was reportedly conquered and resettled by Teleklos. Boiai was said to have been
'synoecized' by the Heraklid Boios at an unspecified, but
presumably early date (Moggi 1976, no. 5). Finally,
Prasiai was an independent member of the Kalaureian Amphiktyony (Strabo 8.6.14, C374), a primarily religious association for the worship of Poseidon centred on what is
now the tourist island of Poros, before Sparta assumed
Prasiai's responsibilities. Unfortunately, though, the
date of the origins of the Amphiktyony is uncertain. Some
would put it as early as the ninth century (Coldstream
1977, 54 n. 65), others as late as the seventh (Kelly
1966). The earliest archaeological evidence from Prasiai

belongs perhaps to the second half of the seventh century.
Apart from these, in some ways the most disappointing
archaeological gap of all is the lacuna in our evidence
for Gytheion between the PG period and the sixth century.
For it must have been through this port that most of the
expensive raw materials and finished manufactures referred
to above (and perhaps some foreign craftsmen too) made
their way to the Spartan basin.

Again, though, as in the third and second millennia
(Chapter 4), Kythera served as a window on the wider
Aegean world and indeed on that disturbed Near East which
indirectly stimulated what is referred to in art-historical
terms as the 'orientalizing' period of Greek history. By
the fifth century Sparta sent out officials called 'Kyth-
erodikai' or harmosts to supervise Kytheran affairs (Chapter 12) and the islanders were regarded as colonists of
Sparta; indeed, a remark attributed to the sage Chilon
(discussed in Chapter 11) suggests that the island had
already become of some strategic concern to Sparta by the
mid-sixth century. But between c.1200 and c.550 the history of Kythera is opaque; archaeologically, there is
nothing known between the thirteenth and the early eighth
centuries. However, Homer ('Iliad' 10.268) does mention
Skandeia, the port of Kythera town, which is almost
certainly to be identified with the Kastri/Palaiopolis
area on the east coast. Kythera town itself, according to
Pausanias (3.23.1), lay ten stades inland and has accordingly been identified with the area centring on the hill
of Palaiokastro.

In the present context, however, undoubtedly the most
intriguing piece of literary evidence is the passing mention by Herodotus (1.105.3) that the temple of Aphrodite
at Kythera town had been founded by Phoenicians. Should
this report be believed? First, let us consider the role
of the Phoenicians. After briefly summarizing the archaeological evidence for the resumption of contact between
Greece and the Near East after the Mycenaean period Boardman (1973, 36) comments: 'It is none too easy to fit the
Phoenicians into this picture of relations in the Aegean
in the Early Iron Age - or at least to fit in the reputation which the Phoenicians had acquired as mariners and
traders.' None the less, he accepts cautiously that 'they
may have been the carriers of what little did travel into
the Greek world from the east before the eighth century.'
None of that little has yet turned up in Lakonia, but a
recent comprehensive survey of the archaeological and literary evidence bearing on the Phoenicians (Muhly 1970)
indicates that, if they were ever active on Kythera, this
should have been between the eleventh and eighth centuries

rather than before or after.

In the light of these conclusions the very absence of direct corroborative evidence from Kythera is perhaps significant. Greek Aphrodite could of course have supplanted the Phoenician Astarte (Biblical Ashtoreth), but nothing is known of the cult before some wholly Greek dedications of the sixth century and the disiecta membra of a Doric temple of c.500 (the site of the temple itself is not yet agreed). The harbour called Phoinikous (probably modern Avlemonas bay) mentioned by Xenophon ('Hell.' 4.8.7) need have nothing to do with Phoenicians. No Phoenician inscriptions have been found anywhere on the island. In fact, the only sign of life in eighth-century Kythera is provided by a provincial Geometric pottery, unrelated to Lakonian LG, and a couple of Argive imports. The latter (pace Coldstream 1977, 84) can hardly be used to support the view (highly improbable on other grounds as we have seen) that Kythera was controlled by Argos at this time. In short, the report of Herodotus is something of a puzzle. The only suggestion I can bring in its support is that it was the Phoenicians who introduced or reintroduced the purple-dye industry to the island (discussed further in Chapter 10).

The rest of this chapter will consider Sparta's external relations and cultural development between c.715 and 650. So far the picture I have painted of the consequences for the Spartans of their victory in Messenia has been fairly rosy. In reality, it was rosy only for some, as the circumstances of the foundation of Taras will adequately reveal. The traditional date of settlement, 706, is not contradicted by the earliest archaeological finds (below). The rest of the ancient evidence, however, is almost entirely worthless, and my tentative reconstruction of the process departs from it in several particulars.

A war of long duration is almost bound to exacerbate, if not create, internal social tensions, and the origins of the colony certainly lie in social discontent, whose focus may have been a group enigmatically known as the Partheniai. We shall never know exactly who they were, but the common opinion of the ancient sources, that they were in some sense impure in birth, deserves respect. The shake-up of the eighth century could well have led to a questioning of fundamental values: why should a family-tree - and pre-eminently descent from Herakles - give a man the right to cheat, oppress, dominate and impoverish his fellows? It is no accident that the Partheniai were contemporaries of Hesiod. For them too land was a part, perhaps the major part, of their grievance. It was, however, probably only one aspect, if a crucial one, of a

broader political discontent, 'political' precisely in the
sense that the birth of a concept of citizenship and the
full development of the 'polis' were phenomena of the decades around 700. This was why, as Aristotle ('Pol.' 1306b
29-31) correctly saw, the Partheniai represented potential
revolution. But there may have been a further contributory grievance, Amyklaian 'nationalism': for the settlers
took with them to Taras the cult of Apollo Hyakinthios.
     Plato ('Laws' 735f.) observed with hindsight that one
solution to such social discontent is to export the dis-
contented, and traditionally this is what occurred in the
case of the Partheniai. My own view, however, is that
Taras was not originally sanctioned by the Spartan state,
but was a foundation as it were 'from below' effected by a
few enterprising families, whose success was only later
given the official seal of approval. The contradictory
evidence concerning the supposed 'oikist' (leader of the
colony) Phalanthos may be thought to support this interpretation. So too may the Delphic Oracle which advised
settlement, not at Taras, but at Satyrion twelve kilometres further south-east in the heel of Italy (Parke and
Wormell 1956, I,71-3; II, no. 46). At any rate LG pottery
has been found here, as it has at Scoglio (or Punto) del
Tonno on the other side of the lagoon entrance from Taras,
and these sites may represent temporary stopping-places
before the occupation of Taras itself (Figure 15). The
latter, however, was the real prize. The best harbour in
Italy (the modern Mar Piccolo), protection by the sea on
three sides and good communications inland - these are
only some of its advantages. The only trouble was that
the native Iapygians were already occupying it. With some
difficulty, however, they were dislodged, and perhaps before 700, to judge from the recent find of Lakonian LG
pottery on the site of the akropolis of the ancient city
(Lo Porto 1971, 356-8). The relations of Taras with
Sparta, though not with the Iapygians, were exceptionally
close thereafter: the archaeological, epigraphical and
literary evidence is at one on this.
     The conquest of Messenia was presumably the main reason
why Taras remained Sparta's only colony, but it would be
wrong to follow the sensationalist bent of our sources and
so isolate Taras from the general wave of agrarian colonization of south Italy and Sicily initiated a quarter of a
century or so earlier. Messenia after all was still unfinished business in 706. Indeed, if we can trust Pausanias and others, the Spartans' search for new land - and
perhaps now also for wider political influence - in the
Peloponnese was still on, and the next target was the Thyreatis or Kynouria. To repeat, I do not believe in the

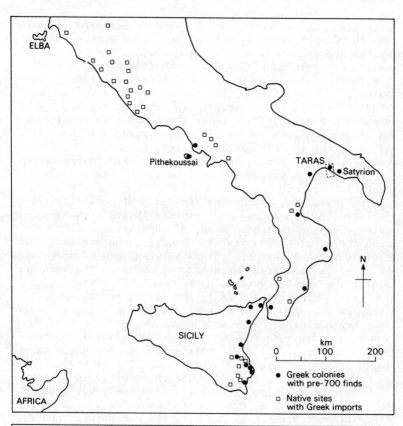

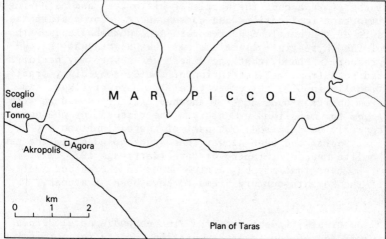

FIGURE 15   The colonization of Taras c.706

pretended Argive control of the eastern seaboard of Lakonia and of Kythera at any time. Nor can I accept that
Sparta and Argos had come to blows before the First Messenian War. It does, however, seem feasible that after
its initial successes in Messenia Sparta, already presumably in control of Skiritis, following the conquest of
Aigytis, should have attempted to seal off its frontier in
the north-east against a power whose might in the second
half of the eighth century is amply attested in both the
literary and the archaeological record. Moreover, the
Partheniai were perhaps not alone in their disappointment
at the unfair distribution of land in Lakonia and most
recently Messenia.

The Thyreatis, because of its relative fertility (especially in olives) and more especially its strategic location, was the appointed scene of physical conflict between the rival Dorian states. However, the earliest more
or less reliably attested clash between them occurred when
the Argives conquered and destroyed Asine in the last decade of the eighth century (Coldstream 1977, 154 and n. 57;
but see Styrenius 1975, 183), and Sparta resettled the
refugees in a new Asine in southern Messenia (Paus. 4.14.
3). Whether or not this action was regarded as provocat-
ive by the Argives, it was also in the reign of Theopompos
(c.720-675) that the first battle for the Thyreatis that I
would accept as historical (Paus. 3.7.5) took place.

Pausanias (2.24.7) is also the only source to mention
the subsequent battle of Hysiai (dated 669), but a fragment of Tyrtaios ('P. Oxy.' 3316)* confirms Sparta's military preoccupation with Argos in the mid-seventh century.
I therefore accept the battle as historical and as having
important implications and consequences. For a start the
site of the battle - near modern Achladokambos and north
of the Thyreatis - clearly shows that Sparta was the aggressor. Second, that the defeat was severe may be inferred both from the institution of the Gymnopaidiai, traditionally in 668, to commemorate it (Wade-Gery 1949) and
from Sparta's avoidance of another military showdown with
Argos for more than a century. The reasons for the defeat
can only be surmised, but part of the explanation may be
that Sparta had been slower than Argos to adapt to the new
hoplite mode of infantry warfare (Cartledge 1977, 25).

However that may be, Argive power in the second quarter
of the seventh century seems to have been at a peak,

*I am greatly indebted to the Finance and General Purposes
 Committee of the Egypt Exploration Society for permission
 to refer to this papyrus in advance of publication.

perhaps under the aegis of its revolutionary king Pheidon (Tomlinson 1972, ch. 6). Sparta's fortunes were in a correspondingly low trough. The demand for the redistribution of land attested by Tyrtaios (as reported by Aristotle) and the murder of king Polydoros, who was credited with attempting to satisfy the demand, are political expressions of grave social conflicts which fit most naturally into this post-defeat context. The effect on Messenian morale can be easily imagined; and it was this combination of circumstances, according to a plausible modern theory, which stimulated the Messenians to revolt. The silence of the ancient sources is far from being a fatal objection to this theory; for with few exceptions they are primarily interested in the web of myth and fantasy that surrounded the supposed leader of the revolt, the Messenian folk-hero Aristomenes. Thus the evidence for the revolt or Second Messenian War is if anything worse than that for the First War, despite our one anchor, Tyrtaios, a participant.

The floruit of Tyrtaios, the second or third quarter of the seventh century, makes it almost certain that the Second War began appreciably later than Pausanias' source believed (685); this accords with the 'tradition' (Paus. 4. 15.3) that the revolt occurred in the reign of Anaxandros, who ruled in the sixth generation before Xerxes' invasion. But there Tyrtaios' direct utility more or less ends, apart from the certain inference from his battle-exhortations that the fighting was between hoplites (a warrior-grave of the seventh century from Pyla in western Messenia may be that of a Spartan) and his mention and perhaps description of a battle at or near a trench (fr. 9; cf. Paus. 4.17.2-9), which may have marked a turning-point in the struggle.

The names of those supposed to have fought on the Messenian side are with one exception superficially plausible, but their alleged participation is perhaps more likely to be a product of the 'Messenian mirage'. Sparta's alleged allies are no less problematic. The Corinthians, whether ruled by the Bacchiads or Kypselos (who became tyrant c.657), would perhaps have in either case sided with Sparta against Argos. The Lepreates of Triphylia might have taken the opposite side to Elis, but Elis, the exception referred to above, was unlikely to have been on the Messenian side at this time. Samos (Hdt. 3.47.1) is at first sight the least likely ally of all, although at least one Lakonian Subgeometric amphora found its way to the island about this time. Perhaps some individual Samians came by ship in the hope of collecting booty. On the other hand, there is nothing intrinsically implausible

in the story that the main focus of resistance was Andania
in north-east Messenia towards Arkadia (site not certainly
identified) and that the last stand was made, not on
Ithome this time, but on Mount Hira not far from Andania.
The Arkadian involvement presaged Spartan reprisals in
succeeding reigns.

The Spartan victory should perhaps be interpreted as a
gradual process of pacification including the spread of
Spartan control to the west coast of Messenia south of the
Nedha, which may not have been completed much before the
end of the seventh century. This would at least accord
with a remark attributed to Epameinondas (Plut. 'Mor.'
194B; Aelian, 'VH' 13.42), that he had (re-)founded Messene after 230 years. I do not, however, think that we
need to postulate a Third ('Hira') War to account for this
figure. Indeed, the loose ends of the conquest can only
be said to have been properly tied up with the treaty of
c.550 between Sparta and Tegea, whose one known clause
(Chapter 9) symbolizes the nerve-wracking consequence of
the Messenian War: Sparta, in G.B. Grundy's adaptation of
an expression of the emperor Tiberius, had 'a wolf by the
throat'.

To conclude this chapter, however, let us look briefly
at Sparta's cultural development in the first half of the
seventh century. It is immediately apparent that this was
as little affected by the almost uninterrupted warfare as
was that of Athens in the fifth. Terpander of Lesbos,
traditionally the first victor in the musical contest at
the reorganized Karneia in 676 (the date worked out by
Hellanikos of Lesbos in the late fifth century), inaugurated a succession of visits by foreign poets who found
Sparta a congenial - and no doubt lucrative - field for
the display of their talents. After c.690 Lakonian vase-
painters under Aegean influence made their first forays
into an orientalizing style, but 'third-rate and unpretentious' (Cook 1972) is probably a fair description of their
products in this unsettled and confusing epoch. However,
as we have seen, at least one Lakonian Subgeometric pot
travelled abroad, and it was presumably pottery of this
transitional phase (described as 'orientalizing Geometric')
which was found at ancient Hippola in the Deep Mani, the
first material evidence of settlement so far south in Lakonia in the historical period. Simultaneously, the Lakonian bronze-workers began to show an increasing interest in
human subjects; perhaps their most engaging product is the
so-called 'Menelaion goddess' of c.675, crude in conception but competent in execution. Following a generation
or more of preparation Lakonian ivory-carving began to
flower shortly before 650. No less technically competent,

if more parochial in flavour, was the output of the coro-
plasts, who were among the earliest in Greek lands to
borrow the Syrian mould and create a local 'Daedalic'
style with strong Cretan affinities. At a humbler level
still, the 'mass-production' of mould-made lead figurines,
perhaps using the ore found near Kardamyli, also began in
the first half of the seventh century: we might single out
the representations of hoplite warriors which were first
dedicated at the Orthia sanctuary around 650. In short,
the cultural picture for Lakonia between c.775 and 650 has
no features in common with the image of sterility beloved
by the ancient and - more reprehensibly - the modern 'mirage'.

NOTES ON FURTHER READING

Perhaps the best discussion of the Greek world as a whole
in the period covered by this chapter is still Starr 1961,
part III; cf. Starr 1977. Bouzek 1969, Snodgrass 1971 and
now Coldstream 1977 deal with all aspects of the archaeological record down to about 700; a comparably comprehensive work for the succeeding period is a desideratum.
Jeffery 1976 is an up-to-date survey, by region, of the
entire Archaic period (to c.500); the chapter on Sparta
(111-32) includes a good discussion of Lakonian art.
    The office of the Pythioi, who were permanent and
hereditary ambassadors to Delphi (Hdt. 6.57, 60; Xen.
'Lak. Pol.' 15.5), may have been instituted in the eighth
century: Cartledge 1978.
    On the (incomplete) 'synoecism' of Sparta see Toynbee
1969, 171-4; Moggi 1976, no. 6 (with very full bibliography). On the status of Amyklai as an 'obe' I agree
with Ehrenberg 1924, 28f. (=1965, 165f.) against e.g.
Grote, who believed that Amyklai was Perioikic.
    The basic study (in default of new information from
grave-groups or stratified settlement-deposits) of
Lakonian LG pottery is Coldstream 1968, ch. 9 (cf. pp.
330, 364f.). I have filled in more details in my
unpublished thesis (1975, 139-67), where I also attempt to
elucidate the 'Transitional' pottery of c.690-650.
    Ephorus (FGrHist 70F216) may have been the first to
write in terms of more than one original war of conquest
in Messenia, but Aristotle ('Pol.' 1306b38) still uses the
singular form, which, historically, is perhaps the less
misleading of the two. Against the notion that the early
history of Messenia was created ex nihilo after 369 see
Shero 1938, esp. 504, 511; Treves 1944. But Pearson
(1962) rightly shows that much of the tradition is
'pseudo-history', and Niebuhr (1847) long ago exposed the

deficiencies of Pausanias' fourth book. For the view that
Tyrtaios is the only real source see the works cited in
Tigerstedt 1965, 347 n. 306. Among the many modern
accounts of the war(s) see Kiechle 1959, 65ff.; Oliva
1971, 102-14; J.F. Lazenby in MME 84-6.

My very brief summary of the physical setting of
Messenia is drawn from W.G. Loy and H.E. Wright, Jr in MME
ch. 3. For some important qualifications of their picture
in detail see Bintliff 1977, II, ch. 5.

On the cult of Helen at the Menelaion see Wide 1893,
340-6; on the type of cult accorded Menelaos see Coldstream 1976, esp. 10, 15; and 1977, esp. 346-8.

The foundation of Taras is discussed by Pembroke
(1970); earlier bibliography in Tigerstedt 1965, 340 n.
261; add now Moretti 1971; Carter 1975, 7-14. The
Spartans were allegedly particularly interested in stories
about the foundations of cities (Plato 'Hipp. Ma.' 285D).
For the close links between Sparta and Taras see e.g.
Jeffery 1961, 279-84 (dialect and script); Pugliese
Carratelli 1971 (cult and myths); Pelagatti 1957 (Lakonian
pottery at Taras). On western colonization in general see
Bengtson 1977, 88-127; the contributions to 'Dialoghi di
Archeologia' for 1969; and Jeffery 1976, ch. 4. The
latest archaeological discoveries are reported in the Acts
of the annual congresses of Magna Graecia Studies held in
Taranto and of the Centre Jean Bérard in Naples.

Concerning the power of Argos in the early seventh
century, Kelly (1976, ch. 6) has mounted a sustained
attack on a widely accepted modern view that Pheidon
should be dated to this period. However, while I agree
that the ancient evidence is hardly inspiring or inspired,
I cannot agree that Hdt. 6.127.3 is a sufficient ground
for dating the great Pheidon to c.600; Herodotus might
after all, as Jeffery (1976, 137) has suggested, have got
his Pheidons muddled.

I have succeeded thus far in confining my notice of the
'Great Rhetra' to a single, oblique reference. For if
anything justifies the description of the study of early
Sparta as 'intellectual gymnastics' (Ehrenberg 1973, 389),
it is surely this document of some fifty words preserved
for us by Plutarch ('Lyk.' 6), over which more scholarly
ink has been spilt than over any other Greek text of comparable length. None the less, for two main reasons, the
'Great Rhetra' must now be pulled out from under the car-
pet, dusted off and, if only briefly, held up to the light
of historical scrutiny. First, it represents in kernel
the political solution which has been precisely characterized by Andrewes (1956, ch. 6) as the 'Spartan alternative
to tyranny'. Second, it was the attainment of internal
political equilibrium at an early date which, as Thucydides (1.18.1) saw, enabled the Spartans to intervene in
the affairs of other states – and, we might add, to control their own Perioikoi and Helots in the manner analysed
in the next chapter. Two questions, however, remain to be
answered: at how early a date was this triumphantly successful solution devised and acted upon, and to what
problems did it offer a solution?

Two overlapping and mutually reinforcing aspects of the
'Spartan mirage' have played havoc with our evidence for
early Spartan political history. The first in point of
time and significance was the 'Lykourgos legend', which
held that Sparta was the paradigm of a state owing all its
institutions to the legislative enactments of a single
lawgiver – in this case to the wondrously omniprovident
Lykourgos, for whom dates ranging (in our terms) from the
twelfth to the eighth centuries were offered. The second
distorting aspect of the 'mirage' was the theory of the
'mixed constitution', developed perhaps in the fifth century but not apparently applied to Sparta until the fourth

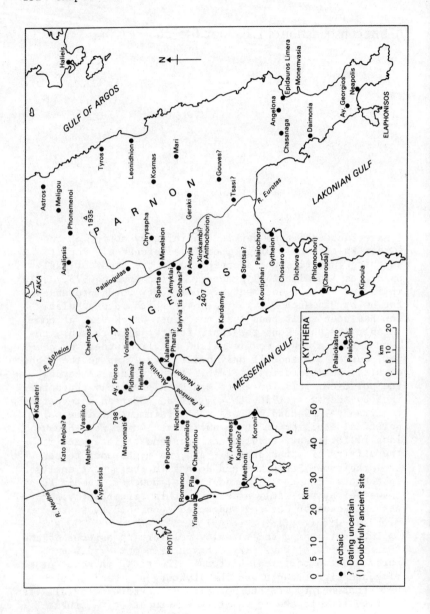

FIGURE 16   Archaic sites in Lakonia and Messenia

(Rawson 1969, 10). This theory contended that the best, because most stable, form of state was either one which combined ingredients from each of the basic constitutional types (monarchy, aristocracy/oligarchy, democracy) in a harmonious whole (the 'pudding' version) or one in which the different elements acted as checks and balances to each other (the 'seesaw' version). The combined effect - and, no doubt, the object - of the 'Lykourgos legend' and the theory of the 'mixed constitution' was to suggest that Sparta had achieved an internal political equilibrium considerably earlier than could in fact have been the case. Indeed, the devoutly pro-Spartan Athenian exile Xenophon could even, by making Lykourgos contemporary with the (Return of the) Herakleidai ('Lak. Pol.' 10.8), contrive to suggest that there had never been stasis or civil strife on the political plane in Sparta since the Dorian foundation.

Happily for us, however, not all of our sources were equally persuaded of the truth of every aspect of the 'mirage', and Xenophon's optimistic and partisan view was eccentric. Even Plutarch was unable to keep stasis (civil strife) out of his biography - or rather hagiography - of the lawgiver ('Lyk.' 5.4f.). More instructive, though, are the sources who were not a party to the 'mirage'. Herodotus (1.65.2) went so far as to say that before Lykourgos' reforms Sparta had suffered the worst 'kakonomia' (lawlessness) of any Greek state, while Thucydides (1.18.1), without mentioning Lykourgos by name, agreed for once with Herodotus that there had been stasis followed by 'eunomia' (orderliness). (I shall bring out the significance of these antonyms presently.) But perhaps the most impressive testimony of all is that of Aristotle ('Pol.' 1306b29-1307a4), who knew of no less than five potentially revolutionary situations in Sparta between the late eighth and early fourth centuries. Had it not been for what Thucydides (5.68.2) calls the 'secretiveness' of the Spartan state, he might conceivably have learnt of more. It is no accident that two of these - the Partheniai affair and a demand for the redistribution of land, both cited in Chapter 8 - fell in the reigns of Theopompos and Polydoros.

The Eurypontid Theopompos and the Agiad Polydoros, who reigned jointly during roughly the first quarter of the seventh century, are the first two individuals known to us as distinct personalities in Spartan history. We need not of course accept all the elaborated details of their reigns, but it was certainly remembered in Sparta that they had played active and decisive roles, and the general tenor of their rule has perhaps been accurately enough conveyed. Theopompos was known to Tyrtaios (fr. 5.1f.) as the general who led the Spartans to victory in the 'First' Messenian War. In much later authors, the first known being Aristotle ('Pol.' 1313a26f.), he displaced the Lykourgos of Herodotus (1.65.5) as creator of the Ephorate. This innovation was represented as a major concession to non- or rather anti-monarchist sentiment and allegedly justified by its author as a pragmatic device to ensure the monarchy's perpetuation. The original purpose and functions of the office are in fact by no means clear, but it seems likely that it did not from the start possess the extensive executive, judicial and administrative powers symbolized by the oaths exchanged monthly between kings and Ephors in the fourth century (Xen. 'Lak. Pol.' 15.7). At any rate, there was no place for the Ephorate in the 'Great Rhetra' (below).

The evidence for the career of Polydoros is of a more unambiguously inflammatory character, but the chief diffiulty in assessing its value is that Polydoros was looked back to as, or transmogrified into a prototype by revolutionary Spartan monarchs of the third century (when, perhaps, his supposed image was first employed as the official state seal). Thus he was alleged to have espoused the cause of the ordinary Spartan and to have initiated some form of land-distribution, only to be murdered for his reformist pains by a disgruntled noble called Polemarchos (Paus. 3.3.3). In reality, his populist politics are unlikely to have been ideologically motivated or even wholly altruistic, although it is open to argument how far they were dictated by reason of state (the Argos crisis) or concern for his personal position as king, which was perhaps being undermined in Sparta as elsewhere by the jealous non-royal nobility. But whatever the motivation, the defeat at Hysiai in 669 - if indeed Polydoros was the defeated general - would have added weight to the opposition, and it is to be assumed that Polydoros' schemes were robbed of fruition by his death. This, at any rate, is how I would explain the demand for land- redistribution recorded by Tyrtaios.

Two events, however, could have served to breathe fresh life into the Polydoran corpse, the revolt of the Messenian Helots and the establishment of tyrannies on either side of the Isthmus of Corinth c.650. These, I suggest, provided the context in which the 'Great Rhetra' was either produced or - if the whole document and not just the appended clause (4) is to be attributed to Theopompos and Polydoros - acted upon. The text may be translated thus:

Having established a cult of Syllanian Zeus and Athena,

having done the 'tribing and obing', and having established a Gerousia of thirty members including the
kings, (1) season in season out they are to hold Apel-
lai between Babyka and Knakion; (2) the Gerousia is
both to introduce proposals and to stand aloof; (3) the
damos is to have power to (in Plutarch's gloss on a
badly garbled Doric phrase) 'give a decisive verdict';
(4) but if the damos speaks crookedly, the Gerousia
and kings are to be removers.
At a moment of supreme crisis at home and abroad this formula offered something, politically, to all the contending
groups. As a result of its enactment the monarchy survived, though with diminished power. The Gerousia (Senate),
which included the two kings ex officio, became the supreme political organ in effect, but its membership was
limited numerically and (except for the kings) formally
subjected to the constraint of public election though not
to public accountability. The non-aristocratic damos was
granted political recognition, indeed formal sovereignty,
but its power of initiative was effectively bridled. Such
a reform might well have been characterized as the institution of 'eunomia', and it is to be noted that towards the
end of the seventh century Alkman (fr. 64) made Eunomia
the sister of Fortune and Persuasion and the daughter of
Foresight. Finally, the authority of Apollo (the 'Great
Rhetra' was represented as a Delphic oracle) and the
prestige of Theopompos and Polydoros were invoked to
provide the necessary cement of loyalty.
   No less important, however, than what the 'Great
'Rhetra' (to us opaquely) states was what it left unsaid.
The exclusion of the Ephorate was presumably due to its
relative unimportance at this date or, what Tyrtaios'
paraphrase of the document (fr. 4) implies, to the stress
placed by official propaganda on the traditional hierarchy
with the kings at the top of the political pyramid. Second, and yet more important, provision must have been made
for the redistribution of land in a separate initiative,
perhaps in the form of a reward offered for success
against the now revolted Messenians. (I cannot agree with
Chrimes 1949, 424 that 'having obed the obes' implies a
redistribution of land.) Thus the carrot of land-allot-
ments in Messenia for the poor, together with the stick of
the likely consequences of defeat for all Spartans alike,
would have helped to ensure that success was achieved. By
tying citizen-rights to the exploitation through Helot
labour-power of the land distributed in kleroi (allotments), Sparta created the first (and only) all-hoplite
citizen army, truly a 'new model'. The elite order of
Homoioi ('Peers') came into being.

Eventual victory in the 'Second' Messenian War and the
spread of Spartan control to all south-west Peloponnese
gave Spartan society an enormous fillip. The second half
of the seventh century witnessed the apogee of Lakonian
ivory-carving, when the products of Spartan workshops
achieved an extraordinarily wide distribution in the Greek
world - to Tegea, the Argive Heraion and Perachora within
the Peloponnese; to Athens and Pherai beyond the Isthmus
of Corinth; to the islands of Delos, Siphnos, Chios, Samos
and Rhodes; and even to Taucheira in north Africa. In the
first half of the sixth century, however, the quantity
(and quality) of ivory artefacts dedicated at the Orthia
sanctuary fell off sharply, and ivory was to some extent
replaced by bone as the medium of fine carving (apart,
that is, from carving in wood, which is attested in the
literary sources but naturally has not survived the Lakonian soil and climate). Since this phenomenon was not confined to Lakonia, it has been suggested that the trade in
ivory tusks may have been interrupted by the fall of
Phoenician Tyre to Nebuchadnezzar of Babylon in 573; the
Syrian port of Al Mina on the Orontes, where actual tusks
have been excavated, may also have been destroyed about
this time.

The leading position occupied by ivory-work in Lakonian
craftsmanship was assumed by the bronzesmiths, but not apparently much before the sixth century, when they produced
a series of fine hammered and cast vessels, also widely
disseminated. Contemporary with the apogee of ivory-
carving was the slow metamorphosis of the Lakonian pottery
from a 'third-rate and unpretentious' fabric into a full-
blown orientalizing black-figure style by c.625. By the
end of the century work of good quality and lively conception was being not only dedicated in Sparta but exported
as far as Sparta's south Italian colony, Taras. The two
delightful cups from Grave 285 at Taranto with their interior designs of sea-fish betray a maritime interest that
is also evident from the well-known ivory of c.625
depicting a warship and, not least, from the poems of the
contemporary Alkman (Huxley 1962, 108 n. 124). The latter
represents perhaps the jewel in the crown of Spartan high
culture.

It was not, however, by sea that the Spartans chose to
extend the long arm of their suzerainty. With Messenia
under their belt one might have expected them to complete
the unfinished business of the Thyreatis or at least to
absorb the east Parnon foreland politically. The power of
Argos, after all, was not what it had been under Pheidon
or at the time of the battle of Hysiai (if these two
were chronologically distinct). Instead, however, Sparta

seems to have elected to repeat the Messenian trick in Arkadia. There were, it is true, grounds for representing the aggression as a 'just war': the Arkadian king Aristo-krates (of Orchomenos or Trapezous), who was the grand-father of the wife of Periander tyrant of Corinth, had fought on the wrong side in the 'Second' Messenian War; and traditionally Sparta had been defeated at Phigaleia, again in south-west Arkadia, in 659 (Paus. 8.39.3). Moreover, Arkadia offered to Messenian refugees a natural haven, if not a continuing incitement to revolt.

However, the Spartan objective was apparently not merely to punish and neutralize Arkadia but to turn the Tegeans, the nearest Arkadians to Sparta with desirable land, into Helots and the Tegeate plain into kleroi. This at least is the inference to be drawn from the story as preserved in our earliest source, Herodotus (1.66), who describes the overconfident Spartans (trusting, typically, in a Delphic oracle) as marching on Tegea with chains to shackle the future Helots and with measuring-rods to parcel out the plain. With true dramatic irony the Spartans, defeated in battle, ended up working the Tegeans' land as war-captives bound in their own chains. A century or more later Herodotus was purportedly shown the very chains hanging as a trophy in the temple of Athena Alea; indeed, they were still on display more than seven centuries later - or so the cicerone assured Pausanias (3.7.3; 8.47.2). So unsuccessful in fact may have been the Spartans' Arkadian venture that the 'Battle of the Fetters' was not perhaps their only defeat here in the first half of the sixth century. Combining scattered references in later sources to regions further to the south-west than the Tegeate plain, Forrest (1968, 73-5) has suggested that Sparta may also have been frustrated in an attempt to annex the Megalopolis plain.

However this may be, it is doubtful whether the defeat or defeats were as severe as Herodotus' Arkadian inform-ants liked to think. For, as Herodotus himself put it (1.65.1), though with infuriating vagueness, the Spartans under the Agiad Leon and the Eurypontid Agasikles (c.575-560) were successful 'in all their other wars'. I have already remarked in Chapter 8 that the construction of the second temple of Orthia at Sparta c.570 is probably to be interpreted in the light of this comment. We might add that the second quarter of the sixth century was also the heyday of the Lakonian painted pottery, which was exported as far north as Olbia in south Russia, as far west as Ampurias in north-east Spain and as far south as Naukratis in Egypt, with especially heavy concentrations occurring at Taras, Taucheira and Samos. However, the only 'other

war' that we may fairly confidently assign to their reign
is the struggle for the control of Olympia, in which
Sparta helped Elis oust the local Pisatan dynasty
(possibly in 572).

Our general ignorance of Spartan foreign policy at this
time is particularly disheartening in view of another
highly controversial statement of Herodotus (1.68.6), that
in the next generation, under kings Anaxandridas and Ariston, Sparta had already 'subjugated most of the Peloponnese'. The context of this statement is the request by
king Croesus of Lydia for an alliance with Sparta against
the rising power of Persia following Sparta's eventual
triumph over Tegea (below). The alliance was granted and
sealed, in suitably archaic fashion, by a prestation.
Croesus had previously donated Lydian gold to the Spartans, who used it to face the statue of Apollo at Amyklai.
Now in return Croesus was sent - though he did not receive
- an elaborate bronze bowl, presumably fashioned by Lakonian craftsmen and perhaps of the type of the stupendous
bowl buried with a Celtic princess at Vix in France c.500.
Thus by c.550, according to Herodotus, Sparta had extended
its control from the southern two fifths of the Peloponnese to at least one of the remaining three, so that its
strength was such as to attract the notice of a foreign,
if philhellene, potentate. Yet all we learn from Herodotus of this sea-change in Lakonian affairs is contained
in his considerably mythical story of the transfer of the
bones of Orestes from Tegea to Sparta, whereafter, he
says, Sparta proved superior to Tegea in battle (1.67f.).
There is no mention of other military exploits, and the
significance of the recovery of the relics is restricted
by him to the military sphere. Ancient and modern scholarship has done rather better than the Halikarnassian.

It is of course hazardous to correct Herodotus from
later sources, but it is reasonable to supplement him in
such matters as diplomatics and constitutional history in
which he displays distressingly little interest. It is
not therefore surprising that he should have omitted to
mention the stele set up 'on the (banks of the) Alpheios',
which recorded the pledge of the Tegeans to Sparta not to
make the Messenians 'useful', i.e. give them citizen-
rights in Tegea (Jacoby 1944). We owe our knowledge of
this stele proximately to Plutarch ('Mor.' 292B), ultimately to Aristotle (fr. 592 Rose); but unfortunately we
know little more than its existence (Bengtson 1975, no.
112). The very place at which it was erected has been
disputed, some (like Beloch) arguing that it was at Olympia, where the gods could act as witnesses and guarantors,
others believing that it was on the borders of Spartan and

Tegeate territory. What does seem probable is that the
document inscribed on the stele should be distinguished
from the treaty of military alliance concluded between
Sparta and Tegea, which was among the earliest (the first
may have been with Elis) of those unequal alliances by
which Sparta built up its commanding position in the
Peloponnese.

As for the recovery of Orestes' bones from Tegea, and
perhaps also those of his son Teisamenos from Achaia
(Paus. 7.1.3), this symbolized and emphasized the shift in
Spartan policy from aggression to peaceful coexistence,
from 'Helotization' to diplomatic subordination. The
Spartans could now give preponderant emphasis in their
propaganda to their claim to be the legitimate successors
to the 'Achaean' rulers of the Peloponnese and even
represent themselves as champions of all Hellas. The poet
Stesichoros (West 1969, 148) lent his voice to the change
of policy; and it may have been about 550 that Agamemnon,
brother of Menelaos and father of Orestes, began to be
worshipped as a hero at Amyklai. If any one Spartan was
chiefly responsible for the new direction, he may have
been Chilon, eponymous Ephor c.556 and one of the 'Seven
Sages' of ancient Greece, to whom may also be given some
of the credit for elevating the status of the Ephorate
(cf. Diog. Laert. 1.68). A tantalizing fragment of a
sixth-century relief bearing the name of [Ch]ilon found at
Sparta is perhaps to be associated with the much later
report (Paus. 3.16.4) that the Spartans established a
hero-cult to Chilon.

Tegea, then, had been 'subjugated' through a quintes-
sentially Spartan combination of magic, military might and
diplomacy. But what about the rest of the Peloponnese,
and in particular Corinth and Argos? Corinth was certainly
allied to Sparta on some basis by c.525, when the two
states undertook a major naval expedition against Poly-
krates tyrant of Samos (below); but we know little or
nothing of relations between the two states before that
date. The alleged Corinthian aid to Sparta in the 'Second' Messenian War is doubtful, and the statement (Plut.
'Mor.' 859D) that Sparta terminated the Kypselid tyranny
at Corinth is incorrect either in fact or in MS. transmission. There is nothing very surprising about this.
Distance and an accident of geography had prescribed different and separate destinies for the two Dorian states
down to the seventh, if not the sixth, century.   However, once Sparta became involved with Argos and concerned
about communication into and out of the Peloponnese,
Corinth was bound to become of particular importance. If
there is anything to Herodotus' statement that Sparta had

'subjugated most of the Peloponnese' by c.550, then it is
possible that Corinth was received into alliance following
Sparta's deposition of Aischines, last of the Orthagorid
tyrants of Sikyon, in c.556. However, the evidence for
this latter transaction is extremely suspect, partly
because Sparta acquired a reputation as a tyrant-slayer,
partly because the sources - a second-century papyrus
perhaps transcribing Ephorus (FGrHist 105F1) and Plutarch
('Mor.' 859D) - are unreliable and far removed in time.
Its date too is uncertain (some prefer c.510), but c.556
receives some support from the mention by the papyrus of
Chilon as acting in a military capacity with king
Anaxandridas.

We are rather better informed on relations between
Sparta and Argos. Not, that is, that we hear directly of
any contact between them after the battle of Hysiai down to
the struggle for the Thyreatis in the mid-sixth century;
but Sparta's resettlement of the exiles from Argive Nauplia at Messenian Mothone (Paus. 4.35.2) probably belongs
to the late seventh century (Huxley 1962, 59f.). However,
the 'Battle of the Champions' in c.545 caught the imagination of Herodotus (1.82) - and indeed remained indelibly
stamped on the consciousness both of the Argives, who
actually proposed a return match on the same terms in 420
(Thuc. 5.41.2), and of the Spartans, who took to wearing
'Thyreatic crowns' at the Gymnopaidiai (Sosibios, FGrHist
595F5); possible representations of these crowns appear in
two bronze figurines found at Amyklai and Kosmas
(Perioikic Glympeis or Glyppia).

According to Herodotus, the Spartans had in fact seized
the Thyreatis before the ritualistic battle, but he unfortunately omits to say how long before. This is important
for the history of Lakonia, because for Herodotus it was
only after Argos had been comprehensively defeated in the
full-scale engagement subsequent to the 'Battle of the
Champions' that Argos was deprived of the territory east
of Parnon to the south of the Thyreatis, the eastern seaboard of the Malea peninsula and the island of Kythera.
If we rule Herodotus' testimony to such an Argive 'empire'
out of court, as I think we should, then we must admit
that we have no direct literary witness to the process
whereby Sparta completed the enlargement of Lakonia. To
be strictly accurate, a reference to it has been detected
in the second-century papyrus cited above, but this is too
fragmentary to illuminate the nature of the process or to
fix the date of its completion. There is, however, a
little indirect evidence - archaeological and epigraphical
as well as literary - which may be thought relevant.

For the Thyreatis itself there is nothing known between,

on the one hand, Spartan campaigns and the 'Geometric'
pottery of the late eighth or early seventh century and,
on the other, a handful of bronzes (one inscribed) and a
stone head of the last third of the sixth century. But
this sixth-century material is wholly Lakonian, which
suggests either that the alleged 'Dorianizing' of Kynouria
by the Argives (Hdt. 8.73.3) had not been a process
affecting high culture or that the Argive veneer was
stripped off remarkably soon after c.545.

As for the east Parnon foreland, there are only two
sites which merit consideration. The first, Prasiai, was
cited in the previous chapter as originally an independent
member of the Kalaureian Amphiktyony, whose role therein
was later assumed by Sparta. If Kelly (1976, 74) is right
in dating the foundation of the Amphiktyony to the mid-
seventh century, this would of course support his view
that Argos was not in control of the foreland at this
time. We need not, however, follow him in thinking that
Sparta's involvement in the Amphiktyony only began after
the defeat of Argos in c.545. At any rate, the only
Archaic finds from the site of which we may speak with
confidence - a four-sided bone seal of the seventh century
and a fine bronze mirror with a handle in the form of a
draped woman of the late sixth - are both of Spartan
manufacture. The other site, the sanctuary of Apollo
Tyritas, lay north of Prasiai on the coast near the modern
Tsakonian village of Tyros. Controlled excavations in
this century followed tardily on the illicit diggings of
the last, but although nothing of the foundations of the
temple was discovered, a handful of architectural fragments indicated that the earliest version was built around
600. What is particularly interesting is that the disc-
akroterion which surmounted the pediment is of undoubtedly
Spartan type (used in at least six other Lakonian sanctuaries, as well as at Bassai and Olympia) and that all the
inscribed dedications (none, though, certainly earlier
than 545) are in the Lakonian local script.

The sole site on the east coast of the Malea peninsula
for which there is archaeological evidence prior to the
fifth century is Epidauros Limera, but even this is hardly
revealing. An island gem of the seventh century is reported
to have been found here, suggesting Aegean contacts; and a
fine handle from a bronze hydria made at Sparta in the
sixth century has turned up at nearby Monemvasia. Let us
therefore move swiftly on to Kythera. Such cultural connections with the Argolis as the island may betray before
650 disappear completely thereafter. A striking, if
crudely executed, bronze figurine of a draped woman datable
c.630 reminds me somewhat of the 'Menelaion Goddess'

(Chapter 8), although its most recent publisher,
J.N. Coldstream (Coldstream and Huxley 1972, 271), thinks
rather of Crete. There then ensues an archaeological and
epigraphical gap of a century or so. To the last third
of the sixth century belong, for example, a marble lion,
which perhaps served as a grave-marker; a bronze figurine
of a draped woman dedicated, presumably to Aphrodite, by
one Klearisia; and a fine bronze head of a youth. Only
the latter reveals strong affinity with the Lakonian
mainland, and the quasi-Lakonian lettering of an inscription from Kastri bearing the single word 'Malos' (c.525-
400) confirms that down to the fifth century Kythera stood
somewhat apart from cultural developments in the rest of
Lakonia. Its political position, however, is another
matter - a salutary reminder that material artefacts do
not yield straightforward political conclusions.

To conclude this discussion, I do not believe it is
possible at present to say when Sparta absorbed the east
Parnon foreland politically into the polis of Lakedaimon.
The same goes for the east coast of the Malea peninsula
and Kythera. The testimony of Herodotus, however, when we
have subtracted the element due to Argive progaganda,
almost proves that the process had been completed by
c.540. Kelly (1976, 74f., 87) has argued that Sparta
would not have moved to annex the Thyreatis until after it
had established its superiority securely over Tegea, since
the route from the Eurotas valley to the Thyreatis passes
uncomfortably close to Tegeate territory. This may well
be so, but geography alone cannot exclude a priori the
possibility that the territory south of the Thyreatis had
been absorbed politically, as it had undoubtedly been
influenced culturally, by Sparta at an earlier date. On
balance, though, I am inclined to think that this
incorporation, like the favourable accommodation with
Tegea, belongs to the reign of Anaxandridas and Ariston
(c.550-520) rather than to the 'other wars' of their
immediate predecessors.

The only external event of the joint reign of Anaxandridas and Ariston related by Herodotus (3.39.1, 44-8.1, 54-8)
- although, as with the battles for the Thyreatis, he does
not introduce the kings into his narrative - is the naval
expedition to Samos in c.525. This was undertaken
ostensibly to restore some Samian aristocrats but perhaps
had longer-range, anti-Persian ends in view. Sparta, as
already noted, was aided by Corinth, who may have provided
the bulk of the 'large' (Hdt. 3.54.1) fleet. Sparta, however, was perhaps not a complete stranger to naval
activity. One of the five Archaic regiments of Sparta was
called Ploas, which may mean 'Seafarers' (Burn 1960, 275).

We have already cited the depiction of a warship at Sparta
before 600. The far-flung export of Lakonian pottery
between c.575 and 550 suggests nautical skill at least on
the part of some Perioikoi. The alliance with Croesus,
moreover, seems to indicate a Spartan preparedness to
undertake an expedition by sea c.550, even if in the event
only a token penteconter actually reached Asia Minor (Hdt.
1.152f.). Finally, the incorporation and control of the
eastern seaboard of Lakonia and of Kythera presumably
involved the use of a fleet. However that may be, an
expedition of the kind undertaken in c.525 certainly
implies military co-operation of some nature between the
Spartans and Perioikoi, for all naval muster-stations or
ports in Lakonia were located in Perioikic territory
(Chapter 10). We are not told where the fleet sailed
from, but there was presumably a harbour of sorts at
Tainaron in c.600, when Arion of Methymna landed there
(Hdt. 1.24.6), and we hear of fleets at anchor off Gytheion, Las and Messenian Asine in the fifth century.

We should not, however, distort the perspective. In
480 Sparta contributed a paltry ten ships to the Hellenic
fleet at Artemision (Hdt. 8.1.2); and the series of
Lakonian bronze figurines of hoplite infantrymen, which
belong principally to the third quarter of the sixth century, confirms that the expedition to Samos was an exceptional undertaking. (I consider the alleged Spartan
'thalassocracy' of 517-515 below.) Most important of all,
though, the naval expedition was also both costly and
unsuccessful. Hence perhaps Sparta's failure to seize the
opportunity to become the dominant naval power of mainland
Greece before Themistokles persuaded the Athenians in the
480s that their future lay on the sea (Thuc. 1.93.3f.).

Regrettably, our main source for the period c.525-480,
Herodotus, was less impressed by this momentous failure
than by the outcome of Anaxandridas' marital irregularit-
ies (5.39f., esp. 40.2). His eldest son and successor,
Kleomenes I, was undoubtedly the most powerful Spartan
king since Polydoros, and his like was not to reappear
until the Eurypontid Agesilaos II. But Herodotus' impres-
sionistic and distorted account of his reign makes it
abundantly clear that his information was derived overwhelmingly from hostile informants – the descendants, we
may surmise, of Kleomenes' half-brothers (Dorieus, Leonidas
and Kleombrotos) and those of the Eurypontid colleague
whose deposition he engineered in c.491 (Damaratos). For
Kleomenes himself failed to leave behind a son and heir,
and, although his daughter Gorgo was married to Leonidas,
in the pages of Herodotus she serves merely to show her
father up rather than to vindicate his sullied reputation.

Moreover, the one man whose descendants would have been
most likely to give Herodotus a favourable account,
Latychidas (Damaratos' cousin and replacement), had died a
disgraced exile (Hdt. 6.72). The extent of Herodotus'
bias against Kleomenes may be gauged from the fact that he
is prepared to present a highly sympathetic picture of a
proven 'medizer' (Damaratos) and an unsuccessful colonizer
(Dorieus). To add to our problems, there are also major
chronological difficulties in his account. Thus, since
Herodotus provides us with practically all our information
on Kleomenes, it is impossible for us to reconstruct with
confidence the main lines of his - and so, in the main,
Sparta's - domestic and foreign policy in the late sixth
and early fifth centuries.

I labour Herodotus' inadequacies because the reign of
Kleomenes was crucial not only for Lakonian but for all
Greek history and as such demands the closest possible
scrutiny. In the course of it Sparta became firmly established as supreme in the Peloponnese and a leader of the
Greek world generally, through the control of what we call
the 'Peloponnesian League' and the crushing of Argos.
Athens, in spite of and to an extent because of Kleomenes'
best efforts, became a democracy (the world's first) and
later, this time with the backing of Kleomenes, set its
face successfully against Persian expansion. Finally, and
more parochially, it was in Kleomenes' reign that the
peculiar system of Perioikoi and Helots elaborated over
the centuries underwent its first real testing on a wider
stage. Since space forbids me to deal in detail with the
reign as a whole, I shall concentrate on these three main
issues.

A.H.M. Jones opens his history of Sparta (1967) by
remarking that 'the Spartans had short memories'. As an
illustration he cites Herodotus' picture of Kleomenes: 'on
a simple point of fact he says that his reign was short
(5.48), while from the information he gives it appears
that he must have ruled for nearly thirty years.' Kleomenes was certainly on the throne in c.517, when the
Samian Maiandrios unsuccessfully appealed to him to eject
the pro-Persian puppet Syloson (Hdt. 3.148), and he may
have acceded before 519, the date given by Thucydides (3.
68.5) for the alliance between Plataia and Athens. For,
according to Herodotus (6.108.2-4), it was 'the Spartans',
then coincidentally in the Megarid under the leadership of
Kleomenes, who had advised the Plataians to seek this
alliance, in order to make trouble for the Athenians. But
the Athenians were not of course obliged to ally themselves to Plataia, and Herodotus' explanation looks
anachronistic: for the real sufferers from such an

alliance would have been the Thebans, whose claim to
control all Boiotia was thereby undermined. If the
Spartans were really in the Megarid to procure an alliance
for themselves with Megara in 519 (Burn 1960, 265) this
would be a further reason for their wanting to keep Athens
- with whose rulers, the Peisistratids, they were apparently then on good terms (below) - well disposed; for
Athens and Megara were traditional enemies. On the other
hand, should Athens and Sparta fall out, a possibility not
to be overlooked given Athens' increasing power and its
hostility to Megara and Aigina (also perhaps already
allied to Sparta), then Thebes would be likely to take
Sparta's side anyway. Herodotus does not attribute the
advice given to Plataia specifically to Kleomenes, but
such a masterstroke of diplomacy would not be inappropriate for a descendant of Chilon (the family-tree is
plausibly reconstructed in Huxley 1962, 149).

The words with which Kleomenes reportedly resisted the
arguments and bribes of Maiandrios are consistent with
Sparta's claim to the hegemony of the Peloponnese, even if
they are in fact the invention of Herodotus: 'it was
better for Sparta that the Samian stranger should be
removed from the Peloponnese' (not just Lakedaimon).
However, according to Eusebius (Chronikon I, 225 Schoene),
or the source upon which the good bishop drew, it was just
about this time that Sparta was enjoying a period of
'thalassocracy', i.e. 517-515. The reliability of the
'thalassocracy list' is highly questionable, at least in
all its details (Jeffery 1976, 253f.), and attempts to
explain the Spartan 'thalassocracy' in terms of its
alleged deposition of Lygdamis, tyrant of Naxos (Plut.
'Mor.' 859D), involve postulating a naval expedition nearly
as far as the one to Samos which Sparta simultaneously
declined to undertake. In fact, Lygdamis is more likely
to have been deposed during the expedition to Samos of
c.525.

If therefore the attribution of a 'thalassocracy' to
Sparta has any justification, or explanation, a more
likely one is to be found in the activities of Dorieus in
the central Mediterranean, unsuccessful though these
ultimately proved. According to an ingenious emendation
of Pausanias 3.16.4f., proposed by Edgar Lobel, Dorieus
took with him to the west men from Perioikic Anthana in
the Thyreatis (modern Meligou?), a community whose existence is otherwise first recorded by Thucydides (5.41.2).
The entry in the sixth-century AD lexicon of Stephanos of
Byzantion under 'Anthana' states that Kleomenes flayed
alive the eponymous hero of the place and wrote oracles on
his skin. This evidence is hardly impeccable, but it is

possible that Dorieus was attempting to play on discontent
in this recently Perioikized region in order to bolster
his frustrated claim to the Agiad throne. As we shall
see, however, there is no discernible trace of Perioikic
discontent in the Thyreatis twenty years later.

The next major episode in Kleomenes' turbulent career
concerned relations between Sparta (and its allies) and
Peisistratid Athens. Herodotus goes out of his way to
stress that prior to the outbreak of actual warfare Sparta
had been on friendly terms with Athens' tyrant rulers (5.
63.2; 90.1; 91.2) and that it was Spartan religiosity, in
the form of unquestioning obedience to the injunctions of
Delphic Apollo, which prompted the change of heart. However, if one thing is clear about Kleomenes' career, it is
his remarkably flexible, not to say unorthodox, attitude
to religion. A man who in 491 could bribe the Delphic
priesthood itself (he more or less admitted his guilt by
his flight from Sparta) was surely not one to be over-
impressed by Delphic commands - unless they coincided with
his own views. Thus the modern suggestion that the
Peisistratid Hippias' medism was the cause of Spartan
hostility may be more than a 'post hoc, ergo propter hoc'
explanation. Interestingly, the first Spartan expedition
to unseat Hippias travelled to Attika by sea. It was led
in c.512 by one Anchimolios or Anchimolos, possibly the
first Spartan navarch (Sealey 1976, 339), presumably in
Perioikic bottoms and perhaps with Perioikic marines. The
expedition, however, was an unmitigated disaster, and its
admiral was killed. About two years later the Spartans
sent a larger force, this time by land and under the
command of Kleomenes (Hdt. 5.64f.). But even this was
successful only through the chance capture of the children
of the Peisistratids.

The status of Athens after the overthrow and expulsion
of Hippias, who duly went over to the Persians, is unclear.
There is no ancient evidence for the modern suggestion
that it became a subordinate ally of Sparta on similar
terms to those allies who later formed the 'Peloponnesian
League'. On the other hand, the head of the Alkmaionid
family, Kleisthenes, and 700 other families did leave
Athens after Kleomenes' personal interventions in c.508
with a lack of fuss surprising if Athens was in no way
bound to Sparta (Hdt. 5.70; 72.1). This, however, marked
the end of Kleomenes' success. However much he may have
been impelled originally by anti-Persian sentiment, his
predilection for the Athenian noble and would-be tyrant
Isagoras (or, so rumour had it, for Isagoras' wife) proved
scarcely politic, his imprisonment in Athens scarcely
flattering. The democratic reforms sponsored by

Kleisthenes (508/7) might well have been passed anyway, but the speed and smoothness with which they were adopted and implemented owed much to the hostility of the Athenian assembly towards Kleomenes' political schemes.

Thus it was specifically to revenge himself upon the Athenian demos, according to Herodotus (5.74.1), that Kleomenes in c.506 mounted the largest Spartan expedition against Athens so far. It comprised all Sparta's Peloponnesian allies, the Boiotians (Thebes and its allies), and the Chalkidians of Euboia, as well as the Spartans (including presumably Perioikic hoplites) themselves. Yet this invasion of Attika too was a complete failure, largely because Damaratos and the Corinthians abandoned Kleomenes before the fighting began. It was not, however, a wholly unproductive failure. The reputations of Sparta and Kleomenes were heavily tarnished, but the law subsequently passed by the Spartan assembly that only one king should command on campaign prevented a recurrence of the fatal disagreement in Attika between Kleomenes and Damaratos. (One thinks, for example, of the situation in 403.) Perhaps more important still, a couple of years or so later (c.504?) a rudimentary formula for collective decision-making was put into operation and the 'Peloponnesian League' more or less properly so called was born, destined for an active life of nearly a century and a half.

To put it another way, the allies of Sparta had won a collective right of veto denied to the Perioikic towns, whose relations with Sparta in other respects provided both the precedent and the model for the series of individual, unequal alliances Sparta had built up in the Peloponnese and outside (Megara, Thebes, Aigina) since around the middle of the sixth century. (I shall return to this point in the next chapter.) We are very poorly informed on the dates at which Sparta had contracted its various alliances, and we know virtually nothing of the obligations and rights of members of the 'League' before the Peloponnesian War. Indeed, our most extensive source is the Athenian Xenophon writing in the 350s, who witnessed and recorded its demise. It may, however, be worth briefly summarizing here what we do know, for there do not seem to have been any momentous innovations between 500 and the 380s (Chapter 13), and it was as leader of the 'League' that Sparta became the automatic choice as leader of the Greek resistance to Persia in 481.

The 'League' was known simply as 'the Lakedaimonians and their allies'. Its members were all officially autonomous allies of Sparta, though Sparta in practice took care to ensure that they were mostly controlled by

pro-Spartan oligarchies of birth or wealth. In peacetime
wars were permitted between members, but if one was
attacked by a non-member Sparta was bound to come to its
aid 'with all strength in accordance with its ability'.
The clause binding the ally to 'follow the Spartans
whithersoever they may lead', wherein lay the ally's formal
subordination, was modified in practice after c.504 to
mean that, if the Spartan assembly voted to go to war, its
decision had to be ratified by a majority decision of a
'League' Congress, in which each ally regardless of size
had one vote. If the decision for war was ratified,
Sparta levied the 'League' army, decided where the combined force was to muster, contributed the commander-in-
chief (normally a king) and provided officers to levy the
allied contingents. Peace, like war, was subject to a
majority vote, but an individual member might claim
exemption on the grounds of a prior religious obligation.
Finally, there was possibly contained in each individual
treaty a clause binding the ally to provide Sparta with
assistance in the event of a Helot revolt.
     The purpose for which the first 'Peloponnesian League'
Congress was convened in c.504 was to debate the Spartan
proposal (not ascribed by Herodotus specifically to
Kleomenes) to reinstate Hippias as tyrant of Athens (Hdt.
5.90-3). This proposal is important for two reasons.
First, it destroys the myth of Sparta's principled
opposition to tyranny. Second, perhaps for the first but
certainly not the last time, Corinth led a majority of
allies to reject a Spartan decision. Hence, with the
Athenian question temporarily shelved, the next major
episode in Kleomenes' reign involved Sparta's attitude
to the Ionian revolt envisaged by Aristagoras (tyrant of
Miletus) about 500. This time Kleomenes' resolve to
resist bribery needed stiffening - or so Herodotus was
told - by his eight-year-old daughter Gorgo, which may
mean that Kleomenes was in fact inclined to support
Aristagoras. Scholarly opinion is rather sharply divided
over the wisdom of Kleomenes' refusal. But the Delphic
Oracle, which had been 'medizing' since c.540, was in no
doubt that Aristagoras' designs were misguided - if, as I
think we should, we accept as genuine the unique double
oracle delivered to the Argives and, in their absence, the
Milesians (Hdt. 6.19; 77). A possible occasion for its
delivery was when Aristagoras was in Sparta canvassing
support; Argos would naturally have been interested in the
transaction.
     Usually, however, the oracle is regarded as post
eventum, the conjoint doom prophesied for Argos and
Miletos arising from the coincidence of their disastrous

defeats in 494 - the former at the hands of Sparta, the latter inflicted by the Persians or rather their Phoenician fleet. But if the double oracle is genuine, then of course we have no sure way of dating Kleomenes' massively successful campaign against Argos. In Herodotus (6.75.3-82) the episode is allowed to float freely in time. On balance I prefer a date late in Kleomenes' reign, after rather than before the Athens affair of c.512-504. But I leave open the question whether Sparta's aim was simply to nullify its major rival for Peloponnesian hegemony or also in the process to remove a possible source of aid and comfort to an invading Persian army (Tomlinson 1972, 96).

In sharp contrast to the invasion of Attika in c.506, the Argos campaign was a purely Spartan affair. For Herodotus describes Kleomenes' army as 'Spartiatai', by which, if he was being precise (but see Westlake 1977, 100), he meant citizens of Sparta as opposed to the Perioikoi (a mixed force should have been called 'Lakedaimonioi'). We are not told exactly how large the force was, but it numbered at least 2,000 since the 1,000 troops retained by Kleomenes after the main engagement in the Argolis constituted a minority of the total (Hdt.6.81). They were accompanied by Helots, perhaps one for each hoplite, whose function was to carry their masters' armour and look after their other needs. The route taken to the Thyreatis from Sparta was presumably the one used in reverse by Epameinondas in 370 (Chapter 13), past Sellasia through the Kleissoura pass and the bed of the Sarandapotamos to the territory of Tegea, rather than the more difficult route over north Parnon via Arachova, Ay. Petros, Xirokambi and Ay. Ioannis to Astros. Herodotus, however, provides no geographical indications until the Spartans reached the River Erasinos, well into Argive territory, to whose god Kleomenes duly sacrificed. Since the omens were inauspicious - or perhaps more prosaically, since the narrow passage between mountains and sea was blocked by the Argives - Kleomenes withdrew to the Thyreatis and took ship for the Argolis. Again, we are given no geographical indications for the point of embarkation, but the bay of Astros alone provides suitable anchorage. This must have been the port of ancient Thyrea, a settlement which, though frequently mentioned by Pausanias, cannot be precisely located. Of the possible sites in the area only Ay. Triada, some three kilometres inland to the south-west of Cape Astros, suits the information of Thucydides (4.57.1) that Thyrea lay ten stades inland. Presumably, therefore, the Perioikoi of Thyrea provided at least some of the ships to transport the Spartan troops, but we learn from Herodotus (6.92.1) that Aigina and Sikyon also lent naval assistance, either further transports or warships to convoy them.

Kleomenes was careful to land well to the east of Argos at Nauplia (robbed of its separate political existence perhaps a century earlier: see above) and in the territory of Tiryns, which was also subject to Argos. The pitched battle took place at Sepeia near Tiryns, and the Spartans won; but by far the majority of the Argive force, to the (surely exaggerated) number of 6,000, took refuge in a sacred grove nearby. Then in what Tomlinson (1972, 94) has rightly called an 'un-Greek' act of treachery and sacrilege, some fifty of the Argives were lured out of the grove by Kleomenes and killed, while the rest were burned to death in the grove itself. The fire, however, was applied by Helots, presumably to absolve the Spartans themselves technically from any possible taint of ritual pollution. Kleomenes then dismissed the majority of his army and, instead of marching on Argos, proceeded to the Argive Heraion, possibly (a suggestion of A. Blakeway) to parley with the men of Mykenai. On being refused permission by the priest to sacrifice to Hera, Kleomenes had the man whipped - again by Helots.

The consequences of the Sepeia campaign made themselves felt during the Persian invasion of 480-479. Argos itself preserved a spineless neutrality, while Tiryns and Mykenai, briefly independent again, sent hoplites to Thermopylai (the Mykenaians only) and Plataia. Their names were duly inscribed on the Serpent Column erected at Delphi. But between Sepeia and Plataia a very great deal had happened. The defeat of the Ionians in 494 paved the way for Persian intervention in first Thrace then the southern Greek mainland. The envoys sent by the Great King in c.492 to demand earth and water (the customary tokens of submission to Persia) were rejected without ceremony by both Sparta and Athens, but they were received treacherously by Aigina. Athens, threatened with the use of Aigina as a base by the Persian fleet, appealed to Sparta. It is not entirely clear that Aigina was already a member of the 'Peloponnesian League' (I personally believe it was), but Kleomenes' response to the appeal of his former opponents and to the medism of Aigina was unambiguous and unhesitating, according to the account of Herodotus (6.48-51; 61.1; 64-67.1; 73). He went in person to Aigina and demanded hostages as a guarantee of Aigina's loyalty, only to be rebuffed - perhaps on a technicality on which Damaratos, hostile to Kleomenes since at least c.506, had advised the leading Aiginetans to insist (but see Carlier 1977, 78f.).

Kleomenes now stretched his cavalier attitude to religion to the limit - or rather beyond it: for he bribed

the Delphic Oracle to pronounce Damaratos a bastard and so
had him deposed. Most Greeks, Herodotus (6.75.3) says,
imputed Kleomenes' gruesome end (below) to this sacrilege,
and the pious Herodotus naturally could hardly have
approved such an action. But even he, despite the hostile
sources he used, explicitly remarked of Kleomenes' first
intervention in Aigina that he was 'striving for the
common good of Hellas' (6.61.1). We of course may feel
free to apply this comment to the sequel also, in which
Kleomenes returned to Aigina with his new co-king
Latychidas and not only extracted the required hostages
(the ten most powerful and wealthy Aiginetan aristocrats)
but actually handed them over to their bitterest enemies,
the Athenians. Nothing was better calculated to prevent
Aiginetan medism, and, when the Persian fleet sacked
Eretria and landed in Attika in 490, Aiginetan aid to
Persia was conspicuous by its absence.

Had Kleomenes died after handing over the hostages, he
might not have received quite so sweeping a 'damnatio
memoriae' at Sparta. Damaratos, after all, did go over to
the Persian side in 491, and it is doubtful whether those
in authority at Sparta at the time thought so highly of
him as Herodotus did, despite his prestigious victory in
the four-horse chariot-race at Olympia in about 500 (Ste.
Croix 1972, 355 n. 5). (Damaratos' direct descendants were
excluded from the Eurypontid throne thereafter until the
elevation of Nabis in the late third century.) Besides,
the Spartans themselves rather curiously ascribed Kleomenes' mode of death to his habit of taking wine neat
(Hdt. 6.84.1), not to his tampering with the Delphic
Oracle. However, when Kleomenes' sacrilege became known
in Sparta, he at any rate feared for his throne (or his
life) and withdrew from Sparta.

According to the manuscripts of Hdt. 6.74.1, Kleomenes
went to Thessaly (Forrest 1968, 90, says to the Aleuadai of
Pharsalos, though on what authority I do not know). But
the emendation of 'Thessalia' to 'Sellasia' (proposed by
D. Hereward) is attractive: Sellasia was the first
Perioikic town Kleomenes would reach on his way north from
Sparta. Sellasia, however, proved too close to Sparta
for Kleomenes' liking (or Thessaly proved too far), and he
is next heard of in Arkadia engaged in the revolutionary
activity of uniting the Arkadians against Sparta and
binding them by the most awful oaths to follow him
whithersoever he might lead them (Hdt. 6.74). Herodotus,
typically, quickly loses interest in this small matter of
royal revolution and, after spending the rest of his space
on Arkadia in discussing a minor point of geography, goes
on to describe Kleomenes' recall and death. We, however,
must fill out the picture.

Arkadia is an upland area of central Peloponnese,
difficult of access and yet of crucial strategic importance. It was no coincidence that the historical dialect
most akin to the language of the Linear B tablets should
have been developed here nor that so many decisive battles
were fought in the plain of Mantineia. For Sparta, once it
had gained control of Messenia and pushed its frontier in
the north-east as far as the northern boundary of the
Thyreatis, Arkadia was the single most important area with
which it had to deal. Its boundaries marched with those of
the Messenians in the south-west and those of the Argives
on the north-east, in other words, with those of Sparta's
most important internal and external enemies. It was
through Arkadia that Sparta was bound to proceed in the
event of war in central or northern Greece. Conversely,
Arkadia served as a buffer-zone against any enemies who
might be interested in invading Lakonia or Messenia. The
full significance of the role of Arkadia was expressed
soon after the battle of Leuktra in 371: Sparta's Arkadian
allies defected, taking with them the Perioikoi of the
Belminatis, Skiritis and Karyatis on the northern frontier
of Lakonia, and constituted themselves the Arkadian League
(Tod 1948, no. 132); Epameinondas led the first-ever
invasion of Lakonia since the Dorian 'invasion' of the
Dark Ages and liberated the Messenian Helots; finally, the
polis of Megalopolis was created out of forty Arkadian
villages as a permanent watchdog on Messenian independence
and a rival claimant to the Belminatis. It is only if we
keep this longer perspective in view that the full import
of Kleomenes' behaviour in Arkadia in 491 can be grasped.
    Kleomenes, however, may not have been responsible for
uniting the Arkadians in the first place. Rather, he may
have placed himself at the head of a 'nationalist' conspiracy, in much the same way as Catiline was forced to
lead the Italians in 63. For Herodotus (5.49.8) makes
Aristagoras in c.500 refer to Spartan difficulties with
the Arkadians, and it was just about then or perhaps ten
or fifteen years later that the coinage bearing the legend
'Arkadikon' was first minted at Heraia. The propaganda
significance of these coins cannot have escaped the
Spartan authorities: the Arkadians were announcing that in
some sense they wished to act and be treated as 'the
Arkadians', whereas Sparta's consistent policy towards
their allies from the mid-sixth century onwards was
(anticipating Rome) to divide and so rule. The really
extraordinary and paradoxical thing, therefore, about
Kleomenes' behaviour was that the very same man who had
been instrumental in keeping the Boiotians divided in 519
should also have been prepared to foster the unity of the

Arkadians some thirty years later.

Herodotus does not explain this volte-face of Kleomenes, but I prefer to think of it as yet another instance
of his political opportunism rather than as a sign of
mental imbalance. In the words of Herodotus (6.75.1),
however, Kleomenes had always been 'slightly touched'; and
on his return to Sparta he went stark staring mad. He
took to poking his staff in the face of anyone he chanced
to meet, until his relatives (one suspects his surviving
half-brothers) clapped him in the stocks. Here he
persuaded his Helot guard to lend him his iron dagger
(some Helots at least were trusted to carry offensive
weapons in Sparta) and proceeded to butcher himself from
the calves upwards. Such a suicide is not, I understand,
unexampled in the psychoanalytical literature, but I
prefer to follow the amateur detectives who suspect foul
play on the part of the Spartan authorities. The case of
the Maigrets would certainly be greatly strengthened if
Sparta in 491 was faced with not only Arkadian dissidence
but a revolt of the Messenian Helots to boot.

Such a revolt is not mentioned by Herodotus. He does,
however, make Aristagoras (in the passage just referred
to) describe the Messenians as 'well-matched' enemies of
Sparta; and it has been argued that a Helot revolt makes a
better explanation than an alleged religious scruple (Hdt.
6.106.3; 120) for Sparta's failure to arrive at Marathon
in time for the historic battle of 490. Moreover, about
twenty years later a Spartan king (Pausanias the Regent)
could plausibly be accused of conniving at a Helot revolt.
However, the Spartans undoubtedly were monumentally super-
stitious (see above all Hdt. 6.82), and we should, I
think, take a lot of convincing that Herodotus ignored,
deliberately suppressed or was ignorant of so crucial an
event in Spartan history. Since I have an open mind on
the question, I shall simply set out the evidence and
arguments that have been mustered in favour of its
occurrence.

First, Plato ('Laws' 698DE) specifically states that
there was a Messenian revolt at the time of Marathon.
Second, if the so-called 'Rhianos hypothesis' (a tissue of
interdependent conjectures without direct external
corroboration) is correct, the war starring Aristomenes
the Messenian and celebrated by Rhianos was a war fought
in the early fifth century, not (as Paus. 4.15.2) the
'Second' Messenian War of the seventh. Third, a dedication of war-spoils at Olympia by the Spartans belongs
epigraphically perhaps to the first, rather than the
second, quarter of the fifth century (M/L no. 22).
Pausanias (5.24.3) apparently knew that the inscription

referred to spoils from the Messenians, but he wrongly
believed it to have been inscribed at the time of the
'Second' or perhaps the 'Third' (the revolt of the 460s)
Messenian War.   Fourth, the bronze tripods wrought by the
Lakonian Gitiadas (flor. c.550) and the Aiginetan Kallon,
which Pausanias (3.18.7f.) saw at Amyklai, cannot both
have commemorated the same Spartan victory over the
Messenians, let alone a victory in the 'Second' Messenian
War; but that of Kallon, who is known to have been active
at Athens in the 480s, could have commemorated a victory
in the early fifth century.   Fifth, the statue of Zeus
made by the Argive sculptor Ageladas could not have been
originally made for the Naupaktos Messenians, as Pausanias
(4.33.2) was told, since Ageladas worked in the early
years of the fifth century, not c.460 or later.   It might,
however, have been commissioned at a time when the
Messenians were in a state of revolt.   (A large dedication
by the Messenians at Delphi in the first half of the fifth
century is even more problematic: Jeffery 1961, 205.)
Finally, Anaxilas, tyrant of Rhegion in the early fifth
century, settled some Messenians at Zankle in north-east
Sicily, according to Pausanias (4.23.6), who, however,
wrongly dates Anaxilas to the seventh century by connect-
ing the resettlement with the 'Second' Messenian War.
     It should be obvious that singly none of these scraps
of evidence is incontrovertible or even compelling; but
taken together they do at least add up to an arguable
case, though not an 'overwhelming' one, as J.F. Lazenby
believes (MME 87).   A Helot revolt in the 490s would have
been the red light as far as Spartan expansion was concerned and a powerful argument for abandoning the extra-
Peloponnesian adventures (as they may have seemed to the
more conservative members of the Spartan ruling class)
favoured by Kleomenes.   As we shall see in Chapter 11,
Sparta was considerably reluctant to commit large numbers
of its troops north of the Isthmus of Corinth in the
defence of Greece in 480-479, and one reason for this
reluctance may well have been Helot disaffection.
     I cannot leave Archaic Sparta and Lakonia without
contributing to the perennial debate on Spartan 'austerity'
or the supposed 'death' of Spartan (or, as I prefer,
Lakonian) art.   One of the most alluring and enduring
aspects of the Spartan 'mirage' has been the idea of an
austere, barrack-like Sparta, hostile to the higher arts.
The 'mirage' as a whole of course was (and is) a myth, in
part a groundless fabrication, partly a half-conscious
distortion of the realities.   But its cultural aspect
seemed more firmly anchored in fact than some others, the
more so because it seemed to be independently confirmed by

Herodotus (2.167.2) and Thucydides (1.10.2). Furthermore, it appeared that participation in the manual crafts was not merely despised in Sparta but legally prohibited to citizens, at least by the early fourth century.

However, this resilient aspect of the 'mirage' suffered a near-fatal blow from the British School excavations at Sparta in the first decade of this century. These proved that the 'austere' Sparta of the myth had had no counterpart in reality before the mid-sixth century at the earliest. The 'mirage' was accordingly revised, and Chilon, a veritable Lykourgos redivivus, was credited with sponsoring c.550 a sort of Spartan Arusha Declaration, a self-denying ordinance through which Spartan society abandoned its fun-loving ways and transformed itself, overnight, into the familiarly philistine barracks. Unfortunately, subsequent archaeological and art-historical research has shown that the revised picture will not do either, at least not when it is presented in this black-and-white form.

In the first place, the literary and archaeological evidence will not support the hypothesis of a sudden and comprehensive change of attitude. It is true that Alkman (c.600) was possibly the last representative of a native tradition of poetic creativity, but it was not perhaps a very deep-rooted tradition in any case; and Sparta continued to be visited by poets at least to the end of the fifth century, for example by Stesichoros, Simonides, Eupolis and Kratinos. But even if creative poetry was no longer being produced by Lakonians after the early sixth century, there was no comparable shutdown in the visual arts. Ivory-work may have ceased by c.550, but this was not due to 'austerity' (see above). Bronze-work continued well after the mid-century, the series of bronze vessels to the last quarter of the sixth century, the figurines into the fifth. Stone sculpture was never highly developed in Lakonia, whether in the form of statues of or public buildings, but c.550 Theodoros of Samos allegedly designed the Skias in Sparta; towards the end of the sixth century Bathykles of Magnesia was commissioned to remodel the Amyklaion and employed Lakonian masons (Jeffery 1961, 200, no. 32); the third Menelaion was built in the first third of the fifth century, perhaps about the same time and for the same reason as the Persian Stoa in Sparta; and in the 480s the Spartans were prepared to pay for the marble group to which the misnamed 'Leonidas' belongs. Besides, the series of stone 'hero reliefs' found all over Lakonia ran from c.550 into the Hellenistic period. The Lakonian painted pottery continued to c.520, its demise, like that of the Corinthian fabric, being due to Athenian

competition rather than Spartan 'austerity'; and black-
painted Lakonian ware of high quality continued to be
produced into the fifth century and found its way as far
afield as Olympia.

Second, the decision not to coin silver, which must
have been taken around 550, should not be interpreted as
either implying an attitude of or leading inexorably to
'austerity'. Coinage was not invented or introduced
elsewhere in Greece for primarily economic reasons, and
its use did not become synonymous with trade until the
later fifth century. The Spartan state could always use
coins minted elsewhere, as other states did, and there is
no evidence that the retention of iron spits as a store of
wealth and standard of value prevented internal economic
exchanges. In any event, Sparta through its control of
the Eurotas and Pamisos valleys was extraordinarily
autarkic in essential foodstuffs; and its possession of
abundant deposits of iron ore within its own frontiers may
have been a contributory factor in the decision not to
import silver to coin.

However, even if there was no sudden death of Lakonian
art c.550, the question remains how, when and why did the
transformation occur that culminated in the philistine
fourth-century Sparta presented by Xenophon, Plato and
Aristotle, in which citizens were debarred from manual
crafts and the products of craftsmen were at a discount?
The answer, I believe, lies in what Finley (1975, ch. 10),
has called the 'sixth-century revolution', a complex and
gradual transformation of the Spartan social system
designed to perpetuate Spartan control over the Helots and
Perioikoi without abolishing the wide and growing disparities within the citizen-body itself. Thus it was the
Spartans, for example, who took the lead in adopting a
simple and uniform attire and 'in other ways too did most
to assimilate the life of the rich to that of the common
people' (Thuc. 1.6.4). The new social system, in operation by the time of Herodotus, was characterized by an
overriding emphasis on military preparedness and a
reduction of non-military wants to the barest minimum. In
this new Sparta there was no longer any room for expensive
private dedications to the gods or the ostentatious
trappings of the 'good life'. Here alone could Wealth be
described by a comic poet as 'blind like a lifeless
picture'.

With the decay of patronage, craftsmanship and attitudes towards it in Sparta took an irreversible dive.
Lakonian craftsmen were not slow to perceive and reflect
the change: as early as c.525 some bronzesmiths emigrated
to a more congenial yet somewhat familiar environment,

Taras in southern Italy; and Lakonia had no part in the
cultural efflorescence of the fifth century. Instead of
conspicuous consumption in food, clothes, personal
possessions or dedications to the gods, the Spartan
plutocrats from c.550 onwards displayed their riches with
enormous success and rare gusto in 'that most expensive,
most aristocratic and most glory-bringing of all events in
the Greek games' (Finley 1968a, 45), the four-horse
chariot-race at Olympia (Ste. Croix 1972, 354f.). For
victory here satisfied the claims both of personal
prestige and of patriotism.

The Spartan social structure, however, was fatally
flawed. The gap between rich and poor Spartans widened,
and eventually by the early fourth century moral pressure
grew inadequate to suppress differences in life-style at
home. The most serious and glaring symptom of internal
contradictions was the catastrophic decline in the full
citizen population, that 'oliganthropia' through which, as
Aristotle ('Pol.' 1270a33f.) laconically put it, 'Sparta
was destroyed.' This will be the major theme throughout
the rest of this book.

NOTES ON FURTHER READING

The older bibliography on the 'Great Rhetra' may be found
in Busolt 1893, 511f. (n. 1), the more recent in Oliva
1971, 71-102. Still fundamental is Wade-Gery 1958, 37-85
(originally published 1943-4). The most recent study I
know is Lévy 1977.

On the historicity of Lykourgos (as opposed to that of
'his' laws) see Toynbee 1969, 274-83; Oliva 1971, 63-70.
The theory of the 'mixed constitution' in antiquity is
discussed generally in Aalders 1968; its application to
Sparta from antiquity onwards is examined in Rawson 1969
(Index s.v.).

On the Ephorate see generally Oliva 1971, 123-31; on
the Ephor-list, Jacoby 1902, 138-42; Samuel 1972, 238-41.

For tyranny in the seventh and sixth centuries see
Andrewes 1956; Berve 1967; on Sparta's avoidance of it
Andrewes 1956, ch.6 (to be read with his earlier study of
'eunomia': 1938). The connection between the institution
of hoplite warfare and the emergence of tyranny is discussed, with differing emphases and conclusions, in
Salmon 1977 and Cartledge 1977.

For all aspects of Lakonian ivory-work see the metic-
ulously thorough, if chronologically over-precise,
Marangou 1969. The study of Lakonian bronze-work is
bedevilled by the problem of stylistic attribution: for

the hydriai see Diehl 1964; for the hoplite figurines Jost
1975, 355-63. Leon 1968 is among other things a pioneer-
ing attempt to isolate regional workshops within Lakonia
and Messenia. The fundamental study of the development of
the Lakonian pottery in the seventh century is still Lane
1934; for the sixth century see now Stibbe 1972. Rolley
1977 provides an admirable conspectus of Archaic Lakonian
art.

On the dispute over Alkman's place of origin see Page
1951, 102-70; for his language see Risch 1954. His date
is discussed in West 1965 and Harvey 1967, 69, on the
basis of a recently published papyrus ('P. Oxy.' 2390).
Treu 1968 is a useful review of all aspects of Alkman's
life and work. The modern literature is exhaustively
cited in Calame 1977.

For Sparta's relations with Arkadia and especially
Tegea in the seventh and sixth centuries see the works
cited in Kelly 1976, 176 n. 13; for the character of the
Tegeate plain see briefly Howell 1970, 88f. Forrest 1968,
ch. 6, is a typically stimulating account of the 'Second'
Messenian War and its Arkadian aftermath.

The 'Bones of Orestes' policy is looked at in Leahy
1955; Griffiths (1976) has detected a trace of it in
Herodotus 7.159 (where he would emend 'Pelopides' to
'Pleisthenides'). The policy is attributed to Chilon by
Forrest (1968, 75-7); for the papyrus in which Chilon is
yoked with Anaxandridas see Leahy 1956 and 1959.

The Argos vs. Sparta struggle for the Thyreatis is
discussed in Tomlinson 1972, 87-90 (but his implication
that the 'Battle of the Champions' took place in the
seventh century is not cogent) and Kelly 1976, 137-9 (but
it is unnecessary to deny that the relationship between
Sparta and Argos after the Spartan capture of the
Thyreatis was for the most part one of mutual hostility).

On Lakonian akroteria of the type found at Tyros etc.
see now Lauter-Bufé 1974; add Catling 1977, 36 (the 'Old
Menelaion' of c.600).

The most recent discussion of the Spartan navarchy is
Sealey 1976, who argues that it did not become a regular,
annual office until after the Battle of Kyzikos in 410.
The expedition to Samos of c.525 is briefly considered in
Jeffery 1976, 216f. Forrest (1968, 80-2) discounts the
view that Sparta was pursuing a consistently anti-Persian
policy from the time of its alliance with Croesus, but his
tentative reconstruction of a loose 'Argive-inclined'
grouping is not an adequate explanation of Spartan actions
either. Perhaps here we must allow purely personal
considerations some weight: the extraordinarily wide
distribution of Lakonian pottery on Samos in the sixth

century (it had been imported since the early seventh) and the dedication of a bronze lion at the Samion Heraion by 'Eummastos a Spartiate' (Jeffery 1976, pl. 14) seem to betoken strong ties of 'xenia' (guest-friendship) between Spartan and Samian aristocrats of the kind attested by Herodotus (3.55.2) for the fifth century. We recall the traditions that Samians had helped Sparta in the 'Second' Messenian War (Chapter 8).

The most stimulating and convincing recent account of Kleomenes' reign is Carlier 1977. He, like Jeffery (1976, 123-7), rightly holds that Kleomenes was a strong king; whether his strength was used for the good or ill of Sparta or indeed all Greece is of course another matter. On all aspects of the origin, character and development of the 'Peloponnesian League' see Ste. Croix 1972, ch. 4.

The Sepeia campaign is handled in Tomlinson 1972, 93-5, and Kelly 1976, 140f.; the epitaph of the Argive Hyssematas (Daly 1939) should perhaps be connected with the battle.

On the role of Kleomenes in Arkadia see Wallace 1954. The fifth-century 'Arkadikon' coinage, however, has been more recently studied by Williams (1965; cf. Kraay 1976, 95-8), and it seems not to have begun until some ten or fifteen years after Kleomenes; it may betoken a religious not a political organization.

Of modern attempts to read back the 'austerity' vaunted by the 'mirage' into the historical record the most successful to date is Holladay 1977a.

10 Helots and Perioikoi

By the time Kleomenes I died, the process of internal
construction in Lakonia, including now what Thucydides
(4.3.2; 41,2) accurately described as 'the land that was
once Messenia', had been completed; and Spartan hegemony
was recognized generally within the Peloponnese and to
some extent outside it. A decade later Sparta was the
automatic choice as leader of loyalist Hellas against the
invading forces of the Persian Empire. Since this
military and political supremacy can only be explained
against its Lakonian background, I propose to pull
together the threads of the foregoing chapters by
discussing systematically the status and functions of
first the mainspring and then the essential complement of
the Spartan power, respectively the Helots and the
Perioikoi. As far as the archaeological and epigraphical
evidence goes, 500 will be taken as an approximate
terminus. But it will be necessary to draw on literary
and environmental evidence from a far wider period than
the seventh and sixth centuries.

I

Plato* had occasion to remark that the Helots afforded the
subject for the liveliest controversy in Greece; the
remark was noted and repeated some six centuries later by
the learned Alexandrian Athenaios. The controversy was
not of course conducted primarily on the moral plane, for
the number of Greeks who argued that slavery was not merely

---

* Where no specific reference is given, the ancient
  sources cited in this Chapter may be found translated
  in Appendix 4.

160

not in accordance with nature but actually contrary to it
and wrong was small; slaves found a place even in some of
the literary utopias which envisaged a general liberation
from backbreaking toil and a superabundance of the good
things of life (Finley 1975, ch. 11; Vogt 1975, ch. 2).
The question rather was one of practical management, and
it was in this sense that in the eyes of Aristotle ('Pol.'
1269), for example, the Helot-system was one of the seven
most defective elements in the Spartan polity.

What struck non-Spartans from at least the fifth
century was, in the first instance, the sheer number of
the Helots in comparison to the surprisingly small, and
shrinking, master class. Secondarily, it was noted that
the Helots were Greeks who, at least in the case of the
Messenians, were being denied their legitimate political
aspirations - political precisely because the Messenian
Helots wished to become the polis of 'the Messenians'.
Modern scholarly controversy, which can afford to stay
neutral on the moral and political aspects, has arisen
chiefly from the inadequacies of the ancient sources.
The origin of the (Lakonian) Helots, a vexed question
already in antiquity, has been considered above (Chapter
7). Here I shall be concerned with the further problems
of their juridical status, their economic functions within
the complex system of Spartan land-tenure, and the way in
which the juridical and economic aspects of Helotage conditioned Spartan political practice.

Unlike the Romans, the Greeks lacked a 'developed
jurisprudence' (Finley 1973, 64). But even the Roman
lawyers were not always able to articulate the complex-
ities of social status and structure in precise and
unambiguous legal language. Particularly instructive is
the case of the late Roman colonate. We need not here
consider its origins, which so nicely express the transformation of economic life in the Roman Empire during the
first three centuries AD. What matters is that after
Diocletian the 'colonus' though formally free was in a
condition so close to slavery that only the (technically
inappropriate) vocabulary of that institution was found
adequate to describe his subject status. The Helot, by
contrast, was formally unfree, but yet he or she
apparently enjoyed aspects of life normally associated
with the status of a free person rather than a slave - or,
to be precise, a chattel slave. Hence there was coined,
perhaps by Aristophanes of Byzantion in the third century,
the expression 'between free men and slaves' to character-
ize the Helots and several other unfree populations
scattered over the Greek world from Sicily to the Black
Sea.

Unfortunately, though, Pollux, a lexicographer of the second century AD, is our only source for this expression, and he fails to tell us exactly in what respects these populations were thought to resemble each other. It seems to me therefore to be in principle wrong to regard this unclear and ambiguous expression as the most useful classificatory label. Rather, I suggest, we should follow the lead of the Spartans themselves and most of our non-Spartan literary sources, who describe the Helots simply as 'slaves', whether using the most general word 'douloi' or terms which more strictly refer to their place of work ('oiketai') or mode of acquisition ('andrapoda'). Indeed, Kritias, the pro-Spartan Athenian oligarch (Chapter 13), reportedly said that in Lakedaimon could be found the most free and the most enslaved of all Greeks. It is this formulation, rather than the one recorded in Pollux, which deserves consideration above all.

For one of the key questions in Greek history, as I see it, is whether the propertied class ('the rich' or 'richest' in Greek parlance) derived their surplus wealth mainly from the exploitation of unfree and especially slave labour. As far as the propertied classes of most Greek states are concerned, the evidence is scattered, allusive, slight. But for the Spartiates (to use the technical term for Spartan citizens of full status) the evidence is relatively full and unambiguous. Spartan citizen-rights were tied strictly to the ability to contribute a certain amount of natural produce to a common mess in Sparta (below). This produce was procured by Helots who were bound, under pain of death, to hand it over to the individual Spartan on whose land they worked. Thus were Spartiates wholly freed from agricultural production and able - indeed, in a sense compelled - to devote their lives to the one practical craft to which no social stigma was ever attached, the craft of warfare.

Two passages will sufficiently illustrate this peculiar feature of Spartan society. The first comes from Xenophon's 'Oeconomicus' (4.20-5), a disquisition on good husbandry probably composed in the 350s. In accordance with the then ideology of the Greek propertied class, Sokrates is here made to commend agriculture as the only one of the mechanic arts worthy to be cultivated. In passing he recounts the story of the visit by the Spartan Lysander to the home of his friend Cyrus, the Persian prince (cf. Anderson 1974, 68f.). What particularly amazed Lysander was not so much the sweet smells and beautiful colours of Cyrus' garden as the fact that Cyrus had actually laid it out and planted it with his own hands. The other passage occurs in the 'Rhetoric'

(1367a28-33) of Aristotle, according to whom the wearing of long hair in the Spartan manner is the mark of a 'gentleman', since long hair is incompatible with manual labour.

What Kritias was saying, then, is that the Spartans were the 'freest' of the Greeks because they had taken the exploitation of slave labour to its logical limit and contrived to perform no productive labour themselves whatsoever. It should be noted in this connection that Aristotle did not criticize the Spartans for thereby securing an abundance of leisure but for misusing the leisure thus obtained. The Spartans, he thought, through devoting themselves exclusively to military matters and neglecting the arts of peace had become little better than wild beasts (passages cited in Ste.Croix 1972, 91). For Aristotle shared the view generally accepted in Greek (and Roman) antiquity that to be a fully free man almost necessarily involved being able to utilize slave labour.

The Helots therefore were properly called slaves in this basic economic sense. But it was also recognized from the fifth century that they differed from the more characteristic chattel slaves in important respects. Since the Spartans had no written laws, we have no Spartan equivalent of the Cretan Gortyn Code inscribed c.450 (Willetts 1967), and we cannot therefore establish precisely the regulations governing the marriages of Helots or their ownership of property. So far as marriages are concerned, in fact, we have just a single reference to Helot wives (Tyrtaios fr. 7) to prove that they were effected, though not necessarily recognized at law. Some kind of family life, however, is implied by the fact that, like slaves in the Old South, they apparently managed to reproduce themselves or at least to maintain themselves in sufficient numbers to constitute a permanent and indeed growing threat to the diminishing body of Spartiates.

This self-reproduction is of great interest in view of the modern debate over the economics of slavery, particularly slavery in the western hemisphere. But already in the eighteenth century David Hume had remarked in his essay 'Of the Populousness of Ancient Nations' that 'the only slaves among the Greeks that appear to have continued their own race, were the Helotes (sic), who had houses apart.' It is uncertain whether their 'houses apart' were all scattered on the kleroi (allotments) to which they were attached or might also be grouped in villages. Strabo's 'katoikiai' could refer to either mode of habitation; Livy's 'castella' could be either forts or farms; and the Helos of Thucydides (4.54), Damonon (IG V.1.213)

and Xenophon ('Hell.' 6.5.32) could be either a village or
a cult-centre. Since the archaeological evidence does not
resolve the matter, we can only speculate that in both
Lakonia and Messenia the Helots were forced to abandon the
villages of their ancestors and kept dispersed on the land
of their masters (cf. Xen. 'Hell.' 3.3.5) as a precaution
against rebellious combination.

It does seem certain, however, that the Helots could in
some sense own or perhaps rather possess personal
property. Whether or not they possessed instruments of
production is unclear and perhaps unimportant, but it
appears that in 425 some Messenian Helots had their own
boats (Thuc. 4.26.6f.); and in 223 or 222 6,000 Lakonian
Helots were allegedly able to raise the five Attic minas
required by Kleomenes III for the purchase of their freedom (Plut. 'Kleom.' 23.1, with Welwei 1974, 163-8).
Moreover, the Helots not only enjoyed private rights of
religious practice, like slaves in other states, but they
were also granted at least one public religious guarantee,
that of asylum at the sanctuary of Poseidon at Perioikic
Tainaron (though this might be violated: Chapter 11).

Such elements of 'freedom' in the Helot way of life may
have suggested the first term of the designation 'between
free men and slaves'. We are more surely informed as to
the reasons why the Helots could not be called 'slaves'
without qualification. The main one, to continue the
quotation from Hume, was that they were 'more the slaves
of the public than of individuals'. That is, relations
between a Spartiate and the Helots attached to his land
were as it were mediated through the state, in the sense
that the Spartiate 'owned' Helots only in virtue of his
membership of the Spartan citizen-body. This is why,
incidentally, Diakonoff (1974) has appropriated the term
'Helots' as a generic classification for state-owned
direct producers in the Ancient East.

Thus the informal agreement existing among other Greek
slaveowners 'to act as unpaid bodyguards of each other
against their slaves' (Xen. 'Hieron' 4.3) was formalized
in Sparta, where the state, represented by the Ephors,
declared war annually on the Helots - a typically Spartan
expression of politically calculated religiosity designed
to absolve in advance from ritual pollution any Spartan
who killed a Helot. The Spartan state alone had the power
to manumit Helots and release them from the land to which
they were forcibly bound (Thuc. 5.34.1 is an example).
And any Spartan who exacted from 'his' Helots more than
the maximum rent was liable to a public curse. Conversely,
every Spartan citizen had the right to use the Helots
attached to the service of any other, in the same way that

he was entitled to use another Spartiate's horses and
country-stores on hunting expeditions.

Following this lead, therefore, Pausanias described the
Helots as 'slaves of the community'. Strabo, however, was
yet more exact: the Spartans, he says, held the Helots as
'in a certain manner public slaves'. The qualification,
which applies to the epithet and not the noun, is crucial.
For although no individual Spartiate owned Helots as other
Greeks owned their chattel slaves, yet it was to an
individual Spartan master that the Helots working a
particular estate handed over their rent in kind, out of
which the Spartiate paid his mess dues and so exercised
the rights of citizenship. It is because the Helots were
thus 'tied to the soil' and bound to pay a rent that the
terminology of serfdom may be employed to describe their
legal status as that of 'state serfs'. That this does not
necessarily imply any close similarity between Helotage
and mediaeval feudalism will emerge as we examine in some
detail the Spartan system of land-tenure.

Let us first be clear that we are being sucked into a
bog: the problem of Spartan land-tenure is 'one of the
most vexed in the obscure field of Spartan institutions'
(Walbank 1957, 628). Part of the reason for this is that
of the surviving sources none was writing before Sparta
lost Messenia in 370. But the major complicating factor is
the twist given to the Spartan 'mirage' in the third
century by the revolutionary kings Agis IV and Kleomenes
III, who claimed, inevitably, to be restoring the
'Lykourgan' system. The essential problems seem to me to
be twofold: from what date was there private and legally
alienable landed property in Lakonia and Messenia? and did
this include, or was it coextensive with, the kleroi
worked by Helots?

The first point to establish is that the literary
sources from at least Tyrtaios onwards are unanimous that
there were rich and poor Spartans. This literary evidence
is fully corroborated by archaeology (from the eighth
century) and epigraphy (from the mid-seventh). Again, we
might cite the string of victories won by Spartans in the
four-horse chariot-race at Olympia. For king Agesilaos II,
according to the presumably well-informed Xenophon ('Ages.'
9.6), pointed out that such victories depended on the
ownership of private wealth; and being the brother of a
victor - or rather victrix (Kyniska) - he should have
known.

The specific problems posed by the sources on Spartan
land-tenure concern above all the precise meanings of
certain technical or semi-technical terms. We are told by
Aristotle ('Pol.' 1270a19-21) that Lykourgos (for

Aristotle an eighth-century figure) had declared it
immoral for a Spartan to buy or sell landed property. It
may be anachronistic to think of ownership in juridical
terms at so early a date, but, given the congruence at
Sparta between what was customary and what was legally
permitted, we might assume that Spartans practically never
bought or sold privately owned land. This assumption
seems to be supported by Aristotle himself, since he then
points out that the lawgiver in effect frustrated his own
intention by allowing anyone complete freedom to donate
his land away from the heirs by gift or bequest.

It is important to realize that Aristotle is here
discussing only one category of land, legally alienable
private property. But in a passage of the Aristotelian
'Lak. Pol.' preserved by Herakleides Lembos (373.12 Dilts)
a different distinction is drawn. While it was deemed
shameful for a Spartan to sell any land whatsoever, it was
forbidden, presumably by law, to sell the 'ancient
portion'. However, although the notion of two different
categories of land is introduced, the two passages are not
formally irreconcilable. For it is not denied that the
'ancient portion' might also be alienated through gift or
bequest. We might recall Aristotle's definition of
ownership as 'alienation consisting in gift and sale'
('Rhet.' 1361a21f.). This 'ancient portion' reappears in
slightly different wording in Plutarch ('Mor.' 238E).

Polybius (6.45.3), however, introduces a further
complication. Writing in the second century and discussing the allegedly unique features of the ancestral
Spartan polity, he says that the first of these,
according to the fourth-century writers Ephorus, Xenophon,
Kallisthenes and Plato, was the landed property régime: no
Spartan citizen might own more land than another, but all
must possess an equal quantity of the 'politike' land.
Unfortunately, 'politike' is ambiguous, since it could be
the adjective of either 'polis' (city) or 'politai'
(citizens). Most scholars have in fact derived it from
'polis' and argued that Polybius provides evidence for a
pool of state property distinct from the land owned
privately by the citizens. It seems to me, however, that
Polybius is most easily interpreted as referring only to
land owned by the citizens. For this would be a natural
distinction to make in the case of the Spartans, whose own
land was not coextensive with the territory of the polis
as a whole, which embraced also the land of the Perioikoi.

At all events, this interpretation would bring Polybius
into line with Plutarch ('Lyk.' 8.3), who, perhaps drawing
ultimately on a common source, agrees with Polybius in the
matter of equal shares. Significantly, though, he adopts

a different criterion of equality, according to yield of produce rather than surface area; and he is far more explicit and detailed than Polybius. In his account Lykourgos conducted a thoroughgoing land-redistribution and carved up Spartan territory into kleroi. Plutarch was uncertain how many of the 9,000 kleroi had been created by Lykourgos (Polydoros had a reputation for distributing kleroi too), but he was certain that 9,000 was the eventual total and that the corresponding number of 9,000 citizens, one per kleros, had remained constant down to the reign of Agis II at the end of the fifth century ('Lyk.' 29.10; cf. 'Agis' 5.2).

The implication that all Spartan land was distributed into kleroi and that these kleroi were somehow in public control is consonant with Plutarch's description of the process whereby a Spartan acquired his kleros: the allocation was made at birth, provided that the 'eldest of the tribesmen' had passed the infant as fit to be reared. Here, however, Plutarch is undoubtedly in error, and the error is instructive. For he has conflated two separate procedures, the enrolment of the new-born into a tribe and the allocation of a kleros. The latter, even if we accept that it was a tribal matter, could only have been effected at a later stage, when a man had passed through the controlled system of public training called the 'agoge' and been elected to a common mess. The simplest explanation of Plutarch's error is to suppose that he has tried to reconcile the fact (made unambiguous by Aristotle) of hereditary succession to a privately owned and legally alienable kleros with his false belief in a publicly owned and controlled system of equal and inalienable kleroi.

This explanation of the error, to whose source I shall shortly return, is confirmed in my view by his description, apparently following the third-century Phylarchos, of the 'rhetra' of Epitadeus ('Agis' 5.3). This measure is said to have provided that anyone who wished might legally dispose of his household and kleros by gift or bequest. Most scholars have automatically identified the freedom of gift and bequest criticized by Aristotle as the consequence of this measure. Aristotle, however, as we saw, attributed the dispensation to Lykourgos, and there is reason to suspect that the 'rhetra' of Epitadeus may be an invention designed to explain away the failure of 'Lykourgos' to foresee the drastic fall in citizen numbers during the fifth and early fourth centuries (Chapter 14). For no matter what measures had been taken to forestall the alienation of kleroi, these had been circumvented long before the date usually assigned to Epitadeus' 'rhetra', the early fourth century. As Forrest (1968, 137) has succinctly put it, 'Epitadeus, if he existed, does not belong to the fourth century or, if he does, did not create the trouble.'

I cannot therefore accept that there had ever been a pool of equal and inalienable kleroi owned or controlled by the state. On the other hand, I do not of course mean to deny that there had ever been a redistribution of Spartan land before the redistributions of Kleomenes III and Nabis in the third century. Some form of distribution was indispensable to provide the economic basis for transforming all Spartan citizens into hoplites in the seventh century. Moreover, if we can give any sense to the expression 'ancient portion', I feel this must refer to the land owned in Lakonia, mostly by aristocrats, prior to the creation of what we might call the 'new portions' in Messenia. An attempt must have been made to achieve a rough equality between these new kleroi, since it was on the produce from a kleros that a Spartan's citizenship and membership of the hoplite army was made to depend – in a manner to be discussed shortly.

For two reasons, however, I do not believe there is any way we can rationally calculate the size or number of the kleroi. First, we lack the requisite ancient evidence for all the relevant factors; in particular, the recent demonstration that the geomorphology of the Eurotas and Pamisos valleys has changed significantly since our period (Chapter 2) makes it impossible to estimate with any precision the ancient agricultural potential of the Spartans' land, besides automatically ruling out of court all modern calculations based on existing conditions. Second, such ancient evidence of a quantitative nature as we do possess is either relevant only to the third-century reforms or, if relevant to the period from c.650 to 370, is not sufficiently reliable or precise. It may none the less be useful to set out this evidence in some detail, if only to demonstrate that the host of wildly fluctuating and mutually incompatible modern estimates are indeed built on sand.

According to Isokrates (12.255), the original number of Dorians who 'invaded' Lakonia was 2,000. This figure can only have been a guess, perhaps related to the number of Spartan citizens at the time (339 BC) – an even smaller figure. Aristotle ('Pol.' 1270a36f.), however, about the same time as Isokrates referred vaguely to a report that there had once been as many as 10,000. Obviously he is referring to the period before 370, when Sparta controlled Messenia as well as Lakonia, and indeed to a time well before 370, since he knew that then there were only about 1,000 Spartan citizens. It would be rash to place much

trust in such a round number thus allusively cited,
although it is possible that Aristotle's 10,000 is a
rounding up of Herodotus' 8,000 given for 480 (Hdt. 7.234.
2). Certainly though Herodotus' figure is the earliest
reliable figure we have.

Whether or not it is absolutely correct, when taken
with Aristotle's figure for the second quarter of the
fourth century it is sufficient to prove that, despite
Plutarch, there was no necessary one-to-one correspondence
between the number of citizens and the number of kleroi.
In other words, even if each Spartan paterfamilias had
been allocated a kleros in the seventh-century distribution, that number of kleroi did not determine the size of
the citizen body for all time. Yet this was precisely
what Plutarch wrongly but revealingly believed. We may
now turn to consider the possible source or sources of his
error.

First, we recall a serious discrepancy between Plutarch
and Polybius. The latter, naming four fourth-century
sources, gave size as the criterion of equality among the
holdings of 'politike' land. Plutarch, however, is
confident that the kleroi were so carved out as to yield
an equal amount of produce, from which the Spartan master
and his wife might receive respectively seventy and twelve
medimnoi of barley and a corresponding amount of fresh
fruits. The simplest explanation of the discrepancy is
that Plutarch has followed the sources implicitly rejected
by Polybius, namely those of the third century who
swallowed or indeed formulated the propaganda of Agis and
Kleomenes. This explanation is perhaps supported by the
number 9,000 given by Plutarch for the kleroi distributed
by Lykourgos and Polydoros. For Agis proposed to raise
the citizen body from 700 to 4,500 by redividing Spartan
land in the Eurotas valley, and this land was thought to
be roughly equal to the land once held in Messenia.

It could of course be argued that Agis' projected
figure was based on the number of citizens known or
believed to have existed in the 'Lykourgan' heyday. But
for me this would only reinforce the suspicion that
Plutarch was using Agis-tainted sources, as there was in
fact no one-to-one correspondence numerically between
citizens and kleroi in the fifth and fourth centuries at
least. A second clue pointing in the same direction is
Plutarch's statement that Lykourgos had also redistributed
the land owned by the Perioikoi into 30,000 kleroi. Since
there is no evidence, and no reason to suspect, that the
Spartans had interfered with Perioikic land before the
third century - apart from assigning 'choice precincts' to
their kings (Xen. 'Lak. Pol.' 15.3) - this figure can only

be explained as a doubling of the 15,000 Perioikic allotments envisaged by Agis. In short, it seems highly
probable that Plutarch's figure for the kleroi and
citizens under the 'Lykourgan' dispensation is a backwards
projection of the figure envisaged by Agis and almost
achieved by Kleomenes.

It is far harder to handle the figure of eighty-two
medimnoi of barley given by Plutarch as the (maximum)
annual rent to be paid by the Helots to a kleros-holder
and his wife. On the one hand, the fact that in Plutarch
the rent was to be paid just to a Spartan master and his
wife corresponds to the situation immediately following or
envisaged in the third-century redistributions rather than
to the one criticized by Aristotle in the 'Politics', in
which the sons of such a couple were falling into poverty
and forfeiting citizen-rights through division of the
inheritance (cf. Chapter 14). Moreover, it was only after
a relatively large number of approximately equal kleroi
had been created that an average rent could have been fixed.
On the other hand, these arguments would apply no less to
the situation following the seventh-century distribution,
and it could be argued further that Agis aimed to produce
kleroi commensurate with the payment of the 'Lykourgan'
mess dues.

For in the case of the latter Agis could have been
genuinely following rather than setting a precedent.
That is, the quantities given by Plutarch ('Lyk.' 12) for
the monthly mess contributions so correspond to those
given by the fourth-century Dikaiarchos (fr. 72 Wehrli)
that both must have been drawn from a common source
(Kritias or Aristotle have been suggested). This does not
of course mean that we may extrapolate from these quantities the size and yield of a 'Lykourgan' kleros. For it
is unclear precisely which land was redistributed in the
seventh century; we do not know the ratio between rent
and yield (the proportion of one half cited in Tyrtaios
fr. 6, even if it is a rent paid by Helots, does not
necessarily apply to the situation after the 'Second'
Messenian War); and the minimum contributions to the mess
do not exhaust the commodities produced on Spartiate land.
None the less, these contributions do provide our best
evidence for the economy certainly of Lakonia and probably
of Messenia too before the third century.

According to Dikaiarchos, the prescribed minimum
contribution was: one and a half Attic medimnoi (roughly
bushels) of barley flour; eleven or twelve choes of wine;
an unspecified weight of cheese and figs; and ten or so
Aiginetan obols to buy extras. Plutarch gives: one
medimnos of barley; eight choes of wine; five minas

of cheese; two and a half minas of figs; and an unspecified sum of money for extras. In other words, Dikaiarchos
has translated Lakonian measures and weights into their
Attic equivalents where he was reasonably sure of the
ratio.   Let us consider each item in turn, incorporating
other literary, archaeological and epigraphical evidence.

Barley today is merely a major feed grain for animals
and is ingested by humans only indirectly; in Lakonia, for
example, it is grown widely, especially in the Malea
peninsula and east Helos plain (ESAG no. 304).   In
antiquity, however, it was used as well for human food as
for animal feed (Moritz 1955; 1958, xxi, 167).   Indeed, it
appears that until perhaps as late as the fourth century
barley, eaten as a 'kneaded thing' (maza: Plut. 'Kleom.'
16.5 etc.), was widely preferred to wheat as food in
Greece, partly for technological reasons and partly
because tastes in food are always partly irrational (the
ancients were aware from experience that wheat was more
nutritive).   The stipulated mess contribution being in
barley suggests therefore that the rule had been established before the fourth century; 'home' rations for kings
in the fifth century were also provided in barley (Hdt. 6.
57.3).   However, by the first half of the fourth century
rich Spartiates were contributing wheaten bread to their
messes (Xen. 'Lak. Pol.' 5.3), although Theophrastos
('Hist. Plant.' 8.4.5; 'Caus. Plant.' 4.9.5) remarked on
the lightness of Spartan wheat at the end of the century.

A Spartan medimnos of barley a month, perhaps seventy-
three or seventy-four litres in volume, undoubtedly
constituted a living ration for an adult male; this can be
seen by comparing our other evidence for rations,
especially those sent over to the men trapped on Sphakteria
in 425, although we must allow for exceptional circumstances here (Thuc. 4.16).   Thus the rent of eighty-two
medimnoi per annum maximum should have fed at least six or
seven persons.   Presumably, if the figure applies to our
period and not just the third century, the surplus was
either consumed by the members of the Spartiate's household or put into a public store.   We are not told how the
barley made its way from field to mess, but there may have
been a central mill at a place near Sparta called 'the
grindings' (Alesiai: not yet certainly located).   Alkman
(fr. 95a) mentions a mill, and stone suitable for mill-
stones occurs near Mistra in the Taygetos piedmont west of
Sparta.

The grapevine can flourish in droughty, rocky and
calcareous soils, on level and sloping ground, and at
considerable altitudes (up to 1,219 m. today in the
Peloponnese).   The Mediterranean type of climate normally

provides sufficient moisture for its spring vegetative
phase and the dry, sunny weather to ripen the fruit. Both
in relief and in climate Lakonia (especially) and Messenia
are admirably suited to viticulture, although we should
note that vines 'require a greater degree of tendance and
control of the environment than any other Mediterranean
crop' (White 1970, 229). The recent discovery of grape-
seeds at the Menelaion site should confirm that the wine
in the stoppered jars found in the Mycenaean mansion was
locally produced. Pedasos (Mothone?) was noted for its
vines by Homer ('Il.' 9.152). By 600 Alkman could write
as a connoisseur of five local wine-growing districts (fr.
92d: Oinous, Dentheliatis, Karystos, Onoglos, Stathmis)
and even suggest an intimacy with viticulture by referring
to the grubs that destroy the 'eyes' of vines (fr. 93).
The districts, however, where they can be securely located,
were in Perioikic territory. Perhaps the Spartans' own
Helot-produced wine was vin ordinaire, a potent enough
brew to dement Kleomenes I if taken neat too often no
doubt.

The fig, like the grapevine, was pre-eminently well
Cheese will have been made from the milk of sheep and
goats rather than cows. 'Pasture' in the northern
European sense does not exist in Greece today, and since
cultivable land is a maximum of 20 per cent of the surface
area per annum livestock may merely graze the stubble to
manure the soil for the next planting. Normally they must
make do with the terrain between the 'cultivable' and the
totally barren (30 per cent of the surface area in 1961),
and on this basis Kythera in 1961 was reckoned to have the
highest proportion of 'pasture' of any eparchy (ESAG no.
319). Ancient conditions will not have differed greatly.
None the less, in 1961 the eparchy of Lakedaimon (roughly
the Eurotas furrow) had the seventh largest number of
goats, and it seems from the Pseudo-Platonic 'Alkibiades'
(1.122D) that Lakonia and Messenia were no less well
equipped with small stock animals in antiquity. Indeed,
it has been suggested that land in Messenia planted to
wheat in the Mycenaean period was turned over to pasture
under the Spartan domination. Apart from cheese, sheep
and goats will have provided skins, wool, hair, animal fat
and, to a minor degree, meat.

The fig, like the grapevine, was pre-eminently well
adapted to the Lakonian and Messenian environment. Today
the first crop in June-July is mostly eaten fresh, the
second in August-October is used for drying. Charmis,
Spartan victor in the prestigious 'stadion' foot-race at
Olympia in 668, is said to have trained on a special diet
of dried figs. Aristophanes (fr. 108) provides a
typically humorous political explanation of the relatively

small size of the 'Lakonian' fig, but this may be a
generic name rather than a reference to the figs actually
grown in Lakonia or Messenia. Theophrastos ('Hist. Plant.'
2.7.1) adds that irrigation improves the fruit of the
Lakonian fig.

The last of the items mentioned by Dikaiarchos and
Plutarch is money. As we have seen, Sparta did not coin
silver as early as most other states - in fact not until
the early third century. Exchanges, however, did take
place in Lakonia, in which iron spits seem to have been
somehow involved. This subject is too complex to go into
here, but Dikaiarchos may have translated into the
Aiginetan standard monetary contributions that were in
fact made in the form of iron spits. It should, however,
be added that at least one Aiginetan coin has been found
in an Archaic context on Spartan territory, at Anoyia in
the Spartan plain (perhaps the Dereion of Paus. 3.20.7).
Spits, square in section, have been excavated at all the
major Spartan sanctuaries, but it is unclear whether they
are monetary or purely functional.

The items mentioned so far exhaust the range neither of
the food consumed in the mess nor of the plants and
animals raised in Lakonia and Messenia by Helots. The
first notable omission is the third member of the
'Mediterranean dietary triad' (Chapter 4), the olive,
whose possibly crucial role in the Dark Ages has been
considered in Chapter 7. In fact, Dikaiarchos does
mention the olive earlier in the same passage, where he
indicates the range of food actually consumed in the
mess. We may add that, according to Thucydides (1.6.5),
the Spartans were the first Greeks to anoint themselves
with olive oil and scrape themselves off after athletic
exercise. This presumably betokens an abundance of the
oil in Lakonia.

The same passage of Dikaiarchos also introduces another
dietary staple, pork, from which the Spartans made their
state speciality, the bloody black broth that so disgusted
a visiting ruler and so delighted Hitler (Rawson 1969, 7,
343). The Spartan kings were privileged to receive the
hides of all sacrificed animals (Hdt. 6.57.1), and
Xenophon ('Lak. Pol.' 15.5) refers to pigs in the context
of royal sacrifices.

Dikaiarchos notes that exceptionally fish, a hare or a
ring-dove might be eaten in the mess. The fish were
presumably sea-fish caught by Perioikoi and perhaps dried,
but the hare and the dove were prizes of a favourite
Spartan pastime, hunting. The chief prize, however, was
the wild boar, to the capture of which the Spartans
apparently devoted considerable thought. The specially

bred 'Lakonian' hound was valued as a scenter; horses,
dogs and provisions were made available on demand to all
Spartans, though they were no doubt owned only by the
rich; and a hunting party was one of the only two
legitimate excuses for being absent from the common meal.
The popularity of boar-hunting with the Spartans is
demonstrated by archaeology. Lakonian artists represented
boars and sometimes hunting scenes in vasepainting,
terracotta, bronze and stone during the sixth century and
later. A funeral mound of c.600, to which we shall be
returning in various connections, contained bones of wild
boar. The chief hunting area near Sparta seems to have
been the region of the lower eastern slopes of central
Taygetos known as Therai (Paus. 3.20.5). The area was no
doubt more densely wooded than it is today.

The horse deserves separate mention, for it occupied a
special place in Lakonian life. Small bronze representations of the animal were fashioned by Lakonian craftsmen
and dedicated in Spartan sanctuaries from c.750. Alkman
(fr. 1.51, 59; 58.2; 60.3) displays a virtuoso familiarity
with the various regional breeds and mentions galingale,
which was particularly used as horse-fodder. Probably it
was in Alkman's lifetime that horses were sacrificed on
the funeral mound just mentioned. Finally, there are the
horses bred for racing. Being extremely expensive to
maintain, horses were the prerogative of the rich and
often aristocratic few. Since they require extensive
pasture and abundant water, conditions in the ancient
forerunners of the modern Helos plain and Pamisos valley
appear to have been most suitable. The Pseudo-Platonic
'Alkibiades' suggests there were a remarkably large number
of horses kept in Lakonia and Messenia, and it is no
surprise to meet a Messenian supplying horses to
Alexandria in the third century (Plut. 'Kleom.' 35.3).

Three more life-sustaining creatures deserve a mention.
The bee, first represented in Lakonian art on a four-sided
ivory seal of 700-675 and beautifully evoked by Alkman
(fr. 89.4), yielded the essential sweetener honey and the
multi-purpose wax. Second, migratory quails were presumably netted in antiquity, as they are shot today, at the
foot of the Tainaron and Malea peninsulas; Xenophon
('Mem.' 2.1.3f.) commented that their sexual ardour made
them easier to catch. Third, the domesticated fowl,
besides providing meat and eggs (the symbol of Helen,
represented for instance on a sixth-century relief from
Sellasia: below), was also a suitable object for
sacrifice.

Finally, let us turn from animal to vegetable. Another
unknown forbidding us to use the available quantitative

evidence as a sufficient basis for estimating the size of
a kleros is the amount of land planted to legumes. That
they were important in the Spartan diet is suggested by
Alkman's references (fr. 17.4; 96) to a porridge of mixed
pulse (perhaps pea, lentil, lupine and vetch), the food of
the common man, and by Theophrastos' citations ('Caus.
Plant.' 7.4.5f.) of 'Lakonian' types of vegetable (lettuce
and cucumber). Alkman also mentions sesame, a soil-
improver whose seeds might be used both to flavour bread
(fr. 19.2f.) and to feed animals. Flax, which is labour-
intensive and requires much water for its growth and
processing, was grown for its fibre in Messenia in late
Mycenaean times, but for the historical period we hear
only of edible linseed (Alkman fr. 19.2f.; Thuc. 4.26.5).
I would guess, however, that the linen used, for example,
in hoplite tunics was locally produced.

Those then are the crops and animals raised by Helots
in Lakonia and Messenia for Spartan use at home and
abroad. We cannot estimate with precision or even roughly
the size of a kleros. It is clear, however, both from the
imbalance in numbers between Spartiates and Helots and
from a crucial passage in Xenophon ('Hell.' 3.3.4-11,
fully discussed in Chapters 13 and 14) that more than one
Helot family worked each kleros. Unfortunately, though,
only one source gives a numerical ratio, and that for a
military not an agricultural context. In 479 each
Spartiate who fought at Plataia was accompanied by seven
Helots (Hdt. 9.10.1; 28.2; 29.1). If the figure has been
correctly transcribed by Herodotus or his copyists, this
would certainly be the largest number of Helots ever
known to have left Lakonia. In fact, to many scholars it
has seemed implausibly high. Clearly it was not demanded
on strictly military grounds, although Welwei (1974, 120-
4) has properly stressed the supply problem of this
campaign and suggested that Helots were used to solve it.
Moreover, even if the Spartans were afraid of revolution
in their rear - a plausible suggestion in view of the
evidence mustered for a possible Helot revolt c.490
(Chapter 9) - it is highly unlikely that they would have
risked taking so many potential enemies with them on a
vital campaign. It is worth remembering Xenophon's
statement that on campaign the Spartans took the precaution of debarring the Helots from the arms-dump. So if
Herodotus' seven-to-one proportion has any validity, it
seems more likely to represent the ratio of the Helot to
Spartan populations as a whole than the proportion at
Plataia.

However that may be, all our evidence indicates that at
least by the fifth century the Helots were vastly more

numerous than the Spartans and that this very numerical
disproportion was an important factor governing relations
between the two. However, the precise character of these
relations is harder to discover. Thucydides in a
celebrated passage (4.80) fully discussed in Chapter 12
regarded the liquidation of some 2,000 Helots in 425 or
424 as an instance, if a spectacularly horrific one, of
the normal precautionary attitude of the Spartans towards
the Helots. Myron too, who is of course a less reliable
witness, treats the killing of Helots as a regular mode of
control. Then there is the evidence for the 'Krypteia',
which has been illuminated by Jeanmaire (1913) with a
wealth of comparative anthropological material. This too
appears to have been a routine institution, whereby those
youths who had passed through the 'agoge' (the state
educational system) completed their apprenticeship by
going out into the country, lying low by day and killing
Helots by night. Plutarch is emphatic that this exercise
in brutality was no part of the 'Lykourgan' order, but
only became general after the revolt following the great
earthquake of c.465. Herodotus, however, in a rarely
noticed passage (4.146.2) almost casually remarks,
ostensibly with reference to a context of c.800, that the
Spartans perform their official killings by night; and
Isokrates (12.181), admittedly with hyperbole, claimed
that only the Spartans denied the wickedness of all
homicide.

Some modern scholars, on the other hand, have preferred
to follow Plutarch and minimize the role played by hatred,
fear and judicial murder in Spartano-Helot relations. As
Grote put it (though he was careful to distinguish between
domestic and agricultural Helots in this regard), 'the
various anecdotes which are told respecting their treatment at Sparta betoken less of cruelty than of ostentatious scorn - a sentiment which we are noway surprised to
discover among the citizens of the mess-table.' This
milder interpretation has been followed most recently by
Ducat (1974), who suggests that it was because the Helots
were in some ways so similar to the Spartans that the
latter were anxious to exaggerate the differences. For
example, it was because the Helots were in a sense 'within
the city' that war was declared upon them annually in
order to render them legally outsiders. And the murder of
Helots, Ducat argues, was essentially a magical rite, a
symbolic representation intended to reaffirm the norm that
Helots were not and could not become Spartans. In short,
the characteristic attitudes of the Spartans towards the
Helots were scorn and contempt. Hence the beatings, the
intoxications, the enforced wearing of a dogskin cap and

rough animal pelts - all measures designed to remind the
Helots of their 'alterity'.

No doubt there is truth in both versions. The main
point, however, remains: Helotage had been initiated and
maintained to serve the class interests of the Spartans.
The proper question to ask then is why the Spartans,
unlike other Greek master classes, found themselves
constantly menaced by revolt and felt compelled to resort
to such extreme repression. There is no single answer.

In the first place, as Finley (1973, 63, 68) has
emphasized, the Helots were in comparison to chattel
slaves a privileged group, enjoying 'all the normal human
institutions except their freedom'. Of course the context
in which these institutions were forced to function was
highly abnormal, but their relative privilege in such
matters as family-life and the possession of personal
property could have encouraged them to lay claim to
greater rights and freedoms, especially since they were
Greeks.

Second, the Messenian Helots, who at least by the time
of Thucydides (1.101.2) greatly outnumbered the Lakonian,
were politically motivated men. In fact, they were
precisely what Vernant (1974, 28) denies to have been
possible in ancient Greece, 'an active and unified social
force, a group of solidary men intervening on the historical stage to orient the course of events in a direction
conformable to their interests and aspirations'. They
lived, moreover, far from Sparta and separated from it by
a formidable mountain barrier. For these reasons no doubt
it was against them rather than the Lakonian Helots that
Spartan repression was more particularly directed. We
should, though, recall that in 465 it was the Lakonian
Helots (if Diodorus may be trusted) who began the revolt,
that in the late fifth and early fourth centuries the
Athenians devoted some attention to disaffecting the
Lakonians as well as the Messenians, that Kinadon's
conspiracy of c.399 may have been a primarily Lakonian
affair, and, finally, that Aristotle's often quoted
comparison of the Helots to 'an enemy constantly sitting
in wait for the disasters of the Spartans' was made after
the liberation of Messenia.

Third, however, and for me decisively, the relationship
between the Spartans and the Helots had been conceived in
conquest, and it was essentially as a defeated enemy that
the Spartans treated the Helots, whose very name perpetu-
ally recalled the fact. The relationship, however, was
dialectical. The militarism which Aristotle deplored was
the price Sparta inevitably paid for maintaining a
uniquely profitable system of economic exploitation.

II

The origins of the Perioikoi, as already stressed in
Chapter 7, were more heterogeneous than those of the
Helots, but their status, as it had been gradually defined
by the end of the seventh century, was no less uniform in
relation to the Spartans. They were the inhabitants of
the towns in Lakonia and Messenia apart from Sparta and
Amyklai, free men but subjected to Spartan suzerainty and
not endowed with citizen-rights at Sparta. Their free
personal status and disfranchisement are not controversial. Disagreement abounds over the character of their
subjection, and the social and political organization of
their own communities.

According to Larsen (1938, 818), the Perioikoi stood
somewhere between Helots and free allies of Sparta.
According to Oliva (1971, 62), they occupied a station
between Spartan citizens and foreigners or allies. The
latter, I suggest, is the more fruitful perspective. For
on the one hand the Perioikic communities were regarded as
'poleis', not only by inexact writers like Herodotus (7.
234), Xenophon ('Hell.' 6.5.21; 'Lak. Pol.' 15.3; 'Ages.'
2.24) and Stephanos of Byzantion, but even by Thucydides
(5.54.1). The same idea that they were in some sense
politically autonomous is conveyed by the formally
incorrect description of Pharai, Geronthrai and Kythera as
'colonies' of Sparta. (However, the apparently corroborative epigraphical evidence for magistracies in Perioikic
towns belongs to the second and first centuries and may
not therefore be relevant to the period before 195, when
Flamininus completed the political liberation of the
Perioikoi from Sparta: see Chapter 15.) On the other hand,
it was a peculiarity of the Spartan polis that its
territory was not identical with the land owned by its
citizens, and that the name of the state was not 'the
Spartiates' but 'the Lakedaimonians', which in military
contexts embraced the Perioikoi as well. Xenophon indeed
several times refers to a mixed force as 'the citizen
army' ('Hell.' 4.4.19; 5.4.41, 55; 7.4.20, 27). In what
then did the subjection of the Perioikoi lie?

The answer, I suggest, is that they were bound, as it
were, 'to follow the Spartans whithersoever they might
lead'. We do not in fact know the terms of any individual
treaties between the Spartans and a Perioikic community,
and their mutual relationship need not ever have been so
formalized. Undoubtedly, though, they were obligated to
submit without question to Spartan direction in foreign
policy, and in this respect their position resembled that
of the allies of Sparta outside Lakonia and Messenia

before the formation of the Peloponnesian League. Indeed,
I would argue that it was Sparta's experience in dealing
with its Perioikoi which provided the model for the Peloponnesian League. Unlike the League members, however, the
Perioikoi never won and may never have sought the right of
collective veto of a Spartan decision provided by a
majority vote of the League Congress. The King's Peace of
386, which guaranteed 'autonomy' to every separate Greek
city, was only once interpreted to support Perioikic
independence from Sparta. And the 'haughty roughness'
(Grote) dealt out by the Spartans to their foreign allies
may have been felt the more strongly by the Perioikoi.

Thus in order to explain their subjection we need not
believe (pace Parke 1931; Bockisch 1965, 131-7) that the
twenty harmosts mentioned in an ancient commentary on
Pindar were imposed on the Perioikoi (the harmosts at
Kythera and perhaps Thyrea and Aulon were exceptions due
to strategic exigencies) nor that the Ephors, as Isokrates
(12.181) claimed, could have any Perioikos put to death
without trial. We do not, however, know when the military
burden was first imposed nor when Perioikoi first fought
with Spartans against an external enemy. The suggestion
that the 'gymnetes' of Tyrtaios (fr. 11.35; cf. 'P. Oxy.'
3316) were Perioikoi is unconvincing. But the bronze
figurines and grave stelai depicting hoplites found in
Perioikic territory (below) suggest a terminus ante quem
of c.525. Our earliest literary evidence concerns the
campaigns of 480-479, but by 418, and probably by 425,
Perioikoi were brigaded individually with Spartiates in
the hoplite phalanx (Chapter 12).

The Perioikoi in question will have been drawn from the
ranks of the wealthy, who, as elsewhere in Greece, will
have included but not been coextensive with the 'true
gentlemen' (presumably aristocrats) who volunteered for
hoplite service in 380 (Xen. 'Hell.' 5.3.9; cf. Plut.
'Kleom.' 11 for this stratum). Again like other Greeks,
these rich Perioikoi will have derived their surplus from
the exploitation of chattel slaves (not Helots: see below).
We have unfortunately no positive ancient evidence that
they did so, but there are four pieces of evidence which
strongly suggest this.

First, a fifth-century inscription cut into the living
rock of Mount Koumaro (ancient Larysion) at Gytheion,
(IG V.1.1155) forbids anyone, whether free or slave
(doulos), to quarry stone. Second, five manumission
stelai of the late fifth and early fourth century from the
sanctuary of Poseidon at Tainaron (IG V.1.1228-32), which
dedicate the freed persons to the god, must be attributed
to Perioikoi. It is true that the transactions are dated

by the eponymous Ephor at Sparta and that Helots used
Tainaron as an asylum, but from all we know it was the
Spartan state alone, and not individual Spartiates, that
could manumit Helots.   Third, a famous anecdote concerning
Agesilaos (Plut. 'Ages.' 26.5 etc.) implies that in the
early fourth century there were no craftsmen among the
Perioikic hoplites; they must therefore have been farmers
but freed by slaves from the necessity to labour constantly with their own hands.   Finally, in c.240 a raid by
the Aitolian League on Lakonia allegedly netted no less
than 50,000 slaves (Plut. 'Kleom.' 18.3).   The raid was
directed at least in part against the Perioikoi (Polyb.
4.34.9), so if the figure is to be trusted it seems
necessary to postulate that some at least of the captives
were slaves of the Perioikoi rather than Helots.

A second related function of the Perioikoi, but antedating the seventh century, was to serve as a kind of
territorial reserve against the Helots.   The general lack
of military co-operation between the Perioikoi and the
Helots against the Spartans may or may not betoken different ethnic affiliations, but it is true that only once
before the liberation of Messenia did Perioikic towns join
a Helot revolt (in c.464) and that in this instance both
were Messenian.   The majority, however, was in Lakonia,
where they served to separate the Helots from the
Arkadians and Argives in the north and to keep an eye on
the lower Eurotas valley from their less favoured situations in Vardhounia and the Tainaron and Malea peninsulas.   Forts at Kosmas and Trinasos prevented the Helots
from communicating with the outside world respectively
across Parnon and by sea.   Similarly in Messenia the fort
at Vasiliko divided the Messenians from the south-west
Arkadians, and Aulon blocked the way to Triphylia and
Elis.   All this may become clearer after the review below
of Perioikic towns archaeologically attested by c.500.

The third main function of the Perioikoi was broadly
economic.   There is no good reason to believe that they
actually paid tribute to Sparta: the 'royal tribute'
mentioned in the 'Alkibiades' (1.123A) is a mystery, and
the comparable reports in Strabo (8.5.4, C365) and
Hesychius (s.v. 'kalame') are inconclusive.   They may,
however, have been required or encouraged to make monetary
or other contributions on an individual and ad hoc basis.
However this may be, it is quite certain that the chief
rock, mineral and marine resources of Lakonia and Messenia
lay in Perioikic territory, that imports to Sparta and
other commercial relations with the outside world had to
pass through Perioikic hands, and that Perioikoi played a
major role in Lakonian craftsmanship.

Most of the marble used for the sculpture now in the
Sparta Museum was won from Spartiate land on the eastern
slopes of Taygetos in a quarry difficult of access between
Anavryti and Mistra. But Lakonia was not distinguished at
any period for its buildings or sculpture of marble.
Subsidiary marble quarries are known at Vresthena in
northern Lakonia, Chrysapha in the west Parnon foreland
and Goranoi in west Vardhounia. In its uppermost course
the marble from Dholiana just north of the Spartan
frontier resembles Pentelic, but in Lakonia it seems only
to have been used at Tyros in the east Parnon foreland.
Transport was presumably too expensive for it to be used
at Sparta. In fact the stone most widely used for
buildings in Lakonia and Messenia was local limestone of
varying quality. The chief sources for other than local
use seem to have been the quarries in north-west Mani at
ancient Thalamai, Leuktra and Kardamyle. Finally, poros,
which was used for monumental carving in Sparta, occurs in
the plain of Molaoi.

Iron ores are widely distributed throughout Lakonia.
Apart from the important deposits at Neapolis (Chapter 7),
we might cite those at Kollinai in the Skiritis and Porto
Kayio (ancient Psamathous) in south Mani. The quantity of
small, mould-made lead figurines dedicated at Spartan
sanctuaries in Lakonia (over 100,000 at Orthia alone) and
exported, probably by Spartan pilgrims for the most part,
to sanctuaries elsewhere in Lakonia (Anthochorion,
Analipsis, Tyros) and the Peloponnese suggest an extensive
local supply of the ore; there were certainly ancient
workings in the Kardamyli district. Finally, O. Davies in
1935 made a tantalizing reference to the known location of
copper ore at Alagonia, at the western end of the Langadha
pass over Taygetos; but the localities in question have
been shown to contain 'very small, low-grade sulfide
deposits with little or no copper mineralization' (MME 232).

Lakonia, then, was remarkably self-sufficient in useful
rocks and minerals as well as agricultural potential, and
overseas trade in essentials was relatively unimportant.
From one standpoint this was fortunate. For although the
borders of Lakonia and Messenia are washed on three sides
by the Mediterranean, communications inland are generally
poor (below), and the number of harbours offering both
protection from winds and heavy seas and a holding
anchorage is small compared to the extent of coastal
frontage. The only harbours of any practical significance
on the long eastern coastline of Lakonia were, north to
south, Astros (ancient Thyrea), Tyros, Leonidhion (ancient
Prasiai), Kyparissi (ancient Kyphanta), and Palaia
Monemvasia (ancient Epidauros Limera). On the Lakonian

Gulf Gytheion was the chief port of Sparta; the next best
anchorages were Neapolis (ancient Boiai) and Skoutari Bay
(ancient Asine). In the Messenian Gulf Kardamyle served
as Sparta's port after Gytheion had become independent in
the second century; Kalamata (ancient Pharai) did not
become important until the modern breakwater was built.
On the west coast of Messenia the best natural harbour was
of course Navarino Bay (ancient Pylos), but the Spartans
made little or no effort to develop its strategic or
commercial potential.

However, despite this dearth of good harbours, there
were still of course Perioikoi who engaged in fishing and
trade. The eonomic significance of fishing in the
Mediterranean world generally is often grossly inflated
(cf. Braudel 1972, 140, 145); and we should regard it as
of secondary importance even for most coastal settlements.
There is, however, one marine resource, the murex mollusc
(trunculus or brandaris), which merits special mention.
As Edward Gibbon remarked, 'by the discovery of cochineal,
etc. we far surpass the colours of antiquity.' But of the
latter 'royal purple', obtained by processing the milky
secretions of the murex, exercises a certain fascination
(Reinhold 1970). Its production in antiquity was
primarily associated with the Phoenicians of Tyre, but
among the Greeks the Lakonians and Tarentines were leading
producers. Murex shells have been excavated in prehistoric
contexts at Kastri on Kythera and Ay. Stephanos, and the
waters off Kythera and Gytheion are still major sources of
the mollusc. I suspect, however, that it was the Phoenicians calling at Kythera in the eighth century or earlier
who firmly established the production of the dye, which in
historical times was used to colour the 'phoinikis' or
short cloak worn by all members of the Spartan hoplite
army (Cartledge 1977, 15 and n. 38).

The problem of Perioikic trade and traders is more
complex. As already remarked, overseas trade will have
been relatively restricted. Apart from the copper and tin
needed for bronze artefacts, it will have been concerned
mainly with the import and export of fine ceramic table-
ware or bronzes for display or votive dedication. This
trade will undoubtedly have been in Perioikic hands to
some extent, but, when it more or less disappeared in the
course of the fifth century, we should not imagine that
this precipitated an economic crisis in the Perioikic
communities, of whom Gytheion was the most important in
this regard. For even if Gytheion had acted as a sort of
'port of trade' linking the closed and archaic Spartan
system with the more open and developed economic systems
of the Greek world, most Perioikic communities were no

doubt dominated by the same land-oriented values as the
Spartans themselves. A possible index of this is the fact
that, although Perioikoi were presumably not forbidden to
handle coined money, pre-Hellenistic coins have been found
on only two Perioikic sites (Prasiai and Kythera). On the
other hand, trade within Lakonia between Spartans and
Perioikoi was crucial, not merely for the procurement of
chariots for horseracing but for the very maintenance of
the military machine. This leads us naturally, and
finally, to consider the role of Perioikoi in Lakonian
craftsmanship.

I have been careful hitherto to speak of 'Lakonian' art
and artefacts. That label must now be unpacked, and the
discussion placed within the modern debate over the status
of craftsmen and craftsmanship in ancient Greek societies
generally. This debate is focused on two main problems:
how typical of Greek sentiment as a whole was the hostile
attitude towards 'banausic' (manual) enterprise manifested
by intellectuals and aristocrats like Sophokles, Xenophon
and Plato? Second, if their attitude was typical, was it
long or recently established? Briefly, my own view is
that the attitude was largely confined to the propertied
classes, whose members did not have to work for their
living, and that it only took on its acrimonious overtones
with the rise of democracy (cf. R. Schlaifer in Finley
1968b, 99ff.). Sparta, thanks to the exploitation of the
Helots, was somewhat peculiar, though not unique, in its
official hostility to manual craftsmen (Hdt. 2.167.2;
Plut. 'Ages.' 26.5). However, as we saw in Chapter 9,
neither the belief of the 'Spartan mirage' in archetypal
Spartan austerity nor its modern substitute, the belief
that Lakonian art suddenly 'died' around 550, is
consistent with the facts. In the same way the problem of
craftsmanship in Lakonian society must clearly be
reappraised.

According to the conventional wisdom, perhaps most
pithily expressed by Cook (1962), craft production at
Sparta and a fortiori in the rest of Lakonia was from a
very early period exclusively in the hands of the
Perioikoi. I have already tried to show elsewhere that
the picture is more complex (Cartledge 1976b); space
forbids much more than a summary of those arguments here.
In the first place, Pausanias expressly distinguishes two
Lakonian craftsmen of the sixth century as Spartan
citizens. Unreliable evidence, no doubt, but I wonder if
they, like the 'local' man Gitiadas, would have secured
such firm remembrance had they been Perioikoi. Second,
there are two scraps of epigraphical evidence possibly
tending to the same conclusion. One of the masons working

at Amyklai under Bathykles at the end of the sixth century
had the extraordinary - indeed, so far unique - name
Technarchos (Jeffery 1961, 200, no. 32), whose suffix is
more usually associated with aristocrats. In the first
quarter of the fifth century a sculptor called Kyranaios
executed an expensive and perhaps royal commission at the
Hyperteleaton sanctuary (Jeffery 1961, 201, no. 43). If
he was a Lakonian, as the script of the inscription may
suggest, his name recalls those like Athenaios (Chapter
11) and Chalkideus (Chapter 12) and seems more appropriate
for a citizen than a Perioikos.

The evidence cited so far hardly constitutes proof that
Spartan citizens had once practised a manual craft.
Inferences from archaeological evidence, however, are more
compelling. To begin with, the dogma that only Perioikoi
were responsible for Lakonian art founders on the rock of
the continuity of Lakonian art from the tenth century.
Spartan citizenship may not have been precisely defined
before the eighth century (the Partheniai episode), but it
is hard to believe both that none of the craftsmen working
in Sparta before the seventh century was a descendant of
the Dorians who had settled Sparta in the tenth and that
all craftsmen working in Sparta in the eighth century were
automatically excluded from the citizen body. At any
rate, we know that cooks, like heralds and flautists,
enjoyed hereditary citizen rights in the fifth century
(Hdt. 6.60).

We need not, however, rely on speculation alone. A
burial-group has been excavated in what was the village of
Mesoa at Sparta, comprising four cist-graves marked by a
terracotta relief amphora of c.600 and covered by an
earthen tumulus (Christou 1964). This group has already
been cited for the bones of horses and wild boar found in
the earth. We can now add that nearby were discovered the
remains of a house-wall and - the point of the story - a
potter's kiln. The location of the graves, the elaborate
nature of the funeral rites, possible ancestor-worship,
the hunting-scene depicted on the amphora - these can only
mean that the occupants of the graves were of citizen
status. Thus, as far as Spartan citizens' involvement in
craft-production is concerned, the proper question to ask
is the one to which I sketched an answer at the end of
Chapter 9.

I do not, however, wish to deny that Perioikoi, at
least from the seventh century, played the major role
therein. Far and away the most important function they
will have performed in this connection was the manufacture
and repair of armour and weapons. Copper and tin for the
bronze protective armour had to be imported, but iron for

swords and spearheads was available locally. Metal-
working in Lakonia, however, remained backward down to the
eighth century (Chapter 7), although it is illegitimate to
infer from the story of the Spartiate Lichas marvelling at
a Tegean blacksmith (Hdt. 1.67) that forges were unknown
in Lakonia as late as c.550. Armour and weapons, I
assume, were manufactured in Sparta itself as well as the
Perioikic centres where iron slag has been found (below).
But a problem arises over the mechanism whereby a Spartan
hoplite acquired his equipment.

Most scholars have assumed that he did so by direct
individual purchase in the same way as hoplites in other
states - and indeed Perioikic hoplites. It seems to me,
however, more likely that the Spartan state made itself
somehow responsible for supplying citizens - as from 424
it certainly supplied Helots and Neodamodeis (Chapter 12) -
with their arms and armour. For then the qualification
for hoplite service for a Spartiate would have been on a
par with that for membership of the citizen body, namely
election to a common mess and the ability to contribute to
his mess the minimum fixed quantities of produce and money
discussed earlier in this chapter.

III

I shall conclude my study of Archaic Lakonia and Messenia
by passing in review the Perioikic sites identifiable
archaeologically by 500. There were many more sites than
the thirty or so for which we have archaeological evidence,
but precisely how many is unclear. Herodotus (7.234.2)
says vaguely that there were many, Strabo that in his day
(the turn of our era) there were about thirty 'polichnai'
apart from Sparta itself. But Strabo was referring only
to Lakonia. In 'ancient times', when Sparta had also
controlled Messenia, there were reportedly around 100
Perioikic communities. This report goes back at least to
Androtion (324F49) in the fourth century, but the eighty
or so known by name, mostly contained in the lexicon of
Stephanos, represent a more likely number.

The vast majority of these were in Lakonia. Their
small size as a rule was a natural consequence of the
restricted quantity and quality of the arable land left to
them after the Spartans had taken the most fertile for
themselves. Indeed, it was no doubt precisely because
their land was less desirable that the Perioikoi had not
been transformed into Helots - a line of argument which
would, incidentally, rule out the suggestion of Hampl
(1937, 35f.) that Perioikoi too had Helots. Sparta did

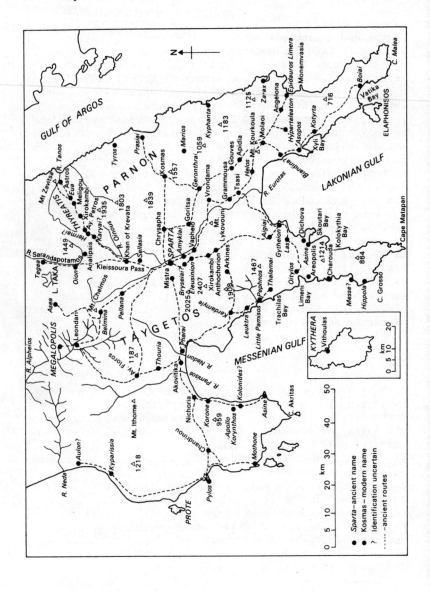

FIGURE 17   Routes in Lakonia and Messenia

not actively encourage, and may have generally discouraged, combinations between the Perioikic communities; it is noticeable that independence in the second century was swiftly followed by some form of confederation. But no attempt was made to disband the 'synoecism' of Boiai (Chapter 9) or the 'Tripolis' in northern Lakonia to which Pellana belonged (Polyb. 4.81.7; Livy 35.27.9).

Where possible, in my survey I shall follow the lines of the ancient routes (Figure 17). For although Lakonia was notoriously hard to penetrate from outside (Eur. fr. 1083; Xen. 'Hell.' 6.5.24; 'Anth. Pal.' 7.723.1), it was of paramount strategic and economic importance to the Spartans to be able to communicate both within Lakonia and with Messenia. The importance can be gauged from the fact that it was the responsibility of the kings, presumably qua generals, to 'give judgment in all matters concerning public highways' (Hdt. 6.57.4). These highways, however, were probably the handful of arterial routes suitable for the transport of Helot produce or military supplies by wooden cart or waggon (cf. Xen. 'Hell.' 7.4.22). Theophrastos ('Hist. Plant.' 3.16.3) mentions a type of oak used for carts in Lakonia. The remainder perhaps approximated more nearly to the Greek norm, being hardly more than footpaths or bridlepaths, many barely suitable even for pack-animals.

The most convenient route linking Sparta with central Peloponnese followed the Eurotas furrow northwestwards as far as the small plain at the foot of Mount Chelmos, the site of ancient Belmina, where it split and continued either to the plain of Asea or to the Megalopolis basin. En route it took in the unidentifiable Charakoma and Perioikic Pellana (Paus. 3.21.3). The latter lay at Kalyvia Georgitsi about twenty-seven kilometres by road from Sparta. The settlement was probably centred on the hill of Palaiokastro, where the walling of a small ruined mediaeval fort may incorporate earlier Greek work and black-painted sherds have been found on the surface. Trial excavations yielded a small black-painted oinochoe and an iron spearhead. The site is favourable, lying in a fertile plain and fed by a nearby perennial spring. Pellana's claim to be the birthplace of the Dioskouroi was challenged by little Pephnos in north-west Mani, but Alkman (fr. 23) sensibly sought a compromise, no doubt chiefly to conciliate the strategically vital Pellana when Sparta was turning its aggressive attentions to Arkadia.

Belmina was also strategically crucial. Mount Chelmos overlooks the whole upper Eurotas valley. On its summit are preserved the extensive remains of fortification walls, some of which go back to the third-century or earlier

'Athenaion' (Polyb. 2.46.5; Plut. 'Kleom.' 4.1). Remains
of house-walls associated with Classical black-painted
pottery were found a short way south, and from the village
of Petrina about four kilometres north-west comes a limestone relief of 500-475 depicting a naked youth with a
snake rearing up before him. This must belong to the
series of such funerary reliefs made in Lakonia in the
last six centuries BC and found all over the region.

To reach Tegea, a route via the old Khan of Krevata and
bypassing Sellasia was followed through the Kleissoura
pass and the bed of the Sarandapotamos. Perioikic
Sellasia, which lay on the border of the territory held
directly by Sparta (Xen. 'Hell.' 2.2.13, 19), was situated
most probably on the hill of Palaiogulas, some twelve
kilometres north of Sparta and close to the west bank of
the Kelephina (ancient Oinous). Excavation has revealed a
rubble circuit-wall and sherds from the fifth to second
centuries. A stone relief of the sixth century, dedicated
by a Pleistiadas to the Tyndaridai (Jeffery 1961, 200, no.
24), was found in modern Sellasia further west.

At the old Khan of Krevata the route joins up with
those leading to the villages of north Parnon and the
Thyreatis; Chateaubriand in 1806 bitterly noted that they
were among the roughest and wildest in Greece. Since
drinking water is not available in the Kleissoura, the
muletrack via Arachova (ancient Karyai) was sometimes
preferred for journeying to Tegea. Ancient Karyai lay on
the border of Lakedaimon (Thuc. 5.55.3), but has not been
certainly located. K. Rhomaios, a native of the area,
initially placed it at Analipsis, the hill about four
kilometres west of Vourvoura close to the junction of the
routes from Sparta to Tegea and the Thyreatis. Later, he
preferred to identify Analipsis with Iasos or Iasaia
(Paus. 7.13.7; 8.27.3). The hill was the site of an
extensive Classical and Hellenistic settlement, encircled
by a wall of polygonal style. Earlier occupation is
attested by Geometric pottery (Chapter 8) and a few
Archaic finds, including terracotta figurines and small
lead wreaths. In the Sarandapotamos river west of Vourvoura a tiny bronze 'bucket' was fished up at the end of
the last century, inscribed 'Alphios' in lettering of
c.500 (cf. Chapter 1).

The pass over Parnon to the Thyreatis continues north-
east from Karyai to Ay. Petros. Just before the crest of
the ridge forming the watershed of water flowing to the
bay of Astros, Tegea and Sparta are three heaps of stones,
each about five metres in diameter, the whole forming a
triangle. Their identification with the Hermai (Paus. 2.
38.7) is not proved, but there was an Archaic sanctuary

here. Rhomaios excavated a schist slab bearing a sixth-century inscription, a small fragment of an Archaic terracotta gorgoneion, a broken spherical aryballos and some scraps of roof-tiles and black-painted pottery.

From Ay. Petros (the site of a well-preserved fourth-century kiln) the route leads to Xirokambi, Helleniko (ancient Eua), Meligou (?ancient Anthana) and Astros (near ancient Thyrea). The sixth-century finds from Meligou and Astros have already been cited (Chapter 9). A secondary route leads from Helleniko via a monastery of St Luke to the foot of Mount Zavitsa, the northern boundary of the Thyreatis. An inscription of c.500 from Mount Zavitsa (SEG XIII.266) marked an Argive cenotaph commemorating an otherwise unrecorded battle with the Spartans, perhaps to be connected with the Sepeia campaign. Communications within the Thyreatis are difficult by land, so most traffic will have been by sea. Ancient Tyros well illustrates the point: it lies between Astros, whose natural lines of communication are to the north, and Leonidhion (ancient Prasiai), whose links are southwards; and the routes across Parnon from the Eurotas valley lead to Astros and Leonidhion.

On the principal pass across Parnon, from Chrysapha or Geraki (ancient Geronthrai) to Leonidhion, lies modern Kosmas, which is possibly to be identified with ancient Glympeis or Glyppia. Bronze figurines have been found sporadically here, the most notable being a resplendent hoplite dedicated to Apollo Maleatas by one Charillos c.525 (Jeffery 1961, 200, no. 37). A considerable scatter of black-painted sherds on the hill Proph. Elias prompted an excavation, which revealed the existence of a Classical fort stocked with iron spearheads and arrowheads, small knives and pointed bronze objects (apparently missiles).

The only other Perioikic site on the east coast of Lakonia known to have been inhabited by 500 is Epidauros Limera (Chapter 9), whose epithet is probably a tribute to its harbour. The town could be reached from Sparta by skirting Parnon via Chrysapha, Goritsa, Geraki and Apidia (?ancient Palaia); ancient wheel-ruts have been detected between Goritsa and Geraki. Chrysapha lies twenty kilometres south-east of Sparta and has been doubtfully identified with ancient Therapne (Appendix 2). About three kilometres south of the village is a hill which is the reported provenance of a fine hero-relief of 550-530 (now in the Pergamon Museum, East Berlin). One of the two dead portrayed holds a pomegranate in her hand, as does one of the two diminutive worshippers; the other worshipper bears a cock. The hill itself is scattered with iron slag and a good deal of Classical pottery, and I would therefore adjudge the site to have been Perioikic.

Geraki has yielded several of the series of hero-reliefs, including what seems to be the earliest of all. Yet more important, however, are the fragments of two Archaic korai, tne only such figures known from Lakonia (Ridgway 1977, 90, 114), and an inscription of c.500 concerning Apelon, the Doric form of Apollo (Le Roy 1974, 220-2). Also worth mentioning are three lists of names of the same date, one certainly a victor-list (SEG XVII.189), the others possibly so (Jeffery 1961, 201, nos 45-6). One of the names recorded is Tebukios, which has been interpreted as an epichoric form of Homeric Teukros. A tomb near Gouves not far away has produced aryballoi described as 'orientalizing' and so possibly Archaic; the settlement to which the tomb belonged probably lay on the Geronthrai-Palaia route. About sixteen kilometres east-north-east of Geraki across Parnon lay ancient Marios. Near the ancient akropolis there are fine springs, and a small bronze horse and another list of names of c.500 were discovered close by. On the akropolis itself some of the roughly squared walling may go back to the first half of the fifth century.

The 'Hyakinthian Way' (Athen. 4.173F) between Sparta and Amyklai, along which the common messes lay, ran on a short distance to Vapheio. A little south of here the road bifurcated, the left fork continuing along the Eurotas to Mount Lykovouni, crossing the river by ruined Vasilo-Perama and thence following the left bank to what is now the Helos plain. Below Vrondama the ancient route can be followed in sections for almost the whole way between Grammousa and Tsasi. About 200 m. west of Tsasi a hill is sprinkled with sherds, including perhaps some Archaic.

Near Tsasi there is a second fork in the road, one branch going eastwards to ancient Helos (general region of Vezani), the other continuing south to Gytheion and skirting the Helos plain. From Vezani the road continued through the pass of Mount Kourkoula to Molaoi and thence either to Epidauros Limera or via Plytra (ancient Asopos) to Neapolis (ancient Boiai).

In the hills surrounding the Molaoi plain, midway between the plain and Monemvasia, lies the village of Angelona. A short distance east of here an Archaic and Classical heroon was excavated, which yielded for example miniature votive kantharoi, a few terracotta figurines and two loomweights. The surface finds were even more impressive, in particular a bronze snake and the base of a marble statue, both late Archaic. The heroon perhaps belonged to the territory of Epidauros Limera.

Not far north-east of Asopos lay the Hyperteleaton, which may once have been attached to Perioikic Leuke or Leukai (Polyb. 4.36.5; 5.19.8; Livy 35.27.3). Numerous inscriptions have been found here, mainly Hellenistic and Roman in date, although some bronze vessels and a stone lustral basin were inscribed before 500 (SEG XI.908). The most interesting Archaic finds, however, are the temple itself, a long narrow structure; and a bronze figurine of an oldish man carrying a hydria, whom one is tempted to identify as the owner of a hydria workshop (but see Rolley 1977, 130 and fig.7).

In the small plain on the coast south of Plytra lies Daimonia (ancient Kotyrta), where a rare black-figure sherd has turned up. In the Vatika plain behind Neapolis a fragmentary Archaic kylix has been reported from Ay. Georgios. Perioikic Boiai will presumably always have been in fairly close contact with Kythera. Iron slag from Vithoulas not far from the northern harbour of Ay. Pelayia corresponds to the slag from Neapolis. The sixth-century finds from Kythera town and a coin-hoard (buried c.525-500) have already been mentioned. Worth adding here is a black-painted mug of c.500 from Gonies inscribed 'hemikotylion' (IG V.1.945).

The direct route from Sparta to Gytheion has been outlined above. An alternative route skirted Taygetos via Bryseiai (not precisely located: see Appendix 2), the Eleusinion at Kalyvia tis Sochas and Xirokambi. The settlement at Anthochorion (Chapter 7) lay about two kilo-metres south-east of Xirokambi. Archaic finds included lead figurines, suggesting the existence of a sanctuary.

Thirty stades before Gytheion, according to Pausanias (3.21.5), to the right of the road lay Aigiai. This has been plausibly located at Palaiochora, where farmers have unearthed Archaic terracottas and bronzes, the latter including a figurine of Zeus (?) and a bowl dedicated apparently to Athena. At Gytheion itself, however, sixth-century archaeological evidence is rather slight: a bronze figurine of Hermes, an engraved gem (perhaps made on Euboia), and two inscriptions in the living rock (one already cited, the other a dedication to Zeus Kappotas). The floruit of the town seems not yet to have arrived.

The obvious route from Gytheion into the Tainaron peninsula, perhaps taken already by Teleklos (Chapter 8), followed the modern road to Areopolis via the Karyoupolis divide. Along this lay ancient Las (modern Chosiaro), whose sixth-century products include a pyramidal stone 'herm' of a ram-headed deity, probably Apollo Karneios, and a fragmentary hero-relief. At Dichova near Kamares on the west coast of the Lakonian Gulf between Ageranos

(probably ancient Arainos) and Skoutari (ancient Asine)
disiecta membra of an Archaic temple to Aphrodite have
recently come to light.

Communications in south Mani were perhaps always
desultory. Between Oitylon (ancient Oitylos) and Mezapos
(ancient Messe?) a sixth-century marble hero-relief (now
in the Sparta Museum) was built into a mediaeval church at
Charouda. It depicts a nude male figure with his hoplite
equipment on the ground before him. Another Perioikic
hoplite, then, but hardly from barren Charouda and so
perhaps from Messe. South of Messe at ancient Hippola,
occupied certainly by the seventh century (Chapter 8),
there has been found Lakonian black-figure pottery of the
sixth.

From Oitylon an ancient road may have run along the
coast to Kalamata (ancient Pharai). Wheel-tracks, but of
uncertain date, have been noted between Koutiphari
(ancient Thalamai) and Platsa; near Levtro (ancient
Leuktra); and north of Kardamyli (ancient Kardamyle). The
main attractions of Thalamai's site were two natural
springs. Sixth-century finds include a Doric capital in
the local limestone and the elaborate handle of a bronze
hydria, but for the historian the main significance lies
in the oracular shrine of Ino-Pasiphae, in which the
Spartans took a direct, political interest (Oliva 1971,
131 n. 1). The cult is attested for the fifth century
(IG V.1.1316), but it is not known when or why the Spartan
involvement began. A fourth-century dedication by a
member of the Spartan Gerousia (IG V.1.1317) presumably
gives a terminus ante quem.

Kardamyle was blessed with a defensible akropolis as
well as the harbour, limestone and lead-deposits already
mentioned. Sixth-century objects from here include a
Doric capital and a bronze figurine of a bull. Another
such figurine has been found in Kalamata, as well as a
sherd from a black-figure krater. In the valley of the
Nedon close by several names of uncertain significance
were incised c.500 on a smoothed surface of rock (Jeffery
1961, 206, no. 5).

From Kalamata main routes radiated north along the
eastern side of the Pamisos valley via Hellenika (ancient
Thouria) and Ay. Floros to the Leondari pass into Arkadia;
north-west to Ithome and the Stenyklaros plain; and west
to Pylos via Akovitika, Nichoria and Chandrinou.

At Ay. Floros was built the temple of the river-god
Pamisos. (Compare perhaps the bucket inscribed 'Alphios'
and Kleomenes' sacrifice to the god of the Erasinos.)
This has yielded the earliest known Messenian inscription,
a dedication of c.550 (Jeffery 1961, 206, no. 1).

Akovitika on the east bank of the Pamisos was of great
prehistoric significance (Chapter 4). In historical times
it was the site of a sanctuary of Pohoidan (Poseidon), the
identification being guaranteed by dedications inscribed
on sixth-century and later pottery. It was presumably
here that the Pohoidaia festival managed by Thouria was
held. Of the other sixth-century dedications particularly
noteworthy are the bronze figurines apparently made by a
school of local craftsmen (Leon 1968).

The latter may also have been responsible for the
bronze figurine of Hermes dedicated to Zeus at Ithome
c.525 (Athens, N.M.7539: Lamb 1926, 138, no. 9; I cannot
accept Miss Lamb's attribution to an Arkadian workshop).
This figurine is perhaps the sole material evidence that
the cult of Zeus Ithomatas was maintained between the late
eighth century (attested by an ithyphallic terracotta) and
the mid-fifth, and one wonders whether a Helot would have
been able to afford so costly a dedication.

Nichoria (?ancient Aipeia) is exceptionally well
situated for both agricultural and strategic purposes, but
was apparently abandoned c.750, perhaps following the
intervention of Teleklos (Coldstream 1977, 164). Chandrinou, however, has produced an Archaic bronze figurine of
a horseman (now in the National Museum, Athens).

To south of Nichoria ran the route to Koroni (ancient
Asine) bypassing the sanctuary of Apollo Korynthos, which
may have been attached to the predecessor of ancient
Kolonides (founded in the 360s). This Apollo received a
sixth-century bronze figurine of a hoplite second in
quality only to the one dedicated to the Apollo of Kosmas.
An inscribed spear-butt of the early fifth century main-
tains the martial flavour. A PC sherd is reported from
Koroni, but there is nothing from the sixth century,
although the harbour may already have been used by the
Spartans before 500 (cf. Hdt. 8.73.3). North of Nichoria
ran another route to the Stenyklaros plain.

From Chandrinou a route led south-westwards to ancient
Mothone, where late Archaic pottery has been found in
cist-graves. A road presumably linked Mothone to Pylos,
whence a coastal route led via Kyparissia (ancient
Kyparissia) to Aulon (Chapter 13). An Archaic head has
been found at Kyparissia, and on the offshore island of
Prote graffiti begin in the sixth century (Jeffery 1961,
206, no. 2). Most of these are concerned with sailing
ventures, but ironically it was the arrival of an
Athenian fleet in 425 which put the area on the map and
gave it a significance most unwelcome to the landlubbing
Spartans.

NOTES ON FURTHER READING

Helots

Most of the ancient sources and a representative selection
of the more influential modern views are brought together
in Toynbee 1969, 195–203, and Oliva 1971, 38–48. For the
use of Helots in war, not directly attested before 494,
see Welwei 1974, 108–74, which also touches on many other
aspects of their status.

The groups of dependent labourers classified as
'between free men and slaves' are discussed in Lotze 1959
(26–47 on the Helots), Finley 1964, and Austin and Vidal-
Naquet 1977, ch. 4. For chattel slavery, with which
Helotage is to be compared and contrasted, see the studies
reprinted in Finley 1968b, and Finley 1976 (a succinct
summary of its essential character). The quantity of
recent excellent work on chattel slavery in the Old South
is prodigious: see the bibliography in Weinstein and
Gatell 1973, 411–39. Degler 1970, a comparative survey of
slavery in Brazil and the southern States in the nineteenth century, is full of suggestive analogies and
contrasts to the ancient experience on such matters as
reproduction, family-life, religion and revolts.

For modern work on Spartan land-tenure see Oliva 1971,
32–8, 48–54; his discussion of the ancient evidence is
less satisfactory. Lotze 1971 tries to determine (1) the
boundaries of the land held directly by Spartan citizens
and the Spartan state; (2) the number of kleroi or at
least citizens; (3) the quantities of produce handed over
by Helots; and (4) the proportion of Spartiates to Helots.
He rightly stresses that the literary evidence is reliable, if at all, only for Agis and Kleomenes, but, like
Roebuck 1945 (on Messenia, mainly after the liberation),
he makes insufficient allowance for our ignorance of
crucial quantitative data; and, like Jardé (below), he is
not aware of the altered geomorphology of modern Lakonia
and Messenia.

On cereal-growing in ancient Greece generally see Jardé
1925; but his attempt (109–15) to calculate the size of
yields in Lakonia and Messenia fails to distinguish
between Spartiate and Perioikic land. The view that there
was a marked shift from pasturage to cereal-growing in the
eighth century has been most persuasively advanced by
Snodgrass (1977, 12–15). The instruments and techniques
involved are discussed in Moritz 1958 and by W. Schiering
in Richter 1968, 147–58.

On olive-cultivation in modern Greece see ESAG no. 316;
also Richter 1968, 137–40 for ancient Greece, and White

1970, 225ff. for ancient Italy.

For early Greek hunting in general see Buchholz 1973.
The 'Lakonian' hound in literature is considered in Hull
1964, 31-4; in visual art by Freyer-Schauenberg (1970).

Perioikoi

Useful summary accounts of their origins, status and
functions may be found in Toynbee 1969, 204-12, and Oliva
1971, 55-62. Gschnitzer 1958, 66ff., 188, is a useful
collection of the ancient evidence, but his interpretation
suffers from the thesis, adopted from Hampl 1937, that the
Spartans were an aristocratic group, the Perioikoi the
Dorian commons. The fullest periegesis of the individual
towns is Niese 1906; see also Boelte 1929, 1303-21.

The military functions of the Perioikoi will be looked
at more fully in Part II. For their economic role see now
Ridley 1973; it seems, however, he has set up an 'Aunt
Sally' by arguing against 'the still standard view that
they were basically an industrial and commercial class'.
For even if most Perioikoi were somehow engaged in
agriculture, this would not exclude the existence of
Perioikic mining contractors, merchants, small traders,
craftsmen and so on. As for Ridley's doubts that the
Perioikoi could have so faithfully reflected Spartan
values, Holladay (1977a, 123) has rightly observed that
'subjected groups have often tended to accept and emulate
the values ... of dominating groups'. I am not, however,
sure I agree with Holladay that life in a Perioikic town
might not have differed substantially from life at Sparta.

Part III
Classical Laconia c. 500–362BC

II The crisis of Lakonia 490-460

Herodotus is generally acknowledged, even by thoroughgoing sceptics like C. Hignett (1963), as our primary
source for Xerxes' invasion of Greece. It is no less
generally recognized, however, that his account of its
immediate antecedents - the period from Marathon to the
Isthmus Congress of 481, punctuated by the death of Darius
in 486 - is wholly unsatisfactory. Herodotus assumes,
perhaps rightly, that a full-scale Persian campaign of
conquest in Greece was inevitable after 490, but instead
of discussing in detail the attitudes and responses of the
Greeks to the barbarian menace he indulges his theological
and dramatic bent by casting Xerxes' expedition in the
form of a tragedy with full supernatural apparatus. Part
of the reason for this one-sided approach was no doubt the
kind of Greek sources he had available or chose to use.
The treatment of the role of Themistokles is only the most
notorious product of biased reporting. However, the
history of Sparta is equally personalized and distorted by
being presented, fitfully, through the medium of Damaratos,
one of Herodotus' most audaciously exploited dramatis
personae (and sufficiently impressive to excite the muse
of C.P. Cavafy).

Damaratos, it will be recalled, had been deposed from
the kingship in c.491 at the instigation of Kleomenes, who
was then - as even Herodotus conceded - pursuing a
thoroughly 'panhellenic', anti-Persian foreign policy.
The motive for Damaratos' opposition to Kleomenes'
coercion of medizing Aigina is not specified and probably
not creditable, but not even Herodotus could turn a blind
eye to Damaratos' subsequent, unambiguous medism. I put
it this way because Herodotus' account of Damaratos'
career after his deposition is quite remarkably sympathetic. Both the alleged suicide of Kleomenes in c.491
(6.84.3) and the death in exile over twenty years later of
Latychidas (6.72.1) are explained as retribution for their

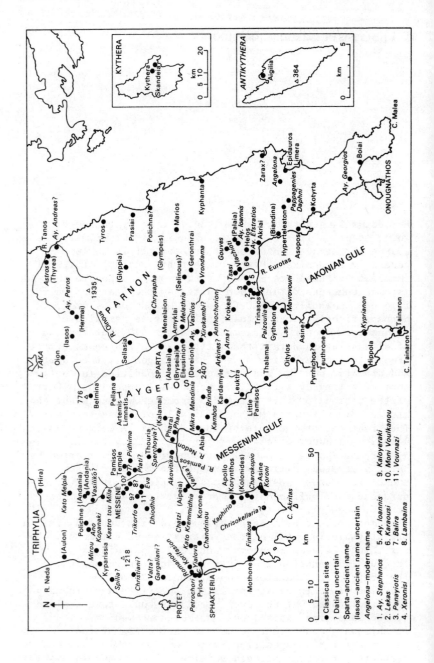

FIGURE 18   Classical sites in Lakonia and Messenia

engineering of the deposition of Damaratos. His self-
imposed exile from Sparta soon after being dethroned is
ascribed to an intolerable insult from Latychidas (6.67),
and he is made to say that the insult will be the source
of countless blessings or (what Herodotus clearly believed)
troubles for Sparta. His flight to Persia is represented
as enforced upon him because the Spartans would not permit
his exile in Elis (6.72), although Herodotus does not say
why they would not nor why Damaratos chose to go first to
Elis (see below). His extremely favourable treatment at
the hands of Darius is recorded without comment (6.70.2;
7.104.2), and he is then introduced at several important
junctures in the narrative of Xerxes' invasion to serve as
a mouthpiece for Herodotus' ideas, even when this results
in the psychologically implausible situation of the
unjustly exiled king lauding Sparta to the skies for
embodying the rule of 'nomos' (law: 7.102.2).

The reason for this favourable and circumstantial
account of Damaratos' medism is doubtless that Herodotus
had talked to Damaratos' descendants in the Troad, where
they were still ensconced in the time of Xenophon (Lewis
1977, 54 and nn. 29-30). But revealing though this is of
Herodotus' historical methods it is less important in the
immediate context than Damaratos' alleged role in bringing
the proposed Persian invasion to the notice of the Greeks.
The chapter describing the concealed message sent by Damaratos to Sparta (7.239) has in fact been suspected as an
interpolation, but it poses no more difficulties than the
formally similar story of how the Milesian Histiaios, also
at Susa, allegedly urged the Ionians to revolt from Persia;
and it accords perfectly with the generally favourable
picture of Damaratos that Herodotus is so anxious to
paint. However, whether or not it was Damaratos' doing,
it is not implausible that the Spartans should have been
the first of the Greeks to hear of the Great King's design
on their land. For as leaders of the Greeks their
reaction to this intelligence would have been one of the
first to be canvassed, and the Greeks, we are told
(7.138.1), had ample advance warning of the invasion.

Xerxes took four years to prepare his expedition, so it
was perhaps not long after 485 that the Spartans sent to
Delphi, as was their wont, to ask Apollo what attitude
they should adopt (7.220). The god's response, in accordance with his general line at this time, was blatantly
medizing: either Sparta would lose a king in battle or the
Persians would overrun Lakonia. Since Sparta had never
yet lost a king in battle, the message was plainly
intended to discourage resistance. It was at this awkward
juncture, I believe, that the Spartans took the extra-

ordinary – indeed, so far as we know, unique – step of
holding repeated assemblies, at which the sole agendum was
'Is anyone willing to die for the fatherland?' (7.134).
Herodotus does not link the news from Susa with these
assemblies. He is primarily interested in the 'wrath of
Talthybios', whereby two Spartan heralds paid the penalty
in 430 for the Spartans' impious treatment of Darius'
herald in 492; and it is somewhat incidental that the
fathers of these two heralds were the men who had volunteered to die for the fatherland between 485 and 481.
However, as the Spartans 'esteemed the things of heaven
more highly than the things of men' (5.63.2), it is just
conceivable that the volunteers, who were leading aristocrats and so not lightly dispensable, were sent as a kind
of expiatory and at the same time apotropaic sacrifice to
Xerxes. Alternatively, and more prosaically, they went as
ambassadors in the ordinary way to discover whether Xerxes
was prepared to consider a diplomatic rather than a
military settlement.

When it was learned that he was not, it is to Sparta's
credit that (so far as we know) no attempt was made to
give earth and water. For most of the Greek states which
had not been incorporated into the Persian empire by
Darius were medizing, whether positively (7.138.2) or
negatively (by remaining neutral: 8.73.3); and there must
have been more than a few Spartans who believed that the
Athenians should suffer for a war they had provoked without consulting the Spartans (8.142.2). As it was, Sparta
was unanimously adopted as leader of the loyalist Greeks
who met at the Isthmus of Corinth in autumn 481 to form
what is usually known today (from Hdt. 7.205.3) as the
'Hellenic League', to distinguish it from the pre-existing
Peloponnesian League and the subsequent Delian League.
Herodotus, however, is typically unhelpful in dealing with
the organization of the loyalist alliance. He speaks
generally of mutual pledges, but mentions only two specific decisions, those to suspend internal disputes and
to send ambassadors to persuade the Argives, Gelon of
Syracuse and the Cretans to join the alliance (7.145).
The remaining details have to be inferred from Herodotus'
narrative.

The Hellenic League was an offensive and defensive
alliance with one state, Sparta, recognized as the overall
leader. If we can believe Herodotus, Sparta had been
regarded as 'leader of the Greeks' since the middle of the
previous century (1.69.2; 141.4; 152.3; 5.49.2); but for
the period 481–479 he simply assumes Sparta's position
(cf. Thuc. 1.18.2), and allows it to emerge indirectly.
Thus the claims of Argos and Athens to joint, and of Gelon

to sole, command are all rejected out of hand by Sparta
and the other allies, if indeed they were seriously (or
actually) put forward; and Spartans hold the supreme
command of either the naval or the land forces and once
(Latychidas briefly in spring 479) of both at the same
time. On the other hand, although the decisions
eventually taken by Spartan commanders are regarded as
final and binding on the other Greek states in the alliance, Herodotus makes it abundantly clear that the
Spartans were by no means always responsible for initiat-
ing strategy and tactics. Indeed, on the central issue of
which Greek state deserved the most credit for preserving
Greek independence, Herodotus silently rejects the claim
of Sparta. The fairness of this judgment may be assessed
from the following account, which will concentrate on the
main engagements and in particular on the way in which
Sparta's conduct of the war was conditioned by its
position in Lakonia and the Peloponnese.

Herodotus does not comment on the choice of the Isthmus
of Corinth as the general headquarters of the loyalists,
but it presumably recommended itself in the first instance
for its geographical centrality. From here the first
allied force of some 10,000 hoplites was sent out by sea
to the Pass of Tempe separating Thessaly from Macedonia,
in order to secure the militarily exposed and politically
divided Thessalians for the loyalist cause (7.173). It
returned a few days later, mission unaccomplished, to be
replaced by the first serious attempt at resisting the
Persians in a joint land-sea operation. It is not,
however, entirely clear that Herodotus fully appreciated
the Persian strategy of keeping the fleet and land-army in
close communication with each other (7.49, 236.2; 8.60a)
or the necessity for the Greeks to counter this strategy
by adopting it themselves (8.15.2). He may therefore have
misunderstood the objective of the defence of the Thermopylai pass from Thessaly into Phokis undertaken in
conjunction with the fleet stationed off northern Euboia.
But even if he did not, his account is full of other
puzzles, which have only been exacerbated by the recent
discovery at Troizen of the possibly forged 'Themistokles
Decree' (Fornara 1977, no. 55).

First, there is the question of numbers. Those on the
Persian side (7.60, 89, 184-6) are of course hugely
exaggerated (Cawkwell 1968); faced with Herodotus'
1,700,000 land troops, one is tempted to remind him of his
own scathing comment that 'neither the Ionians nor any of
the other Greeks know how to count' (2.16.1). But this
comment is even more apropos when we consider his woeful
mishandling of the numbers on the Greek side at Thermopylai.

He quotes (7.228) an honorific inscription which quite
plainly states that 4,000 Peloponnesians had fought there,
but later (8.25.2) appears to take this figure as the
number of those (not only Peloponnesians) who died in the
pass. Moreover, in his own enumeration of the Greek force
sent to Thermopylai (7.202) the Peloponnesian contingent
adds up to only 3,100. The simplest explanation of the
discrepancy is that Herodotus in his enthusiasm for the
derring-do of Leonidas and his 300 picked Spartiates has
forgotten the 900 or 1,000 'Lakedaimonians' (i.e.
Perioikoi) mentioned in Diodorus (11.4.2,5) and Isokrates
(4.90). These Perioikoi would be the first known from
literary evidence to have participated with Spartans on
campaign.

The other major problem concerns the composition of the
Greek forces under Leonidas' command. The presence of
eighty hoplites from Mykenai is to be explained as a
consequence of the liberation of this town by Kleomenes
from Argos, which in 480 was in effect medizing. The
absence of men from Tiryns is slightly surprising,
especially as they turn up alongside the Mykenaians at
Plataia. But the biggest question-marks are these: why
was more than half the Peloponnesian contingent drawn from
Arkadia, while Corinth, in whose territory lay the general
headquarters, provided a mere 400 men (some hoplites may
of course have been serving at Artemision)? And why did
Sparta send even fewer of its citizens than Corinth? The
first of these questions, both of which are unanswerable,
is less crucial than the second, which introduces the
'final problem' of Thermopylai.

According to Herodotus, the Spartans through Leonidas
(who had succeeded his half-brother Kleomenes) claimed that
this force was merely an advance guard (7.203). The Spartans would be sending a full contingent when the Karneia
was over; the other allies, a minority of whom were
Dorians, were to follow suit after celebrating the Olympic
Games (7.206). However, Leonidas clearly interpreted his
mission as being in effect akin to that of a Kamikaze
squadron. For although he took with him 300 men, which
was the number of the Hippeis (the crack royal bodyguard
selected from the ten youngest age-classes), he deliberately chose men who already had sons and so men who were
not all Hippeis. Had he really been meant to hold the pass
until the Karneia and the Olympics were over, he would
presumably have taken, if not more troops, at least the
best Spartan warriors rather than the best of those who
had sons. Here is the first concrete sign of that drastic
fall in citizen manpower which had become critical by 425.

Sparta has therefore been accused of pursuing a narrow

and Peloponnesian policy in sending an inadequate force to
Thermopylai. To this charge, however, three replies are
possible. First, it might be argued that the force was
adequate for its stated purpose, and that the cardinal
though excusable error was that of Leonidas in posting the
unreliable Phokians to guard the pass (discussed in Gomme
1956, 397f.) through which the Greek position was eventually turned. Second, believers in the authenticity of the
Themistokles Decree or disbelievers in Herodotus' chronology could point out that Themistokles had already
persuaded the Athenians to envisage the abandonment of
Attika even before the defence of Thermopylai was undertaken, whereas in Herodotus the retreat to the Isthmus
appears as the necessary consequence of the pass being
forced sooner than anticipated. Third, those who still
think that Leonidas' force was inadequate and are not
convinced that the Themistokles Decree is authentic can
yet argue that Sparta' policy was narrow and Peloponnesian
from necessity rather than choice and that with the con-
straints imposed Sparta did the best possible.

For, as even Herodotus' generally unsympathetic account
makes clear, Sparta genuinely did have difficulties in the
Peloponnese at this time, not only from Argos, but also
from Peloponnesian League allies. Some time in the 480s
Tegea was hostile to Sparta (9.37.4); in 479 Elis (significantly, the first refuge of Damaratos) and Mantineia
were suspiciously late for Plataia, apparently because
their leaders had been medizing (9.77); and within a
decade all these were in open revolt from Spartan hegemony
assisted by a somewhat revitalized Argos. Besides − a
point Herodotus fails to mention − Perioikic Karyai is
reported, admittedly only by Vitruvius (1.1.5), to have
medized. The strategic importance of Karyai to Sparta has
been emphasized already, an importance symbolized by the
fact that Spartan girls participated in the cultic dancing
at the temple of Artemis Karyatis (Burkert 1965, 172).
Here we need only repeat that Karyai lay on the border
with Tegea and en route to medizing Argos.

Seen in this light, the despatch of 300 picked citizens
and a king in effect to their deaths acquires an almost
heroic aura; and this is certainly how the behaviour of
these men struck most other Greeks (cf. Simonides fr. 26
Page) − and indeed the Persians. We, however, should not
forget the Perioikoi, who alone remained with the
Thespians and the reluctant Thebans to withstand the final
assault, nor indeed the Helot shield-bearers (8.25.1, with
Welwei 1974, 125 and n. 21), not all of whom emulated the
one who took to his heels after leading his blinded master
to the fray (7.229.1).

The Greek fleet at Artemision was commanded by Eurybiadas, who like his predecessor at Tempe and Anchimolios
in c.512 was not of royal blood. A mere ten of the 271
ships were provided by the Lakedaimonians, and these were
presumably manned by Perioikoi or Helots. The skirmishes
with the Persian fleet, weakened already by losses in
storms, were surprisingly successful from the Greek
standpoint, but the forcing of Thermopylai rendered the
station at Artemision untenable. Withdrawal was anyway
apparently greatly to the taste of Eurybiadas, who cuts a
poor figure in Herodotus. For even before the defeat at
Thermopylai he had contemplated withdrawal (8.4.2) and had
had to be bribed to stay put (8.5.1,3). Then, after
ruling out fighting off Attika (8.49.1) and voting to
fight 'on behalf of' or 'at' the Isthmus (8.56), he is
only reluctantly persuaded to remain at Salamis (8.64.1).
Presumably he shared the views of most Peloponnesians, who
were now encamped under the command of Leonidas' brother
and successor Kleombrotos at the Isthmus and desperately
throwing a fortification wall (which has left no certain
archaeological trace) across its six-kilometre narrowest
width (8.40.2, 71). Herodotus, however, insists, rightly,
that such a wall would have been futile without a fleet to
counter the Persians at sea. Indeed, it is on this very
point that he felt 'constrained to deliver an opinion,
which most men, I know, will dislike, but which, as it
seems to me to be true, I am determined not to withhold.
... the Athenians were the saviours of Greece' (7.139).
By this he means that without the Athenian contribution to
the fleet the Spartans would have had their allies removed
from them one by one as the Persian fleet sailed at will
round the Peloponnese (cf. Thuc. 1.73.4).

In case any reader might be either unclear as to what
Herodotus' view of the matter was or doubtful as to its
truth, Herodotus makes his point in several ways in
addition to this directly expressed personal judgment.
For example, he puts into the mouth of Damaratos the
advice to Xerxes to occupy Kythera (7.235). This would,
he says, distract the Spartans, without whose aid the
cities of the other Peloponnesian Greeks would be easily
taken. Scholars like Fornara (1971, 33f.) have thought
this passage was written by Herodotus in or after 424,
when Kythera was in fact seized by the Athenians and the
spectre of a Helot revolt was raised in the minds of the
Spartans (Thuc. 4.53-6). But Kythera had already been
taken by the Athenians under Tolmides in 456 (Chapter 12),
and Damaratos is made to imply that Chilon in the mid-
sixth century had already anticipated such a use of
Kythera by a foreign power. Above all, if there had

indeed been a Helot revolt in the late 490s, then
Damaratos' advice (or at least the idea he is made to
express) would have been particularly opportune. Xerxes,
however, seems to have been anxious to settle matters once
and for all with the Greek fleet. At least this would
help to explain his rash plunge into the straits of
Salamis and his ensuing defeat. Sparta needless to say
did not contribute greatly to that defeat with its sixteen
ships (8.43). But at least their flotilla had managed to
round the awesome Cape Malea, unlike the considerably
larger and avant-garde (Thuc. 1.14.2) Kerkyraian fleet,
which after putting in at Pylos and Tainaron pleaded
inability to pass Malea as its excuse for absence from
Salamis (7.168; cf. 4.179.2 for the wind off Malea).

The other main way in which Herodotus brings out the
futility of the Spartans' faith in the Isthmus wall is
again through a speech, this time of a more Thucydidean
character and placed in the mouth of the Tegean Chileos,
said to be the foreigner with the greatest influence at
Sparta (9.9.1). The occasion of Chileos' homily is the
Athenian threat to come to terms with the Persians in 479
if the Spartans persist in their failure to send troops
into Boiotia; and, like Herodotus himself, Chileos argues
that the Peloponnese cannot be protected by the Isthmus
wall alone. The alleged cause of the Spartan delay was
not this time the phase of the moon (Marathon) or the
Karneia (Thermopylai) but the Hyakinthia. However, on
hearing the words of Chileos, whose Tegean nationality
will have carried as much weight as his personal influence, the Spartans moved swiftly, thereby illustrating
Thucydides' general rule (1.118.2) that they were
'traditionally slow to go to war, unless they were forced
into it'. The compulsion in this case was a combination
of Athenian blackmail and Peloponnesian unrest.

The details of the Spartans' eventual response give us
our greatest insight to date into the Spartan state at
war. The Ephors made the decision to despatch the troops.
Pausanias, son of the now dead Kleombrotos and Regent for
his under-age cousin Pleistarchos, was given the command,
in which he associated with himself Euryanax, the perhaps
illegitimate son of his uncle Dorieus. Five thousand
Spartiate soldiers were sent off overnight, perhaps 1,000
from each of the five Spartan villages, putting into
practice their deliberately fostered familiarity with
movement in darkness (Xen. 'Lak. Pol.' 5.7; Plut. 'Lyk.'
12.14). They constituted about two thirds of the
Spartiates of military age (20-59), if 'Damaratos' was
correct in saying that the Spartan citizen-body in 480
numbered 8,000 (Hdt. 7.234.2). Two thirds was a normal

figure for a state's full levy on an allied campaign
(Thuc. 2.10; 3.15). To each of the 5,000 there were
reportedly attached seven Helots, but I have suggested in
Chapter 10 that this figure is inflated. More likely to
be right is the figure of 5,000 given for the Perioikic
hoplites who were sent off after the Spartiates the
following morning. Since these are said to have been
picked men (9.11.3), it is possible that they had been
quartered in Sparta for the duration of the war and had
been training with the Spartiates. Herodotus, unfortunately, is not interested in such mundane details, and he
fails to elucidate the relationship between the Spartiate
and Perioikic troops at the battle of Plataia itself
(9.28, 47f. etc.). But perhaps the fact that the two
contingents were despatched separately is enough to show
that Perioikoi and Spartiates were not yet commingled in
the same regiments as they were (or so I argue in Chapter
12) at Mantineia in 418. Each Perioikic hoplite had just
one batman (an inference from Hdt. 9.29, 61.2), possibly
his personal slave. This was the usual ration, obtaining,
for instance, for the Spartiates at Thermopylai.

The route out of Lakonia taken at least by the 5,000
Spartiates went via Orestheion, which appears to have been
situated in the centre of the Oresthis in Arkadian
Mainalia (Thuc. 4.134.1; 5.64.3) and to have been the same
as the Oresthasion of Pausanias (8.44.2) that was later
called Oresteion (Paus. 8.3.2). If these identifications
are correct, then the Spartans were following the route
taken by Agis in 418, not, as has been suggested, to avoid
the Argive frontier, but because this was the easiest way
out of Lakonia for an army travelling with waggons.
Although Orestheion must have lain a short distance south-
west of Megalopolis (not of course built until the 360s),
it seems not to have been unusual for Spartan armies to
march north-north-west to here and yet still turn back
eastwards towards Tegea (A. Andrewes in Gomme 1970, 91-3).

The bulk of Pausanias' Lakedaimonian army waited at the
Isthmus for the other Peloponnesians to rally to the
loyalist cause (9.19.1), but 1,000 men were sent on ahead
into the Megarid (9.14.1). Mardonius, the Persian general
left behind by Xerxes, had meanwhile withdrawn to Plataia,
and here after much manoeuvring for position and preliminary skirmishing (the problem of supplies was perhaps the
greatest the Greeks as a whole ever faced) the Greek and
Persian forces eventually met in a decisive battle. The
Helots are reckoned among the 'light-armed troops' by
Herodotus (9.28.2, 29.1, 61.2), but even if armed they did
no fighting and served as supply troops, armour-bearers
and baggage-carriers (Welwei 1974, 63, 120-6). The

laurels clearly belonged to the heavy-armed citizen
hoplites, above all the disciplined and skilful Spartans.
The generalship of Pausanias has been criticized, but it
was well thought of at the time (Thuc. 1.130.1). The
seers on both sides also deserve a mention, honourable in
the case of Teisamenos, who with his brother had been
received into Spartan citizenship perhaps at Pitana
(Huxley 1975a, 29f.) shortly before 480, a unique grant in
the view of Herodotus (9.35.1); slightly less honourable in
that of Hegesistratos, another Eleian, who seems to have
put the liberation of his own city from Spartan domination
before the 'common good of Greece' and so hired himself
out to the Persians (9.37). Herodotus' casualty-figures
(9.70.5) seem improbably low, but they may not have been
meant for grand totals. Apart from anything else, both
here and in describing the Spartans' burial arrangements
(9.85) he has again forgotten the Perioikoi. Finally, the
booty. We do not know if the Spartans had yet created the
office of the 'booty-sellers' (Pritchett 1974, I, 90),
because Herodotus is only interested in an earlier stage
in the booty's distribution. Pausanias ordered the Helots
to bring in the Persians' gold and silver articles (9.80.
1; cf. 7.119.2, 190; 8.8, 41; 9.106), but they allegedly
managed to withhold a fair amount and later sold what they
could not hoard to the Aiginetans, who had not participated at Plataia (9.85.3). The Aiginetans paid knock-down
prices, since the Helots could not tell gold from bronze.
Thus Herodotus, but the whole story is revealed as a
malicious Athenian joke by Herodotus' obviously false view
that it was from this bargain purchase that the Aiginetans
became extremely wealthy. The innocence of the Helots,
though, is perhaps true to life, but whether they could
have been involved in such a sale of valuable metal-work
is more than doubtful.

According to the loyalist mythology, the remainder of
the retreating Persian army was defeated at Mykale, on the
mainland of Asia Minor opposite Samos, on the same day as
Mardonius was beaten at Plataia (9.100). The leader of
the Greek fleet was Latychidas - the first (and nearly the
last) Spartan king to be appointed admiral - who had
succeeded Eurybiadas in spring 479. Despite the fervent
appeals of an Ionian delegation for 'the Greeks' to
liberate Ionia (8.131.1f.), the fleet had proceeded from
Aigina with the utmost caution and at first only as far as
Delos. Here it was greeted with further 'Hellenic'
appeals from a Samian delegation, through whom Samos was
admitted to the Hellenic League (9.90-2). After yet more
indecision the Greek force, more than half of which was
provided by Athens, at last engaged the Persians on land

at Mykale and won. 'Ionia therefore on this day revolted
a second time from the Persians' (9.104). Next on the
agenda were the Hellespont and the islands (9.101.3).

Now for the first time the Spartans, represented by
Latychidas, were faced with a wider issue than resistance
to a Persian invasion; and, if Herodotus' account is
accurate, they failed the test signally. A proposal was
made by 'the Peloponnesians' to remove the Ionians from
Asia and settle them in the coastal towns of the mainland
Greek medizers (9.106.2f.). This was scarcely diplomatic.
The Ionians' fears of such a transfer had been aroused in
499 by Histiaios, who had lied to them that Darius planned
to place them in Phoenicia (6.3); and in 494 and 490 the
Milesians and Eretrians respectively had indeed been
resettled by the Persians (6.20, 101.3). The 'Peloponnesian' proposal was, however, in line with a strand of
Spartan thinking stretching back to the origins of Graeco-
Persian relations. For although the Spartans had repeatedly claimed to champion all Greeks against Persia, Mykale
was in fact the first time (despite Hdt. 3.56.2) that they
had fought the Persians in Asia, which the Great King in
some sense considered his own preserve (e.g. Hdt. 1.4;
9.116.3).

The speech attributed to Eurybiadas after Salamis
(8.108) precisely captures this Spartan attitude: he would
not follow Themistokles in advancing to destroy the
Hellespont bridge, but he did envisage challenging the
Persian king for his empire at some future date. Likewise
Latychidas, after the 'Peloponnesian authorities' had
withdrawn their proposal to transfer the Ionians to European Greece and the islanders had been admitted to the
Hellenic League (9.106.3), yet declined to follow the
Athenians in liberating the cities of the Hellespont. The
attitude of Herodotus himself emerges from his description
of an essentially Athenian force at Sestos as 'the Greeks'
(9.116.3), but he would have given a more balanced picture
if he had remarked upon the importance of the Hellespont
for the Athenian wheat-supply: Sestos was the 'meal-table
of the Peiraieus' (cf. Ste. Croix 1972, 48).

It is at this point that Thucydides takes up the story
in his tantalizingly brief excursus on the 'Pentekontaëtia'
(1.89-118), the fifty or so years prior to what has come
to be known as 'the' Peloponnesian War. For Herodotus,
everything after the liberation of Sestos was 'after the
war against the Medes' and so outside his brief. However,
apart from a score of references in passing to individual
incidents after 479, he does also make a general comment
on this period: as in the forty or so preceding years
'Greece suffered more misery than in the 600 years before

Darius was born, partly from the wars against the Persians, partly from its own internal struggles for supremacy' (6.98.2). It is precisely the latter, seen from the standpoint of Athens' growing power, with which Thucydides' excursus is concerned; and he begins it with a richly symbolic episode, the rebuilding of the walls of Athens masterminded by Themistokles.

In Herodotus Themistokles is presented in an ambiguous light, thanks to the generally hostile sources the historian chose to follow. Thucydides, silently reacting as so often against his predecessor, put the record straight at the end of another excursus (1.126–38), to which we shall return in a different connection. Two sentences in his encomium are particularly relevant here: 'in estimating what was likely to happen his forecasts were always more reliable than those of others ... he was particularly remarkable at looking into the future and seeing there the hidden possibilities for good or evil' (1.138.3). Written with hindsight, this can only mean that in Thucydides' view Themistokles had in effect foreseen (among other things) the Peloponnesian War. He realized, in other words, that Sparta not Persia was the more likely to pose a threat to Athens in the long run. Indeed, Themistokles seems to have come to this conclusion as early as 479.

Herodotus (8.124) gives us only half the story, when he describes how in the winter of 480–479 Themistokles had been fêted in Sparta and granted a guard of honour to escort him from Sparta to the Tegean border. For in 479, despite his alleged appeal to the common good of the Hellenic League, Themistokles was prepared to risk an open breach with Sparta by resisting with trickery the 'request' made by the Spartans, at the urging of their allies, that the Athenians should not rebuild their walls (Thuc. 1.90–3). One suspects that Themistokles will have gained from his two visits to Sparta a rather different impression from the one held by the international aristocrats who were welcomed to the annual Gymnopaidiai festival; and one wonders whether that 'guard of honour' might not have been designed to ensure that Themistokles went where the Spartan authorities wished (cf. Thuc. 2.12.2). In the light of his subsequent career it is not irrelevant to observe that his trips through the Peloponnese will have taken him through Arkadia and the Argolis.

So far in this chapter I have stuck closely to Herodotus and Thucydides. Hereafter, although I shall generally attribute the greatest weight to the testimony of the latter, it will be necessary to use other sources, ranging in date from the fifth century BC to the second century AD. It is often difficult to evaluate their

reliability when they include events omitted by Thucydides.
For example, did Themistokles really propose the burning
of the Greek fleet (except presumably the Athenian ships)
at Pagasai in 480-479 (Plut. 'Them.' 20.1) or even just
the Spartan ships at Gytheion (Cic. 'Off.' 3.11.49)? Did
he, presumably early in 478, oppose the Spartan proposal
to expel the medizers from the Delphic Amphiktyony (Plut.
'Them.' 20.3f.)? However, whether he did any of these or
not, it is clear that he took no part in the 'Delian
League', whose foundation constituted for Thucydides the
second major step in the growth of Athenian power between
478 and 431.

The details of the 'constitution' of the League need
not concern us here, except in so far as the Spartans
attempted to use it as a propaganda weapon against the
Athenians perhaps from as early as 465. What does concern
us are the immediate circumstances in which the League was
founded. Sparta, as we have seen, had been less than
responsive to the Ionians' appeals for aid towards their
liberation from Persia. But it would be a mistake to
regard Spartan foreign policy as clearcut and monolithic
at this or any subsequent time until perhaps the second
decade of the fourth century (Ste. Croix 1972, 151). In
479 Sparta was faced with three choices: to continue the
war against Persia by sea, as the Ionians had requested;
to extend the crusade against the medizers north of the
Isthmus with a view to possible consolidation of Spartan
influence here on a permanent basis; or to adopt a 'little
Spartan' policy and concentrate on retaining the Peloponnese in a pacified and submissive condition. In practice,
the first two options were successively exercised, but
with such signal lack of success that the third was
brought into play perforce.

Regent Pausanias seems to have stood for the first
option. In 478 he led the Hellenic League in a naval
expedition of liberation first to Cyprus and then to
Byzantion. From the latter, however, he was recalled by
the Spartan authorities to stand trial, and here our
source-problem begins in earnest. For our primary account
is the excursus mentioned above, whose Herodotean flavour
and un-Thucydidean linguistic usage have provoked the
suggestion by Westlake (1977) that Thucydides is here
reproducing, with uncharacteristic credulity, the account
of a written source, perhaps Charon of Lampsakos.

However that may be, Pausanias at this first trial was
apparently condemned for various acts of injustice against
individuals but acquitted on the more serious charge of
medism (for which Thucydides says there seemed to be very
good evidence, although Herodotus, 5.32, preferred to

suspend judgment). The next year Pausanias returned to
the Hellespont off his own bat, allegedly intending to
make himself governor of Greece in the Persian interest.
The Athenians, who had clearly been the ones to object to
his behaviour in 478 and were now leaders of the Delian
League, this time drove him out of Byzantion. Indeed,
Herodotus (8.3.3) links the behaviour of Pausanias in 478
with the seizure of the hegemony of the Greeks by the
Athenians. In Thucydides (1.95) the loss of hegemony is
accepted philosophically by the Spartans, but a remarkable
passage in Diodorus Siculus (11.50), a first-century
historian who mainly reproduced the fourth-century Ephorus,
throws much light on internal Spartan wrangling. On
losing the hegemony a great majority of the Spartan
citizen body, above all the younger men, was in favour of
declaring war on Athens to recover it, but they were
dissuaded by a distinguished member of the Gerousia.

After his expulsion from Byzantion, Pausanias took up
residence in the Troad. It is unfortunately unclear how
long he remained here, but before his return Latychidas -
and with him the second of Sparta's three options in
foreign policy - had also fallen out of favour with the
home authorities. Again, there is an uncertainty over the
date (476/5, according to Diod. 11.48.2), but it seems
clear that when on campaign against the medizing Thessalians
Latychidas was discovered to have embezzled public funds
(Hdt. 6.72). Recalled to Sparta, found guilty and
banished (though not perhaps formally deposed), he went
into exile at Tegea, where he died in c.469. The significance of his chosen place of asylum will emerge
shortly.

Between 474 and 470 Pausanias was summoned back to
Sparta and summarily incarcerated. He was, however,
released, but his offer to stand trial again was turned
down because neither the state nor his personal enemies
had sufficient evidence to condemn the victor of Plataia
and the only active king of Sparta. Such evidence,
though, was not long in appearing, and Pausanias was
accused not merely of medism this time but also of
intriguing with the Helots, to whom he was said to have
offered citizenship as well as freedom. The charge of
medism, according to Thucydides or his (written?) source,
was the one that sealed his doom; but modern scholarship
has generally, if sometimes intemperately, placed greater
emphasis on the other one (Oliva 1971, 146-52; Welwei
1974, 122 n. 7). As with Kleomenes and the Arkadians in
c.491, Pausanias' offer to the Helots, whatever it was,
would have been at the least a potent method of silencing
his enemies.

There may, however, have been more to it that that.
For I find it extraordinary that Pausanias should have
gone to the sanctuary of Poseidon at Tainaron to incrim-
inate himself in the naive manner described by Thucydides.
Rather, I would connect his presence there with the
sacrilege to which the Spartans themselves attributed the
great earthquake of c.465, the dragging of Helot suppliants
from Poseidon's altar to be murdered. The information that
the Tainaron sanctuary could be used as an asylum by
Helots is interesting in itself (Boemer 1960, 18f; cf.
Hdt. 2.113.2, for an Egyptian sanctuary for deserting
slaves). But the real question is why the Spartans should
have attributed the earthquake to this particular affront
to Poseidon (who was generally held to be responsible for
sending earthquakes). I suggest that the 'secretiveness'
of the Spartans (Thuc. 5.68.2) may have concealed from
Thucydides or his source an abortive Helot uprising of
c.470, in which Pausanias was somehow implicated.

One argument in favour of this hypothesis is based on
Aristotle's general statement that the Helots as it were
lay in wait for their masters' misfortunes. For the late
470s and the early 460s (the general period in which the
death of Pausanias, synchronized with the flight of
Themistokles to Persia, is to be placed) threw up the
greatest crisis the Spartans had faced since their
decisions first to base their power and wealth on the
exploitation of Helots and then to protect their economic
base with a network of alliances in the Peloponnese. Such
a crisis would help to explain the extraordinarily savage
reprisals taken against Pausanias, treatment which even
Delphic Apollo, usually so agreeable to the dictates of
the Spartan authorities, found himself unable to sanction.
Moreover, as Thucydides (1.132.5) parenthetically observed,
the Spartans were habitually cautious in taking action
against any Spartan citizen regardless of his rank -
another hint that the problem of citizen numbers was
already being felt before the mid-fifth century.

The crisis is summarily and artistically referred to by
Herodotus (9.35.2) in one of his rare flash-forward
passages. Teisamenos, the Eleian seer who had won Spartan
citizenship (above), helped Sparta to five victories.
The first and last were Plataia in 479 and Tanagra in 458-
457. Sandwiched between these, presumably in chronological order, are a battle near Tegea against the Tegeans
and Argives, one at Dipaieis (or Dipaia) against all the
Arkadians except the Mantineians, and one at 'the Isthmos'
against the Messenians. Our other sources do not elucidate the background or dating of these battles, and it is
chiefly due to the scholarly acumen and ingenuity of

Andrewes (1952) and Forrest (1960) that a coherent account
can be attempted.

In the 480s Tegea had been hostile to Sparta, and
Forrest believes that with Tegea we should understand the
whole Arkadian League. Andrewes argued that during and
immediately after the Persian Wars Tegea was reconciled to
Sparta once more. However, the retirement of Latychidas
to Tegea by 475 suggests that hostility continued.
Indeed, it may not be fanciful to connect the presence of
Latychidas with the Arkadian troubles. The issue was
presumably the same as it had been in the 490s: the
Arkadians wished to be recognized and treated as such,
whereas Sparta preferred to divide and rule, fostering
above all the rivalry and mutual suspicion between
Mantineia and Tegea. Latychidas, the creature of Kleomenes, will not have been above using the same tactics as
his mentor to effect his recall, whatever his private
feelings about the justice of the Arkadian cause may have
been.

Elis and Mantineia had arrived late for Plataia. It
was alleged that their generals had favoured the Persian
cause, an allegation perhaps to be connected with the fact
that Damaratos had regarded Elis as a congenial asylum.
But the establishment of a democracy at Elis before 470
(A. Andrewes in Gomme 1970, 60f.) suggests that there were
wider and deeper socio-political issues involved as well.
Mantineia too received a democratic constitution,
certainly before 421 (Thuc. 5.29.1) but not necessarily as
early as Elis. Forrest would also place the synoecism of
Tegea around 470. This extraordinary conjunction of
political revolutions coincided with the revitalization of
Argos, which fought with Tegea against Sparta. Whether
Forrest (1968, 100) is right to postulate an actual
alliance against Sparta between Elis, the bulk of the
Arkadian cities and Argos I am doubtful. But his suggestion that the hand of Themistokles lay heavy on this anti-
Spartan activity is cogent. He was apparently a convinced
democrat and certainly since 479 an opponent of Sparta.
After his ostracism at Athens (late 470s?) he based
himself at Argos, from where he made frequent trips around
the rest of the Peloponnese (Thuc. 1.135.3): as Tomlinson
(1972, 106) tersely remarks, 'there is no reason to suppose that he was engaged in mere sightseeing.'

Space forbids discussion of internal political developments at Argos since its defeat at Sepeia in 494 or of the
circumstances and date of Themistokles' ostracism. But I
would like to apply the 'hand of Themistokles' hypothesis
to a remarkable piece of inscriptional evidence from Argos
(Jeffery 1961, 169, no. 22). Some time around 470

epigraphically, the Argives erected in their agora a
bronze tablet in honour of Gnosstas, their proxenos
(political representative) in the Perioikic town of Oinous,
which has not been certainly located but presumably lay
near the river of the same name. That the tablet should
refer to Gnosstas as 'Oinountios' (of Oinous) and not
'Lakedaimonios' has rightly been interpreted as a deliberate affront to Sparta. But the fact that the Argives
should have thought it worth while to make a citizen of an
otherwise insignificant Perioikic town their proxenos has
not received the comment it deserves. Gnosstas may not in
fact have been the only Perioikos who acted as proxenos
for a foreign state; a fourth-century proxeny-list from
Keos (IG XII.5(1).542) has been restored to include a
citizen of Kyphanta. But his favoured treatment, I
suggest, could represent a deliberate attempt to create or
exploit sympathy for Argos at least among the Perioikoi of
northern Lakonia, perhaps with a view to detaching them
from their Spartan allegiance. We recall the medism of
Karyai about a decade earlier.

At any rate the Spartans certainly felt sufficiently
strongly about the activities of Themistokles to suspend
their latent hostility towards the Athenians and co-operate
with them in hounding Themistokles out of Greece. As we
have seen, his flight to Asia Minor is synchronized with
the death of Pausanias, but this scarcely helps us to
penetrate the chronological obscurity, since the date of
his flight is perhaps the major difficulty of the first
half of the Pentekontaëtia (White 1964, 140). If there
was a change to a more oligarchic régime at Argos in the
early 460s following on the defeat of the Tegeans and
Argives by Sparta, and if Themistokles left Argos as a
result of the change, then the battle near Tegea could
have occurred about 470. The next battle took place at
Dipaieis in west Arkadia (for its suggested site see
Howell 1970, 100, no. 49) and is apparently synchronized
by Diodorus (11.65.4) with the great earthquake of c.465.
An interval of about five years allows plenty of time for
Mantineia and Argos to abandon the entente of c.470, but
our sources give no other insight into the reason for the
Spartan victory. Archidamos, to whom a stratagem perhaps
to be assigned to the battle is attributed by Polyainos
(1.41.1), must have been in command of the Spartan forces.
He had reigned de facto since Latychidas' exile, de iure
since the latter's death (Diod. 11.48.2; cf. 12.35.4). His
Agiad co-king Pleistarchos may still have been under age.
At all events it was reputedly the resolution and authority
of Archidamos which saved the day for Sparta immediately
after the great earthquake of c.465 (Diod. 11.63.5-7;

Plut. 'Kim.' 16.6f.; Polyain. 1.41.3).

This earthquake is directly relevant to the major themes of this book in two main respects. First, it is said to have caused enormous loss of life at Sparta and so has been held in varying degrees responsible for the catastrophic drop in citizen numbers (Chapter 14) and for a major reform of army organization. Second, it either occasioned or intensified the Helot revolt otherwise known as the Third Messenian War, a revolt rightly characterized as 'not only the greatest upheaval in Sparta during the classical period, but one of the most significant social outbreaks in ancient Greece altogether' (Oliva 1971, 163). For these reasons the earthquake and revolt deserve the closest possible scrutiny, but, unlike many of my predecessors, I shall try not to allow the chronological problems to overshadow the more important – and, I believe, more problematic – issues.

The relationship between the earthquake and the revolt is made unambiguous by Thucydides' use of a relative clause indicating simultaneity (1.101.2). Thucydides, however, also says that the revolt lasted ten years (1.103.1), as does Diodorus (11.64.4). Since on this reckoning the revolt would still have been in progress at the time of the Battle of Tanagra in 458 or 457, it has been felt that Thucydides' text must have been corrupted either palaeographically or by the 'editorial' insertion of the ordinal 'tenth' to accord with the text of Diodorus. The latter explanation of the alleged corruption is not cogent: in the Pentekontaëtia excursus Thucydides gives only seven figures indicating duration of time, but three of these concern the duration of sieges and two of them (our passage and 1.117.3) are precisely parallel in form (after so much time the besieged were unable to hold out and surrendered). Thus the corruption, if it is a corruption – as on balance I am inclined to believe, principally because of the strict chronological sequence adhered to by Thucydides in the Pentekontaëtia excursus as a whole – must be explained palaeographically; and 'fourth' or 'sixth' seem to be the most plausible emendations of 'tenth', giving a terminal date for the revolt of c.460. What is not permissible, however, is both to maintain that the text of Thucydides should not be tampered with and at the same time to ignore his explicit statement of simultaneity between the earthquake and the revolt, in order to put its outbreak back to c.469 and so link it directly with the death of Pausanias. There may have been an abortive Helot rising at the time of the death of Pausanias, but Thuc. 1.103.1 is not evidence for it.

More important, however, is the problem how far Diodorus can be used to supplement or correct Thucydides. For although his account (11.63f., 84.7f.) is far more detailed and even circumstantial, it is also at variance with that of Thucydides in crucial respects. According to Thucydides, the Helots, most of whom were of Messenian origin, revolted immediately after the earthquake and seceded to Ithome, supported by the Messenian Perioikoi of Thouria and Aithaia. The siege went on for some time until the Spartans, feeling their inadequacy in this department of warfare (cf. Hdt. 9.70.1f.), summoned their allies, especially the Athenians, who they thought were experts in taking fortified positions by assault. When, however, the siege did not have quick results, the Spartans suspected the Athenians of revolutionary sym- pathies towards the Helots and dismissed them forthwith. With their remaining allies (below) they compelled the rebels to surrender after a siege lasting ten (or, as I prefer, four or six) years in all.

According to Diodorus, however, great earthquakes (in the plural) hit Sparta and continued for some time, razing the dwellings to their foundations and killing more than 20,000 'Lakedaimonians'. The (Lakonian) Helots and the Messenians, emboldened by this loss of life, joined together in revolt. Their first idea, to march upon Sparta itself, was thwarted by Archidamos, whereupon they decided to secure a strong base in Messenia (Ithome). The Spartans summoned their allies (only the Athenians are named), but after some fighting in which the Athenians at first distinguished themselves the Spartans dismissed them for sympathizing with the rebels. Then and only then the Spartans and the remaining allies marched to lay siege to Ithome, whereupon the (Lakonian) Helots revolted in full force in support of the Messenians. After ten years the Messenians from Ithome were sent away under a truce; the ringleaders of the Helots were punished (presumably with death).

Other sources provide further details, some of which are journalistic, some plausible but problematic. None, however, resolves a major inconsistency between Thucydides and Diodorus. For the former the revolt was a Messenian, indeed almost a 'nationalistic', affair. Diodorus, on the contrary, distinguishes between the Messenians and the (Lakonian) Helots throughout and ascribes a not insignif- icant role to the latter. It has been suggested that Ephorus made the distinction because he was writing after the liberation of the Messenians in 370, at a time when the only Helots were the Lakonians. But even if this suggestion is true (it is certainly plausible), it is unclear why Ephorus or his source should have invented a distinct role in the rebellion for the Lakonian Helots. I have already intimated in Chapter 10 that modern scholars have underestimated the potential hostility of the Lakonian Helots towards the Spartans; this Diodoran passage is one of the pieces of direct evidence to be adduced in favour of my view. For only the Lakonian Helots would have been in a position to take such quick advantage of an earthquake in Sparta, and it will have been they who communicated the news of their masters' disaster to their brothers on the other side of Taygetos.

For the rest, Thucydides' more sober account is surely preferable, although his severe concision requires expansion and exegesis. In the first place, it is implausible that all the Messenian Helots should have revolted and then retired at once to Ithome without a blow being struck. More likely only a proportion rebelled and only a proportion of these resorted to Ithome after skirmishing in the fields. This at any rate would make sense of Herodotus 9.64.2, where we learn in passing that the Spartan credited with felling Mardonius at Plataia was himself killed 'in Stenyklaros' during 'the Messenian War' together with the detachment of 300 men under his command. Such a feat could have been effected by an ambush of Helots armed with agricultural implements. On the other hand, Teisamenos' victory 'at the Isthmos' (9.35.2) is presented as if it were a regular pitched battle. The reading 'Isthmos' has in fact usually been emended to 'Ithome', but the Isthmos in question could be the nearly continuous Skala ridge stretching from Ithome to Taygetos and dividing the upper (Stenyklaros) plain of the Pamisos valley from the lower (Makaria). Either way, however, the Helots would seem to have required less rustic weapons. These could have been supplied by their Perioikic supporters or conceivably by dissident Arkadians or Eleians.

As for the allies on the Spartan side, I assume that hoplites among at least the Perioikoi either volunteered or were drafted as a matter of course, and I suspect that the 'planters' of Mothone and Asine were conspicuously loyal to Sparta. But of Sparta's foreign allies apart from the Athenians (who require separate treatment) we hear explicitly only of Aigina (Thuc. 2.27.2, 4.56.2) and Mantineia (Xen. 'Hell.' 5.2.3), who were members of the Peloponnesian League, and of the Plataians (Thuc. 3.54.5). If the revolt was on a smaller scale than Thucydides implies, then there may not have been need for help from other allies, and Thucydides does say that the Athenians were summoned specifically for their reputed skill in siege-warfare. Probably, though, it is just by chance that other allies, especially those of the Peloponnesian League, are not recorded. We may, however, suggest some special reasons for the presence of those that are known. The Plataians may have acted out of a double sense of gratitude, to the Spartans for suggesting their alliance with Athens in 519/8 (Chapter 9), to the Athenians for being good allies. The Aiginetans were no doubt jealous and fearful of the growing naval power of the Athenians and perhaps also anxious to atone for their non-appearance at the Battle of Plataia. The Mantineians had declined to join the rest of the Arkadians against Sparta at Dipaieis and so were possibly particularly reliable at this time.

The Helot revolt among other things marked a turning-point in relations between Athens and Sparta. In 479 the Spartans had been secretly angered by Themistokles' circumvention of their wish that the walls of Athens should not be rebuilt. Probably in 478-477 a majority of them had been dissuaded only with difficulty from voting to declare war on Athens. In c.465, if Thucydides (1.101. 2) is to be believed, they had actually voted to send help to Thasos in its revolt from Athens and had only been prevented from sending it by the earthquake and Helot revolt. This vote of assistance has been doubted, but Ste. Croix (1972, 178f.) has argued cogently that Thucydides is to be believed. The Athenians, however, unquestionably were not aware of the Spartan vote when they themselves agreed, perhaps after heated debate (Plut. 'Kim.' 16.9), to send 4,000 hoplites under Kimon to Ithome in c.462.

Kimon, son of Miltiades, was the leading Athenian general of the day, vanquisher of the Persians at the famous Battle of the Eurymedon (c.469). Correspondingly, he was the foremost Athenian supporter of the 'dual hegemony' thesis, according to which Athens should lead the Greeks by sea, Sparta by land. Significantly in the 470s he had named one of his sons Lakedaimonios, just as the Spartan Perikleidas called a son of his Athenaios (Thuc. 4.119.2); Perikleidas was the ambassador who successfully sought Athenian aid in c.462 (Aristoph. 'Lys.' 1138). This amicable policy was in shreds after the Spartans dismissed the Athenians, alone of their allies, from Ithome.

The probable reason for Spartan suspicion has been admirably expressed by Ste. Croix (1972, 179f.): 'the ordinary Athenian hoplite ... may well have been shocked when he arrived in Messenia and found that the revolting "slaves" of the Spartans were Greeks, the majority of them Messenians, who had never lost consciousness of the fact that their ancestors had been citizens of the polis of Messene, and were now fighting for their freedom and the

right to be "the Messenians" once more.' Thereafter the
Athenians and Spartans were openly hostile. The Athenians
allied themselves first with Sparta's major Peloponnesian
enemy, Argos, and then with one of the more prominent
groups of former medizers, the Thessalians. Moreover,
they had been made forcibly aware of Sparta's Achilles
heel, the Messenian Helots, and it was not long before
they sought to exploit it (Chapter 12).

I have set out above the problem posed by Thucydides'
text for dating the end of the revolt. My preference for
an emendation giving a terminal date of c.460 will be
further reinforced in the next chapter. However, as with
the campaign of Theopompos in the 'First Messenian War'
(Chapter 8), we can only guess at the manner in which the
rebels were forced to capitulate. There is no archaeological evidence for a stone-built fortification on the
mountain before the fourth century; but Ithome is (with
Akrocorinth) one of the two best natural fortresses in the
Peloponnese, so a palisaded camp will have been adequate
to keep at bay an army self-confessedly incompetent at
sieges. Besides, there is a well within twenty metres of
the summit. Thus we must suppose that the Spartans and
their allies gradually cut off sympathetic sources of
supply and starved the Helots out.

Under the terms of the surrender the rebels (only the
Messenians, not the Lakonians, according to Diod. 11.84.8
- divide and rule?) were permitted to withdraw from the
Peloponnese (Sparta's preserve) on pain of instant
enslavement should they set foot within it again. These
terms have been seen as mild and an indication of Spartan
weakness. But there may in fact have been relatively few
Helots involved at the finish, and Sparta could hardly
have anticipated either the brilliant move of the Athenians in settling them at Naupaktos or the havoc the
Naupaktos Messenians would wreak in Messenia after the
Athenian seizure of Pylos in 425 (Chapter 12). Indeed,
'dual hegemony' theorists in Sparta may have misguidedly
hoped that a gesture of leniency towards the Helots might
help to reconcile Sparta to Athens. Nor should we under-
estimate the power of religion or rather superstition.
For the Helots had cleverly placed themselves as
suppliants under the protection of Zeus Ithomatas, mindful
perhaps of the Spartans' own explanation of the great
earthquake as caused by the wrath of Zeus' brother
Poseidon. However, even if the terms given to the rebels
do not necessarily imply Spartan weakness, it still
remains to consider the argument for weakness drawn from
the alleged effects of the earthquake.

A full statement of this argument is Toynbee 1969,

346-52, but I find most of his views unconvincing. In the
first place, he starts by saying (rightly) that 'the
meagreness of our information makes it impossible to reach
any sure conclusion about either the statistical facts
themselves or their demographic, social, political and
military consequences.' Yet a few pages later he con-
cludes that 'these facts and figures' (i.e. his inferences
from the meagre information) 'are illuminating' and help
to explain several major cruces of Spartan history between
c.460 and 432. Second, the sources are in fact not only
meagre but unreliable. The ancients, as David Hume so
elegantly demonstrated ('Of the Populousness of Ancient
Nations'), had a notorious weakness for large figures, and
Diodorus' 'more than 20,000' fatalities need not be taken
at its face value, even if we could be sure what he or his
source meant by 'Lakedaimonians'. Toynbee tries to save
his credit by arguing that the casualties were principally
women and very young children - hence Archidamos' ability
to rally the male warriors against the encroaching Helots.
But if about half the total population of citizen status
had really been wiped out (the total of 35,000-40,000 is
extrapolated from our only usable figure, the 8,000 adult
male warriors cited by 'Damaratos'), and if the proportion of the casualties among the women and very young
children was relatively even higher, then the catastrophe
would have been still more immense and its effects yet
more long-lasting than even Toynbee depicts them.
    I do not of course wish to deny that the earthquake
brought death and destruction to Sparta. But elementary
comparative demography shows that, other things being
equal, a population which suffers even a major loss of
life from a disaster quickly reconstitutes itself; we
might perhaps compare the recovery of Argos by 460 after
losing perhaps as many as 6,000 hoplites at Sepeia in 494.
Transparently, then, at Sparta other things were not
equal, and the constant and eventually catastrophic
decline in the number of male Spartan citizens - from
8,000 in 480 to at most 1,500 in 371 - cannot be
attributed to the earthquake alone. Neither can the army
reform, which, as we shall see in the next chapter, was
certainly carried out between 479 and 418 but not
necessarily nearer 460 than 420.

NOTES ON FURTHER READING

Most of the essential secondary literature has been cited
in the text. Here follow just a few supplements. For a
fuller citation of the ancient sources for the Pente-

kontaëtia reference should be made to the invaluable
indices compiled by R. Meiggs and A. Andrewes in Hill
1951.

A new commentary on Herodotus by W.G. Forrest is in
hand. The Hellenic League is most usefully discussed by
Brunt (1953/4); cf. Ste.Croix 1972, 301f. On all aspects
of the Delian League and subsequent 'Athenian Empire' see
Meiggs 1972. For the 'final problem' of Thermopylai see
Hope Simpson 1972.

For the Thucydidean chronology of 465-431 see Deane
1972; but I cannot follow him in retaining 'tenth' in
Thuc. 1.103.1 and dating the Helot revolt 464-455/4. See
rather Bayer and Heideking 1975, 120f., 130-4.

The history of Argos 494-461 is succinctly handled in
Tomlinson 1972, 96-109.

12 The Athenian wars c. 460-404

The war between Sparta and Athens and their respective
allies, which broke out in 431 and ended definitively in
404, is generally known today as 'The Peloponnesian War'.
The very title is not the least remarkable achievement of
its historian. For that it should be viewed as a single
war temporarily interrupted by a 'phoney' peace, that this
was 'the' war of the two fought in the fifth century
between these antagonists, and that it should be seen
primarily from the Athenian side - these are the legacies
of 'Thucydides the Athenian' (1.1.1; 5.26.1 - where no other
indication is given, the references in brackets in this
chapter are to Thucydides), who undertook his history 'at
the very beginning of the war in the belief that it was
going to be a great war and more worth writing about than
any of those which had occurred in the past'. As M.I.
Finley has observed in his introduction to the 1972
reissue of the Penguin Classics translation of Thucydides,
'no other historian can match this achievement; no other
war, for that matter no historical subject, is so much the
product of its reporter.'

Thucydides had his rivals, above all Ephorus, who
survives for us mainly in the garbled version of Diodorus.
But it is a measure of Thucydides' impact in his own time
that men like Xenophon, Kratippos and the unknown author
of the 'Hellenica Oxyrhynchia' fragments (if indeed he was
not Kratippos) preferred to complete rather than rewrite
his unfinished manuscript. With scarcely a dissenting
voice (Dionysios of Halikarnassos being a notable case in
point) the judgment of posterity on Thucydides as an
historian has echoed that of his continuators, whether
explicitly (for instance Lucian, Hobbes and von Ranke) or
implicitly. Until, that is, the present century, when
something of a reaction against Thucydides appears to have
set in, some tudents preferring the broader vision of his

main predecessor Herodotus, others stressing his subjectivity, yet others querying his self-proclaimed accuracy,
and all in some way touching upon 'the' Thucydides problem, that of the order of composition and degree of
revision of the work as we have it.

My own view is that, for all its narrowness of outlook,
subjectivity of interpretation, inaccuracy in detail
and self-inconsistency due to lack of final revision, the
history of Thucydides must be the bedrock of any account
of Greek history from 433 to 411 (where it abruptly ends).
Moreover, I agree with Ste.Croix (1972, 5-34) that
Thucydides has a claim to both originality of thought and
permanency of value in his unswerving insistence, for
purposes of historical interpretation, on the amorality of
interstate relations.

Reliance on Thucydides for 'the' Peloponnesian War,
however, cannot automatically be extended to his account
of the period before 433. The contemporary historian par
excellence, Thucydides mainly confines his treatment of
the preceding half-century to a prefatory excursus (1.89-
118), which is both sketchy and chronologically fluid -
oddly, because these are precisely the defects he berates
in the work of his only forerunner in this field,
Hellanikos (1.97.2). The difficulties posed by his
excursus have been sampled in the previous chapter, but
these pale when we turn to consider the role of Sparta in
the origins, character and even duration of the so-called
'First' Peloponnesian War of c.460-445.

This does not mean that we should not base ourselves on
Thucydides here too, but it is necessary to invert his
perspective. For he viewed this war solely in the context
of the growth of Athenian power, whereas we shall attempt
to see both of the Peloponnesian wars and the fourteen
years of genuine, if uneasy, peace which separated them
from the Spartan side of the barricades - as Thucydides
himself was more able to do during his enforced exile from
Athens between 424 and 404 (5.26.1). Hence the deliberately unfamiliar title of this chapter, modified from
Thucydides (5.28.2; 31.3, 5). No attempt, however, has
been made here to give as complete as possible an account
of the formulation and execution of Spartan domestic and
foreign policy between c.460 and 404. Rather, the
literary, epigraphical and (scanty) archaeological
evidence pertaining to Lakonia and Messenia in this period
has been set out in the belief that any account of Spartan
policy should start from a consideration of developments
within the polis-territory as a whole.

The dominant section of Spartan opinion in the late
460s was not necessarily anxious to effect a rift with

Athens. But whatever its intentions, the rift was
occasioned by the dismissal of Kimon from Ithome and the
discrediting at Athens of his 'dual hegemony' thesis.
Once this policy had been jettisoned, the newly radical-
ized Athenian democracy warmly embraced the intervention-
ist ideas apparently fathered by Themistokles. An
alliance was concluded with Argos (Hill 1951, I.4.5),
which had recently recovered control of the Argolis and
lovingly nursed longstanding grievances against Sparta,
both specific (possession of Kynouria: 5.41.2) and general
(hegemony of the Peloponnese: cf. 5.28.2). Shortly after,
Megara seceded from the Peloponnesian League – the first
state to do so, unless Mantineia, Tegea and Elis really
had concluded an offensive alliance with Argos in the late
470s – and made a full offensive and defensive alliance
with Athens (Hill 1951, I.4.8). Hence, according at least
to Thucydides (1.103.4), Corinth's 'bitter hatred' for
Athens, exacerbated by the Athenian masterstroke of
settling Naupaktos at the mouth of the Corinthian Gulf
with the Helot rebels from Ithome (Hill 1951, I.4.7:
perhaps in 460). An Athenian inscribed relief of c.450
depicting a seated goddess (IG I^2.37) has been interpreted
as evidence of an actual treaty of alliance between Athens
and the Naupaktos Messenians (Meritt 1944, 224-9).

No doubt Corinth, which was now threatened at either
end of the Gulf named after it, was anxious to induce
Sparta and the Peloponnesian League to declare war on the
Athenian alliance. Sparta, however, was not lightly to be
drawn into a war not of its own seeking; and although
Thucydides (1.18.3) describes the Pentekontaëtia as a
period in which Sparta and Athens were for the most part
'either fighting each other or putting down revolts among
their allies', the 'First' Peloponnesian (or Athenian) War
should be understood mainly as a conflict between the
Athenian alliance and Sparta's Peloponnesian League
allies. The informal character of the struggle is implied
in the scholarly controversy over the precise date at
which the war may be said to have begun (Holladay 1977b).
Whatever the solution to that, it seems clear that
Sparta's direct involvement before the battle of Tanagra
in 458 or 457 was negligible. Not even after the Athenians had reduced Aigina by siege in 457/6 and compelled it,
though nominally still within the Peloponnesian League, to
pay tribute (Hill 1951, I.5.3) did Sparta engage more
energetically.

On one level the reason for Spartan abstention is quite
straightforward. The Athenians' alliance with Argos
(followed perhaps by a minor victory over a Spartan force
at Oinoe in the Argolis: Meiggs 1972, 459-62) and their

occupation of the passes through Mount Geraneia in the Megarid (1.107.3) made it virtually impossible for the Spartans to venture north of the Isthmus and return to Lakonia without risking a full-scale battle. Also perhaps relevant in this context is Thucydides' reference (1.118. 2) to the 'internal/domestic wars' by which Sparta was hindered from resisting the increase of Athenian power. On another level, however, this geographical and also perhaps political constraint only makes Sparta's two forays into central Greece during the 'First' Peloponnesian War the more problematic and potentially revealing.

The first of these was undertaken in the early 450s, ostensibly to aid Doris, the supposed motherland of the Dorians (1.107.2; 3.92.3), against Phokis. Phokis, it has been suggested, had seized Delphi, as it certainly did in 449. However, powerfully though the Spartans could be affected by ties of sentiment and religion, it is unlikely that they were not moved equally by considerations of prestige and profit (cf. 5.105.3f.). The defection of Megara, the siege of Aigina (then still in progress) and a defeat suffered by the Corinthians in the Megarid (Hill 1951, I.5.4) constituted a powerful challenge both to the unity of the Peloponnesian League and to Sparta's leader-ship of it. So powerful indeed that, notwithstanding the recent earthquake and Messenian revolt, Sparta was prepared to send out of Lakonia 1,500 of 'its own' hoplites. Despite the arguments of Holladay 1977b, Thucydides' elliptical account must surely presuppose a decision taken by Sparta and then the Peloponnesian League as a whole, although I agree that this was not necessarily a decision for war specifically against Athens. However, more important for us perhaps are the two other facets of Sparta's action.

First, what is meant by 'its own' hoplites? In 3.92.5 Thucydides uses this expression to distinguish Spartiate from Perioikic colonists of Herakleia Trachinia; but such a distinction would be inappropriate here, where the contrast being drawn is between the troops contributed by Sparta and those by its allies. As in 5.57.1 and 5.64.2, therefore, where by 'themselves' Thucydides does not refer only to Spartiates, he is describing a mixed force of Spartiate and Perioikic hoplites. Still, even if not all and perhaps not even half of the 1,500 were Spartiates, the total is high as a proportion of the allied force as a whole, indeed 'about the highest ... that was likely to occur' (Ste.Croix 1972, 209). This, I believe, not only underlines the importance of the expedition of 458-457 in Spartan eyes, but also supports the views tentatively advanced in the last chapter that the earthquake had not

had catastrophic demographic effects and that the Helot
revolt was over by c.460.

The second major point of interest concerns the routes
whereby the allied force made its way into and out of the
Peloponnese. The Isthmus being blocked, it has been
inferred from Thuc. 1.107.3 that it went north by sea
across the Corinthian Gulf, perhaps from Pellene or
Sikyon, to modern Itea and thence via Amphissa to the
upper Kephissos valley. The knife-edge victory over the
Athenian alliance at Tanagra in Boiotia (Hill 1951, I.5.7)
facilitated its return by land through the Isthmus, but it
is significant of the prevailing strategic situation that,
even if Delphi had been temporarily liberated from Phokian
control, the dedication offered by the Spartans and their
allies for Tanagra was apparently made not at Delphi but
at Olympia alone (M/L no. 36).

In a broader perspective the Athenian defeat at Tanagra
was but a momentary set-back in a quinquennium or so of
resounding success. From the Lakonian point of view the
most portentous Athenian undertaking in this period was
the Periplous or 'sailing-round' of the Peloponnese by a
fleet under Tolmides (Hill 1951, I.5.11). Thucydides
(1.108.5) gives the barest of summaries, but he does at
least record that Tolmides fired the Spartan dockyards.
These can only have been at Gytheion, as Diodorus (11.84.
6) states in his much more circumstantial account under
the year 456/5; a recent sonar search offers some confirmation of the ancient report (Strabo 8.5.2, C363) of built
docks here (Edgerton and Scoufopoulos 1972). They may
have been inaugurated under the influence of Athens'
construction at Peiraieus (1.93) or at the urging of
regent Pausanias, but they can hardly have been a hive of
activity as far as the actual construction or refitting of
Spartan warships was concerned, given the dearth of these
before the final phase of 'the' Peloponnesian War.

The rest of Diodorus' narrative of Tolmides' expedition
is of uneven value. An alleged motive of personal rivalry
between Tolmides and Myronides (who by defeating the
Boiotians at Oinophyta in 457 had won Boiotia for Athens)
is given undue prominence. But to his credit Diodorus
does stress that Lakonia and Messenia had never before
been ravaged and that such an exploit would depress yet
more the Spartans' prestige (11.84.3) - and so, though
Diodorus does not draw the conclusion, further
'destabilize' the tottering Peloponnesian alliance.

Tolmides indeed may have had even more far-reaching
intentions. For apart from Gytheion he attacked and
briefly held Kythera and Boiai in Lakonia (Paus. 1.27.5)
and Mothone in Messenia (Diod. 11.84.6) and then sailed

round to Naupaktos. Diodorus is wrong to say (11.84.7)
that it was Tolmides who planted the freed Messenian
rebels here, at least at this date, but Tolmides may well
have anticipated Demosthenes (below) in believing that the
Naupaktos Messenians could contribute essentially to a
strategy which would distract, though not necessarily by
itself defeat, Sparta. We recall the alleged advice of
Damaratos to Xerxes to seize Kythera in 480. Thus it
seems to me that the modern debate about the tactic of
'epiteichismos' (or 'epiteichisis'), the occupation and
fortification of a promontory or island in the enemy's own
territory, may have sometimes been misconceived. The
question is surely not whether this tactic was discussed
as a possibility at Athens so early as 432 (1.142.2; cf.
122.1) but why, since it was an obvious possibility for a
naval power (Ps.-Xen. 'Ath. Pol.' 2.13), it was not in
fact employed until 427. The answer, implied by Thuc.
4.3.3, seems to be that permanent occupation of a piece of
enemy territory was considered too expensive; but Tolmides,
I suggest, was among the first to draw the correct lesson
from the great Helot revolt and to advocate 'epiteichismos'
as a peculiarly effective way of exploiting the antagonism
between the Spartans and the Helots.

Perhaps in 449 the Spartans made their second excursion
north of the Isthmus in the 'First' War. By then, however, the international situation had radically changed.
In 451 a Sparta which had never been able, even if it had
wished, to prosecute the war vigorously made a truce for
five years with an Athens then perhaps influenced by the
returned Kimon (Hill 1951, I.5.17; Piccirilli 1973, no.
20). Soon after, early in 450 rather than late in 451,
Sparta granted to Argos the Thirty Years' Truce (cf. 5.14.
4; 28.2) that Argos itself had spurned in 481 (Hdt. 7.
148.4).

This stalemate between the great powers was symbolized
by the 'Second Sacred War' (Hill 1951, I.7.1): after
Sparta had (again?) wrested Delphi from Phokian control,
Athens promptly returned it to their Phokian allies. In
447, however, the equilibrium was shattered. Defeated at
Koroneia, the one victory over Athens that the Boiotians
could boast before 424 (3.63.3; 4.92.6), the Athenians
were swiftly relieved of Boiotia. Worse followed in the
shape of the revolt of Euboia, an island whose economic,
strategic and psychological significance for Athens was
laid bare in the closing phase of 'the' Peloponnesian War.
At Sparta the tails of the 'hawks', those who since 478-
477 had resented and feared the growth of Athenian power
and wished to see it cut down to size, were up; and when
Megara too, perhaps on cue, revolted from Athens (1.114.1),

the way was open for a full-scale Peloponnesian League
invasion of Attika (Hill 1951, I.7.4-5), the fifth such
incursion by Dorians (cf. Hdt. 5.77), the first by the
League properly so called. But with Athens apparently at
his mercy king Pleistoanax tamely withdrew from Attika and
was later exiled on a charge of having been bribed by the
Athenians (2.21.1).

The real bribe, however, may not have been monetary but
'the offer to surrender, or to discuss the surrender of,
Megara, Troizen and Achaia' (Gomme 1956, 74; cf. Ste. Croix
1972, 196-200). For in the winter of 446-445 Sparta and
Athens concluded a Thirty Years' Peace whereby each side
recognized the hegemony of the other, on land and by sea
respectively (Hill 1951, I.7.7). Athens, we note,
retained Naupaktos and - a major gain from the war -
Aigina. Argos was not a party to the treaty, but specific
provision was made for the eventuality of its establishing
friendly relations with Athens (Paus. 5.23.4).

Sparta entered into the peace from a bargaining
position crucially weakened by what some Spartans took to
be the too ready compliance of Pleistoanax and his
adviser. The peace, however, might have been expected to
preserve the status quo about the Isthmus that had been so
rudely disturbed by the defection of Megara. In the
event, it lasted for only fourteen of its intended thirty
years. For in 432 Sparta voted that the Athenians had
broken their oaths and in 431 began 'the' Peloponnesian
War by invading Attika once again. 'What made war inevitable', wrote Thucydides (1.23.6), 'was the growth of
Athenian power and the fear which this caused in Sparta',
a judgement he repeats in different words and with some
amplifications. It was not, he says (1.88), the specific
grievances which Sparta's allies Corinth, Megara and Aigina
brought forward against Athens so much as Athens' growing
power that influenced the Spartan vote for war. By 432,
he adds (1.118.2), Athens' power had reached the point
where it had begun to encroach upon and disrupt the
Spartan alliance, particularly the Peloponnesian League, a
situation Sparta found intolerable. Again, looking back
from the vantage point of 413, Thucydides (7.18.2) says
that the Spartans themselves then thought that in 432 the
fault (sc. for breaking the peace) lay more on their side
and that 'there was some justice in the misfortunes they
had suffered' since 431, a remarkable admission on many
counts, not least because it involved the retrospective
recognition that Apollo's approval (1.118.3) had not
turned the conflict into a 'just war' (contrast the view of
Thucydides' Corinthians: 1.123).

The judgment of Thucydides on the origins of the war is

still today, no less than in antiquity, monumentally
controversial (e.g. Sealey 1975). But readers of Ste.
Croix 1972 should at least be convinced that, whether or
not Thucydides was right, his judgment is at least
consistent with his portrayal of Sparta's behaviour in
432. That is to say, in contrast to 479, when it was
'chiefly because they were urged on by their allies'
(1.90.1) that the Spartans had tried to prevent the
rebuilding of Athens' walls, in 432 they took their decision for war chiefly through fear for their own position,
specifically for fear that the Peloponnesian League might
break up and so expose Lakonia to the kind of devastating
invasion that did in fact occur in 370. In this judgment
I believe Thucydides to have been essentially correct,
although his own jejune narrative of the period 445-433
has made some historians wonder why he could have thought
Athens' power was growing then.

The answer to this apparent puzzle is, I suggest, to be
found in Thucydides' attitude to the challenge to Athenian domination in the Aegean thrown down by Samos between
440 and 439. He bestows his longest treatment of any
episode in the Pentekontaëtia on this challenge (1.115.2-
117), which (in the words of Athenian democrats in 411)
had 'come very close to depriving the Athenians of their
control of the sea' (8.76.4f.; cf. 73.4; 86.4; 98.4). In
other words, if even the most powerful of Athens' subject-
allies could not shake the grip of Athens on its Empire,
there was small chance of any other ally's loosening it.
Thus the suppression of Samos, together with the terms of
surrender imposed (the Samians 'pulled down their walls,
gave hostages, handed over their fleet, and agreed to pay
reparations in instalments at regular intervals'), could
be seen as a great advance in Athenian power. The effect
at Sparta will have been to play once more into the hands
of the 'hawks'. Indeed, it is probable that already in
441-440 the Spartans had voted to aid the Samians and so
break the peace after only four years. To the arguments
of Ste.Croix (1972, 117, 143, 200-3) we may perhaps add
one drawn from the special relationship between Sparta
and Samos - or rather between certain Spartan and Samian
aristocrats - that had existed perhaps since the Second
Messenian War.

In 432 the immediate occasion of Sparta's vote was
Corinth's bringing into the open at Sparta its grievances
against Athens over its colonies Kerkyra and Poteidaia.
Corinth was not the only ally of Sparta with grievances,
but Thucydides underlines Corinth's cardinal role within
the Peloponnesian League by writing speeches for 'the
Corinthians' alone of the allies both at the meeting of

the Spartan Assembly which voted for war (1.68-71) and at
the subsequent Peloponnesian League Congress which confirmed the Spartans' decision (1.120-4). How far Thucydidean speeches correspond to speeches actually delivered
is another of those eternally vexed problems of Thucydidean scholarship, but fortunately in the case of the
first Corinthian speech we need not trouble ourselves too
much over this, given Thucydides' own personally expressed
judgment of why Sparta voted for war. Instead, we may
select what seem to me the two most revealing points made
by 'the Corinthians' - that, if Sparta does not vote for
war, they will look for 'another alliance' (1.71.4); and
that Sparta's 'whole way of life is out of date when
compared with theirs (sc. the Athenians')' (1.71.2; cf.
70).

The first of these points raises the whole question of
diplomatic relations within the Peloponnesian League and
between the League or its individual members and Athens or
Argos. An ancient commentator on 1.71.4 inferred that
Corinth was threatening to secede from the League and ally
itself with Argos, and his view receives prima facie
support from the diplomatic situation in 421 (below).
However, as Ste.Croix (1972, 60) has pointed out, in 432
Argos' truce with Sparta still had more than a decade to
run and in the event Argos showed no sign of willingness
to break it. His alternative suggestion, that Corinth
contemplated a separate alliance with Athens, may seem
somewhat implausible. But students of Middle Eastern
affairs in late 1977 were presented with a no less extraordinary diplomatic volte-face; indeed, there was even
talk of a 'separate peace' between Egypt and Israel, which
could hardly be said to be less ideologically and politically opposed to each other than Corinth and Athens.

The second point, about the archaic character of the
Spartan way of life, takes us back to the alleged 'death'
of Spartan high culture. It was argued at the end of
Chapter 9 that this process had been either misdescribed
or misconstrued but that by the time of Herodotus Spartan
society had been reorganized along almost exclusively
military lines, partly to palliate the disparities of
private wealth among citizens and so abort civil strife,
partly to compensate for shrinking citizen military
manpower in face of the Helot threat. It is therefore
entirely appropriate that Thucydides' Corinthians should
draw an analogy between archaism in politics and archaism
in the arts and crafts: for, according to Herodotus (2.
167.2), the Corinthians - upper-class Corinthians, that
is - were of the Greeks the least unfavourably disposed
towards the practitioners of manual crafts, the Spartans

the most contemptuous of all. Herodotus himself adds a
telling commentary on the anachronistic ossification of
Sparta society. For Sparta is the only Greek state which
he treats 'ethnographically' by describing some of the
'customs of the Spartans' (6.56-60) as if they were a
'barbarian' or non-Greek people. Indeed, he specifically
remarks of one aspect of the elaborate funeral rites of
Spartan kings that it was common to pretty well all non-
Greek peoples.

It was also suggested in Chapter 9 that the military
reorganization of Spartan society was to be associated
with the remarkable passion for horseracing attested by
the outstanding record of rich Spartans in the four-horse
chariot-race at Olympia between c.550 and 370. The palm
or rather wreath must go to Euagoras, who in the late
sixth century won at three successive Olympics with the
same team of mares (Hdt. 6.103.4). But no less noteworthy
in its own way, and for our purposes yet more informative,
is the curriculum vitae of Damonon and his son preserved
on a stele of the third quarter of the fifth century,
precisely the period to which the remarks of 'the Corinthians' refer (Jeffery 1961, 196f., 201, no. 52; Schwartz
1976). The stele, originally set up in the sanctuary of
Athena on the Spartan akropolis, records among other
victories the well over thirty won by Damonon in horse-
races at Lakonian festivals held in both Spartan and
Perioikic territory: the Pohoidaia at Sparta, Helos and
Thouria; the Athenaia and Ariontia (?) at Sparta (?); the
Eleusinia at modern Kalyvia tis Sochas; the Lithesia near
Cape Malea (?); and the Parparonia in the Thyreatis (on
the site of the great victory over the Argives in c.545).
One can think of few better ways by which a Spartan might
at once take advantage of the political unification of
Lakonia and Messenia and emphasize his economic superior-
ity over his Perioikic rivals and subjects. As if to ram
the point home, Damonon stresses that his victorious teams
were bred in his own stables.

Thucydides' Corinthians were of course concerned not
with local Lakonian economics and politics but with the
effect of the Spartans' outmoded way of life on their
perception (or lack of it) of shifts in the contemporary
diplomatic constellation. Thucydides himself, however,
clearly believed that their general point had a yet wider,
indeed almost a universal, application. For the contrast
between stick-in-the-mud Sparta and go-ahead Athens drawn
by 'the Corinthians' in 432 is one to which he recurs in
different contexts and for various purposes throughout his
history. One of the most revealing of these passages
occurs near the end of the work as we have it (8.96.5):

'Athens, particularly as a naval power, was enormously
helped by the very great difference in the national
characters - her speed against their slowness, her enterprise as against their lack of initiative. This was shown
by the Syracusans (sc. during the Sicilian expedition of
415-413, below), who were most like the Athenians in
character and fought best against them.'
     In fact, though, the Spartans were not absolutely slow
and in the type of situation exemplified in 432, when they
felt 'compelled' to go to war in the sense that the
alternatives to fighting were intolerable, they had never
been slow at all (1.118.2, with Ste.Croix 1972, 94f.).
And although Thucydides' retrospective judgment on the
degree of Spartan success down to 411 does of course hold
good, it is doubtful whether even he would have predicted
this in 432 on the basis of the difference in national
characters. At any rate, it is certain that the Corinthians had no such notions in 432. On the contrary they,
like the majority of Greeks, confidently expected that, if
the Spartan alliance invaded Attika annually shortly
before the grain-harvest, Athens would be unable to hold
out for more than three years at the outside (7.28.3; cf.
4.85.2; 5.14.3). It was not the least of the many para-
doxes of 'the' Peloponnesian War that this confidence was
largely misplaced. Let us therefore briefly review the
strategy of the war.
     On the Spartan side there is relatively little contro-
versy. Since the Persian Wars of 480-479 it had been
dogma, both inside and outside the alliance, that an
invasion of Attika was the optimum method of bending
Athens to its enemies' will. Moreover, in 432, Sparta as
aggressor was bound to adopt such a primarily offensive
strategy aimed at eliminating the threat posed by Athens
to its hegemony of the Peloponnesian League; and as a land
power heading an alliance mostly composed of primarily
land-orientated states Sparta was bound to play to its
strength. The Athenians, it was calculated, would either
refuse a pitched battle and so lose their crops and be
starved into submission or be demoralized into risking a
battle they would assuredly lose. The naval aspect of
Spartan strategy was emphatically secondary for the simple
reason that the Spartan alliance could not pack enough
nautical punch and lacked sufficient expertise in naval
warfare to threaten Athenian supremacy at sea. As late as
411 the inhabitants of Iasos on the south coast of Asia
Minor could not believe that the fleet advancing on them
was not Athenian (8.28.2). Instead, therefore, the
Spartans relied on words rather than deeds to break the
cohesion of the Athenian war-effort. To exacerbate

existing discontent within the Athenian Empire, they proclaimed that their aim in the war was to liberate Athens' allies from the yoke of the 'tyrant' city (esp. 2.8.4).

The strategy of Athens, by contrast, remains controversial. Thucydides' representation of it cannot be fully discussed here because it forms part of the wider problem of the composition of the history. But the narrower question, that of the balance intended or struck by Athens between offence and defence, must be raised. To Thucydides the architect of Athenian strategy at the outbreak of war was Perikles, who spoke first at a meeting of the Assembly called when the Peloponnesians were on the point of invading Attika in 431 and gave the Athenians 'just the same advice as he had given before. This was that they were to prepare for war and bring into the city their property in the country. They were not to go out and offer battle, but were to come inside the city and guard it. Their navy, in which their strength lay, was to be brought to the highest state of efficiency, and their allies were to be handled firmly, since, he said, the strength of Athens came from the money paid in tribute by their allies, and victory in war depended on a combination of intelligent resolution and financial resources' (2.13.2; cf. 65.7). The allied tribute was of course employed to finance the fleet, but what is left unclear in Thucydides is what role or roles Perikles envisaged for the fleet thus financed and mobilized. Was it to be used mainly defensively to keep the allies in hand and so preserve Athens' lifeline, the sea-lanes along which travelled the merchantmen carrying wheat from the Crimea to the Peiraieus? Or did Perikles also plan a major offensive role for fleets to be sent round the Peloponnese in order to ravage and even occupy the territory of Sparta's coastal allies and that of Sparta itself?

In the early books Thucydides lays the emphasis squarely on the first of these alternatives in line with the overwhelmingly defensive aura he imparts to Periklean strategy as a whole. The only passage with a different colouring is 3.17, but its authenticity is often - and reasonably - contested. In Book 6, however, after describing the Athenian armada prepared against Sicily in 415 as 'by a long way the most costly and the finest-looking force of Greek troops that up to that time had ever come from a single city' (6.31.1), he points out that in numbers of ships it was no larger than the Athenian fleet of 430. From this and other indications scholars have inferred that Thucydides underestimated the role Perikles had allotted to sea-borne raids (cf. Westlake

1969, 84-100).

That may be true, but we should not, I think, allow this to outweigh Thucydides' view that Periklean strategy taken as a whole was preponderantly defensive in intention. For if we follow his judgment on the origins of the war (as interpreted above), it was enough for Athens as the aggrieved party to 'win' the war if it simply survived the annual Spartan onslaughts by land and, by keeping a firm hold on its alliance, maintained a supply of foreign grain sufficient to feed a population temporarily deprived of part of the produce of its own territory. Indeed, this is precisely what Perikles is made by Thucydides to say to the Athenian Assembly in 432, 431 and 430 (1.144.1; 2.13. 9; 62.1; cf. 65.7), when he recommended his strategy as one that entailed suffering but would enable Athens, not to win an outright victory, but to 'win through' (cf. Ste. Croix 1972, 208).

And so it proved, at least in the first phase of 'the' Peloponnesian War from 431 to 421, which is sometimes known as the 'Archidamian War'. Thucydides of course could never have used this title (and in fact refers descriptively to 'the Ten Years' War': 5.25.1; 26.3). For not only did Archidamos die about halfway through the decade, but, if Thucydides represents him with substantial fidelity (see, however, Westlake 1968, 123-5), he actually opposed the majority Spartan view of Athens in 432 and advised that war should at least be postponed until Sparta was ready for it (1.80-5, esp. 83). It is of course possible that Thucydides the 'artful reporter' (Hunter 1973) used Archidamos to foreshadow dramatically the actual course of the initial phase of the war. On the other hand, as a guest-friend of Perikles and the most experienced Spartan general (though not in warfare against Athens), Archidamos was perhaps the best placed of the Spartans to evaluate the relative strengths of the two sides; and his experiences as general in the 460s may well have made him a 'dual hegemony' theorist and a supporter of the Thirty Years' Peace.

However that may be, Archidamos led the first three invasions of Attika, until in 427 he stood down in favour of the Agiad regent and in 426 was replaced by his son and Eurypontid successor, Agis II. The invasion of 430, though only lasting about forty days, was the longest of all (2.57.2), while the first, taking a maximum of thirty-five, is said to have continued 'a long time' (2.19.2). They were so short simply because they could last only as long as did the supplies the Peloponnesians brought with them or found in Attika. It was part of the amateurism of hoplite warfare that an army was expected to live

literally from hand to mouth (Pritchett 1974, I, ch.2).
In these circumstances it is not surprising that the
invasions did no permanent and irretrievable damage, and
that the damage they did cause was as much psychological
as material.

Indirectly, however, they were responsible for the
devastating effects of the greatest unforeseen accident of
the Ten Years' War, the plague which first hit Athens in
430 (2.47.3-54; 3.87; cf. 6.12.1; 26.2; and generally
1.23.3). The concentration of population in the city of
Athens in insanitary conditions aggravated the plague's
virulence, and this further sapped the morale of a people
already severely depressed by seeing their property
destroyed under their noses. In fact, so powerful became
the depression that envoys were sent to Sparta to treat
for peace (2.59.1; 4.21.1), until a speech of Perikles
(2.60-4; cf. 65.2), combined with 'hawkish' Spartan
intransigence, convinced the Athenians that such diplomacy
was pointless.

Not everything, however, went the way of Sparta in the
first years of the war. For apart from mounting annual
counter-raids on the Megarid and reducing Poteidaia
eventually in 429 Athens had been notably active by sea
round the Peloponnese. In 431, shortly after the first
Peloponnesian invasion of Attika had begun, an Athenian
fleet of 100 ships carrying 1,000 hoplites was despatched
(2.23.2). Diodorus (12.43.1) mentions an attack on the
Argolis, but Thucydides chooses to record only the raid on
Perioikic Mothone in Messenia. The town was apparently
fortified but not garrisoned, since the Spartans sent a
mobile detachment ('phroura') under the brilliant Brasidas
to defend it (2.25.1f.). Gomme (1956, 84f.) did not
believe that the Athenians intended Mothone to become
their first 'epiteichismos', and he is probably right,
since Mothone is rather far from the main object of such a
tactic, the Helots working the central Pamisos valley. It
is, however, highly significant, in the light of subsequent events, that among Athens' allies at Mothone were
Messenians from Naupaktos. Moreover, after the Peloponnesians had withdrawn from Attika the Athenians 'established and garrisoned positions both by land and sea, with
the intention of keeping these up for the duration of the
war' (2.24.1). One of these positions was certainly
Salamis (2.93.4); others may have been Aigina, from which
the Athenians expelled the inhabitants in 431 and replaced them with their own colonists (2.27.1; cf. 8.69.1),
and Naupauktos itself (2.69).

In 430 precisely the same response was made to the
second Peloponnesian invasion of Attika (2.56), but this

time Thucydides gives more details. First stop was
Epidauros, which lay en route to Argos and was friendly to
Sparta; then Troizen, Halieis and Hermione; and finally
Lakonian Prasiai. Like Mothone, Prasiai was seemingly
fortified but ungarrisoned; but the Spartans appear not to
have sent a defence force and the Athenians captured and
sacked the 'polisma' (2.56.6). Although Prasiai lay at the
end of a difficult route of communication with the Eurotas
valley, there was little profit in occupying it permanently. Naval raids were the best way of harming one of
Sparta's more important Perioikic subjects, and to judge
from some lines of Aristophanes' play 'Peace' (242f.)
invoking 'thrice-wretched Prasiai' they seem to have been
effective.

In 429 the Spartans did not invade Attika, and the
Athenians did not send a fleet round the Peloponnese until
early in Thucydides' 'winter' (November to February).
Instead, the Spartans laid siege to Plataia, whose
eventual capitulation in 427, followed by a notorious
instance of Spartan bad faith (3.68.4), helped to thwart
Athenian designs on Boiotia in 424. The fleet that went
round the Peloponnese late in 429 (thereby incidentally
helping to diminish the terrors of Cape Malea outside the
official sailing season) was commanded by Phormion, who
used Naupaktos as a base to block fleets sailing from
Corinth (2.83) and resoundingly demonstrated Athenian
naval superiority by crushing a much larger Peloponnesian
fleet.

Against the view of Brunt (1965, 271) that 'if
Perikles set high hopes on the effectiveness of such
attacks (sc. by sea on the Peloponnesian coast), this
only shows that ... he overestimated the potency of
maritime superiority', I would point out first that the
Spartans were persuaded to prepare a second fleet against
Phormion in 429 precisely because they thought they might
thereby 'make it more difficult for the Athenians to send
their fleets round the Peloponnese' (2.80.1). In 428
their resolve can only have been confirmed by an Athenian
expedition under Phormion's son which ravaged several
places in 'Lakonike' (3.7.1-2) and a later one of 100
ships (as in 431 and 430) which landed at will in the
Peloponnese and ravaged the Spartan Perioikis (specifically so called by Thucydides at 3.16.2). Second, the
decision of the Spartans in 426 to found a colony in
Trachis (Herakleia Trachinia: 3.92-3) should be taken as
a firm indication that they were by then aware that land
invasions of Attika would not alone win the war. For
Herakleia was envisaged partly as a base for naval
operations against Euboia, and partly as a way-station en

route to Athens' allies in Thrace. As Gomme (1956, 395)
remarks, 'clearly we can see the mind of Brasidas behind
this.'

The Athenians' use of 'epiteichismos' on the island of
Minoa off Megara in 427 (3.51) marked a turning-point in
the Ten Years' War. Thucydides, as we have noted,
represents Athenian strategy in the first years as
essentially that of Perikles. The great man, however,
died of the plague in 429, and Thucydides in the course of
a summary of Perikles' influence written at least in part
after 404 commented that his successors as democratic
leaders entirely reversed the essentially defensive
direction of his strategy (2.65.8). This judgment is
hardly sustained even by Thucydides' own narrative, at
least of the Ten Years' War (Gomme 1951, 70f., 76-80), and
Perikles' followers, if not Perikles himself, may well
have contemplated 'epiteichismos'. Thucydides, though,
tells us nothing about any debates over strategy there may
have been in Athens after Perikles' death, so we can only
guess that in 427 'epiteichismos' had been promoted from
a longer-term to a short-term objective. Among the men
elected general who actively favoured this tactic I would
single out Nikias, who completed the first 'epiteichismos', and Demosthenes. Between them, by employing the
tactic in Messenia and Lakonia, they very nearly won the
war for Athens in the full sense, although the element of
chance should not be overlooked. Historians have perhaps
underestimated the extent to which such a tactic was the
logical one to employ against Sparta in the light of its
geographical situation and the course of its history since
the Persian Wars.

Demosthenes makes his first appearance in Thucydides in
the summer of 426 as one of the commanders of a fleet sent
round the Peloponnese (3.91.1). His career as general in
Aitolia in 426-425 was chequered, though ultimately
successful, but its main significance for the future was
that it brought him (like Tolmides and Phormion before
him) into a close working relationship with the Naupaktos
Messenians, for whose strategic and tactical skills he
conceived a healthy respect. It was they who persuaded
him to undertake the Aitolian campaign on the grounds that
the Aitolians constituted a threat to Naupaktos (3.94.3;
95.1); one of their number acted as guide (3.98.1); their
hoplites played a crucial role in the decisive battle with
the Aitolians and Peloponnesians (3.108.1); finally, and
not least, their Doric speech was for the first time used
to confound Doric-speaking adversaries, in this instance
the Ambrakiots (3.112.4). It was perhaps to mark these
exploits that the Naupaktos Messenians erected a monument

in the Athenian portico at Delphi (M/L, p.244). A
similar offering at Olympia is perhaps to be dated about
five years later (M/L no.74).

With 425 we reach the episode which more than any other
before the abortive conspiracy of Kinadon in c.399 unmasks
the realities of life in Lakonia and Messenia and so
exposes Spartan priorities in decision-making to the
glare, as unusual as it was unwelcome, of publicity: the
Pylos affair - or 'disaster' as it seemed to the Spartans
(4.15.1; 7.71.7). Reverting superficially to the pattern
established in 431 and 430, the Spartans led an invasion
of Attika in the spring, to which the Athenians responded
with an expedition round the Peloponnese (4.2.1f.). For
once, however, Thucydides permits us some insight into the
character of Athenian policy since Perikles' departure.
This Athenian fleet had for its main objective an intervention in Sicily (where Athenian forces had been engaged
since 427), but en route to Sicily it was to settle the
vicious civil war in Kerkyra that had raged since 427, and
en route to Kerkyra it was envisaged that Demosthenes
might make some special use of the fleet on the Peloponnesian coast (4.2.4). 'No wonder', comments Gomme (1956,
438), 'that Athens had little success in Sicily.' What
concerns us is the role of Demosthenes.

According to Thucydides (4.3.2), who seems to have had
Demosthenes for a source, he had joined the expedition
expressly to conduct an 'epiteichismos' at Pylos on the
west coast of Messenia. The discrepancy between this
specific statement and the vague wording of 4.2.4 is
ambiguous: Demosthenes may have wished to keep secret the
location of his intended fortification or he may have felt
that the majority of the Athenian Assembly would not share
his views on Pylos. At any rate, neither his two fellow-
commanders nor the junior officers nor the other ranks
were convinced by the array of arguments he adduced in
situ in support of his project (4.3.2f.): that Pylos
possessed abundant timber and stone; that its situation
was naturally strong; that it was unguarded; that it had a
harbour close by; and finally that the Naupaktos Messenians, who knew the terrain and spoke the same language as
the Spartans, would both provide a reliable garrison and
do great damage to the surrounding country. The last of
these arguments strongly suggests that Demosthenes was
acting on the advice of the Naupaktos Messenians, whose
motivation is implicit in Thucydides' description of Pylos
as lying in 'the land that was once Messenia' (4.3.3; cf.
41.2). (Thucydides is wrong, however, to place Pylos at
400 stades from Sparta; by the easiest route via Oresthasion in south-west Arkadia it is some 600 stades or 90

kilometres.)

In the event, the only unanswerable argument in Demosthenes' favour was provided by an opportune storm, the second most portentous accident of the Ten Years' War. The Spartans at the time (May/June) were celebrating a festival and, confident that they would easily storm the Athenian fortification (it had been hastily erected and was manned by a few soldiers; there was not much grain in the place), merely informed the Peloponnesians, who were then encamped in Attika, of the occupation. Agis, however, perceptively and promptly withdrew from Attika, and a Spartan force was immediately despatched to Pylos, where it joined up with the nearest of the Perioikoi (presumably those of Mothone and Kyparissia). The other Lakedaimonians who had returned from Attika (presumably Lakonian Perioikoi) were slower to respond (4.8.1). Sparta's Peloponnesian allies were also summoned and the Peloponnesian fleet of sixty ships was recalled from Kerkyra.

Against them the Athenians despatched a fleet of fifty ships from Zakynthos, including some from Naupaktos, to supplement the five left with Demosthenes when the rest had continued on to Kerkyra. The reinforcements anchored off the unguarded island of Prote which served as the harbour of Kyparissia. Before their arrival, however, and presumably by prior arrangement, Demosthenes was joined by forty hoplites of the Naupaktos Messenians. The Spartans meanwhile sent over hoplites in relays to garrison the island of Sphakteria, Thucydides' ignorance of whose topography argues against autopsy (4.8.6, with Gomme 1956, 484). When their fleet arrived, some ships were detached to fetch timber from Asine for siege-engines (4.13.1); there are the remains of extensive oak-forests on the hills west of modern Koroni.

This stalemate continued until the Athenians by a victory at sea as it were put the Spartans permanently in check by taking their queen. For cut off on Sphakteria was one of the relays of hoplites, 420 men (4.8.7,9). The significance of the composition of this garrison for the organization of the Spartan army and the development of Spartan society will be considered at length below. In the immediate context what matters is the electrifying effect the potential loss of citizen hoplites had on the Spartan authorities. Treating the matter as a 'disaster', they concluded a local armistice and sent ambassadors to Athens to negotiate for the release of 'the men'. The terms of the armistice (4.16) were manifestly one-sided, only one clause – that forbidding the Athenians to land on Sphakteria – restricting the Athenians' freedom of movement. The Spartans on their side handed over all their

remaining ships at Pylos and further agreed to place in
Athenian custody all their warships from elsewhere in
'Lakonike' (meaning presumably those at Asine and perhaps
also Gytheion); in all sixty ships were surrendered.   They
contracted not to attack the Athenian fortification and to
send over to the blockaded garrison on Sphakteria only
moderate and perishable rations (two Attic choinikes of
barley meal, two kotylai of wine and some meat for each
soldier; half-rations for each servant).

The speech written by Thucydides for the ambassadors to
Athens (4.17-20) is the most telling possible comment on
the course of the war to 425, and best illustrates the
foresight displayed in their different ways by Perikles
and Demosthenes.   Yet again one wishes one could be sure
how closely Thucydides stuck to the original.   The
ambassadors begin with 'the men on the island' (4.17.1;
cf. 19.1), their chief though not their only cause for
anxiety.   They continue with an unmistakable reminiscence
of the fundamental provision of the Thirty Years' Peace,
over whose alleged breach Sparta had gone to war in 431:
'You (sc. Athenians) are now in a position where you can
turn your present good fortune to good use, keeping what
you hold....'   The idea had already been present to the
Spartans' mind in 427 (3.52.2), and it is even possible
that they had actually made a proposal for peace on these
terms towards the end of 426 (Gomme 1956, 391).   Anyway, a
little later in the speech the idea is made explicit by an
appeal to the 'dual hegemony' thesis: 'if we, Athens and
Sparta, stand together, you can be sure that the rest of
Hellas, in its inferior position, will show us every
possible mark of honour' (4.20; cf. Aristoph. 'Peace'
1082).

To bring out the full import of this speech the comment
of Gomme (1956, 459f.) cannot be bettered: after 'a war
begun with so many hopes, such high-sounding promises,
such favour from the greater part of the Greek world, and
continued with a series of miserable failures and but one
success, the inglorious victory over Plataia', the Spartans, for the sake of a handful of men, were reduced to
making 'an empty and, almost certainly, a vain offer' (sc.
of peace, alliance and friendship: 4.19.1).   So much for
the avenging of the injuries done by Athens to Sparta's
allies.   So much for the 'liberation' of the Greeks from
the Athenian yoke.

The rest of the story is more quickly told.   The
Athenian Assembly, then influenced mainly by Kleon (whose
stature cannot be truly grasped because of Thucydides'
transparent animosity towards him), refused to negotiate.
The armistice at Pylos ended, and the Athenians robbed

Sparta of its (mainly allied) fleet by refusing to hand
back the ships in their custody. The Athenian blockade of
Sphakteria was prolonged, however, both by the difficulties of the Athenians' own position (esp. 4.29.1) and by
desperate Spartan counter-measures. The most notable, and
drastic, of the latter was the unprecedented offer of
freedom to any Helot who would take over supplies (4.26.5).
    Eventually Kleon secured an extraordinary personal
command, resigned to him by Nikias, and, thanks chiefly to
the experience of Demosthenes (4.30.1) and the local knowledge of the Naupaktos Messenians (4.36.1), succeeded in
storming the Sphakteria garrison remarkably quickly. To
the astonishment of the Greek world (nicely captured by
the anecdote in 4.40.2) the 292 survivors, of whom only
about 120 were Spartan citizens (4.38.5), surrendered
rather than fight to the death. They were taken back to
Athens and used as hostages for Sparta's good behaviour;
their physical presence is attested by the find of one of
their shields in the Agora, where it had originally been
hung in the Painted Stoa (Cartledge 1977, 13 n. 14). It
was these prisoners, or rather the Spartiates among them,
who did most to hamstring the Spartan effort in the
remainder of the Ten Years' War.
    Sparta's troubles, though, had only begun. The fort-
ification at Pylos was garrisoned with Naupaktos Messenians, who, as Demosthenes had predicted, channelled their
'nationalist' aspirations, knowledge of the terrain and
Doric speech into successful guerrilla warfare, of which
the Spartans had had no previous experience. So successful
indeed was this warfare that the Messenian Helots began to
desert in sufficient numbers to conjure up the spectre,
always lurking in the Spartan subconscious, of a full-
scale Helot revolt (4.41.3).
    For some time, perhaps until the conclusion of an
armistice in 423, the Spartans continued to send embassies
to Athens to get back Pylos and 'the men' (cf. Aristoph.
'Peace' 665ff.). But the Athenians not unnaturally were
at first unwilling to do any deals. Rather they redoubled
their efforts at 'epiteichismos'. Later in 425 a large
fleet under Nikias attacked the Corinthia and Epidauros;
and Methana between Epidauros and Troizen was permanently
fortified (4.45.1f.). It has been suggested that Nikias
was merely anxious not to be outshone by Kleon and Demosthenes, but his exploits of 424, for which the ground had
been carefully prepared, argue that he had perceived the
wisdom of their strategy and felt it could profitably be
extended to Lakonia.
    For 424 was the first year of the war in which the
major sea-borne campaign was directed specifically against

Lakonia. Nikias' colleague in joint command of a fleet of sixty ships was Autokles son of Tolmaios. He may have been a relative of Tolmides (Davies 1971, no. 2717), and, if so, the kinship may not be irrelevant, since the primary objective of the expedition was the capture of Kythera, a feat Tolmides had accomplished in c.456-455. It appears from an inscription that Nikias received 100 talents for the expedition and that it departed in about the second week of May, a favourable time for the rounding of Malea with the Etesian wind blowing from the north-east.

Thucydides notes that the inhabitants of Kythera are Lakedaimonian Perioikoi, who are governed by an officer (called 'harmost' in a fourth-century inscription: IG V.1. 937) sent out annually from Sparta with a garrison of hoplites from the mainland. He does not say when the Spartans had instituted this method of control, which was not normally applied to other Perioikic communities; but, if it did not go back to the mid-sixth century, Tolmides' Periplous provides an obvious occasion. Certainly it appears to have been a necessary precaution (if an inef-fective one) during the Ten Years' War, since Nikias had been able to enter secretly into discussions with 'some Kytherians' (4.54.3).

It is tempting to infer from a general remark of Thucydides (3.82.1) about civil strife progressively con-vulsing practically the whole Greek world after 427 that these fifth-columnist Kytherians were in some sense democratically inclined. But they may simply have wished to use the Athenians to secure independence from the Spartans, who, as is implied by the alleged advice of Damaratos to Xerxes, were well aware of the strategic implication of Kythera's geographical situation. For apart from being a port of call for merchantmen from Egypt and Libya, Kythera also offered a convenient base for raids on Lakonia by sea, the only method of harming the region, as Thucydides (4.53.3) emphatically notes - since, that is, the land-route through the Peloponnese was normally shut off. In 424 Kythera was besides the one link the Athenians needed to complete a chain of bases around the Peloponnese: Aigina, Minoa, Methana, Pylos, Zakynthos, Naupaktos and Kerkyra were already in their control; Nisaia off Megara was soon to be added (4.69).

Nikias divided his fleet in two and made separate landings, the main one at Skandeia, which he occupied and garrisoned, the other at 'the part of the island that faces Malea' (4.54.1), that is either at Ay. Pelayia on the north-east (Gomme 1956, 733) or near Diakophti much further south (G.L. Huxley in Coldstream and Huxley 1972,

38). The latter force advanced on (and presumably took) the upper town of Kythera itself, notwithstanding the Spartan garrison, which indeed is conspicuous by its absence from the narrative and had perhaps been withdrawn to forestall a repetition of the Sphakteria débâcle.

Using Kythera as a base, the Athenians made wide-ranging raids on most of the coastal settlements in the Lakonian Gulf over a period of seven days. Asine (near Skoutari bay: this is the only certain reference to Lak-onian Asine in ancient literature), Helos, Kotyrta and Aphroditia are mentioned by name (4.54; 56.1). To increase the Spartans' embarrassment, the Athenians also made raids round Malea on the eastern coast of Lakonia, first at Epidauros Limera and then at Thyrea. The latter had a double point, because Aiginetan refugees had been settled here in 431. Thyrea was captured, looted, burnt and not apparently rebuilt. All Aiginetan captives were put to death at Athens, but the commander of the Spartan garrison and some Kytherian hostages suffered the milder fate of the 'men from the island' (4.57.3f.). Finally, Kythera became a tribute-paying member of the Athenian Empire at the rate of four talents a year, although no record of actual payments survives on stone.

To counteract these raids, the Spartans could not follow the example of the Corinthians in 425 and muster a single force for a decisive battle (4.42-4), but, as in 431 for Mothone, despatched mobile garrisons to various key points (e.g. Thyrea, as we have seen). They also took the extraordinary step of raising a small force of cavalry and archers, a sign of the exceptional nature of the situation as it was apprehended at Sparta. For, as Thucydides is careful to remark - and to underline by employing his favourite comparison between the Spartan and Athenian national characters - the Spartans were now more timid and hesitant than ever. They had suffered a great and unex-pected disaster on Sphakteria; Pylos and Kythera were in enemy hands: and the Athenians were making lightning raids on their own territory (4.55.1f.). Indeed, the situation was so grave that the Spartans feared 'there might be a revolution'. It is probable that, as in 425, what the Spartans mainly feared was a Helot revolt, but Thucydides' wording does not exclude civil strife within the Spartan citizen body, the one thing the 'Lykourgan' system was at such pains to prevent.

In this desperate crisis even the cautious Spartans were bound to review critically the course of the war so far and to draw radical conclusions. Such was the fertile soil into which Brasidas could sow the seeds of a new and more profitable approach. The ground for his Thracian

expedition had been laid by the foundation of Herakleia
Trachinia and by the long since (1.56.2) wavering loyalty
of Athens' Thracian allies, whose importance lay chiefly
in their control of crucial raw materials like shipbuild-
ing timber. Even so Brasidas failed to receive the whole-
hearted Spartan support that he required and - so Thucydides (4.81.2) fervently believed - richly deserved. The
reason emerges later: the 'leading men' of Sparta were
jealous of Brasidas, and besides it was not clear to them
how Brasidas' Thracian excursion would help to secure
their main objective in the war since 425, the return of
'the men from the island' (4.108.7).

It is of course regrettable for the historian of
ancient Sparta at this and many other junctures that
'Sparta did not wash her linen in public'(Gomme 1956, 358;
cf. Brunt 1965, 278-80). But it seems certain that it was
a mixture of this selfish jealousy with patriotic prud-
ence, actual necessity and perhaps financial stringency
which explains the composition of Brasidas' army - 700
Helots and 1,000 Peloponnesian mercenaries. The Helots
selected presumably had had some military experience as
armour-bearers and were of proven loyalty, but this time
they were equipped as hoplites by the state, the first
known instance of this remarkable procedure; and they were
despatched, if Thucydides is right, expressly because the
Spartans were anxious to get some Helots out of the country (4.80.5). The reason for their anxiety is given
earlier in the same chapter, when Thucydides repeats
(there are clear signs of a lack of revision at this
point) that the Spartans were afraid of a Helot revolt,
and then goes on to retail what is possibly the single
most illuminating episode bearing on Spartano-Helot
relations (4.80.2-4).

With Pylos in Athenian hands, Thucydides says, the
Spartans wanted a good pretext for sending some Helots out
of Lakonia or (Thucydides' Greek is ambiguous) they had
good reason to send them. For they feared the unyielding
character of the Helots (or, according to a variant reading, their youthful impetuosity). Then Thucydides inserts
the famous parenthesis already considered in Chapter 10
(again, however, the Greek is ambiguous): 'Spartan policy
is always mainly governed by the necessity of taking
precautions against the helots' (Ste Croix) or 'most of
the relations between the Lacedaimonians and the Helots
were of an eminently precautionary character' (Gomme).
Even if Gomme's interpretation of Thucydides' word-order
is correct, I would still subscribe to the broader version
of the generalization.

Next, Thucydides describes the Spartans' action. They

made a proclamation that the Helots should select from
among themselves those who thought they had best served
Sparta in the wars. The implication of the proclamation
was that these Helots were to be freed (like those who had
volunteered to take over provisions to Sphakteria), but
the real intention was to sort out the most obdurate
dissidents, who, the Spartans anticipated, would be the
first to put themselves forward. The Helots selected
about 2,000 from their number, who crowned themselves with
wreaths and made a progress of the local sanctuaries as if
they were freed. The Spartans, however, 'liquidated' them
(presumably at night), and no one knew how (a journalistic
exaggeration designed to convey the secrecy and enormity
of this mass execution; Plutarch, 'Lyk.' 28.6, makes the
educated guess that the Krypteia was responsible). No
doubt this 'necessary' measure was to some degree exceptional, and a reflection of the critical post-Pylos
situation in Lakonia; but, I repeat, Thucydides chose this
episode as a vehicle for his generalization about relations between Spartans and Helots, so we should concentrate on its 'normal' features. These I take to be,
first, the fact that these relations were based on fear
and, second, the willingness of the Spartans to go to
extreme lengths of cruelty to maintain their Helot base
intact.

Brasidas' Thracian campaign was triumphantly successful, not least because he made great play with Sparta's
'liberation' propaganda (4.85.1-5; 86.1, 4f., 108.2; 114.
3; 121.1) and because he was believed - somewhat naively
(cf. 4.87.4-6) - to be sincere. Other significant features were his repeated use of marching by night (including
one of the rare Greek attempts at surprise attack on a
defended town) and the foreshadowing of the widespread
Spartan use of governors known as 'harmosts' to control
supposedly friendly or allied states (4.132.3). The home
authorities, however, were insufficiently impressed,
despite Brasidas' masterstroke of capturing Amphipolis
(Thucydides' failure to save it led to his exile and no
doubt helps to explain his admiration for Brasidas); and
in spring 423 they concluded a one year's armistice (4.
117f.; Piccirilli 1973, no. 25) with an Athens chastened
not only by its Thracian setbacks but by its defeat at
Delion in Boiotia also in 424 (4.89-101.4).

The armistice is interesting primarily as an anticipation of the full peace that came two years later, many of
whose clauses it shares. Again, as in 425, the Spartans
were chiefly anxious to recover 'the men' (4.117.2), but
the terms reflect the improvement in Sparta's position
since then. For example, although each side was to keep

what it held, and thus the Athenians were to retain Pylos
(or Koryphasion, as the Spartans called it; cf. 4.3.3; 5.
18.7), they were not to venture beyond Bouphras (Voïdho-
koilia Bay?) and Tomeus (inland - but where?); and as for
the Athenians on Kythera, they were not to enter into any
communication with 'the alliance' (presumably the Peloponnesian League, but just possibly Sparta's other Perioikic
'allies' as well). On the other hand, the sixth clause
exposes Sparta's Achilles heel: neither side was to
receive deserters, whether free or slave (i.e. Helots
above all).

Not all Sparta's allies 'signed' the armistice,
although those who did so included the all-important
Isthmus block. Less surprisingly, Brasidas refused to
countenance what he saw as an impediment to his projects
and a poor return for his labours, and he proceeded at
once to breach it in spirit if not also in the letter
(4.123.1). This naturally fuelled the arguments of those
Athenians like Kleon who had not favoured the armistice,
and after its expiry Kleon led an army in August 422
specifically to recover Amphipolis. Overconfident and
inexperienced, he was soundly defeated by Brasidas, but
both generals died in the battle, and at a stroke two
important obstacles to the conclusion of a full peace were
removed. Negotiations to that end were begun in winter
422-421 and concluded, to the satisfaction at least of the
principals, in mid-March 421.

Thucydides sums up the considerations that weighed most
with the Athenians and Spartans, although the text of the
relevant chapters (5.13-17) is certainly interpolated to
some extent. With two exceptions Thucydides adds nothing
to the reasons influencing the armistice of 423. The
first exception is that 'the men from the island' are now
said to have included 'leading' Spartan citizens (5.15.1),
an expression which an ancient commentator glosses by
saying that they were related to 'leading' Spartans, i.e.
men formulating and executing policy. The second
additional reason is the 'Argos question'. The Thirty
Years' Truce of early 450 between Sparta and Argos was
soon to expire, and the Spartans judged, wrongly in the
event, that it would be impossible to fight Argos and
Athens at once. They also suspected, rightly, that some
Peloponnesian states planned to go over to Argos. In
particular, though Thucydides does not explicitly say as
much, Sparta was threatened by the attitude of Mantineia.
This important state had carved out for itself a small
'empire' in south-west Arkadia, had recently crossed
swords with Tegea (4.134.1) and had built a fort in
Parrhasia threatening the strategically crucial Skiritis

(5.33.1, with A. Andrewes in Gomme 1970, 31-4).

The Spartans, in short, whose territory was menaced from the south-west (Pylos), the south-east (Kythera) and the north (Skiritis), were more 'compelled' (in the Thucydidean sense) to make peace than the Athenians. There is also perhaps a hint in Aristophanes ('Peace' 622ff., with Ehrenberg 1962, 89) of Perioikic discontent with the war. So, to stiffen Athens' resolve, they threatened an invasion of Attika, but an invasion on a new, improved model: 'orders were sent round to the cities to prepare for building permanent fortifications in Attika' (5.17.2). The lesson of Pylos and Kythera had been learned, even if it was not to be acted upon for another eight years.

The basis for the negotiations in 422-421 was the same as that of Sparta's proposals for peace in 425: a return to the status quo of 431 and by implication of 445. The only difference was that in 421 the Spartans were not only prepared but able openly to ride roughshod over the wishes both of their allies and of their recent adherents in the Thraceward area (Ste. Croix 1972, 18, 157-9). This emerges starkly from the clause in the 'Peace of Nikias' (as it is usually called, after one of its chief sponsors) permitting Athens and Sparta to change any other clause by mutual agreement (5.18.1; cf. 23.6). This clause above all aroused consternation in the Peloponnese (5.29.2; cf. 30.1), and it was small wonder Athens insisted that Sparta's allies should swear separately to abide by the peace (5.18.9): this would prevent Sparta from concealing which of its allies declined. In practice these were the Boiotians, who refused to give up the fort of Panakton on the frontier with Attika (5.18.7; with 35.5; 36.2; 39.2f.; 40.1f.; 42.1f.); the Corinthians, who in fact objected to the losses they had incurred (5.30.2-4) but claimed publicly to be opposing Sparta's attempt to 'enslave' the Peloponnese (5.27.2); the Eleians, who considered the long-contested Lepreon in Triphylia on the border with Messenia to be theirs (5.31.1-5); and the Megarians, who wished to recover Nisaia (5.17.2).

Space forbids a listing of all the other clauses in the Peace of Nikias (Piccirilli 1973, no. 27). We may single out the one which both bears immediately on the main theme of this book and nicely illustrates the inefficacy of the peace. Athens contracted to return among other places Koryphasion (Pylos) and Kythera and to restore any Spartan prisoners of state held in Athens or Athenian territory (5.18.7). In fact, though, neither Pylos nor Kythera was returned, and it took yet another agreement, between Sparta and Athens alone, for Sparta to retrieve 'the men'.

This second agreement, concluded perhaps in late March
421, was a defensive alliance to last fifty years concur-
rently with the Peace of Nikias.

One of the main reasons for the alliance is implicit in
a unilateral clause binding the Athenians to aid Sparta
'if the slave population (sc. the Helots) should revolt'
(5.23.2). The other reasons are given by Thucydides in a
passage which most unfortunately is corrupt (5.22.2).
When emended in accordance with Gomme's plausible suggestion, it reads like this (with my exegetical notes in
parenthesis): the Spartans thought that the Argives (who
had refused to renew their Thirty Years' Truce with them)
would be least dangerous to them without Athenian aid and
that the rest of the Peloponnese would be cowed (because,
if they attacked Sparta or its loyal allies, they would be
faced by both Athens by sea and Sparta by land); for, if
it had been possible, the rest of the Peloponnesians
would have gone over to the Athenians. The Spartans, in
other words, anticipated that the opposition to their
hegemony of the Peloponnese would crystallize around a
potentially resurgent Argos (5.28.2) and saw that, to
safeguard their own narrow interests, it was imperative to
forestall a renewal of the alliance between Athens and
Argos. As it turned out, however, the alliance between
Sparta and Athens was no less inefficacious than the Peace
of Nikias.

The diplomatic manoeuvrings after March 421, which
radically dislocated the pattern of alliances since 445,
are too complicated to discuss here (see now Seager 1976);
discussion is anyway frustrated by the state of the first
eighty-three chapters of Thucydides' fifth book ('the odd
man out in style and technique, apparently not revised
even to the standard of Book VIII': Dover 1973, 20).
Clearly, though, the second phase of 'the' Peloponnesian
War opened like the first against a background of strong
dissatisfaction with Sparta's leadership among its allies.
Indeed, even stronger, since in 421 Mantineia actually
seceded from the Peloponnesian League, the first state to
take this drastic step since Megara in c.460. It naturally turned to Argos, chiefly because the latter, on the
advice of Corinth, had passed a decree 'inviting any Greek
state that chose, provided that such a state were independent and would deal with other states on a basis of legal-
ity and equality, to enter into a defensive alliance with
Argos' (5.27.2; cf. 28). The lead of Mantineia was followed by Corinth and Elis, but Megara and Boiotia held
aloof, expressly because they thought the Argive democracy
would be less congenial to their own oligarchies than Sparta
was (5.31.6; cf. generally 1.19). Tegea too held true to

Sparta, vitally so, since the Corinthians and Argives
believed that, if they could win over Tegea, they would
have the whole Peloponnese (5.32.3). It would be hard to
cite a more spectacular dividend of Sparta's policy of
'divide and rule' in Arkadia; a major factor in Tegea's
loyalty was precisely Mantineian disloyalty.

Sparta was not backward in reasserting its supremacy.
Probably soon after the middle of March the perhaps 500
or so survivors among Brasidas' 700 Helot hoplites returned from Amphipolis. The Spartans voted to liberate
them (a vote was needed because they were 'in a manner
public slaves') and allowed them to live where they wished
(normally Helots were, as it were, tied to the soil) - so
long, that is, as they undertook garrison duty at Lepreon
(5.34.1). This was not the first time Helots had been
liberated, but it is the first time that we get an indication of what liberation might mean in practice.

Despite much modern scholarship, there is no evidence
and no reason to believe that they received grants of land
in Triphylia, and the direction to garrison Lepreon
implies that these men were not made citizens, even of
inferior status. Other ex-Helots sent to Lepreon,
however, had been made precisely that, as their title
Neodamodeis (virtually 'new citizens') signifies.
Thucydides infuriatingly provides no information on their
origins or status, but it is a fair inference from the
fact that Brasidas took unliberated Helots to Thrace that
there were no Neodamodeis available in 424. The further
facts that we hear of Neodamodeis only between 421 and
370-369 and that they appear exclusively in military contexts suggest that they were a systematically trained body
first raised between 424 and 421 following the success of
Brasidas' Helots and intended solely to compensate for
that deficiency of manpower which, as the Pylos episode
demonstrates, had by 425 become critical. Their special
name will have been devised to differentiate them by
origin and status from the hoplites who had entered the
army via the agoge and participated in the common messes
and Assembly. They will have differed from the 'Brasideioi' and the Helots sent to Sicily in 413 (below) in
being manumitted prior to enrolment in the army.

The Spartans, then, held on to Lepreon, and in the
summer of 421 they demolished the Mantineians' Parrhasian
fort (5.33.1). But this was the limit of their success.
In particular, they were aggrieved that Athens had not
evacuated Pylos (5.35.6; cf. 39.3). After much negotiation the Athenians were in fact persuaded to withdraw at
least the Naupaktos Messenians, the other (sc. Messenian)
Helots and the deserters from Lakonike (?Lakonian Helots)

who had taken refuge there (5.35.7). But in winter 419-
418 some of these, perhaps only the Naupaktos Messenians,
were returned (5.56.2f.), and they remained until Sparta
recaptured Pylos in 409 or 408.

More grave even than this was the disunity within the
Spartan citizen-body. There had from the start been a
'hawkish' faction opposed to the conclusion of the Peace
of Nikias (and presumably yet more so to the alliance
with Athens). This faction had considerable success in
the elections to the Ephorate for 421-420, and ironically
its hand will have been much strengthened by the return of
'the men from the island', who would naturally have
supported a strong anti-Athenian line. Hence, I believe,
the remarkable punishment some of the latter incurred,
probably in the summer of 421. Being 'leading men', they
were already holding public offices, but they were behav-
ing in such a way that the highest Spartan authorities
feared internal revolution and deprived them of their full
citizen rights (5.34.2). In particular, they were forbidden to buy and sell, a prohibition to whose significance
we shall return in Chapter 14.

Argive prospects of fulfilling their most cherished
ambition, the hegemony of the Peloponnese (5.40.3), could
hardly, one would have thought, have been rosier. They
chose paradoxically to play safe. Having failed to renew
their truce with Sparta before it expired, in 420 they
sent 'fresh' proposals to Sparta (5.41.2): Kynouria was to
be restored to them as the price of their standing aside
from the conflict within the Peloponnesian League. When
the Spartans refused even to discuss its restoration, let
alone submit to independent arbitration, the Argives
proposed a 'romantic and preposterous combat' (Tomlinson
1972, 120) - a re-run 'Battle of the Champions'! The
Spartans were not amused, although in their anxiety to
secure Argive neutrality they did at least draft the terms
of a new agreement (5.41.3). This, we infer, would have
been concluded but for the timely intervention of Alkibiades, who used his family connections with Sparta and his
ample diplomatic skills to effect a rift between Sparta
and Athens and bring Athens into alliance with Argos,
Mantineia and Elis. Corinth, however, withdrew from this
axis (5.48.2; 50.5), consistently enough since its aim had
probably been simply to bring pressure on Sparta to abandon the foreign policy of 421.

In the summer of 419 the Argive alliance tried to
coerce pro-Spartan Epidauros. The Spartans marched out in
full force, apparently for the first time in their history,
but they got no further than Leuktra (probably near modern
Leondari in ancient Aigytis) on their frontier opposite

Mount Lykaion; and 'no one, not even the cities which had
sent contingents, knew what was the aim of the expedition'
(5.54.1). This passage contains two major difficulties.
First, who were 'the cities'? Andrewes (in Gomme 1970, 74)
argued that the reference is to the loyal members of the
Peloponnesian League, but I share the view of Ste. Croix
(1972, 345f.) that the Perioikoi are meant. For this
expedition, like the one against the Parrhasian fort in
421, was a purely Lakonian affair, and the Spartans'
paramount consideration was secrecy. Thucydides was not
alone in referring untechnically to the Perioikic communities as 'cities', and such an unquestioning duty of
obedience corresponds to what else we know of relations
between Sparta and the Perioikoi but is not appropriate to
the relationship of Sparta to its Peloponnesian League
allies since c.504.

The second main difficulty is to decide what was the
true aim of the expedition – and indeed of a subsequent
expedition in the same summer, which this time only got as
far as the Lakonian frontier at Karyai (5.55.3), the first
recorded use of the more direct route from Sparta to Tegea
(Figure 17). The answer, I suspect, is that they were
designed not so much to relieve Epidauros as to secure
Sparta's northern frontier against the kind of diplomacy
illustrated in the 470s by Gnosstas' proxeny of the Argives
at Oinous (Chapter 11). Alkibiades will not have been
less astute in this than Themistokles. However that may
be, in winter 419-418 the Spartans felt compelled to send
in a small garrison to Epidauros. This, however, the
Argives regarded as a breach of their alliance with Athens
(5.47.9), while the Athenians in reply ostentatiously drew
attention to Sparta's failure to implement all the provisions of the Peace of Nikias (5.56.3). In 418, with the
renewal of fighting between the Argives and the Epidaur-
ians, the Spartans decided to try conclusions with the
Argive alliance.

In midsummer after the grain-harvest they again marched
out in full force 'themselves and the Helots' (5.57.1).
This expression, used by Thucydides only here and at 5.64.
2 introduces one of the two main problems plaguing discussion of this crucial campaign, that of terminology.
'Helots', it has been suggested (Andrewes in Gomme 1970,
79), includes Neodamodeis as well as Helots proper, unless
(what is unlikely) Sparta maintained a reserve of trained
but not liberated Helots. Alternatively these Helots were
not combatants but assigned to the necessarily large
baggage-train (Welwei 1974, 127). But what is meant by
'themselves'? Thucydides of course refers to the Spartan
forces of 418 collectively as 'the Lakedaimonians', but

this term as used by and of the Spartans was always potentially misleading, since it could refer either to the
Spartans alone or to the Perioikoi alone or to a mixture
of the two (Toynbee 1969, 159-61). In 418, it has been
argued, the term achieved one of its most impressive and
disturbing feats of deception, the hoodwinking of Thucydides himself.

This brings in the second main problem of interpretation, that of numbers. Thucydides was struck by the size
of the forces put into the field by both sides in 418. He
describes the first Spartan force led out by Agis,
together with its Peloponnesian League allies, as 'the
finest Greek army that had ever been brought together'
(5.60.3), and he goes out of his way to give as detailed
and accurate an account of the numerical composition of
the second Spartan force (the one that fought the Battle
of Mantineia) as 'the secrecy with which Sparta's affairs
are conducted' (5.68.2) made feasible. Yet most modern
scholars have refused to accept Thucydides' figures as
they stand and have accused the historian, albeit reluctantly, of committing a fundamental category error. Both
of these major problems must be tackled here, for on their
resolution or at least illumination depends our evaluation
of the changing military role of the Perioikoi since 479.

The first phase of the campaign of 418 may be ignored,
beyond noting that Agis' conclusion of a four-month truce
with Argos on his personal initiative led to his being
tried and heavily fined (5.63.2-4, with Ste. Croix 1972,
351). So we begin with Thucydides' repeated observation
that Agis' army at Mantineia was perceptibly larger than
the opposition (5.68.1; 71.2). This provides the surest
indication that something is awry either in the transmission of Thucydides' text or in his calculations. For if
the aggregate strength of the 'Lakedaimonians' comes out
at only 4,484 (5.68.3), then they together with their
Arkadian allies (only the Heraians, Mainalians and
Tegeans) should have been far too inferior numerically
either to have camouflaged their inferiority in such a way
as to deceive Thucydides' informants (the historian was
not himself an eyewitness apparently) or to have won the
decisive victory they did. Wherein does the error lie?

To oversimplify grossly, two main solutions have been
proposed. The first, and most popular, holds that the
error springs partly from confusion over Spartan technical
terminology (Toynbee 1969, 396-401; and more tentatively
Andrewes in Gomme 1970, 111-17). Thucydides, it is
contended, wrongly speaks of the highest multiple of the
Spartan 'enomotia' (platoon) as the 'lochos' (battalion),
when he ought to have called it 'mora' (brigade). Thus,

since there were two inter-linked 'lochoi' in each 'mora',
of which there were seven at Mantineia (one of Brasidas'
veterans and Neodamodeis, six of the Spartiates and Perioikoi brigaded together), Thucydides has almost precisely
halved the true total of 'Lakedaimonians' - almost,
because the 600 Skiritai and the 300 Hippeis are not to be
included in the organization by 'morai'. The second solution (Forrest 1968, 132-5) rescues Thucydides' credit to
some extent by postulating that in 418 Spartans and Perioikoi were not yet brigaded together in the 'mora', as
they certainly were by 403 (Xen. 'Hell.' 2.4.31), and that
Thucydides' figures should be taken as referring only to
Spartiates.

The difficulties in the way of accepting either solution are wellnigh insuperable. Against the first, for
example, and leaving aside Thucydides' putative confusion,
it can be urged that there is no positive evidence for the
'mora' before 403 and that Xenophon in his 'Constitution
of the Spartans' ('Lak. Pol.' 11.4) implies that there
were four, not two, 'lochoi' to each 'mora'. Thus,
although both Thucydides' and Xenophon's analyses yield
the same total number of the smallest constituent units
('enomotiai') in the 'Lakedaimonian' army, they arrive at
this figure by different computations, each of which is in
its way unsatisfactory. Against the second solution it
may be argued that Thucydides' failure to remark on the
numbers and organization of the Perioikoi in the situation
of 418 practically constitutes criminal negligence and,
more decisively, that there is some indirect evidence that
the Spartiates and Perioikoi were indeed brigaded together
by 418.

On balance I find the latter objections the weightier,
and it may be added that a simple emendation of Xenophon's
text, suggested well over a century ago (Welwei 1974, 129
n. 40), would remove the contradiction between him and
Thucydides over the number of 'lochoi' in a 'mora'. Moreover, as we shall see, the adoption of the first solution
facilitates a coherent reconstruction of Lakonian social
and military history since 479.

The indirect evidence just mentioned is as follows.
First, a barbed shaft loosed by Thucydides (1.20.3)
against an unnamed predecessor: 'it is believed, too,
that the Spartans have a company of troops ('lochos')
called "Pitanate". Such a company has never existed.'
The unnamed predecessor is of course Herodotus (9.53.2),
who mentions the 'Pitanate lochos' in his description of
the Battle of Plataia. Herodotus, as we have remarked, is
notoriously unreliable on technical matters, and Aristotle
(fr. 541), when describing a Spartan army organized into

five 'lochoi', does not mention one called 'Pitanate'.
However, since one of Aristotle's five is variously transcribed as 'Messoatas' or 'Messoages', and clearly derived
its name from the 'obe' or village of Mesoa, Herodotus may
plausibly be understood as 'giving a common-sense explanatory paraphrase of an esoteric technical term' (Toynbee
1969, 372), whereas Thucydides' criticism though formally
justified would be pedantic. In 479, then, the Spartiates
were organized in five 'obal' regiments, as they had been
probably since the 'Lykourgan' reforms of the mid-seventh
century. But by 418 there were six 'Lakedaimonian' regiments and by 403 the 'mora' was in existence, a mode of
organization that we know from Xenophon ('Hell.' 4.5.10f.)
cut across local demarcations. Can we date the transition
from 'obal' to 'moral' army more precisely than 'between
479 and 403'?

Here we invoke the other two pieces of indirect evidence. Xenophon in his 'Lak. Pol.', which was written in
the second quarter of the fourth century, attributed the
institution of the 'moral' army to Lykourgos; in itself
obviously false, this attribution seems progressively more
implausible the nearer the date of the change is brought
to 403. Second, and more decisively, Thucydides in describing the Spartans' attempted defence of Sphakteria in
425 says that 'they sent the hoplites across to the
island, choosing the men by lot from each battalion
('lochos') of their army ... the one that was caught there
numbered 420 hoplites, with Helots to attend on them'
(4.8.9); later he tells us that of the 292 survivors from
the 420 about 120 were Spartiates, the rest Perioikoi
(4.38.5). Toynbee's explanation of the 420 (1969, 373f.,
376f., 382f., 391) as the sum of one 'enomotia' of thirty-
five men from each of twelve 'lochoi' possesses what
Einstein called the 'beauty' of the truly fruitful scientific hypothesis. For Toynbee's analysis of the 'enomotia'
as consisting of one man from each of the forty active-
service Spartan age-classes (20-59 inclusive) 'is as
secure as any hypothesis about the Spartan army can hope
to be' (Andrewes in Gomme 1970, 115). In 425, therefore,
Sparta would have called up thirty-five of the forty age-
classes, and the presence of Perioikoi in the garrison was
a consequence of the fact that they were now brigaded with
Spartiates in the twelve 'lochoi' of the 'moral' army (two
'lochoi' to each of the six 'morai'). Thus the terminus
ante quem for the army reform would be 425.

I cannot, however, follow Toynbee in linking the reform
exclusively with the great earthquake of c.465, since I
believe he has exaggerated its demographic effects (Chapter 11). On the other hand, he is surely right in arguing

that the purpose of the reform was to ease the share of
the military burden borne by Spartiate hoplites and shift
it more on to the shoulders of the Perioikoi. In 480
there had been a rough total of 8,000 Spartiates of military age. In 425 the potential loss of about 120, albeit
men of high social status, caused the Spartans to sue for
peace. Moreover, even though these men had surrendered to
save their skins, they, unlike the men who for one reason
or another had failed to die at Thermopylai, were neither
ostracized socially nor made to feel compelled to commit
suicide. Similarly, the two Spartan commanders who
refused to obey orders at Mantineia (5.72.1) were merely
banished. Finally, since at Mantineia five sixths (5.64.3)
of a full Spartiate call-up amounted to only about 3,000
men, the total number of Spartiates of military age had
dropped by a little over half in about two generations.
A drastic step like the army reform was needed to compensate for this decline of Spartiate military manpower,
since other measures (Chapter 14) were proving manifestly
inadequate.

Regrettably, we are wholly ignorant of the provision
made for the training of those Perioikoi who now found
themselves brigaded with Spartiates in the 'mora', and we
can only guess at the proportion they comprised of the
'Lakedaimonian' complement (against Toynbee's suggested
ratio of 6:4 see Welwei 1974, 130 n. 64). It is certain,
however, that the Perioikoi as a whole were well equipped
to handle a larger share of military responsibilities. Of
the notional 100 Perioikic communities some forty are
attested archaeologically in the fifth and fourth centuries (Figure 18). This would give an average requirement
of no more than 100 hoplites per community, if we assume
that Thucydides has roughly halved the true figure for the
'Lakedaimonians' at Mantineia. We may single out in this
connection the Skiritai of northern Lakonia, whose troops,
presumably armed as hoplites, were stationed in a position
of honour on the extreme left wing; and also Eualkes of
Geronthrai, who lost his life in the battle and was
proudly commemorated with the laconic epitaph 'Eualkes in
war at Mantineia', exactly as if he had been a Spartiate
(Jeffery 1961, 197f., 202, no. 60).

Victory for the Spartans at Mantineia was hardly won
and dearly bought. But victory in 'the greatest battle
that had taken place for a very long time among Greek
states' (5.74.1) repaired the damage done to Sparta's
reputation in 425 (5.75.3) and re-established its hegemony
of the Peloponnese (5.77.6). Argos, rent by civil strife,
withdrew from its alliance with Athens, Mantineia and
Elis, and in winter 418-417 made a treaty with Sparta

(5.77, 79). The two parties moreover made a joint
resolution not to enter into diplomatic relations with
Athens until it had abandoned its fortified posts in the
Peloponnese (5.80.1), namely Pylos, Kythera and Epidauros.
Mantineia too was reconciled to Sparta and, on condition
of relinquishing its Arkadian 'empire', made a special
separate treaty (5.81.1; Xen. 'Hell.' 5.2.2). The position of Elis in uncertain, although it may have rejoined
the Peloponnesian League by 413 (7.31.1; cf. 6.88.9).

Sparta's buoyancy is shown by the confident way in
which in 417 it intervened, on the side of oligarchy, in
Sikyon, Argos, Achaia and Tegea (5.81.2; 82.1; 82.3). The
only failure was at Argos, where a democratic restoration
brought the state back into alliance with Athens. Thucydides mentions almost in passing a winter campaign of the
Spartans against the Argolis in 417-416, their capture of
Hysiai and massacre of the free population (5.83.1f.). He
is also careful to remind readers of the continued occupation of Pylos, noting that in 416 the Athenians there
captured a great deal of plunder from Spartan territory
(5.115.2).

In short, 'all of Alkibiades' fine plans for completing
the humiliation of Sparta had gone astray' (Gomme 1970,
147; cf. K.J. Dover in Gomme 1970, 242, 248), and he
required a fresh initiative to re-establish his charisma-
tic authority with the Athenian people. Weariness with
fighting Sparta, the rise of a new inexperienced generation, the fabled wealth of Sicily, the eagerness of
Alkibiades himself - these and other factors opportunely
conspired to recommend the 'Sicilian Expedition', to which
Thucydides devotes most of his sixth and seventh books.
His admiring comment on the quality of the armada that
left Peiraieus in 415 has already been quoted in a
different connection; his final remark on the expedition
was that 'this was the greatest Greek action that took
place during this war, and, in my opinion, the greatest
action that we know of in Greek history' (7.87.5).

For the Athenians, however, it began as it ended,
disastrously. On the eve of sailing many of the Herms
were inauspiciously mutilated. There were also alleg-
ations in circulation, directed chiefly against Alkibiades,
concerning a plot to establish a tyranny and the profan-
ation of the Eleusinian Mysteries. (Intriguingly, one of
those eventually convicted, an uncle of Alkibiades, owned
a male Messenian slave: Pritchett 1953, 288, X.9; 1956,
278; it would be pleasant indeed to know how and why a
Messenian had exchanged serfdom in his native land for
chattel slavery at Athens.) Then, shortly after the
expedition sailed, its prime mover was recalled to stand

trial for his alleged profanity.

Here began Sparta's involvement, since Alkibiades jumped ship en route back to Athens, made his way to Sparta and (so Thucydides' account goes, but Alkibiades may have been his source) persuaded the Spartans to engage Athens on two fronts (6.89-92). At a crucial juncture in 414 they sent Gylippos to bring reinforcements to the beleaguered Syracusans (6.93.2); he sailed with two Corinthian and two Lakonian ships from Messenian Asine (6.93.3; 104.1) and slipped through the Athenian blockade to swing the balance in the Syracusans' favour (7.1.3f.). In 413 the Spartans sent a further force of 600 of the best Helots and Neodamodeis (7.19.3; 58.3). At the same time they implemented a decision at last taken in 414 (6.93.1f.), to effect an 'epiteichismos' in Attika (7.19.1). The turning-point in 'the' Peloponnesian War had been reached.

Any lingering sympathy the Spartans may have had for the Peace of Nikias was killed in 414. After a lull of two years the Spartans had invaded the Argolis twice that summer (6.95.1; 105.1). To the first invasion the Argives replied with a profitable reprisal against the Thyreatis, but on the occurrence of the second the Athenians despatched a fleet not directly to the Argolis but against the east coast of Lakonia (6.105.2). It landed at Epidauros Limera, Prasiai and elsewhere (perhaps Kyphanta and Zarax) and laid waste the land in flagrant breach of the peace.

This violation, together with the continuing raids from Pylos and Athens' refusal to submit to arbitration, persuaded the Spartans that now, in contrast to 432, justice and religion were more on their side (7.18.2f.). A further incentive to action was provided by Demosthenes in 413. En route to Sicily he first ravaged Epidauros Limera (cf. 7.20.2) and then established a fortified post 'opposite Kythera' on 'a kind of isthmus' (7.26.2: probably near what is now the island of Elaphonisos). The chief interest of this intended counterpart to Pylos is that Demosthenes thought it worth while trying to disaffect the Helots of Lakonia too. The fort at Trinasos (Paus. 3.22.3) north-east of Gytheion, whose remains perhaps go back to the fifth century, should probably be interpreted as a Spartan precaution against just this contingency. A final fillip to the Spartans was given by the result of the Sicilian expedition in 413 - 'to the victors the most brilliant of successes, to the vanquished the most disastrous of defeats' (7.87.5). No less brilliantly Thucydides twice (7.71.7; 86.3) illustrates the meaning and irony of the Athenian defeat by comparisons with Sparta's Pylos/Sphakteria disaster.

In a general reflection on the significance of the
Spartan 'epiteichismos' at Dekeleia (7.27f.) Thucydides
comments that it was 'one of the chief reasons for the
decline of Athenian power' (cf. Xen. 'Por.' 4.25). Looking back on the invasions of Attika in the Ten Years' War,
he points out that they had been short and had only temporarily interrupted the Athenians' access to some of
their land, whereas between 413 and 404 they were permanently deprived of all of it. For Dekeleia was equidistant
(at about eighteen kilometres) from the Boiotian frontier
and Athens, and from here Agis could see not only Athens
itself but the grain-ships arriving in Peiraieus (7.19.2;
cf. Xen. 'Hell.' 1.1.35). Agis, moreover, had the power
to send troops where he wished, to raise fresh forces and
to levy money; indeed, to begin with he had more contact
and influence with Sparta's allies than did the home
government (8.5.3).

Hence one ancient name for the final phase of 'the'
Peloponnesian War is the 'Dekeleian War'. The rest of
this account, however, will concentrate on an alternative
title, the 'Ionian War' (8.11.3), for two reasons: by more
of those ironies mentioned earlier in this chapter 'the'
Peloponnesian War was decided not by land in mainland
Greece but at sea, specifically at the Hellespont; and it
was decided less by Peloponnesian prowess than by Persian
gold.

The Sicilian disaster excited the optimistic belief
among the Greeks (not including Thucydides) that the war
would soon be over. In particular, both Athens (8.1.2)
and 'the city of the Spartans' (8.2.3: an unusual expression) expected the arrival shortly in the Aegean of a
Sicilian armada. Not for the first time, however,
Sparta's hopes of Sicilian ships were disappointed (for
431 see 2.7.1 with Gomme). So in 413-412 a total of 100
was ordered from the Peloponnesian alliance, this being
the greatest number it had actually managed to deploy in
the Ten Years' War (2.66.1). Of these one quarter was to
be built in Lakonia, presumably at Gytheion. Athens in
its turn fortified Sounion to give protection for grain-
ships from the Black Sea (cf. Xen. 'Hell.' 1.1.26) or
Egypt (8.35.2), withdrew from its 'epiteichismos' in the
Malea peninsula (cf. Xen. 'Hell.' 1.2.18) and concentrated
on ensuring the loyalty of its wavering Aegean allies
(8.4).

These energetic preparations recalled 431 (8.5.1), but
the ensuing struggle was a far more patchy affair than the
Ten Years' War. Thucydides' account breaks off in mid-
flow in 411, although it ends appropriately with one of
the chief reasons why Sparta did not make more rapid

headway (8.109.2). We shall return to this after a few
brief remarks on Thucydides' main surviving continuator,
Xenophon, on whom we must principally rely for the rest of
the period treated in this book.

Another Athenian writing as a political exile, Xenophon
was, however, a historian of a very different stamp from
his predecessor, and judgment of his value has usually
been passed in the form of a comparison between them.
Since Niebuhr ('his history is worth nothing; it is untrue,
written without care, and with perfect nonchalance') and
Grote ('to pass from Thucydides to the Hellenica of
Xenophon is a descent truly mournful') comparison has
usually been greatly to Xenophon's disadvantage. But just
as there has been something of a reaction against
Thucydides of late, so there has been one in favour of
Xenophon (most recently Higgins 1977). I agree with the
revisionists that Xenophon should be read according to his
own lights and not as a Thucydides manqué, but as a historian I am not yet convinced that his allegedly allusive,
ironic manner and anti-imperialist message are sufficient
compensations for his undoubted brevity, omissions and
partisanship (whatever its higher motivation may have
been). In particular, the discovery of fragments of the
'Oxyrhynchus historian' has damaged, perhaps irretrievably, Xenophon's reputation for accuracy (Bruce 1967;
Koenen 1976). On balance, therefore, I regard the transition from Thucydides to Xenophon as a descent, though not
perhaps a mournful one.

To return to Thuc. 8.109.2, we find there Tissaphernes,
governor of the southern of the two Persian provinces in
Asia Minor, hurrying to the Hellespont in summer 411 to
patch up his relationship with the Peloponnesians and in
particular to prevent them coming to an arrangement with
his northern counterpart and rival, Pharnabazus. Both
Persians had reason to support Sparta against Athens,
since the latter by developing an Empire had dried up a
source of Persian tribute and diminished the Great King's
prestige (8.5.4f.; cf. Ste.Croix 1972, 313). Specifically,
Athens had aroused Persian ire by reneging on its treaty
of perpetual friendship with Darius II and backing the
rebel Amorges, perhaps early in 414. On the other hand,
it was not in the Persians' interest that a defeated
Athens should simply be replaced by another Greek super-
power with imperial and 'Panhellenic' ambitions. Sparta,
in other words, should be supported, but rather in the way
that a rope supports a hanging man. This was particularly
the policy adopted by Tissaphernes (8.29; 46; 87.4; cf.
Xen.'Hell.' 1.5.9), allegedly at the instigation of the
resilient Alkibiades.

Sparta for its part was no stranger to dealings with
Persia. To look no further back than 432, Archidamos, who
laid such stress on Sparta's lack of cash, had envisaged
receiving aid from this source (1.82.1), and in 431 and
430 Spartan embassies had been despatched to the Great
King (2.7.1, with Diod. 12.41.1; 2.67.1, with Hdt. 7.137).
In 428, however, the Spartan navarch Alkidas had shown
himself remarkably timid and dilatory, even for a Spartan,
and failed to capitalize on Mytilene's revolt from Athens
by co-operation with Tissaphernes' predecessor (3.31.1); a
Spartan inscription of perhaps 427 (M/L no. 67), which
records contributions to its war-fund in Persian darics
and other media, suggests that more could have been
achieved. Moreover, Spartan diplomacy perhaps fell short
of its usual professional standards in dealing with
Persia, as the Athenians discovered in 425 when they
captured a Persian messenger on his way to Sparta. For
his despatches (in Aramaic) revealed that the Great King
was at a loss to know what the Spartans wanted of him:
each embassy, he claimed, told a different story (4.50).
That, however, is the last we hear of Spartano-Persian
relations until 412, an instance of a general deficiency
in Thucydides which presumably he would have remedied had
he lived to complete his work (Andrewes 1961).

In 412 there began 'the most noteworthy example of
foreign assistance' to a Greek state at war (Pritchett
1974, I, 47), the Persian subsidy of the Peloponnesian
fleet from 412 to 404. Pritchett most helpfully tabulates
this aid, with references to the ancient sources (apart
from Andok. 3.29 and Isokr. 3.97, who overestimated the
total at 5,000 talents or more). However, as Pritchett
notes, it was not until Pharnabazus in 410 took over the
role of chief provider from Tissaphernes that the aid made
any real difference militarily. For Tissaphernes had been
so far successful in his double dealing that in 412 the
Spartans formally sold the Asia Minor Greeks to Persia for
gold (8.58; cf. 84.5) and yet, although in 412-411 they
mustered large fleets including a sizable number of Lakonian ships (8.42.4; 91.2), in 411 were defeated at
Kynossema (8.104-6) and in 410 at Kyzikos (Xen. 'Hell.'
1.1.17-23). Indeed, after this second defeat the Spartans
were apparently so demoralized that they offered to call
off the war: each side was to keep what it held, except
that the Peloponnesians would withdraw from Dekeleia if
the Athenians would abandon Pylos (Diod. 13.52f.; Philochoros 328F149).

The Athenians, despite just having experienced unprecedented political upheaval at home (8.47-98), looked this
gift horse in the mouth and were never again presented

with so favourable an opportunity to make peace with
honour. For although the democracy of strategically
pivotal Samos remained magnificently loyal to the bitter
end (Xen. 'Hell.' 2.2.6), Athens' other major Aegean
allies one by one fell prey to oligarchic counter-
revolutions and defected to Sparta (esp. Chios: 8.15.1;40;
and Euboia: 8.95.2; 96.1). In 409 or 408 the Spartans at
last recovered Pylos (Xen. 'Hell.' 1.2.18; Diod. 13.64.6),
and perhaps Kythera simultaneously; and in 407 the
Persian prince Cyrus, then aged sixteen, was sent down
from Susa with a general command of the Asia Minor provinces (Xen. 'Hell.' 1.4.3; cf. 'Anab.' 1.9.7). It was his
friendship with the extraordinary Spartan Lysander that
sealed Athens' fate (cf. Thuc. 2.65.12) and incidentally
marked the final abandonment, despite the protests of the
Spartan navarch Kallikratidas in 406, of Sparta's preten-
sions to 'liberating' the Greeks.

In 407 and above all 405 Lysander received from Cyrus
the wherewithal to equip, train and maintain a fleet
adequate to defeat Athens. Notwithstanding Athens' base
at Sestos, occupied since 411 (8.62.2f.), Lysander gained
the final victory at Aigospotamoi in the Hellespont in 405
(Xen. 'Hell.' 2.1.20-30; contrast Diod. 13.106). This was
a triumphant confirmation of the Mytilenaians' prediction
of 428 that 'it is not in Attika, as some people think,
that the war will be won or lost, but in the countries
from which Attika draws its strength' (3.13.3-5). For
Lysander was master of the narrows, and Athens, its Black
Sea wheat-supply cut off, was starved into submission by
spring 404. After fruitless negotiations Athens lost its
walls, its fleet and its Empire and became a subject-ally
of Sparta (Xen. 'Hell.' 2.2.19-22; Plut. 'Lys.' 14).

One of the Peloponnesian admirals at Aigospotamoi may
have been a Perioikos from Zarax or Tyros (M/L, p. 289).
If so, he was a worthy successor to those Perioikoi who
since 412 had been entrusted with important naval missions
(8.6.4; 22.1) and an appropriate personage to end a
chapter one of whose main themes has been the increasingly
crucial military role of Sparta's Perioikic subjects.

NOTES ON FURTHER READING

The period covered by this chapter is perhaps the one to
which most modern research in Greek history has been and
is still directed, so these bibliographical notes may seem
even more inadequate than the rest. A useful recent text-
book on the fifth century is Will 1972, esp. 149-70
('First' Peloponnesian War), 313-39 (Ten Years' War), 340-

92 (421-404). Unfortunately, this was written before the publication of Ste.Croix 1972 and Meiggs 1972, which in their very different ways have between them created a new groundwork on which future scholarship must build. The former, unlike Kagan 1969, ranges far beyond its ostensible subject.

The commentary on Thucydides begun by A.W. Gomme and continued by A. Andrewes and K.J. Dover is presupposed throughout; commentary on Book 8 (by Andrewes) should appear soon. To the enormous secondary literature on Thucydides cited in Ste.Croix 1972, 295f., add now esp. Dover 1973 (an unorthodox and challenging pamphlet), Hunter 1973 (which perhaps overstates the reasonable case that Thucydides' literary artistry tends to turn not only the reader but the historian himself into the obedient servant of his own point of view), and Edmunds 1975 (esp. ch. 2 for Sparta).

Thucydides' handling of prominent individuals is treated in Westlake 1968; the most relevant Spartans are Archidamos, Brasidas (whose name, incidentally, may be connected with Prasiai) and Gylippos. Ramou-Chapsiadi 1978 appeared too late to be considered in the present work.

For the 'First' Peloponnesian War in general see Kagan 1969, 75-130; on Sparta's role therein Holladay 1977b. The terms of the peace of 445, the essential background to 'international' diplomacy down to 421, if not 404, are set out in Ste.Croix 1972, 293f., and, with extensive bibliography, in Piccirilli 1973, no. 21.

The Samian rebellion is discussed in detail by Kagan (1969, 170-8) and Meiggs (1972, 188-94).

On the Ten Years' War generally see Kagan 1974, which though detailed is perhaps insufficiently critical. Spartan strategy is admirably analysed in Brunt 1965; see also Cawkwell 1975.

Kagan (1974, 218-59) describes rather than analyses the Pylos/Sphakteria episode; more critical is Westlake 1974, but he underemphasizes the sharpness of the change in Spartan attitudes to the war after 425. A historical and topographical study of Thucydides' account of the Pylos campaign by J. Wilson is announced for 1979.

An interesting sidelight on the situation of Kythera in the late fifth century is thrown by recent Anglo-American excavations at Kastri; the Kytherians were using Attic and Corinthian as well as mainland Lakonian pottery (Coldstream and Huxley 1972, 159-65; 306f.). However, the Attic imports are not necessarily to be explained solely in terms of the Athenian occupation: Attic black-painted amphorai of the fifth century have been excavated at

Gytheion too (AD 21B, 1966, 157).

For comments on Sparta's relations with central and north Greece in the fifth and early fourth centuries see Andrewes 1971, 217-26; I would only add that the father of Chalkideus ('the Chalkidian', frequently mentioned in Thuc. 8) was perhaps one of those who favoured expansion by land to the north.

Bibliography on the Peace of Nikias and other treaties projected or concluded may be found in Bengtson 1975; on those including provision for arbitration in Piccirilli 1973. On the authenticity and function of the documents inserted verbatim by Thucydides see Meyer 1970 (a photographic reproduction of the first edition of 1955). Particularly problematic are the alliance between Athens and Sparta in 421 and the Spartano-Persian treaties of 412-411 (below).

A wide range of modern theories on the origins and status of the Neodamodeis is well discussed in Oliva 1971, 166-70. But he fails to explain their title satisfactorily, as does Welwei 1974, 142-58, which in other respects supersedes previous treatments. The suggestion that regent Pausanias envisaged the creation of Neodamodeis in the 470s has been advanced by Cawkwell (1970, 52) and followed apparently by Lazenby (1975, 249f.). But Pausanias is said to have offered the Helots full citizenship, and an offer to transform them merely into Neodamodeis seems insufficient to have aroused such violent opposition and served as a pretext for his murder. Sparta was not of course alone in freeing slaves for war: a particularly interesting parallel is Chios, which is specifically compared to Sparta for the size of its slave population in relation to the free (Thuc. 8.40.2) and which apparently freed slaves for service in the fleet in the late fifth century (Welwei 1974, 4 n. 12; 93 n. 104; 179 n. 8).

The battle of Mantineia is discussed in relation to the army reform in Toynbee 1969, 396-401. Other discussions of the reform, in addition to those cited in the text, are Anderson 1970, 225-51; and Welwei 1974, 128-31, 138-40 (with most of whose conclusions I agree).

The most recent biography of Xenophon in English is Anderson 1974. Though dismissed by Higgins (1977, xiv) as unoriginal, Anderson does at least share Higgins' respect for Xenophon. The only full commentary in English on the 'Hellenika' is Underhill 1900, which though thorough and sensible is naturally out of date, especially in the eyes of those who wish to argue that the 'Hellenika' is a unity (Baden 1966) and that Xenophon's historiographical intentions have been misprised (Higgins 1977, 99-127). My own view coincides with that expressed in summary by G.L.

Cawkwell (introduction to the 1972 reissue of the Penguin
Classics 'Anabasis'): the 'Hellenika' is essentially the
memoirs of an old man.

On the role of Lysander between 407 and 404 see Lotze
1964; this also discusses clearly the chronological problem of 410-406, on which see further Lotze 1974.

Lewis 1977 is an important contribution to Spartan
history of the late fifth and early fourth centuries. We
agree substantially on basics: a large subject population
of Helots was 'the major determining fact about Sparta'
(27); and 'the Athenians would have had no difficulty in
winning the Peloponnesian War decisively, had they done a
little more to promote helot revolt' (28). But we differ
considerably in emphasis and detail. I cannot, for
example, regard the first two Spartano-Persian accords of
412-411 (Thuc. 8.18, 37) as genuine treaties. Nor am I
persuaded of the existence of a 'Treaty of Boiotios' of
408-407 between Sparta and Persia, as reconstructed by
Lewis (123-34). For if Sparta made its peace overtures to
Athens in 410 and 408-407 partly to recover Spartiate
prisoners (126), this seems an unlikely time for Sparta to
be concerning itself about the liberty and autonomy of the
Asiatic Greeks. And as Lewis himself rightly remarks of
Spartan 'panhellenism' (144), 'I would not argue that it
took precedence in Spartan policy over her need to retain
supremacy in the Peloponnese and internal stability in
Laconia and Messenia.'

13 The reduction of Lakonia 404-362

The essential backdrop to this chapter is provided by
Thucydides' comment on the stasis or civil strife at
Kerkyra in the 420s (3.82.1): 'thereafter practically the
whole Greek world was similarly convulsed, the democratic
leaders calling in the Athenians, their oligarchic opponents the Spartans.' So far as 'the' Peloponnesian War is
concerned, the comment applies particularly to its final
phase, in which stasis was a major contributory cause of
Athens' defeat. Stasis, however, did not subside with
the conclusion of the war. Rather, it burst out anew,
the rule of the 'Thirty Tyrants' at Athens being but the
best-known instance. Indeed, the history of the whole
period spanned by the long adult life of the Athenian pub-
licist Isokrates (436-338) can be written largely in terms
of what might be called the Greek disease (Fuks 1972).
   Even Sparta, as we shall see, was three times on the
verge of catching the infection. What makes this so
remarkable and revealing is that it was precisely for its
vaunted freedom from stasis within the citizen body that
the Spartan political and social system had come to exercise such fascination over oligarchs in other states - men
like Kritias, bloodstained leader of the 'Thirty Tyrants'
who wrote both a verse and a prose 'Constitution of the
Spartans' (we drew on the latter in Chapter 10). Another
such 'Lakonizer', if a politically more moderate one, was
Xenophon, whose unsatisfactory 'Hellenika' is our main
literary narrative source for the period under review
here.* Occasionally our other literary sources -

* Where no other indication is given, all references
  in brackets in this chapter are to the 'Hellenika'.
  It should be pointed out here that many of the dates
  given in this chapter are more or less controversial.

267

especially Diodorus, using Ephorus, and Plutarch, who drew
on several fourth-century sources including Xenophon and
Ephorus - provide correctives and supplements. But these,
like the relevant epigraphical and archaeological evidence,
rarely bear on our main theme, which is the way that
Sparta's progressive failure to maintain its grip on
Lakonia and Messenia and on the Peloponnesian League led
to its demotion from a position of supremacy in the Greek
world east of the Adriatic to the status of an irretrievably second-rank power.

Spartan might since the end of the seventh century had
been based on the exploitation of Helot labour-power in
Lakonia and Messenia, aided and abetted by a complex
organization of Perioikic intermediaries (Chapter 10).
From the mid-sixth century Sparta had extended its suzerainty to the greater part of the Peloponnese and, with the
establishment of the Peloponnesian League in essentials by
500, had since then held sway through a combination of
military muscle and diplomatic support for allied oligarchies (Thuc. 1.19, 76.1, 144.1).

Victory over Athens in 404 stimulated a temporary
attempt to extend the system in a modified form to the
members of the old Athenian Empire. Narrow oligarchies,
frequently only of ten men ('dekarchies'), were established and propped up by garrisons under Spartan governors
known as harmosts ('fixers'); tribute in military service,
cash and kind was now payable to Sparta. The best documented and historically most decisive example of such
counter-revolution is of course the reign of the 'Thirty'
at Athens, but it is convenient first to consider the
experience of Samos, since it reintroduces the victor of
Aigospotamoi.

Lysander had done more than any other Spartan to win
'the' Peloponnesian War through his understanding with
Cyrus. He also it was who most favoured the policy of
imperialist expansion by means of puppet dekarchies, for
the installation of which he had prepared the ground since
407. Following Athens' capitulation in 404, Lysander
naturally turned his attention to Athens' staunchest
democratic ally, Samos, whose control was besides of major
strategic importance. After a siege lasting the whole
summer Samos was taken, the democratic régime terminated,
the oligarchs recalled. The Akanthians in 423 had honoured their 'liberator', Brasidas, with a crown as if he
were a victorious athlete (Thuc. 4.121.1). The restored
Samian oligarchs honoured Lysander as if he were a god
(Plut. 'Lys.' 18), the first attested instance of divine
worship of a living mortal in Greece. Undoubtedly
Lysander's reputation has suffered from posthumous

defamation (Prentice 1934); but such adulation in his
lifetime tells us more about Samian politics than about
Lysander's qualities.

For whatever we think of his Samian settlement his
treatment of Athens was hardly prudent. The terms of surrender imposed in April 404 had included no explicit constitutional provision beyond the requirement to recall
exiles. Among the latter was Aristoteles, a creature of
Lysander and later one of the 'Thirty' (2.2.18), spiritual
kin to those among the 'Four Hundred' extreme oligarchs
who in 411 had been prepared to sell Athens and its allies
to Sparta in return for Spartan support for their rule
(Thuc. 8.40.2). It was on behalf of such men that Lysander sailed from Samos to Athens and, using the threat of
force and the pretext that the Long Walls had not been
pulled down as prescribed, had a decree passed establishing a board of thirty legislative commissioners (Lysias
12.44, 72, 77; 13.28; Plut. 'Lys.' 15).

The pro-Spartan character of what soon degenerated into
the tyranny of the 'Thirty' had been apparent from the
start. It was not long before the new régime stole
another leaf from the Lysandrean book and through his
influence received from Sparta a 'Lakonian' garrison of
700 men (probably Neodamodeis: Anderson 1974, 50) under a
Spartiate harmost (2.3.13f., 42; 4.4, 6, 10). In the
event, however, at least in Xenophon's account (and he
seems to have been present), the garrison was indirectly
a major cause of a split within the ranks of the 'Thirty'.
For Kritias used it to kill and rob the rich, whatever
their political persuasion or social standing (2.3.14, 17,
21), and this alienated Theramenes (2.3.38-40, 47-9), the
very man responsible for negotiating with Lysander in 405-
404 (2.2.16) and securing the subjection of Athens to
Sparta (2.3.38).

Theramenes' impious execution particularly excited the
sympathy of Xenophon (2.3.55f.), but more disturbing to
thinking Spartans was the fact that not only their traditional enemy Argos (Diod. 14.6.2) but also their allies
Corinth, Megara and Thebes were openly flouting a Spartan
decree forbidding any state to harbour Athenian refugees
(2.4.1, with Aesch. 2.148; Isokr. 7.67; Diod. 14.6, 32.1;
Plut. 'Lys.' 27.5-7). The disobedience of Corinth and
Thebes was particularly alarming since they had opposed
Sparta's treatment of Athens on its surrender and had
advocated that Athens be totally destroyed (2.2.19f.; cf.
3.5.8). Sparta, on the other hand, had proposed its
demilitarization and incorporation in the Peloponnesian
League, partly perhaps in recognition of its past services
to Greece, but surely also in order to undercut Thebes'

growing influence north of the Isthmus. The relations
between Sparta, Athens and Thebes shaped Greek interstate
politics down to the 360s.

Immediately, it was very largely due to Theban aid that
a mere seventy or so democratic exiles under Thrasyboulos
were able to seize the Athenian frontier fort of Phyle in
winter 404-403 (2.4.2-7) and then to collect a sufficient
force, composed chiefly of 'the men in the Peiraieus', to
defeat the 'Thirty' in an urban encounter (2.4.10-19).
The survivors of the 'Thirty' fled to Eleusis, where they
set up a separate polity, and were replaced by the 'Ten'.
Both sets of oligarchs scurried to Sparta for further help
(2.4.28; 'Ath. Pol.' 38.1). The Spartans replied by loan-
ing 100 talents to the oligarchs 'from the city' for the
hire of mercenaries and by despatching Lysander by land as
harmost and his brother Libys by sea as navarch to Attika.
Lysander went straight to his friends at Eleusis and began
to raise a large force of Peloponnesian mercenaries; Libys
blockaded the Peiraieus according to plan. But then there
occurred one of those startling reversals of Spartan
foreign policy whose causes, despite recent attempts to
analyse Spartan decision-making in terms of 'factions'
(Hamilton 1970; contra Thompson 1973), can only be surmised.

Agis had by now (403) returned to Sparta from Dekeleia
and was presumably in broad agreement with the line Sparta
had taken towards Athens since April 404. His Agiad co-
king Pausanias, however, having first convinced a majority
of the five Ephors, led out two 'morai' of 'Lakedaimonians.'
at the head of a Peloponnesian League force. There was
some fighting between the Peloponnesians and the Peiraieus
democrats, in which the two Spartiate polemarchs and other
Spartiates were killed; but Pausanias entered none the
less into secret negotiations with his opponents, and the
deputation they sent to Sparta had the blessing of the two
Ephors on the campaign, both of whom supported Pausanias'
conciliatory policy.

Faced with a rival deputation from the 'city' oligarchs,
the Spartan Assembly instructed a fifteen-man commission
to come to an agreement with Pausanias over the settlement
of Athens. The upshot was the restoration of full democracy and the proclamation of a general amnesty (2.4.43),
the first known in history, followed two years later by
the political reunification of Attika. One small way in
which the democrats thanked their Spartan liberators was
by erecting in the Kerameikos a fine tomb for those Spartans they had killed in the Peiraieus (Willemsen 1977).

The tomb, Xenophon notes (2.4.33), lay outside the city
gates - in fact on the road to the Academy in what has
been called the Westminster Abbey of Athens. There were

fourteen burials in all, the corpses being laid out with
their heads resting on stone 'pillows' and pointing
towards the street. In the approved 'Lykourgan' manner
the burials lacked grave-goods, apart from one which
contained merely a strigil. The tomb was originally
marked by an inscribed marble block over twelve metres
long and by three stelai. The stelai and most of the
block are now lost, but the names of the two polemarchs
cited by Xenophon are wholly preserved.

Reaction to Pausanias' settlement extended along a
spectrum from democratic jubilation at Athens (Lysias 13.
80) through mixed feelings at Thebes and Corinth (neither
of which had sent forces for Pausanias' army, probably
because they feared a Spartan take-over of Attika) to
outright hostility from Pausanias' enemies at Sparta. The
latter succeeded in having him put on trial for retreating
from Athens after an indecisive battle (Paus. 3.5.2), but
despite the fact that even Agis voted for condemnation he
was acquitted. More important, the Lysandrean form of
imperialism through narrow oligarchies was definitively
abandoned (Andrewes 1971, 206-16).

The following year (402) Sparta took two decisions with
vital long-run consequences. The first was to 'bring the
Eleians to their senses', as Xenophon (3.2.23) paraphrases
the resolution of the Ephors and Assembly. The immediate
issue was the one that had divided the two states since
the Persian Wars, namely how far Elis should be allowed to
extend its direct political control over what it took to
be its own 'perioikic cities' in Eleia and Triphylia. But
the Spartans and particularly Agis were also anxious to
punish Elis for its defection from the Peloponnesian
League in 420 and subsequent failure to meet its League
obligations in the war, and for two insults delivered in
virtue of its custodianship of the panhellenic sanctuary
of Zeus at Olympia.

The 'liberation propaganda' which the Spartans now
officially resuscitated was therefore so much window-
dressing, and the undeceived Boiotians and Corinthians
significantly refused again to contribute contingents to
the League force (3.2.25). A weak and cautious Athens,
however, did follow the Spartans' lead, and the campaign,
which extended over two years, was brutally successful.
In economic terms it provided a veritable 'harvest for the
Peloponnese' (3.2.26; cf. Pritchett 1974, I, 78). Politically, Elis was stripped of all its dependencies apart
from Olympia and compelled to conclude a treaty of peace
and alliance on those terms (3.2.30f.).

After this, according to Diodorus (14.34.2f.), the
Spartans took the opportunity of tidying up some loose

ends from the great Helot revolt of the 460s. The
Messenians settled by the Athenians at Naupaktos and on
Kephallenia were now expelled and sailed away, some to
Sicily (ironically to become mercenaries in the service of
Sparta's ally Dionysios I, tyrant of Syracuse since 405),
some to Cyrenaica.

The second major decision taken by the Spartans in 402
was to send official support to Cyrus in his bid to oust
his elder brother Artaxerxes II, who had succeeded to the
Persian throne some two years earlier (3.1.1; cf. Diod.
14.19.2). The Spartans were of course deeply indebted to
Cyrus (1.5.2-9; 6.18; 2.1.11-14; 3.1.2), but we may suspect that they also hoped to repair the damage done to
their credibility as liberators by the treaty of 412-411
and Lysander's dekarchies. For the Greek cities of Asia
had revolted from Tissaphernes to Cyrus (Xen. 'Anab.' 1.1.
6). Be that as it may, the aid they sent was slight,
thirty-five Peloponnesian ships under the navarch Samios
or Pythagoras (Sealey 1976, 349f.) and 700 hoplites under
the Spartiate Cheirisophos (Xen. 'Anab.' 1.4.2f.). These
hoplites were not Spartan citizens, Perioikoi or even
Neodamodeis but probably Peloponnesian mercenaries (Roy
1967, 300), and they formed a small proportion of the
10,000 or so hired altogether, more than half from over-
populated Arkadia and Achaia.

This was not the first time Greek mercenaries had been
extensively used in a Persian dynastic struggle, but the
'Ten Thousand' were the largest body of Greek mercenaries
yet recruited for a single mission. As such their significance can tend to be overrated, especially since our
information on their vicissitudes comes chiefly from
Xenophon's 'Anabasis', a first-hand account but written up
several decades later. None the less this work does
reveal that Sparta had sent out as Cheirisophos' under-
study a Perioikos, Neon, an 'Ulsterman' from Messenian
Asine ('Anab.' 5.3.4; 6.36 etc.); it provides a wealth of
detail on conditions in the western extremities of the
Persian Empire; and, above all, it supplies the essential
linking material omitted from the 'Hellenika' in the
abrupt transition from the restoration of democracy at
Athens in 403 (2.4.43) to Sparta's declaration of war on
Tissaphernes in the autumn of 400 (3.1.4).

Cyrus had been unnecessarily killed and so defeated at
Cunaxa in Mesopotamia in 401. Six out of the eight Greek
generals of the 'Ten Thousand', including their supreme
commander Klearchos (a Spartan exile), had been treacherously murdered by Tissaphernes, who had wisely chosen the
path of loyalty to Artaxerxes. Only with great hardship
did the 8,000 or so survivors struggle back to the Black

Sea and Greek civilization in 400.

Their reception here, however, was not all they might have hoped. In particular, the navarch Anaxibios and Aristarchos, harmost of Byzantion, did not shrink even from selling 400 of them into slavery ('Anab.' 7.1.36; 2. 6). One would therefore be forgiven for thinking that the official attitude of Sparta towards the sizeable remnant of the 'Ten Thousand' in the summer of 400 was at best negative, at worst actively hostile; and that Sparta wished thereby to make some amends to Artaxerxes for supporting Cyrus. However, three chapters and a few months later another extraordinary volte-face in Spartan foreign policy is reported ('Anab.' 7.6.1): two Spartiates arrive from Thibron to announce that the Spartans have decided to fight Tissaphernes and Pharnabazus. Thibron himself arrives in the spring of 399 with 1,000 Neodamodeis and 4,000 other Peloponnesian troops (3.1.4) and promptly absorbs the remainder of Cyrus' Greek mercenaries into his own force (3.1.6; 'Anab.' 7.8.24).

Xenophon's account of the background to this change of heart is plausible enough so far as it goes, but his order of narration has obscured a vital connection. Tissaphernes, in high favour with Artaxerxes, was given command of Asia west of the Halys river (3.1.3; 2.13). His demand that the Ionian cities should be subject exclusively to him and his attack on Kyme provoked two Ionian embassies to Sparta (3.1.3; 2.12), whose aid was sought in its capacity as 'leader of all Greece' (cf. 'Anab.' 6.6.9, 12, 13; 7.1.28). The Spartans replied first with a diplomatic note (Diod. 14.35.6) reminiscent of their response to Cyrus the Great on behalf of Croesus in c.550 (Hdt. 1.152) and then by despatching Thibron (above). What Xenophon fails to do, however, is link this aggressive anti-Persian policy with the death of Agis and the role played by Lysander in the unexpected accession of Agis' brother Agesilaos (3.3.1-4). Perhaps Xenophon was unwilling to admit any evidence that might detract from his picture of Agesilaos the 'panhellenist' fervently seeking the liberation of the Asiatic Greeks, an image which the king himself was anxious to foster. At any rate, the most economical explanation of this turn of events is that Lysander hoped to use Agesilaos and the new policy to regain the ground he had lost to Pausanias since 403.

Instead of spelling this out, Xenophon follows his description of Agis' funeral ('more awful than befits the mortal estate') and Agesilaos' elevation with what is perhaps the most remarkable episode in all Lakonian history, the conspiracy of Kinadon (3.3.4-11; cf. Arist. 'Pol.' 1306b34-6). I am still unclear why Xenophon

mentions this incident, which at least in his account had
no serious or obvious consequences, while he omits others
that are blatantly material to his chief interests. But,
whatever his intention, he has certainly succeeded in
exhibiting in a brief compass the variegated social
structure of Lakonian society at the turn of the fourth
century. For this reason discussion of the conspiracy's
social implications has been postponed to the next chapter. Here follows just an annotated summary.

The conspiracy was uncovered within a year of Agesilaos'
accession. This timing is not likely to be fortuitous.
For apart from the succession crisis provoked by Agis'
death, his funeral would have provided a marvellous
opportunity for a prospective revolutionary to test the
political temperature, since the elaborate ritual prescribed by Spartan custom involved the congregation at
Sparta of not only the Spartiates but Perioikoi and Helots
too, presumably heads of households, and their wives
(Tyrtaios fr. 7; Hdt. 6.58.2f.). It was then, I suggest,
that Kinadon began to plot.

Exactly what Kinadon hoped to achieve by his revolution
and how extensive and advanced the plot was when it was
betrayed to the Ephors - these are unclear. What is
certain is that his prime target was the Spartiates, citizens of full status. The conspiracy was to begin in
Sparta, presumably with the murder of suitably prominent
Spartiates, perhaps even of Agesilaos (from whom Xenophon
may have heard the story, which begins with Agesilaos'
ill-omened sacrifices). The Ephors were allegedly terri-
fied by what they considered a potent plan, but their
smooth and instant response suggests the existence of a
well-oiled counter-insurgency machine. In fact, it was
precisely because Kinadon had himself been employed on
similar missions in the past that the Ephors could now
send him, without arousing his suspicions, to Perioikic
Aulon in north-west Messenia to arrest some named Aulon-
ites and Helots.

The significance of this tactic, however, is unfortunately ambiguous (see Chapter 14), and the status of these
Helots at Aulon is problematical. Some like Welwei (1974,
109 n. 5) think that, exceptionally, the Aulonite Perioikoi could have Helots working for them. This I find
intrinsically improbable and suggest that it was precisely
because these named Helots were at Aulon and not working
their masters' kleroi in, say, the adjacent Soulima valley
that they were detailed for arrest. The site of Aulon too
is uncertain; indeed, it may have been a region rather than
a town, as its name meaning 'Hollow' suggests. But
Xenophon provides a strong hint that there was a Spartan

garrison here, perhaps under a harmost. For Kinadon is
ordered to bring back also a lady, presumably a prostitute,
whose physical charms were corrupting older and younger
'Lakedaimonians' alike. By this I think we should understand Spartiates or at least Neodamodeis as well as Perioikoi. The presence of a garrison on the Triphylian
border is easily explicable in terms of the recent
troubles with Elis, and there is besides archaeological
evidence, which may go back to the fourth century, for a
fort in just about the right place - at modern Vounaki
(MME no. 601).
     Ostensibly to accompany, but in fact to arrest, Kinadon
the Ephors sent six or seven 'younger'or 'young' men
(Xenophon uses both words). Since the selection of this
squad was by pre-arrangement entrusted to the eldest of
the (three) Hippagretai (cf. Xen. 'Lak. Pol.' 4.3), we may
assume that these men were Hippeis. We should not,
however, simply infer from this that Hippeis were regularly used to arrest Helots and Perioikoi, let alone that
they were the mainstay of the Krypteia. Rather, the
choice of members of the royal bodyguard is an index of
the Ephors' apprehension and may even imply that Agesilaos
himself was actively involved in the counter-measures,
although Xenophon only says vaguely that the Ephors had
consulted some Gerontes. In case of trouble, however, the
Ephors also detailed a 'mora' of cavalry as a back-up
force. This is our first evidence that the cavalry, which
had first been regularly raised in 424, was also organized
in 'morai'.
     All went according to the Ephors' plan. Kinadon was
arrested outside Sparta and confessed the names of his
closest confederates. The latter were then arrested too.
Intriguingly, they included a seer, Teisamenos, whom it is
tempting to see as a descendant of the Teisamenos who
gained Spartan citizenship before the Battle of Plataia
(Chapter 11); perhaps this citizenship was somehow of an
inferior kind. All those detained had their hands bound
and their necks put in dog-collars and were thus dragged
around Sparta under the whip and the goad. 'So they met
their punishment' is Xenophon's laconic coda. We may
suspect, however, that they were executed, though perhaps
only after due process.
     Xenophon's account continues with Sparta's response in
396 to the news of a Persian naval build-up in the Aegean
(3.4.1). By this time Sparta had been fighting in Asia
Minor for three years. Thibron had been replaced in the
autumn of 399 by Derkylidas (3.1.8), a skilful diplomatist
and general, typically Spartan in his religiosity (3.1.17;
2.16) but ostentatiously unSpartan in his Sisyphos-like

cunning (cf. Ephorus 70F71) and bachelor status (to which
we shall return in Chapter 14). He raised the number of
his troops to about 1,200, some 400 of whom were allocated
to garrison-duty in the cities which he and Thibron had
liberated from Tissaphernes and Pharnabazus. In winter
399-398 he concluded a truce with Pharnabazus to avoid
billeting his troops on the liberated cities (3.2.1; Diod.
14.38.3), and this was renewed in spring 398 after ratif-
ication by a three-man commission sent out by the Ephors
(3.2.6, 9).

By 397, however, Pharnabazus and Tissaphernes had overcome their mutual suspicion (3.1.9) and were actively co-
operating (3.2.13). In particular, Pharnabazus had
secured money from Artaxerxes to put in commission a fleet
of 300 Phoenician ships under the Athenian Konon (Diod.
14.39; cf. Isokr. 9.55; Plut. 'Ages.' 6.1; Nepos, 'Con.'
2; Paus. 1.3.1). This important development is omitted by
Xenophon, although he does give us the name of the Spartan
navarch for 398-397, Pharax (3.2.12, 14). In summer 397 a
further truce was concluded by Derkylidas, this time with
Tissaphernes as well as Pharnabazus (3.2.20); but Xenophon
does not make it clear whether the Spartans formally
accepted the Persian terms for peace (abandonment of Asia,
withdrawal of harmosts and garrisons from the Greek
cities), and Diodorus (14.39.6) merely says that after the
truce both sides disbanded their armies.

Thus Xenophon contrives to omit the naval, and obscure
the diplomatic, background to the Spartan decision to send
out Agesilaos to Asia in 396 (3.4.2; cf. Xen. 'Ages.' 1.
7). He does, however, stress the vigorous support for the
expedition expressed by Lysander (cf. Plut. 'Lys.' 23.1),
who is said to have wished to re-establish dekarchies.
According to Xenophon, indeed, it was actually Lysander
who suggested the composition of Agesilaos' force: thirty
Spartiate advisers, including himself, 2,000 of the Neodamodeis and 6,000 allied troops (3.4.8).

We note the omission of Spartiate or Perioikic hoplites
and second the large number of Neodamodeis (3,000 in all
were employed in Asia). Xenophon's partitive genitive 'of
the Neodamodeis' and Plutarch's description of the 2,000
as 'picked men' ('Ages.' 6.4) confirm that Sparta had
enormously increased its reserve of Neodamodeis since 413,
doubtless because the huge influx of wealth in the form of
Persian subsidy (Lysander was said to have brought back
470 talents in 405-404) and imperial tribute made such an
increase financially feasible (Welwei 1974, 149 n. 44,
151, 157, 159). They were perhaps recruited from Helots
who had seen active service as batmen and armour-bearers.
As far as the allies are concerned, Xenophon crucially

fails to mention here that Corinth, Athens and Thebes on various pretexts refused to contribute troops (cf. Paus. 3.9.1-3). He does, on the other hand, record that the leaders of the Boiotian League prevented Agesilaos from sacrificing at Aulis, like a second Agamemnon, prior to sailing (3.4.4).

Agesilaos' programme was nothing less than to make the Greek cities of Asia autonomous like those in mainland Greece (3.4.5). Such a provision for the autonomy of mainland cities, great and small, had been written into the treaty of 418-417 between Sparta and Argos after Mantineia (Thuc. 5.77, 79), but the Eleians would not have been alone in suspecting that in practice 'autonomy' would be interpreted to coincide with the Spartans' conception of their own best interests. It was at the least a flexible notion, as many mainland Greeks were to learn to their cost. In 396, however, Agesilaos gave no hint that less than ten years later he would preside over the resale of the Asiatic Greeks to Persia. Rather, he seems to have aimed to surpass the 'Ten Thousand' in taking the war deep into the Great King's territory.

At least this is the picture presented by Xenophon; less committed sources like the 'Oxyrhynchos historian' (12.1) gave a more restricted interpretation. Once the personal rivalry between Agesilaos and Lysander had been resolved by the despatch of the latter to the Hellespont (3.4.7-10; cf. Plut. 'Lys.' 24.1), Agesilaos made Ephesos his base for a highly successful campaign first against Pharnabazus' Phrygia in 396 and then against Tissaphernes' Caria in 395 (3.4.12-15, 21-4). Tissaphernes was beheaded on Artaxerxes' orders; his successor, Tithraustes, offered Agesilaos a financial inducement to quit Asia, backed by a guarantee of autonomy for the cities if they would pay the 'old tribute' to Persia.

The 'Oxyrhynchos historian' (12.1) and Diodorus (14.80. 8) speak of a truce between Agesilaos and Tithraustes, but in Xenophon Agesilaos stalls by saying that he must wait for instructions from Sparta and moves north again into Pharnabazus' territory (3.4.26). Here his instructions from Sparta arrived, perhaps no more unexpected than they were welcome. For he was put in charge of both land and sea operations, the first time a king had been given such a joint command (Plut. 'Ages.' 10.9f.). Xenophon does not explain why Agesilaos put such energy into raising a fleet of 120 triremes, which he placed under his brother-in-law Peisandros (3.4.28f.). The answer is provided by the 'Oxyrhynchos historian' (15): Konon had caused the key base of Rhodes to revolt from Sparta.

It can hardly have been coincidental that Tithraustes

in 395 should have decided to emulate Artaxerxes' grandfather and namesake (Thuc. 1.109.2) by distributing cash
to potentially friendly Greeks on the mainland. Only this
time the boot was on the other foot, and it was against
rather than to the Spartans that the money was disbursed.
For it was distributed to politicians in Thebes, Corinth
and Argos on condition that they persuaded their cities to
make war on Sparta. Xenophon (3.5.1) naively or disingen-
uously implies that it was this money that indirectly
brought about the grand coalition of these three with
Athens. But the wiser or less biased 'Oxyrhynchos historian', who also provides the essential background for
Athens' decision, expressly rebuts this view by pointing
out that anti-Spartan Athenians had long been awaiting a
suitable opportunity to bring about such a conjuncture
(7; cf. 18; Lehmann 1978).

     The immediate occasion of the alliance and the ensuing
'Corinthian War' was Sparta's intervention on the side of
Phokis in its struggle with East or perhaps West Lokris,
which had allegedly been instigated by Thebes (3.5.2; cf.
'Hell. Ox.' 16–18). According to Xenophon's one-sided
account, the Spartans actually welcomed the occasion or
pretext ('prophasis') to campaign against Thebes: the
timing was convenient, and they (and Agesilaos above all)
wished to punish Thebes for its disloyalty and constant
opposition since 405–404 (3.5.5). The Ephors therefore
proclaimed a levy, and, as in 403, Lysander was sent
ahead, with king Pausanias commanding the Lakedaimonian
and Peloponnesian League force to follow and liaise with
him (3.5.6f.). Lysander was immediately successful in
detaching Orchomenos from the Boiotian League, and the
Thebans responded by seeking an alliance with Athens.

     At this point in his narrative Xenophon rises above
his usual level to write for the Theban ambassadors
collectively a thoroughly Thucydidean speech nicely
conveying the diplomatic and military realities (3.5.8–15).
Not every detail, however, can be trusted, and the Thebans'
misrepresentations should perhaps be put down to Xenophon's
hostility towards Thebes. They begin by explaining away
their state's desire for the destruction of Athens in 405–
404. They stress the hatred of Sparta felt by the Argives,
Eleians, Corinthians, Arkadians and Achaians and by the
cities tyrannized by harmosts (including Helot harmosts),
garrisons and dekarchies. (In fact, the dekarchies had
been abolished nearly a decade earlier and, despite
Lysander, not reimposed; and if there is any truth in the
allegation that Helots became harmosts, these would have
been strictly 'nothoi', sons of Helot mothers, rather than
Helots in the full sense: Welwei 1974, 132. Demosthenes,

18.96, however, does list a string of places under
harmosts and garrisons.) The Thebans then try to excite
those Athenians, probably a majority (cf. Seager 1967,
115), who dreamed of restoring their empire (cf. 3.5.2);
and they conclude optimistically by noting a contrast
between Spartan and Athenian imperialism: whereas Athens
had had a navy to control its shipless subjects, the
Spartans are themselves few and rule men who are not only
many times more numerous but also no worse armed than
they. The significance of this closing reference to the
small number of the Spartiates (they alone are meant) is
that it ties in with one of the main points in Xenophon's
account of Kinadon's conspiracy.

The Athenians found the Thebans' arguments cogent and
in or about August 395 concluded defensive alliances for
ever with Boiotia and Lokris (Tod 1948, nos 101-2). The
alliances soon bore fruit. Lysander, who had not waited
for Pausanias, was killed at Haliartos (3.5.17-21; cf.
Plut. 'Lys.' 29; Paus. 3.5.4f.), and Pausanias rather than
continue the battle asked for a truce to pick up the dead
(3.5.21-4). For arriving too late, for arranging a truce
instead of fighting (contrast 6.4.15; 7.4.25!) and for
allowing the Athenian democrats to escape (in 403!)
Pausanias was arraigned on a capital charge (Ste. Croix
1972, 351). Anticipating condemnation, he fled, like
Latychidas before him, to Tegea, where he lived for at
least another fifteen years as a suppliant within the
sanctuary of Athena Alea and devoted part of his leisure
to the composition of an anti-Lykourgan tract. After the
death of Lysander it was 'discovered' that he too had
wished to modify the 'Lykourgan' constitution. Perhaps it
was not so surprising that Agesilaos, faced with political
revolution from above as well as below within five years
of his accession, should have been such a stickler for
unquestioning obedience to 'the laws' - at least so far as
they were conformable to his own inclinations.

Meanwhile back in Phrygia Agesilaos in autumn 395
resumed his onslaught on Pharnabazus' domain (4.1.1ff.;
but see 'Hell. Ox.' 18.33-20.38). Much booty was taken
and sold (4.1.1, 26), more cities were won over, until in
394 Pharnabazus consented to a conference with Agesilaos
(4.1.31-9). Xenophon artistically points up the contrast
between the simplicity of the Spartan king and the pomp of
the oriental potentate, but cannot disguise the pointless-
ness of the exercise, whose only positive result was that
Agesilaos became the guest-friend of Pharnabazus' son.
But Xenophon does at least permit the judicious reader to
pass a critical judgment on Agesilaos' conduct by juxta-
posing the king's visionary design of detaching a large

chunk from the Persian Empire (4.1.41) with the fear of
the Spartans at home for the safety of their own city,
threatened as it was by the coalition of Boiotia, Athens,
Corinth and Argos (4.2.1).

By this fear I think we should understand Xenophon to
mean that the Spartans dreaded an invasion of Lakonia.
For this is precisely what he makes a Corinthian speaker
advocate a few sections later (4.2.11f.), using a vivid
entomological simile. The Spartans, says Timolaos (one of
those in receipt of Persian money in 395), should be
fought in their own territory or as near to it as possible,
just like wasps, who cause no trouble when they are smoked
out of their nest but sting if allowed to swarm. Moreover, like the Theban ambassadors at Athens, Timolaos
emphasizes the small number of the Spartans, whom he compares to rivers - small at their source but swollen by
tributaries as they proceed away from it. His implication,
incidentally, that it will be possible to pass through
Arkadia unhindered also ties in with what the Thebans had
said and is a valuable corroboration of Arkadian dissatisfaction with Spartan hegemony.

The Spartans, however, had other ideas. 'Slow to war
unless compelled to it', they had sent a message to Agesilaos ordering his instant return from Asia (4.2.2; cf.
Plut. 'Ages.' 15.2) and now proclaimed a levy under Aristodamos, guardian of Pausanias' under-age son Agesipolis
(4.2.9). Aristodamos speedily marched out to north-east
Peloponnese, picking up some Tegean and Mantineian troops
en route but failing to receive any from Phleious (4.2.16),
which pleaded exemption legitimately enough on religious
grounds but had other reasons for neutrality (Legon 1967,
329f.). The ensuing battle at the Nemea River, the
largest inter-Greek battle yet, resulted in a convincing
victory for the Spartan side. We need not linger over the
tactics, revealing though they are of the changed military
conditions of the fourth century (Anderson 1970, 144-7,
181-4). However, scarcely less of a battleground is the
interpretation of the 'about 6,000 Lakedaimonian hoplites'
(4.2.16) who were engaged, and this problem is relevant to
our main concerns. For what we want to know is how many
of these were Spartiates.

It is as well to make clear at once that certainty is
impossible. To begin with, Xenophon's description of the
'Lakedaimonian' contingent draws no other distinction than
that between the 6,000 or so hoplites and the 600 or so
cavalry. Welwei (1974, 152), mainly following Busolt,
allows for the 300 Hippeis (cf. Thuc. 5.72), some 600
Skiritai (cf. Thuc. 5.68.3), about 1,500 Neodamodeis and
five 'morai' of about 3,300-3,500 men in all. (The sixth

'mora' was in garrison at Boiotian Orchomenos: 4.3.15; cf.
2.17.) I agree with him (140 n. 75) against Toynbee
(1969, 380) and Andrewes (in Gomme 1970, 113) that there
could have been a sizeable number of Neodamodeis present,
since not all of them had been sent to Asia in 399 and
396. But I would prefer to increase his estimate for the
number of Spartiates and Perioikoi in the five 'morai' by
about 1,000, to give a 'mora' of about 900 men. Such a
figure is attested in Polybius (fr. 60 B-W) and other
sources and is appropriate to an emergency for which
Sparta probably mobilized thirty-five of the forty active-
service age-classes (Toynbee 1969, 379); in any case we
should expect the 'morai' at the Nemea River to have been
significantly larger than the one of about 600 which was
performing only garrison duty at Lechaion in 390 (4.5.12:
below). Of these putative 4,500 or so hoplites in the
'morai' perhaps 2,500 were Perioikoi, 2,000 Spartiates.
This may represent a drop of about one third on the number
of Spartiates at Mantineia (in a possibly greater levy).

It was perhaps fortunate that of 'their own men' (not
necessarily just Spartiates) the Spartans lost a mere
eight in the battle (4.3.1; cf. Xen. 'Ages.' 7.5). This
cheerful information was conveyed by Derkylidas (perhaps
Xenophon's source) to Agesilaos, who had promptly obeyed
the summons from Asia, crossed the Hellespont from Abydos
to Sestos and followed Xerxes' route through Thrace to
Amphipolis (4.2.3-8). His other news was less heartening:
most of Thessaly had revolted from Sparta to Thebes after
the battle of Haliartos (Diod. 14.82.5f.). Agesilaos
succeeded none the less in forcing a passage by defeating
the Thessalians in an engagement in which his cavalry did
particularly well (4.3.9: this was not of course Spartan
cavalry, but horsemen hired in Asia - 3.4.2, 16, 20; 4.2.
5).

Agesilaos' pride, however, was soon humbled. On 14
August 394 he learned of Peisandros' disastrous defeat at
sea off Knidos by Konon and Pharnabazus (4.3.10-14). For
background and descriptive details we must turn to other
sources than Xenophon ('Hell. Ox.' 19ff.; Diod. 14.79, 81,
83; cf. Underhill 1900, 129f.). From these we learn that,
apart from the admiral's inexperience, the Spartan defeat
was due to the vast superiority in numbers of the Phoenician fleet which Konon had raised by at last securing
adequate finance from Artaxerxes.

Xenophon's silence on the Knidos sea-battle is to this
extent understandable, that he had left Asia with Agesilaos and was personally involved in the third major
battle of 394, at Koroneia in Boiotia (4.3.15-22);
Polyain. 2.1.23). The 'Lakedaimonians' under Agesilaos'

command comprised a 'mora' which had crossed over from the
Corinthia after the Nemea River battle by sea (the passage
through the Isthmus, as in the 'First' Peloponnesian War,
being blocked), half of the 'mora' stationed at Orchomenos,
and those of the 3,000 Neodamodeis sent to Asia who had
not either been killed or left behind there on garrison
duty. Xenophon twice describes the battle as 'unlike any
other in my time' (4.3.16; 'Ages.' 2.9). He probably had
in mind the nature of its progress, and especially Agesilaos' heroic response to the manoeuvres, rather than its
magnitude or importance. For although it was another
victory for the Spartan side, it no more decided the
Corinthian War than the Nemea River battle. Phokis and
Orchomenos were secured, but no strategic position for
effective action in central Greece. The rest of the land
actions in the war centred about Corinth.

In 393 or 392 stasis produced one of the most interesting political experiments in the history of the independent Greek city-states, the 'union of Corinth and Argos' -
or rather perhaps the conclusion of an isopolity (mutual
citizenship) agreement between them (4.4.6; 8.34; Diod.
14.92.1). Xenophon sees this entirely from the side of
the Corinthian oligarchs, and one suspects that Pasimelos
(4.4.4; 7.3.2) was one of the 'Lakonizers' from whom he
gathered much of his information when he was living at
Corinth after 371. But bloody though the circumstances of
the 'union' perhaps were (4.4.3-5), the mass of the Corinthians are unlikely to have shared the view of their
oligarchic opponents that for the next seven years their
status was no better than that of resident aliens. From
the Spartan standpoint the 'union' was a disaster. It
meant the breakdown of a policy dating at least from 494,
whereby an isolated and hostile Argos should serve to keep
Corinth loyal and the Isthmus passage secure.

Xenophon's chronology for the next few years of the war
is confused and confusing, since he treats land-operations
from 393 to 388 in one piece without clear divisions
between years before returning to the war at sea from 394
to 387. Diodorus is, as usual in this respect, of little
or no help. Not even Xenophon and Diodorus, however, can
completely obscure a vital connection. In 393 the war was
for the first time brought to Sparta's own territory. In
392 Sparta through Antalkidas reversed its policy of the
past seven years and once more sought to ingratiate itself
with Persia at the expense of the Asiatic Greeks.

Following the Knidos sea-battle Konon and Pharnabazus
'sailed around' the Aegean, driving out Spartan harmosts
and giving the cities the twofold assurance that their
citadels would no longer be garrisoned and that their

autonomy would be respected (4.8.1f., 5). Sparta in fact
lost much of its Aegean empire, as we learn also from
Diodorus (14.84.3f.) and Pausanias (6.3.16). A decree of
Erythrai honouring Konon (Tod 1948, no. 106) will not
have been unique; and Athens was quick to begin the
process of restoring its power in the Aegean (Tod 1948,
no. 110: a decree of perhaps 393 honouring Karpathos) and
to attempt to win over Dionysios of Syracuse from the
Spartans (Tod 1948, no. 108). The coinage bearing the
superscription SYN and linking cities from Byzantion to
Rhodes is perhaps the token of an anti-Spartan league
based on Thebes (Cawkwell 1963).

In spring 393 Pharnabazus and Konon sailed through the
Aegean to Melos, which they planned to use as a base for
ravaging Lakonia (4.8.7). In Xenophon's account the idea
was conceived by Pharnabazus as a means of retaliation
against the Spartans for the losses Derkylidas (3.1.9ff.)
and Agesilaos (3.4.12ff.; 4.1.1ff.) had inflicted on his
province. It is, however, worth considering the possibility that the plan was suggested to Konon by the Messenian exiles in his entourage (cf. 'Hell.Ox.' 20.3); Konon
would then be in a direct line of descent from Demosthenes
(Chapter 12).

However this may be, Pharnabazus and Konon attacked
Pharai (modern Kalamata) at the head of the Messenian Gulf
and ravaged its land, the first attack on Sparta's home
territory since the Athenians' unsuccessful attempt to
recapture Pylos in 409-408. They then made landings at
various points on the coast (presumably of Lakonia as well
as Messenia) and did as much damage as possible. This was
not, however, as much or as serious as they would have
liked, for they were hampered by the lack of suitable
harbours to use as bases (cf. Chapter 10), by the defence
forces sent by the Spartans (presumably mobile detachments
like that commanded by Brasidas at Mothone in 431), and by
the shortage of cereals (it was the time of year when, as
Alkman fr. 20.3-5 had noted, hunger was never far away).
So, following the example of Nikias in 424, they sensibly
decided to conduct an 'epiteichismos' on Kythera.

A landing was made at Phoinikous (probably modern
Avlemonas Bay). The citadel of Kythera town was captured,
allegedly at the first assault, and the Kytherians or some
of them were sent away under a truce to the Lakonian mainland (4.8.8; Diod. 14.84.5). The absence of the Spartan
harmost and a Lakedaimonian garrison is, as in 424,
remarkable and probably to be explained on the same lines.
Konon then repaired the fortifications, left behind a
garrison of his mercenaries under an Athenian harmost (so
described by Xenophon) and sailed for the Isthmus, which

the anti-Spartan coalition had made its GHQ.

What Xenophon and Diodorus may have omitted as relatively insignificant is an attack by Konon on Antikythera
(known by various names in antiquity). This small island
(Chapter 2) lies equidistant from Kythera and Crete and
could be reached from the former before the first meal of
the day was taken, according to the fourth-century 'Periplous' of Pseudo-Skylax. Its main town, Aigilia, was fortified in the fifth century, either by the Spartans or
possibly by Nikias. The reasons for thinking that Konon
took an interest in the site are twofold. First, sling-
bullets inscribed 'of the king' have been found here (Foss
1975, 42), together with spearheads and many black-painted
sherds. Second, at some time between 400 and 350 the
akropolis walls were reconstructed and an enceinte-wall
added, enclosing an area of some 300,000m^2. The presence
of walling of such quality demands an explanation in the
absence of evidence for ancient occupation from the rest
of the island, and Konon, as we have seen, had the men and
equipment to repair the walls of Kythera.

Konon's arrival first at Corinth and then, after an
absence of twelve years, at his native Athens raised the
war on to a new plane. For the Persian money he brought
enabled the anti-Spartan coalition temporarily to gain the
mastery of the Corinthian Gulf (4.8.10) and for the next
four years to maintain a permanent force of mercenaries in
the Corinthia, while at home the Athenians could now fully
rebuild the walls they had been compelled to dismantle in
404 (4.8.10; cf. Tod 1948, no. 107; Pritchett 1974, II,
121 n. 22). The Spartans were nevertheless far from
incapable of responding. In 392 they won the Battle of
the Long Walls of Corinth (4.4.6-13) and in 391 they
actually captured Lechaion, Corinth's Peiraieus on the
Corinthian Gulf, and garrisoned it (4.4.17, with Underhill
1900, 139f. on the chronology).

In the interval between these military successes,
however, they had undertaken a drastically new diplomatic
initiative, compelled to do so, as suggested earlier, by
the 'epiteichismos' on Kythera (which had followed so soon
after Kinadon's abortive rising and the machinations of
Pausanias and Lysander). In Xenophon (4.8.12-17) the
Spartans apparently intended to enter into purely bilater-
al negotiations with Tiribazus, who seems to have succeeded
Tithraustes (cf. 5.1.28). In the event they found themselves attending at Sardis an international conference
that included representatives of their Greek enemies, the
Athenians, Boiotians, Corinthians and Argives. Antalkidas
proposed peace with Persia on condition that all Greek
cities and islands should be autonomous, but on the under-

standing that the Spartans would not dispute ownership of
the cities of Asia with the Great King - a return, in
other words, to their position of exactly twenty years
previously. Not surprisingly, the other Greek representatives demurred, partly because these terms involved the
abandonment of the Asiatic Greeks to Persia, but mainly
because the 'autonomy' clause threatened their own vital
interests - Athens' control of Lemnos, Imbros and Skyros,
crucial for its wheaten lifeline; Thebes' control of
Boiotia; and the 'union' of Corinth and Argos. Tiribazus,
on the other hand, was impressed, secretly gave Antalkidas
some money and publicly arrested Konon. Artaxerxes,
however, was not yet ready to settle.

A few months later, early in 391, the Spartans tried
again to make peace and convened a conference at Sparta,
this time not only without involving Persia but also
seeking to meet the other Greeks' objections halfway.
Andokides (3), our only source, is the earliest surviving
writer to use the expression 'Common Peace' to describe
'a general treaty based on the principle of autonomy'
(Ryder 1965, 33). But it was precisely the 'autonomy'
clause which once again proved to be the stumbling-block.

The attitude of Agesilaos to the initiative spearheaded
by Antalkidas is unclear. Plutarch ('Ages.' 23.2) says that
the two were personal and political enemies, but the difference between them may only have been one of emphasis.
For Agesilaos the application of the 'autonomy principle'
in Sparta's favour throughout mainland Greece seems to
have been the paramount consideration. Ideally perhaps he
would have preferred not to renege on the Asiatic Greeks;
but, as the events of 387-386 and following were to
demonstrate, if they had to be sacrificed on the altar of
mainland Greek 'autonomy', then Agesilaos would not shrink
from applying the knife - indirectly, through Antalkidas,
for whom peace was a commodity to be bought at this price.
It is tempting to link the latter's fervour with a curious
piece of information in Plutarch ('Ages.' 32.1), that in
370 he sent away his children for safety to Kythera.
Perhaps he had friends there whose property and lives were
menaced by the 'epiteichismos'.

The fluctuating fortunes of the remainder of the Corinthian War by land and sea from 391 to 387 (4.4.15-7.7; 4.
8.17-5.1.24) need not long delay us, since, despite the
occupation of Kythera, Lakonia as such played little or no
role, at least in our preserved accounts. Indeed, Xenophon refers to Lakonia just once (4.7.6), in the context
of an Argive counter-raid presumably against Kynouria
during an expedition against the Argolis led by Agesipolis
in 388. For the rest, apart from a Peloponnesian League

campaign against the Akarnanians led by Agesilaos on
behalf of the Achaians in 389 (4.6.1-12), regular fighting
on the mainland was confined to the Corinthia. Here one
famous episode requires our attention.

In May/June 390 Agesilaos commanded the first major
Spartan offensive of the war, an attack on Corinth itself
(4.5.1). The Corinthians feared that the city would be
betrayed to Agesilaos, who was accompanied by Corinthian
oligarchic exiles, and so summoned to their aid Iphikrates
and his mercenaries, who were in garrison at nearby
Peiraion protecting Corinth's communications with Boiotia
and Athens (4.5.3; Xen. 'Ages.' 2.19). Iphikrates had
been despatched to the Corinthia by the Athenians in 393
and placed in command of a 'Foreign Legion' of mercenaries
(Androtion 324F48; Philochoros 328F150). Thanks to
Persian money he was able to keep a more or less stable
force in commission for four years, but it was his brains
rather than Persian gold that welded this force into a
powerful tactical unit. Not only did he introduce significant modifications of equipment, blending the hoplite
with the light-armed infantryman to produce the peltast,
but he also proved an excellent disciplinarian and field
commander. His finest hour came in 390.

Agesilaos' expedition against Corinth coincided with
the Hyakinthia festival, and it was customary for Amyklaian Spartans to return to celebrate it wherever or for
whatever purpose they happened to be away from home (4.5.
11). They were therefore granted the usual dispensation
and were escorted by the 'mora' of about 600 hoplites on
guard at Lechaion and by a small contingent of cavalry to
within four or five kilometres of Sikyon. Here the commander of the 'mora' entrusted the Amyklaians to the
cavalry commander and set out back to Lechaion; but en
route he was ambushed by Iphikrates, and the 'mora' was
cut to pieces (4.5.12-17). Xenophon's account of the
number killed is not self-explanatory: although a few, he
says, escaped to Lechaion, yet only about 250 were killed.
Perhaps he means to refer only to the Spartiate casualties. At any rate, the Spartans could no longer afford to
be scornful of peltasts, as they had been the previous
year (4.4.17). For this destruction was a 'disaster of a
kind unusual for the Spartans' (4.5.10), and Xenophon
highlights its magnitude by remarking that the sons,
brothers and fathers of the dead men rejoiced at the news.
This response presages the reaction to the far greater
disaster at Leuktra in 371.

Agesilaos, one minute receiving a Boiotian embassy
treating for peace, next minute is leading back the remains of the destroyed 'mora' to Sparta, shamefacedly

taking care not to pass by Mantineia in daylight and so
present the Mantineians with a chance to mock (4.5.18).
Thereafter there was a stalemate on land, and Iphikrates
next turns up in the Hellespont in 389-388, commanding
eight ships and about 1,200 peltasts, with which he defeats the Spartan harmost Anaxibios (4.8.34-9). He had
been sent there because the Athenians were afraid of
losing the control of the Hellespont won for them in 389
by Thrasyboulos, the resistance leader of 403. In fact,
Thrasyboulos had gone some considerable way towards laying
the basis for a renewal of the fifth-century Athenian
Empire (4.8.25). However, the Athenians' naval resurgence
since 393 had led them to overplay their hand. In 390
they entered into a treaty with a revolted vassal of
Persia, King Evagoras of Cyprus (Bengtson 1975, no. 234);
in 389 they intervened on the side of democracy at Klazomenai (Tod 1948, no. 114). The Great King therefore was
more sympathetic to the Spartans when in 387 Antalkidas
(navarch since 388) once again brought proposals for a
Common Peace.

Antalkidas first obtained an alliance with Persia, a
necessary precaution in case the Athenians should refuse
to accept the peace (5.1.25). To make doubly sure of
Athenian compliance, Antalkidas with Syracusan and Persian
help gathered the largest fleet in service since 394 (eighty
or more ships) and regained control of the Hellespont;
the Athenians were thereby threatened with a repetition of
the aftermath of Aigospotamoi (5.1.28f.). The complaisant
attitude of Argos was secured by the threat of a full-
scale Spartan invasion (5.1.29). The Thebans, concerned
as ever for their hegemony of the Boiotian League, attempted to resist the 'autonomy principle', but Agesilaos had
war declared on them too, and they tamely submitted to the
dismemberment of the League (5.1.32f.). The Corinthians
at first refused to withdraw the garrison sent by Argos
(cf. 4.4.6; 5.1), but like the Argives and Thebans yielded
to Agesilaos' threat of force; the 'union' of Corinth and
Argos was terminated, the Corinthian exiles restored
(5.1.34).

The peace to which all Greeks from 386 were formally
party contained three clauses: the Greek cities of Asia
were to be the King's, as were Klazomenai and Cyprus; all
other Greek cities, great or small, were to be free and
autonomous and to keep their own territory, except Lemnos,
Imbros and Skyros; any state refusing to accept these
terms would be liable to attack by the King. Officially,
these terms had been 'sent down' by Artaxerxes to be
rubberstamped by the Greeks meeting at Sardis, and so one
name for the peace was the 'King's Peace'. Informally,

and more informatively, it was known as the 'Peace of
Antalkidas' (5.1.35). For as Agesilaos reportedly
remarked in its defence (Plut. 'Ages.' 23.4; 'Artax.' 22.
4; 'Mor.' 213B), the Spartans were not 'medizing' so much
as the Persians were 'lakonizing'.

In other words, this was an arrangement sponsored by
the Spartans mainly in their own selfish interests. The
past three years of fighting had brought them no advantage
over the Greeks, and the anti-Persian policy of the 390s
had merely contributed to the resurgence of Athens.
Hence the abandonment of the Asiatic Greeks in favour of
concentrating first on re-establishing Spartan suzerainty
in the Peloponnese and then on extending it north of the
Isthmus. As Ryder (1965, 39) well puts it, 'the King's
Peace had been devised by the Spartans as an acceptable
basis for Persian intervention.... It was, then, naturally
suited primarily to the interests of the Spartans and
Persians.'

The new Spartan policy was at first triumphantly
successful, although its success should not be put down to
the peace as such, whose direct influence, as Seager
(1974) has demonstrated, was intermittent and superficial.
Rather it was because Sparta was still the single greatest
military power in mainland Greece that by 379 the Spartans
could seem to have 'at length established their empire in
all respects well and securely' (5.3.27). Isokrates in
his 'Panegyrikos' of c.380 (4.126) summarized the main
events leading to this position. Mantineia had been
destroyed (385), the Kadmeia (akropolis) of Thebes had
been occupied and garrisoned (382), Olynthos and Phleious
were being besieged (from 382; both submitted in 379),
Amyntas (III) of Macedon, Dionysios of Syracuse and the
Great King were being aided. Diodorus (15.23.3f.),
amplifying Xenophon and Isokrates, adds a curious explanation: 'the Spartans had constantly applied themselves to
securing an abundance of population and practice in the
use of arms, and so were become an object of terror to all
because of the strength of their following.' If Diodorus
(or his source) meant an abundance of population in Lakonia and Messenia, this can only refer to Helots and
Perioikoi. Moreover, as we shall see in the next chapter,
a far greater thinker than he rightly attributed Sparta's
eventual eclipse precisely to its lack of manpower,
meaning of course citizen manpower.

We need not, however, confine ourselves to the matter
of Spartiate manpower to detect signs of Spartan weakness.
For the above summaries of Sparta's position in 380-379
present a one-sided picture of the period 386-379. For
example, in 384 Athens concluded a perpetual alliance with

the important island of Chios (Tod 1948, no. 118); six
years later this alliance could serve as a model for the
series of alliances comprising the Second Athenian Confederacy, a new improved version of the fifth-century Empire.
In 383 Athens allied itself with the Chalkidian League
headed by Olynthos (Tod 1948, no. 119). The possibility
of such a compact was one of the chief arguments used by
the Akanthian delegate at a Spartan assembly of that year
to win Peloponnesian support against Olynthian encroach-
ment (5.2.15f.). By 382 the first certain innovation in
the 'constitution' of the Peloponnesian League had been
made (5.2.21f.; cf. 5.3.10, 17; 6.2.16): in lieu of men an
ally might now contribute a fixed amount of cash. The
measure would of course have benefited Sparta by providing
the money to hire the now obligatory mercenaries; but the
very fact that mercenaries were necessary is an indication
of the war-weariness of the allies. Nor was it only they,
it seems, who found the repeated demands on their manpower
excessive. In 381, according to Diodorus (15.21.2), more
than 1,200 'Lakedaimonians' were killed at Olynthos. This
figure is probably exaggerated, but it cannot be coincidental that in 380 Sparta, for the first and only time on
record, was forced to rely on volunteers to make up the
'Lakedaimonian' force (5.3.9). Apart from men of inferior
Spartan status (Chapter 14), the volunteers also included
'men of quality' from the Perioikoi, men, in other words,.
whom one would have expected to be called up rather than
able to volunteer.

Over and above these difficulties, there is evidence
that Agesilaos' policy - for such it surely was - was far
from unanimously popular in Sparta. Diodorus (15.19.4)
speaks of principled disagreement between Agesilaos and
Agesipolis, but since Agesipolis cheerfully executed Agesilaos' policy towards both Mantineia and Olynthos (cf.
generally 5.3.20) it is better to think of Agesipolis as
the figurehead around whom opposition to so strong a king
as Agesilaos naturally tended to crystallize (cf. Carlier
1977 on the position of Damaratos vis-à-vis Kleomenes).
This opposition surfaced most noticeably in 382 after
Phoibidas' seizure of the Theban akropolis (5.2.32) and in
381 over the forcible restoration of a handful of oligarchic exiles to democratic Phleious (5.3.16). In both
cases - as indeed in all cases down to the end of Agesilaos' reign - the opposition was either won over or silen-
ced. But Sparta's internal and external enemies can only
have been heartened by such discord.

Already before 379, then, there were hints that the
feet of the Spartan colossus might be of ceramic composition. Within a decade the feet had crumbled, and the

giant had been toppled from its pedestal. At the beginning of the process of disintegration stands the liberation of the Kadmeia, which provoked from Xenophon the
nearest he could muster to a direct criticism of Agesilaos.
Its seizure in 382 by Phoibidas, he now says (5.4.1), was
an act of impiety. The Spartans had broken their oath of
386 to leave the cities autonomous, and it was for this
that they were punished by the Thebans, who inflicted on
them (in 371) their first-ever defeat. Xenophon does not
actually say that Agesilaos ordered or suggested the seizure; rather he casts a slur on Phoibidas' character (5.2.
28). But he does make it clear that Agesilaos virulently
hated Thebes (5.1.33) and that he condoned the action on
narrowly utilitarian grounds (5.2.32); and he records that
in 378 Agesilaos installed Phoibidas as harmost of Boiotian Thespiai (5.4.41). It may not therefore be accidental
or irrelevant that Xenophon reports the following message
sent by Agesilaos in 396 (3.4.11): 'he (Tissaphernes) by
his perjury has made the gods enemies to himself but allies
to the Greeks.'
   We, however, may beg to differ from Xenophon's pious
interpretation of Spartan history after 382. A more obvious secular reason for the 'retribution' Sparta suffered
through the Thebans is Agesilaos' unreasoning hostility
towards them. According to a post eventum rationalization
of a familiar type, one of the 'rhetrai' of Lykourgos forbade the Spartans to make war continuously on the same
enemy (Plut. 'Lyk.' 13.10; 'Pelop.' 15.3; 'Mor.' 189E,
213E, 217D, 227D). Had the law-abiding constitutionalist
Agesilaos known of the 'rhetra', no doubt he would have
avoided this particular error; but as it was from 379
until 366 apart from short breaks in 375-374 and 371-370
Sparta waged war constantly against Thebes.
   Since Agesipolis had died at Olynthos in 380 (5.3.19;
cf. Tod 1948, no. 120), only the second Spartan king known
to have died on campaign, and since Agesilaos speciously
pleaded to be excused from the command on the grounds that
he was beyond military age (5.4.13), the war-effort was at
first led by Agesipolis' younger brother and successor
Kleombrotos. His campaign of 379-378 effectively strengthened Sparta's hold on Boiotia and so served to keep the
Athenians neutral, as they were as yet unwilling to take
the Thebans' side in a war that might spill over into
Attika (5.4.14-19).
   All this good work, however, was undone by Sphodrias,
harmost of Thespiai (5.4.15), who in 378 made an abortive
attempt to capture the Peiraieus (5.4.20). Precisely what
Sphodrias' thinking was and who conceived the scheme will
always be uncertain, but the consequences were clear cut

and instructive. Sphodrias was put on trial at Sparta
but, remarkably, was acquitted, thanks to Agesilaos (esp.
5.4.26), on the highly revealing ground that Sparta needed
soldiers like him (5.4.32). The Athenians, no longer so
impressed by their latter-day 'dual hegemony' theorists
like Kallistratos (cf. 6.3.10-17), voted that the Spartans
had broken the King's Peace (Diod. 15.29.7) and initiated
moves resulting in alliance with Thebes and other states
prior to the foundation early in 377 of the Second Athenian Confederacy (Tod 1948, no. 123; cf. 121-2).

The geriatric Agesilaos was once more galvanized into
activity. Both in 378 (5.4.35-41; Diod. 15.32) and in 377
(5.4.47-55; Diod. 15.34) he led Peloponnesian League forces
into Boiotia. Presumably he too was responsible for a
major reorganization of the League designed perhaps to
emphasize the burden carried by the Spartans and so to
restore their prestige as leader when their harshness was
pushing the allies in the direction of Athens (Diod. 15.31.
1f.). Neither invasion, however, was a startling success.
Indeed, the retreat in 377 may have been hastened by
allied discontent (Plut. 'Ages.' 26.6; Polyain. 2.1.7, 18,
20, 21); and Diodorus (15.34.2) portentously comments that
the Thebans for the first time found themselves not inferior to the Spartans. In 376 Kleombrotos fared even worse,
ostensibly because he felt unable to force the passes of
Kithairon (5.4.59; cf. Ste. Croix 1972, 194). Thwarted by
land, the Spartans and their Peloponnesian League allies
decided to try their luck at sea and, as in 404 and 387,
starve Athens into submission (5.4.60). Yet again, their
luck was out, and the Athenians won their first solo naval
victory since 'the' Peloponnesian War, off Naxos in 376
(5.4.61).

The reminiscence of 'the' Peloponnesian War does not
end there. For the Athenians in 375 complied with a
Theban request to 'sail round' the Peloponnese in order to
forestall another invasion of Boiotia by the Spartans, who
would be unable both to guard their own country and that
of their neighbouring allies and to attack Thebes in sufficient force (5.4.62f.). The ploy succeeded, and the
Thebans used the breathing space first to win the Battle
of Tegyra against 1,000 'Lakedaimonians' from the Orchomenos garrison (Diod. 15.37.1; 81.2; Plut. 'Pelop.' 16f.;
with Anderson 1970, 162-4) and then to reconstitute the
Boiotian League, on harsher lines (6.1.1; cf. Isokr. 14.8).

Plutarch's comment on the Tegyra battle, which is
chiefly remarkable for Pelopidas' use of the Theban 'Sacred Band', deserves quotation: 'this battle was the first
to reveal to the other Greeks the secret that it was not
only the Eurotas or the country between Babyka and Knakion

(sc. the place where the Spartan Assembly met) which produced martial and bellicose men.' Soon after, Sparta
rebuffed the request of their Thessalian proxenos to
amputate the rising power of Jason of Pherai in Thessaly,
on the grounds that they lacked a sufficient reserve of
forces (6.1.2-17). They also participated in the second
Common Peace, of 375-374 (Bengtson 1975, no. 265). This
time it was the Athenians, alarmed by the growth of Theban
power and finding the cost of war excessive, who hosted
the conference, and they were gratified to have their hegemony of the sea recognized by Sparta (Nepos, 'Timoth.' 2.
3). As for the Thebans, they had their control of Boiotia
acknowledged, if only de facto (Diod. 15.38.1-4).

However, the peace soon broke down, with Athens and
Sparta fighting over Kerkyra (6.2.3-26), and Diodorus'
'common anarchy' (15.45.1) seems a more appropriate label
for the situation than Common Peace. The chief significance of the Kerkyra struggle from our standpoint is that
in 373 the democrats lured their Athenian allies to aid
them with the bait of their island's geographical situation, pointing out that it was strategically placed for
operations not only against the Corinthian Gulf but also
against the 'Lakonian land', i.e. Messenia (6.2.9). In
372 Iphikrates, having swallowed the bait, made preparations to use his large fleet precisely for the latter
purpose (6.2.38). Xenophon maddeningly gives no details
of his successful operations, but it may plausibly be suggested that there was a connection between his raids on
Lakonia (or at least the imminent threat of them) and the
next Common Peace, sworn at Sparta early in 371 (Bengtson
1975, no. 269).

The initiative for this peace came either from Athens
(6.3.2) or from Persia (Diod. 15.50.4), or perhaps from
Persia prompted by Sparta, if Antalkidas really was again
'with the King' in 371 (6.3.12). Xenophon underlines the
importance of the occasion by writing speeches for three
of the Athenian ambassadors. Kallias, the Spartans' proxenos, orotundly but unconvincingly argues that the common
heritage of Athens and Sparta demands common action (6.3.
4-6). Autokles seeks to split from Sparta its Peloponnesian League allies (whose representatives were present)
by delivering a concerted attack on Sparta's one-sided and
self-seeking interpretation of the 'autonomy principle'
(6.3.7-9). Finally, Kallistratos bluntly advocates the
'dual hegemony' thesis as a way of reconciling the pro-
Athenian and pro-Spartan factions at loggerheads in each
Greek city (6.3.10-17).

The Spartans voted to accept a peace whose main difference from that of 386 was that Sparta was no longer to be

its unofficial guarantor. In fact, there was to be no
guarantor at all. Thus although Sparta as heretofore
swore to the peace on behalf of its allies, its hold on
them was appreciably enfeebled. None the less, when the
Thebans as in 386 and 375-374 claimed the same prerogative
of swearing in relation to Boiotia, Agesilaos as in 386
refused to permit it (6.3.19). This time, however, there
were no second Theban thoughts, and the Thebans remained
isolated outside the diplomatic framework.

This was a considerable coup, welcomed by the anxious
Athenians (6.3.20). But Xenophon has omitted what is for
us perhaps the most interesting detail of all, the heated
exchange between Agesilaos and one of the Theban representatives, Epameinondas, which is recorded by Plutarch
('Ages.' 27.5-28.3; cf. Nepos, 'Epam.' 6.4; Paus. 9.13.2).
The context is no doubt Agesilaos' refusal to allow the
Thebans to swear on behalf of Boiotia. Epameinondas
counters with the demand that all cities must be of equal
status. Agesilaos, ignoring Epameinondas' appeal to universally applicable standards, repeats his demand that
Boiotia be autonomous. Epameinondas replies with a telling question: is it not just for Lakonike to be autonomous too? Agesilaos doggedly reiterates his previous
demand, to which Epameinondas answers that the Thebans
will allow Boiotia to be autonomous - if Agesilaos will do
the same for Lakonike. The reference unmistakably is to
the status within Lakonia of the Perioikic 'poleis'.
Agesilaos was incensed, but yet at the same time delighted
to have a pretext for declaring war on Thebes.

This anecdote, in so far as it redounds to the credit
of Epameinondas, is perhaps ben trovato, but a more hum-
drum variant of it appears in Diodorus (15.51.3f.). Here
the same question about Boiotian autonomy is put to the
Thebans rather later, just before the invasion leading to
the Battle of Leuktra, and the Thebans reply that they
never meddle in Lakonike. The essential point is the same
in both accounts and one which suggests to me that some
Perioikoi had seen how to turn Sparta's cherished 'autonomy principle' against its principal champions uncomfortably close to home. Perhaps they were the same Perioikoi
who, as we shall see, played a crucial role in bringing
a Theban army into Lakonia in 370.

The 'Spartano-Boiotian War' (Diod. 15.76.3) which followed the exclusion of Thebes from the (first) peace of
371 was largely Agesilaos' idea. This we learn from
Plutarch ('Ages.' 28.6), not Xenophon, who merely says
that 'the Assembly' of the Spartans dismissed as rubbish a
call for Kleombrotos' army in Phokis to be disbanded (6.4.
2f.). If Xenophon (6.1.1) is right, Kleombrotos had been

in Phokis with four 'morai' since 375, but it is perhaps
more likely that he was only sent out to aid Phokis against
Thebes early in 371. Anyway, in the summer of that year,
acting on the Spartan Assembly's decision, he invaded
Boiotia and led his army on a circuitous route (designed
to secure his communications with the Peloponnese) to
Leuktra in the territory of Thespiai (6.4.3f.). According
to Diodorus (15.1.2; 50.2), everyone expected the Spartans
to defeat the Thebans. This statement, however, is no
less suspect than that of Thucydides on attitudes to
Sparta and Athens in 431. For Diodorus' account of the
preliminaries to the decisive battle is wholly incompatible with that of Xenophon and is based on pro-Theban
sources concerned to magnify the Theban victory.

As for the battle itself, the best account from the
Theban side is given in Plutarch ('Pelop.' 23); Xenophon's
is patchy and written from the Spartan side only (6.4.13-
15), while that of Diodorus (15.50-5) is largely a rhetor-
ical set-piece. To be brief, the outcome was decided on
the Spartan right, where the only real fighting occurred,
between the 6,000 or so Theban hoplites under Epameinondas
(Diod. 15.52.2), massed at least fifty deep (6.4.12), and
the 2,250 or so 'Lakedaimonians', who were drawn up twelve
deep. The figure for the 'Lakedaimonians' is computed as
follows: thirty-five year classes were called out (6.4.
17), giving an 'enomotia' of thirty-five, each of which
was drawn up in three files abreast to give a depth of
twelve (6.4.12). Since there were sixteen 'enomotiai' to
a 'mora' (according to the scheme accepted in Chapter 12),
the four 'morai' at Leuktra comprised 2,240 men.

Now we know that there were about 700 Spartiates present (6.4.15), few or none of whom except the commander of
cavalry were cavalrymen (6.4.10f.). So, if 300 of them
were the Hippeis (restored in the text of 6.4.14), and if
(as I believe) the Hippeis were drawn up separately from
the 'morai', then only 400 of the c.2,250 in the 'morai'
were Spartiates, the rest being Perioikoi and perhaps men
of inferior Spartan status. In other words, the proportion
of Spartiates in the 'morai' had fallen catastrophically
since the Battle of the Nemea River in 394, and before the
Battle of Leuktra the total number of Spartiates cannot
have exceeded 1,500 compared to the 8,000 of a century
earlier. No doubt poor generalship and inferior tactics
contributed largely to the Spartan defeat. But the adverse
effect on morale of this tiny and shrinking handful of
Spartiates dominating a League force of perhaps 10,000
hoplites (Plut. 'Pelop.' 20.1) should not be overlooked.
Even Xenophon does not hide the fact that some of the allied troops were actually pleased with the result (6.4.15).

Diodorus in line with his pro-Theban stance put the
'Lakedaimonian' casualties impossibly at 4,000. Xenophon
(6.4.15) more plausibly estimates the 'total Lakedaimonian' deaths to be 1,000. Of these about 400 were
Spartiates, including Kleombrotos (Plut. 'Ages.' 28.8;
Diod. 15.55.5) and a polemarch (6.4.14). Rather than
fight to recover the corpses, as some Spartans wished, the
surviving polemarchs wisely decided to ask for a truce.

The news of the disaster was brought to Sparta on the
last day of the Gymnopaidiai festival, which the Ephors
ordered to be completed as usual (6.4.16). The relatives
of the dead, at least the male relatives, were reportedly
cheerful, those of the survivors miserable - in some cases
with more than usually good reason, since, as Plutarch
('Ages.' 30.2-6) tells us in his considerably more
detailed account, there had been many 'tremblers'
(cowards) at Leuktra, including some 'top people'. With
legalistic nicety Agesilaos ordained that the rigorous law
affecting 'tremblers' should be suspended for a day
('Ages.' 30.6; 'Mor.' 191C, 214B), giving the same reason
as he had for urging the acquittal of Sphodrias. Presumably therefore these men were included in the second
Spartan force which was hastily despatched under Agesilaos'
son Archidamos to unite with the remnant of the Leuktra
army (6.4.18).

We do not know how many died on the Theban side,
although at least one of their leaders was killed (Tod
1948, no. 130). We do, however, know that the Thebans
were not quick to capitalize on their stunning victory.
'If the battle of Leuctra marks a revolution in the art of
generalship, it is because of the way it was won, not the
way that it was followed up' (Anderson 1970, 205). One
reason was that Sparta's control of Lakonia and the Peloponnesian League did not at first appear to have been
shaken (6.4.18; 5.1); another was the continuing Athenian
suspicion of Thebes (6.4.19f.); a third was the ambiguous
attitude of Thebes' northern ally Jason (6.4.20-32). The
immediate upshot was that the Spartans and their allies
were permitted to withdraw from Boiotia and a conference
was convened at Athens, where the representatives swore a
fourth Common Peace (6.5.1-3).

There are considerable problems over what this peace
was and whether Sparta was involved. Xenophon, our only
source, is inadequate. If it was a renewal of the King's
Peace of 386, Theban adherence would be surprising. On
the other hand, if Athens was aiming to use the conference to entice the Peloponnesian League allies away from
Sparta, then Spartan adherence would be somewhat odd.
Whatever the truth (cf. Ryder 1965, 71-3), Elis at least

refused to swear the oath, since this would have implied
support for the autonomy of the Triphylian towns of whose
control they had been deprived by Sparta in 400 (6.5.2;
cf. 3.2.30f.). This is the first spark of what in 370
became a forest-fire of disaffection with Spartan rule,
fuelled as usual by stasis.

'The cities', says Diodorus (15.40.1), 'fell into great
disturbance and civil strife, especially in the Peloponn-
nese.' He gives five concrete examples: Phigaleia,
Sikyon, Megara, Phleious and Corinth. To these we may add
Mantineia (6.5.3-5), Tegea (6.5.6-10; Diod. 15.59) and
Argos (Diod. 15.58; with Tomlinson 1972, 139f.).
Isokrates in his 'Archidamos' of c.366 (a speech put in
the mouth of Agesilaos' son) refers to this farflung
revolutionary upheaval at length and with horror (6.64-9).
From the Spartan viewpoint by far the most important
defections were those of Mantineia and Tegea. For as a
result of their joint action Arkadia, which had been 'not
much more than a geographical expression' (Jones 1967,
131), now became (with a couple of exceptions) a political
unit, the Arkadian League (cf. Tod 1948, no. 132). What
the 'Quadruple Alliance' of 420 had hoped for had become
a reality. Sparta was now faced by enemies all along its
northern frontier.

Clearly a show of such strength as Sparta could muster
was obligatory, and Agesilaos once more emerges to command
an almost entirely Lakonian force in Arkadia well after
the end of the normal campaigning season (6.5.10). He
captured Eutaia, a small town on the Arkadian side of the
Lakonian border (6.5.12; cf. Paus. 8.27.3) and then
advanced through Tegeate territory to Mantineia, only to
be forced to retire in the face of overwhelmingly large
numbers of Tegeans, Mantineians, Argives and Eleians.
Diodorus (15.62.3-5) adds the vital information that the
Argives and Eleians, rebuffed by the Athenians, had secured an alliance with Thebes (cf. Xen. 'Ages.' 2.24).

Following Agesilaos' withdrawal, the states bordering
on Lakonia and Messenia urged on the Thebans an immediate
invasion by land of Lakonia, the first time such a tactic
had been proposed since 394 (4.2.12) and the first time
ever that it had really been feasible. All stressed the
size of the forces at the Thebans' disposal, but the
Arkadians added that Lakonia was short on military manpower (6.5.23). The Thebans, however, remained reluctant.
Lakonia, it seemed to them, was extremely hard to penetrate
(cf. Eur. fr. 1083; Diod. 15.63.4), and its frontiers were
garrisoned at Oion in the Skiritis and Leuktron (or Leuktra) above Maleatis (for its probable location see
Andrewes in Gomme 1970, 31-4). They also thought that

their allies were exaggerating the Spartans' weakness and
that nowhere would they fight better than in their own
territory (6.5.24). At this critical juncture some
people arrived from Karyai, supporting the Arkadians'
argument from the Spartans' lack of manpower and offering
to act as guides (6.5.25). Since Xenophon says 'there
were also present some of the Perioikoi', I infer that
Karyai had already defected from Sparta. We recall its
alleged 'medism' in 480 (Chapter 11). Their urging,
together with their allegation that their fellows were
already refusing to obey the Spartiates' summons to aid,
finally convinced the Thebans to invade Lakonia.

The main sources for this - the first, as it turned
out - invasion of Lakonia by Epameinondas are Xenophon
(6.5.25-32), Diodorus (15.63.3-65.5) and Plutarch ('Ages.'
31f.; 'Pelop.' 24). As usual, their accounts diverge
considerably in detail, and I present a conflated version
with some critical or exegetical supplements. The
invasion was mounted on four fronts. The Argives entered
through the Thyreatis (already perhaps in the Arkadian
League: cf. Tod 1948, p. 99), presumably along the Astros-
Karyai road (Chapter 10; Figure 17). Somewhere en route
they stormed a garrison under the Spartiate Alexandros.
The Boiotians took a road that led to Sellasia, no doubt
along the River Sarandapotamos to Karyai and thence
through the waterless Kleissoura pass (hence the need for
guides). The Arkadians crossed the frontier further west
and confronted the garrison of Neodamodeis (their last
mention) and Tegean exiles stationed at Oion under the
Spartiate Ischolaos. He and most of his troops were
killed, and the Arkadians advanced to join up with the
Thebans (and presumably the Argives) at Karyai. Thence
they proceeded to Sellasia, which they burned, looted and
probably (cf. 7.4.12) captured from Spartans. Finally,
the Eleians crossed into Lakonia through the Belminatis
(cf. Plut. 'Kleom.' 4.1) and followed the easiest route to
Sellasia along the Eurotas valley. Perhaps therefore
Belmina, like Karyai, had already been liberated from
Spartan control; at any rate, a few months later, as we
shall see, Pellana, not Belmina, was garrisoned to hold
the line at this point of entry into Lakonia.

The reunited invaders made camp in the plain north of
Sparta in the sanctuary of Apollo at Thornax on the left
bank of the Eurotas. Some hoplites had been posted to
oppose them on the right bank, so the invaders proceeded
south through the Menelaion area to a point on the other
side of the river from Amyklai, on the way burning and
plundering houses full of valuables (a hint of the relax-
ation or evasion of the 'Lykourgan' discipline). They

then with difficulty forded a Eurotas swollen with melted
snow (the invasion had begun at the winter solstice of
370) and reached Amyklai, which had presumably been evacuated. Here the Arkadians occupied themselves with looting
the houses, whereas the Thebans cut down many trees (cf.
Polyb. 5.19.2), presumably olives, to build a palisade.
It was while the invaders were thus engaged that allies
from Phleious slipped past them and made their way to
Sparta. Prevented by the Arkadians and Argives from
entering Lakonia by land, the Phleiasians - like the
allies from Pellene, Sikyon, Corinth, Epidauros, Troizen,
Hermione and Halieis before them - had been forced to take
ship to Prasiai and then make the difficult crossing over
Parnon to the Eurotas valley (7.2.2f.).

Sparta itself was in turmoil. Agesilaos had at his
disposal only a few hundred Spartiates, whom he stationed
at various points to guard the unwalled city. (The wall
of which good traces survive to this day was not completed
until 184.) The Spartan women, already unbalanced by the
deaths of their men at Leuktra, were now running amuck at
the sight of the smoke caused by the invaders. The Perioikoi had not contributed to the full extent of their
manpower, and some of those who had been enlisted were
deserting. An extraordinary proclamation was therefore
made inviting Helots to join the ranks on the understanding that they would be liberated. More than 6,000 of
them - presumably only Lakonian Helots (below) - accepted
the offer with alacrity, indeed with alarming alacrity,
since they swamped the Spartiates and probably the Perioikoi too. Worst of all, there was disaffection within
the Spartan ranks, and two conspiracies had to be suppressed. Certainly some of those involved were Spartiates, since we hear that for the first time ever Spartiates were put to death without trial (Plut. 'Ages.' 32.
11). But perhaps the majority were men of inferior
Spartan status, following the trail blazed by Kinadon.

Despite its dire situation, however, Sparta was not
taken, and Epameinondas turned his attention to the
southern part of the Eurotas valley. It seems that by no
means all the Perioikoi had deserted Sparta, for any of
their towns that were unwalled were looted and put to the
torch. Gytheion, however, which presumably was fortified,
was besieged for three days and perhaps taken. If so,
Sparta was temporarily without a convenient outlet to the
sea. But this was a trifling inconvenience compared with
the immediate sequel, a sequel which Xenophon could not
nerve himself to record, although he could not completely
conceal its occurrence. I refer of course to the liberation of the Messenian Helots.

They had naturally revolted en masse some time after
Leuktra (7.2.2; Xen. 'Ages.' 2.24), in company, I assume,
with the Perioikoi of Thouria and Aithaia as in c.465.   In
369, however, Epameinondas took the step essential for
transforming the former Helots and the expatriates who
flooded back to their homeland into 'the Messenians'. He
supervised the (re)founding of the city of Messene (perhaps at first called Ithome) on the west side of Mount
Ithome, drew up the citizen-register and divided up the
land (Diod. 15.66.1, 6; Plut. 'Ages.' 34.1; 'Pelop.' 24.9;
Paus. 4.26.5-27). The remains of the magnificent enceinte
walling are to this day a massive testimonial to his
achievement.

The loss of the Messenian Helots was the greatest blow
the Spartans had ever suffered. It meant the definitive
end of their status as a first-rate power. Not unnaturally therefore they were angry, chiefly with Agesilaos, at
losing a territory which was as populous as Lakonia and
which they had exploited for some three and a half centuries (Plut. 'Ages.' 34.1). Perhaps no less difficult to
stomach was the blow to their pride. For as Isokrates'
Archidamos (6.28) nicely put it, what was most painful was
not being unjustly robbed of Messenia but seeing their own
slaves becoming masters of it.

In fact, by no means all Messenia was removed at a
stroke from Spartan control; nor did the citizens of
Ithome/Messene immediately control all that was so
removed. For the 'plantation' towns of Mothone and Asine
(Paus. 4.27.8), together with Koryphasion (Pylos) and
Kyparissia (Diod. 15.77.4), remained Perioikic, while the
other Perioikic towns became independent cities in their
own right. None the less, the Spartans had lost the most
fertile and directly controlled portion; and the crucial
strategic link between Messenia and Arkadia, hemming in
Lakonia, had been forged. The men of New Messene also
took out diplomatic insurance by allying themselves to the
Arkadian League and probably to the Thebans too.

In this nadir of their fortunes the Spartans went craw-
ling to the Athenians for help. This they received - but
too little, too late (6.5.33-51). Soon after, in the
spring of 369, they revived the precedent of 421 and
sought an alliance with the Athenians (7.1.1-14: it is
here that we get our only certain reference to Helot
sailors; cf. Welwei 1974, 158f.). Again, however,
although the alliance was concluded, its practical effect
was minimal. The Thebans once more penetrated the Peloponnese, despite an attempt to block them at the Isthmus,
in which 1,000 of the 6,000 or more Helots enlisted for
the defence of Sparta took part (Diod. 15.65.6).

Moreover, the Arkadians were able to make two raids against Spartan territory, probably in the spring and autumn of 369. First, Lykomedes of Mantineia, the guiding spirit of the Arkadian League, led 5,000 elite troops against Pellana, which was garrisoned by 300 or more 'Lakedaimonians' (Diod. 15.67.2). The town was taken by storm, the garrison killed, the land ravaged; perhaps the fourth-century tombstone of Olbiadas (IG V.1.1591) is to be associated with this raid. Second, the Arkadians made an expedition against Asine 'in the Lakonian land' (7.1. 25). Some have thought Xenophon was referring here to Lakonian Asine, but whether or not we consider it possible or likely that the Arkadians could have marched past Sparta, Lakonian Asine was too petty a prize. Messenian Asine, on the other hand, had remained loyal to Sparta and was the nearest enemy town to New Messene. That Xenophon meant this Asine is corroborated by the presence there of a garrison commanded by a Spartiate - or rather a man who had somehow 'become a Spartiate'. (Perhaps he was by origin a 'nothos' or 'trophimos' foreigner: cf. Chapter 14.) The garrison was defeated, its commander slain and the suburbs of Asine ravaged. But the town itself seems to have remained intact and loyal, and perhaps it was in response to this failure that the buffer-towns of Kolon-ides (near Longa) and Korone (modern Petalidhi) were built (Figure 18).

In 368 the fortunes of the Spartans revived somewhat. Despite their refusal to countenance the 'autonomy' of New Messene, Persian money was deployed on their behalf to raise a large force of mercenaries (7.1.27). They also received a supporting band of mercenaries from Dionysios of Syracuse, which Archidamos used to recapture Karyai (7. 1.28). Emboldened by this success, he then made inroads into south-west Arkadia, laying waste the land of the Parrhasioi and Eutresioi (7.1.29). When the Arkadians finally gave battle, they were defeated (7.1.30-2), and the Spartan losses were so slight that the encounter became known as the 'Tearless Battle' (Diod. 15.72; Plut. 'Ages.' 33.5-8). The sequel, however, was considerably lachrymose. For the Arkadians, no doubt at the urging of their Messenian allies (cf. 7.1.29), decided to block Sparta's access to south-west Arkadia for good by founding Megalopolis (Diod. 15.72.4: Paus. 8.27.1-8; Moggi 1976, no. 45). In the process, according to a plausible emend-ation of Paus. 8.27.4 (cf. Andrewes in Gomme 1970, 34), the Arkadians deprived Sparta of part if not the whole of Aigytis and Skiritis: Oion, Malaia, Kromoi (Kromnos), Belmina and Leuktron were among the forty communities incorporated in Megalopolis.

The period 369-362 somewhat recalls 421-418, in that it was one of kaleidoscopically shifting alliances, intermittent warfare and periodic revolutions rounded off by a major but indecisive pitched battle. The difference was that Thebes, not Sparta, was calling the tune. Of Sparta's allies in 369 only the Phleiasians remained consistently a loyal. Elis, however, rejoined the fold to oppose the common enemy, the Arkadians (7.4.19). On the other hand, in 366 Corinth took the initiative in opposing Sparta, as in c.504, 440, 432, 404 and 395 - but this time with decisively deleterious effect. For in leading the movement to make a separate peace with Thebes, it brought about the effective end of the Peloponnesian League (7.4. 7-9). If Thebes had been diplomatically isolated in 371, how much more true was this of Sparta from 366. The irony was that Sparta found itself in this position because it had abandoned the 'autonomy principle' and refused to recognize either New Messene or Megalopolis.

The year 365 was one of mixed luck for Sparta: Sellasia (7.4.12) and perhaps Pellana too (cf. 7.5.9) were recovered, but Koryphasion and Kyparissia were liberated by the Arkadians (Diod. 15.77.4). In reprisal Archidamos in 364 apparently sought to re-establish Sparta's position in Aigytis and maybe also Skiritis. At the request of the now allied Eleians he took the field with 'the citizen troops' (7.4.20) - in fact with a force that included Perioikoi as well as Spartiates (7.4.27).

Having captured Kromnos, he left three of the twelve 'lochoi' there as a garrison and returned to Sparta. Scholars like Anderson (1970, 226) believe that this way of describing a quarter of the Lakedaimonian hoplite army (cf. 7.5.10), taken with the fact that in the 'Hellenika' Xenophon does not speak of 'morai' after Leuktra, indicates a further reorganization of the army in the 360s. However, Polybius (fr. 60 B-W) mentioned the 'mora' in a passage probably describing the army of Kleomenes III (236-22) or Nabis (206-192); and Xenophon's 'Lak. Pol.', which portrays the organization by 'morai', was probably written in the 350s. Whatever the truth, the Kromnos garrison was besieged by the Arkadians, and in an attempt to relieve it Archidamos was wounded and at least thirty 'Lakedaimonians' were killed. The latter included 'almost their most distinguished men', presumably Spartiates. A truce was made, but the siege was only raised by a third expedition, this time by night. Even so more than 100 Spartiates and Perioikoi were captured - and then either ransomed or killed, Xenophon does not say.

In 364-363 the simmering tension between democrats and oligarchs and between Mantineia and Tegea boiled over into

open conflict within the Arkadian League. The attitude of
the Thebans was crucial, and Epameinondas prepared the
ground for Theban intervention by condemning a truce made
between the Arkadians and Eleians and supporting the
action of the Theban governor at Tegea in violating it (7.
4.33-40). Rival deputations were sent - by the Tegeans to
Thebes, by the Mantineians, Eleians and Achaians to Athens
and Sparta - and in 362 Epameinondas for the fourth time
brought an army across the Isthmus.

Both Athens and Sparta responded positively too;
indeed, the Athenians planned to go by sea to Lakonia and
join forces with the Spartans there before marching north
to Arkadia (7.5.7). But Epameinondas learned of the plan
and pre-empted it by a rapid advance to Tegea. His opponents meanwhile decided to take their stand at Mantineia.
Remarkably, Agesilaos (now over eighty) was given command
of the Spartan force, but when he reached Pellana he heard
that Epameinondas had for a second time invaded Lakonia
(7.5.9), no doubt by the route he had taken in 370-369.
So he sent on to Mantineia his cavalry and three of the
twelve 'lochoi' (7.5.10) and managed to regain Sparta
before Epameinondas arrived. Thwarted here, Epameinondas
too proceeded to Mantineia, where he decided to risk all
on a big battle. The Theban side won, but Epameinondas
himself was killed (7.5.22-5), and the outcome, in Xenophon's famous concluding words, was even greater disturbance in Greece than before (7.5.27).

Our story, however, does not end there. The two sides
concluded a Common Peace on the battlefield, for the first
time without Persian intervention (Bengtson 1975, no. 292).
But it was an entente from which Sparta deliberately
excluded itself, since participation would have entailed
the formal recognition of an independent Messene (Diod.
15.89.1f.; Polyb. 4.33.8f.; Plut. 'Ages.' 35.4). This
futile gesture of defiance, for which Agesilaos deserves a
large measure of the blame, is an appropriate symbol of
Spartan weakness in 362.

NOTES ON FURTHER READING

Bibliography on Xenophon is given in the notes to Chapter
12. The 'Lak. Pol.' has been discussed most recently by
Higgins (1977, 65-75). I agree that the essay was composed in one piece in the 350s, but I cannot accept Higgins'
view that it is a consistent and subtle critique of the
Spartan polity. For modern work on the notoriously problematic fourteenth chapter, which I believe was provoked
by Sparta's downfall after 371, see Tigerstedt 1965, 462-4

n. 530.

The development of the 'Second Spartan Empire' from 404 is discussed in Parke 1930. Bockisch 1965 is a full treatment of Sparta's use of harmosts down to 386 but contains several inaccuracies of interpretation and detail. The same is true of her more recent and again fully documented study of the Spartan crisis (1974) whose principal merit is to bring out the universally decisive importance of stasis. On Lysander see the literature in Tigerstedt 1965, 407 n. 17; add Habicht 1970, 6-9, on his apotheosis at Samos.

The downfall of the 'Thirty Tyrants' at Athens is exhaustively discussed in Cloché 1915.

On the composition and terms of service of the 'Ten Thousand' see Roy 1967. The increasing use of mercenaries in Greek inter-state warfare from the late fifth century is documented and analysed in Parke 1933.

Sparta's relations with Persia from the support given to Cyrus down to the King's Peace have been most recently, and acutely, discussed by Lewis (1977). I cannot, however, agree with his view, even in its relatively weak form (144), that Sparta's 'Panhellenism' was substantially genuine and altruistic.

The reign of Agesilaos has been challengingly reviewed by Cawkwell (1976), but I find myself unable to follow him in exonerating Agesilaos from responsibility for Sparta's downfall (see further Chapter 14). Most of the factors which I feel he has not sufficiently accounted for are conveniently listed in Coleman-Norton 1941, 72 n. 10; but add the internal opposition to Agesilaos' foreign policy discussed by Smith (1953/4).

The outbreak of the Corinthian War is discussed in Perlman 1964. For all set-piece battles in this and subsequent wars down to 362 see Anderson 1970, although I cannot follow his account of the reorganization(s) of the Spartan army (229-51). On the career of Iphikrates see Pritchett 1974, II, 62-72.

On 'Common Peace' in general see Ryder 1965; bibliography on the individual peaces may be conveniently found in Bengtson 1975. The connection between the occupation of Kythera and Antalkidas' abortive negotiations in 392 was noticed independently by Lewis (1977, 144).

Spartan politics from 386 to 379 are analysed, not wholly convincingly, in terms of three factions by Rice (1974, 1975). See rather Ste. Croix 1972, 133-6, an admirable treatment of the trials of Phoibidas and Sphodrias.

Concerning the revolutionary upheavals after Leuktra, I am not convinced by the attempt of Roy (1973) to retain Diodorus' date of 374 for those listed at 15.40. See

rather Fuks 1972, 35-7 n. 66. However, for the confused
chronology of 370-362 I follow Roy 1971 rather than
Wiseman 1969.

For the status of Messenia following the liberation of
the Helots see Roebuck 1941; and briefly Lazenby in MME
89ff. The extent of the territory controlled by New
Messene and the related economic questions are considered
in Roebuck 1945 (relevant also to the period before 370).

Part IV
Results and prospects

14 The decline of Spartiate manpower

In the second book of his great work entitled 'Matters
relating to the polis' (our 'Politics') Aristotle first
examines and rejects the ideal states of Plato, Phaleas
and Hippodamos and then turns to consider the three pol-
ities which had commonly been accounted the best of those
actually existing: Sparta, Crete and Carthage. He pre-
faces his detailed discussion of Sparta with the general
observation that any law shall be adjudged good or bad
according as it is or is not consonant first with the laws
of the truly ideal state (as conceived by Aristotle) and
second with the idea and character of the polity proposed
to the citizens by their lawgiver.

In relation to his ideal state Aristotle finds Sparta
defective on the grounds that the lawgiver (meaning
Lykourgos) concerned himself with only a part of virtue,
the military part, and neglected the arts of peace. But
no less harsh are his criticisms of the failure of Spartan
laws to bring about even the defective kind of polity the
lawgiver had proposed. These criticisms are directed
especially to seven aspects of Spartan social and political organization: the Helots, the women, the Ephorate,
the Gerousia, the common meals, the system of naval command and public finance. We have glanced earlier at those
concerning the Helots. Relevant here are those directed
against the organization of the common meals and more
especially the position of women. For under the general
heading of the women he produces his most damning criticism of all ('Pol.' 1270a29-32). In a country capable of
supporting 1,500 cavalrymen and 30,000 hoplites the militarily active citizen-body shrank to less than 1,000; and,
as events showed, the state was not capable of withstand-
ing a single blow but was destroyed through lack of manpower ('oliganthropia').

Clearly, Aristotle's estimate of Sparta's citizen

military potential is appropriate only to the period
before the loss of the Pamisos valley, and the 'single
blow' is the defeat at Leuktra in 371. Probably too the
figure of less than 1,000 militarily active citizens was
borrowed from Xenophon's evidence for the Spartiate
effective at Leuktra. Aristotle therefore expressly
linked Sparta's defeat at Leuktra and consequent 'destruction' with its deficiency in citizens. He is in fact the
only surviving source to make this theoretical connection
and, if that was all there was to it, his explanation
would be vulnerable to the objection that it was not a
shortage of Spartiate warriors but inadequate generalship,
military conservatism and poor morale that brought about
the Leuktra débâcle. However, the strength of Aristotle's
analysis is that, in shining contrast to all our other
ancient sources, he does not merely note or explain away
Spartiate oliganthropy but interprets it squarely as a
function of the Spartan system of land-tenure and inheritance. As we shall see, this sociological rather than
moralizing approach saved him from the error of Xenophon
and others who ascribed Sparta's downfall to a random
'exogenous variable'. For Aristotle the failure lay
within the system itself, which necessarily produced the
historically decisive oliganthropy. In this penultimate
chapter I shall try to demonstrate that Aristotle was
right both in fact and in interpretation and to explain
why official measures to combat oliganthropy proved in the
end a failure.

It must be stressed at once that the oliganthropy for
which we have evidence concerns only the adult male citizens of full status. We have no figures for the categories of men below the status of 'Homoioi', who, like the
Roman 'capite censi' or 'proletarii', did not originally
form part of the regular army. Even for the Spartiates,
however, we have at most four texts which give, or can be
made to yield, concrete, if hardly cast-iron, totals. The
8,000 of 480 (Hdt. 7.234.2), which is corroborated by the
5,000 of 479 (9.10.1, 11.3, 28.2, 29.1), had become about
3,500 by 418 (Thuc. 5.68, as interpreted in Chapter 12).
The 2,500 or so of 394 (extrapolated from Xen. 'Hell.' 4.
2.16) had fallen by nearly a half to a maximum of about
1,500 in 371 ('Hell.' 6.1.1; 4.15, 17). This then is the
scale and pace of Spartiate oliganthropy in the last 100
years of Spartan greatness. Can we say when and why it
became first critical and then apparently irreversible?

The tying of citizenship and so membership of the hoplite army to land ownership and minimum contributions to a
common mess (Arist. 'Pol.' 1271a27-38) will possibly have
encouraged a general 'malthusianism' from the seventh

century, especially if I am right in thinking that the
kleroi then distributed became to all intents and purposes
private property and so subject to the normal Greek practice of partible inheritance. In particular, though, rich
Spartiates, like rich men elsewhere in Greece, will probably have tried harder than most to limit their male offspring, so as to bequeath their considerable property
intact. A further inducement to this end will have been
the fact that in Sparta daughters as well as sons were
entitled to a share of the paternal inheritance.

However, we lack relevant evidence to substantiate
these hypotheses before the mid-sixth century, when the
Ephors intervened to force the Agiad king Anaxandridas to
divorce a loved but barren wife - or rather to take a
second, bigamously (Hdt. 5.39f.). This could of course be
explained by reason of state, but it was also around 550
that Sparta abandoned its aggressively imperialistic
policy of expansion by land in the Peloponnese, and there
may have been a demographic factor in this change of
course (Toynbee 1969, 314). Even if we do not believe
Cicero's report ('De Div.' 1.112; cf. Pliny 'NH' 2.191) of
a serious earthquake at Sparta about this time, the Spartans may already have been alarmed by the disparity in
numbers between themselves and the Helots.

In the late sixth and early fifth centuries the Agiads
Kleomenes I, Dorieus and Pleistarchos all failed to leave
a son - or at least, in Dorieus' case, a legitimate one
(White 1964, 149-51). By the same general period, we
happen to hear, the line of one Glaukos had become extinct
(Hdt. 6.86). An inscription of about 500 (IG V.1.713)
suggests that women who died in childbirth were by then
exempt de facto from the prohibition on named tombstones
(Plut. 'Lyk.' 27.2). In 480 the 300 Spartans selected to
fight with Leonidas at Thermopylai had already produced
male issue (Hdt. 7.205.2). A decade later the authorities
moved most circumspectly against the regent Pausanias,
because 'it was the custom of the Spartans not to act
hastily in the case of a male Spartiate' (Thuc. 1.132.5).
This formulation, though softened at the edges, recalls
Agesilaos' reason for supporting the acquittal of Sphodrias in 378 (Xen. 'Hell.' 5.4.32) and for exonerating the
'tremblers' at Leuktra (Plut. 'Ages.' 30.6; 'Mor.' 191C,
214B).

Taken together, these scraps of evidence fully support
the brilliant suggestion of Daube (1977, 11) that around
500 Sparta, in common with other Greek states, took legal
steps to stimulate the procreation of embryonic warriors.
Daube explains this development in terms of the military
threat to Greece from the Persian empire, and this is no

doubt partly right. But since the measures taken at
Sparta were more extreme than elsewhere, it seems necessary to postulate that the Helots rather than, or in
addition to, the Persians prompted their passage. If we
were to assign them to a specific date, 490 comes to mind.

The measures in question involved above all the legal
obligation on men to get married (Plut. 'Lys.' 30.7; cf.
'Lyk.' 15.1; Stob. 'Flor.' 67.16; Pollux 3.48; 8.40).
Under the law bachelors suffered a diminution of full
civic rights and a fine, together with public disgrace and
ridicule. They were excluded from the Gymnopaidiai festival (Plut. 'Lyk.' 15.2) and so, I assume, from the holding of offices connected with its celebration. On public
occasions not only would younger men not rise to offer
them their seats, but the bachelors were obliged to surrender theirs to their juniors, a terrible humiliation in
gerontolatrous Sparta (Xen. 'Lak. Pol.' 9.5; Plut. 'Lyk.'
15.3; 'Mor.' 227EF; cf. Hdt. 2.80.1). Each winter they
had to walk naked around the Agora, compounding the agon-
ies of the cold (-6.3°C has been recorded in Sparta) by
singing a song to the effect that they were being justly
punished for breaking the law. But perhaps the most
powerful evidence for the strength of the opprobrium
heaped on bachelors is the assimilation of their social
status to that of the 'tremblers' (Xen. 'Lak. Pol.' 9.4f.).
Laws in Sparta were of course unwritten, but, other things
being equal, we should expect the force of example and the
pressure of peer-group conformism in such a disciplinarian
and public culture to have been at least as efficacious as
any written law. Thus the fact that we do hear of confirmed bachelors - including, as we shall see, a man occupying high public office - suggests that other things were
not always equal.

The whole point of this elaborate legal, ritual and
customary apparatus was of course to force adult male
citizens to procreate within the accepted framework of
marriage. But monogamy within what we call the nuclear
family is only one among many possible variants of pairing
relationship contrived for the procreation of legitimate
offspring and so for the transmission of hereditary private property; and Sparta was notorious in antiquity for
its seemingly lax attitude to monogamy (Oliva 1971, 9).

It might happen, says Xenophon ('Lak. Pol.' 1.7-9; cf.
Plut. 'Lyk.' 15.11-18), that an old man had a young wife.
Such a husband was permitted to introduce into his house
a younger man to beget children for him by his wife (a
kind of anticipation of our AID system). Conversely, a
man who did not wish to marry (perhaps a bachelor, but
presumably a widower) might have children by a married

woman, if he could secure her husband's consent. Xenophon
claimed to know of many similar pairing arrangements. One
of these may have been what Polybius (12.6b.8) calls the
honourable custom whereby a man who had produced enough
children might pass his fertile wife on to a friend.

It is unclear whether such marital practices had legal
as well as customary sanction. However, since Plutarch
('Lyk.' 15.16; 'Mor.' 228BC) denies the possibility of
adultery (between citizens, that is: contrast Hdt. 6.68.3;
69.5) in Sparta, and since Xenophon does not mention
adultery at all, it is tempting to connect this in Greek
terms extraordinary state of affairs with the legal crack-
down on bachelors. It may also have been in the early
fifth century that fathers of three sons were exempted
from military service, fathers of four or more from all
state burdens (Arist. 'Pol.' 1270a40-b7; cf. Aelian 'VH'
6.6).

Be that as it may, the measures certainly failed to
produce the desired effect. In 425 the eagerness of
Sparta to sue for peace to recover the mere 120 or so
Spartiates captured on Sphakteria (Thuc. 4.38.5) unambiguously signifies extreme concern over manpower-shortage.
For even if some or all of these captives were leading men
or related to leading men, as a scholiast believed, and
even if there had been a peace movement in Sparta well
before the Sphakteria disaster, the change of official
attitude compared to that of implacable hostility towards
the survivors of Thermopylai is starkly apparent. Some
scholars, notably Ziehen (1933, esp. 231-5), would attribute the change largely to the great earthquake of c.465.
But, as I have suggested in Chapter 11, the demographic
effects of such a natural disaster should have worked
themselves out by 425. Far more important, as should
emerge, was one of the penalties imposed on the returned
Sphakteria hostages in 421, deprivation of their right to
buy and sell real property (Thuc. 5.34.2, with Gomme 1970,
36).

By 425, then, Spartiate oliganthropy had become critical. It cannot be merely coincidental that immediately
thereafter 'Brasideioi' and Neodamodeis appear in the
ancient sources, that in 418 these ex-Helots fight as hoplites at Mantineia and that by the same date (at the very
latest) Perioikoi are brigaded with Spartiates in the
regular hoplite phalanx. Between 418 and 394, however, if
our estimates are approximately correct, there apparently
supervened a generation or so in which the pace of oliganthropy slackened somewhat. Appearances, though, may be
misleading, since the number of Spartiates at the Nemea
River may have been artificially bolstered by a determined

resort to 'Homoioi by adoption' (the 'mothakes') and/or by
enlisting Hypomeiones ('Inferiors'). For what is meant by
these terms we must now return to Xenophon's remarkable
account of Kinadon's conspiracy in c.399 ('Hell.' 3.3.4-
11) and consider its social implications.

The informer, so he told the Ephors, was taken by
Kinadon to the edge of the Agora in Sparta and asked to
count the Spartiates, who numbered only about forty all
told (one king, the five Ephors, the twenty-eight Gerontes
and five or six others). Those, Kinadon pointed out, were
the enemies, whereas the other 4,000 or more persons in
the Agora were to be considered allies. Kinadon then took
the informer on a guided tour of the streets of Sparta,
where again the Spartiates in their ones and twos were
contrasted with the many 'allies', and then of the country
estates, where it was noted that on each there was but one
enemy, the Spartiate master, and many 'allies' (i.e. the
Helots and any private slaves there may have been).

The Ephors then asked how many people Kinadon had said
were implicated with him. The answer was, a few but
trustworthy individuals, who themselves added, however,
that the ensemble of Helots, Neodamodeis, Hypomeiones and
Perioikoi were potential accomplices. For whenever among
these groups any mention was made of Spartiates, no one
could hide the fact that he would gladly devour them -
even raw.

This obviously tendentious account - neither the
informer nor Xenophon's source (if they were different
persons) nor Xenophon himself supported Kinadon's cause -
poses three main difficulties. First, were Kinadon and
his intimates right to imply that all the subordinate
classes of population within the Spartan state were bitterly hostile to the ruling Spartiates? Second, did
Kinadon's plan embrace Messenia as well as Lakonia or did
his plot have 'an essentially Laconian character', as suggested by Vidal-Naquet (in Austin and Vidal-Naquet 1977,
258)? Third, who are these Hypomeiones - a group explicitly attested only in this one passage of Xenophon and in
no other author?

In the first place, it was clearly in the interests of
Kinadon and his confidants to exaggerate the extent of the
hatred for the Spartiates. Thus we surely need not accept
that even a majority, let alone all, of the Neodamodeis
and Perioikoi were so cannibalistically inclined. This
does not of course mean that there were not some Neodamodeis who were disenchanted with their semi-liberated status
and some Perioikoi who desired full citizen rights at, or
(more likely) independence from, Sparta. But most of the
Neodamodeis and at least the hoplites among the Perioikoi

(like Eualkes of Geronthrai: Chapter 12) presumably
regarded it as a privilege to be counted as 'Lakedaimonian'
warriors. To the Hypomeiones we shall return presently.
The attitude of the Helots is linked to the second of the
problems under discussion.

A priori, perhaps, we would expect most Helots to be at
least ill-disposed towards the Spartiates, although we
must draw a distinction between the domestic and the agricultural Helots. Again a priori we might imagine that the
Messenian Helots would be more hostile than the Lakonians.
However, in favour of Vidal-Naquet's interesting suggestion (above) is the geographical consideration that the
country estates nearest to Sparta were of course in Lakonia, and that it was in Lakonia too that the vast majority
of the Perioikoi lived. Moreover, Kinadon was sent by the
Ephors, after they had learned of the plot, to arrest some
named Helots at a Perioikic town in Messenia, a dangerous
tactic, one would have thought, if there had been a serious risk of a rising of the Messenian Helots and Perioikoi. On the other hand, however, it might also be argued,
as Vidal-Naquet himself notes, that the Ephors were seeking to divide the potential enemy's front by setting Lakonian and Messenian Helots and Perioikoi at each other's
throats; and we might add that, if Kinadon did have purely
Lakonian aims, he was apparently depriving himself of one
of his most potent levers against the Spartiates, Messenian 'nationalism'. It is best therefore to leave open the
question of the intended geographical application of
Kinadon's plans.

This leaves for consideration the identity and status
of the 'Inferiors' and a possible motive for Kinadon's
behaviour. We may begin with Kinadon himself. Xenophon
does not expressly say that he was an 'Inferior', but he
implies this in two ways. First, he notes that he was not
one of the Homoioi or 'Peers', the citizens of full status.
Second, he reports Kinadon's alleged reason for plotting
as his wish to be inferior to no one in Lakedaimon. In
fact, unless Kinadon wished to make himself tyrant or
institute an egalitarian democracy, what he probably said
was that he did not want to be one of the 'Inferiors' or
perhaps that he wished to abolish the status of 'Inferiors' altogether.

Now we know that Kinadon was not consigned to
'Inferior' status for want of physical robustness or moral
fibre, since Xenophon emphasizes that he was suitably
endowed in both these respects and yet was not one of the
Homoioi. On the other hand, it appears from another
passage of the 'Hellenika' (6.4.10f.) that physical and
moral debility were grounds for degradation. For the men

enrolled specially for cavalry, not hoplite, service in
the emergency of 371 were 'the most physically incapable
and the least ambitious'. In other words, men who had
failed to pass through the agoge or had not subsequently
been elected to a common mess and so were automatically
ineligible for regular hoplite service became 'Inferiors'.

Some of the plotters, however, as Kinadon revealed to
the informer, were enlisted men (I prefer this translation
of 'syntetagmenoi' to Underhill's 'definitely organized
conspirators') and had hoplite weapons. Kinadon could
of course have been referring to Neodamodeis and Perioikoi,
but as leader he must surely have had arms of his own.
Thus, if he was in fact an 'Inferior', as I believe, then
some 'Inferiors' at least could be enlisted for hoplite
service. This will have been less hard to arrange if the
state anyway provided weapons and armour to Spartiates
(Chapter 10). The enlisted men, however, would have
comprised relatively few of the revolutionaries: the
'masses', Kinadon said, would seize their weapons from the
'iron store'. This, I think, must be a reference to the
central military arsenal in Sparta. For the great quantities it contained of daggers, swords, spits (for cook-
ing), axes, adzes and sickles (for cutting down the
enemy's crops) are explicitly contrasted by Kinadon with
the civilian tools used in agriculture, carpentry and
stonemasonry.

To return to the enlisted men among the 'Inferiors',
these would have acquired their degraded status solely by
reason of their poverty, being men of Spartan birth on
both sides who had perhaps completed the agoge and even
been elected to a common mess but then found themselves
unable to maintain the stipulated mess contribution. Also
to be assigned to the 'Inferiors' are those who had been
temporarily or permanently deprived at law of their full
citizen rights, whether for cowardice in battle (the
'tremblers'), alleged revolutionary designs (the returned
'men from the island' in 421) or other misdemeanours.

More problematic, however, are the two or possibly
three other categories whose names are attested but whose
status as 'Inferiors' is uncertain. Xenophon ('Hell.' 5.
3.9) refers once to foreigners of the category 'trophimoi'
and to the 'nothoi' of the Spartiates, some of whom volunteered, apparently as hoplites, for the Chalkidian campaign of 380. The latter are described as 'exceedingly
fine-looking men not without experience of the good things
of the city', which perhaps means that, like such 'trophimoi' foreigners as Xenophon's own sons, they had gone
through the agoge. Phylarchos (81F43), Plutarch ('Kleom.'
8.1) and Aelian ('VH' 12.43) mention also the category

'mothakes', possibly to be identified with the 'mothones'
cited by lexicographers and scholiasts.

If these disparate sources can be reconciled, it may be
that the 'nothoi' were bastards of Spartiate fathers and
Helot or Perioikic mothers and that they, like the 'trophimoi' foreigners, formed part of the wider category of
'mothakes'/'mothones'. The shared characteristic of the
latter was perhaps that, regardless of their status at
birth, they had been raised with and put through the agoge
with the sons of men of full status. Since such distinguished figures as Lysander and Gylippos were believed to
have been 'mothakes', clearly 'mothax' origin was not
necessarily incompatible either with Spartiate birth on
both sides (Lysander indeed was a Heraklid) or with adult
Spartiate status. The 'nothoi' and 'trophimoi' foreigners, however, were presumably disqualified from Spartiate
status by their illegitimate or foreign birth and so
remained 'Inferiors' for life.

However this may be, we have no positive indication
whatsoever of the size of the 'Inferior' group in 399 (or
any other time of course). Still, if 'Inferiors' could on
occasion be enlisted as hoplites, the continuing drastic
fall in the size of the 'Lakedaimonian' army in the fourth
century must mean either that they did not then form an
abundant reservoir of military manpower or that the Spartiates were unwilling to draw upon it extensively. Whatever the true number of 'Inferiors' may have been, by 371
there were not many more than 1,000 Spartiates all told.
Since this was presumably a matter of no small concern to
the Spartan authorities, or at least Aristotle clearly
thought it ought to have been so, we must ask what were
the countervailing factors over which they had insufficient control.

First, those of demography. The incidence of exclusive
homosexuality and bachelorhood, and their effect on the
birthrate, are not quantifiable, but the ability of a confirmed bachelor like Derkylidas to shrug off the potent
sanctions of civic disgrace and reach the political
heights suggests that this factor may not have been negligible. Habitual intermarriage among a small group of
families, without replenishment from outside or below
(Herodotus, 9.35, was struck by the small number of outsiders to acquire Spartan citizenship), should also have
tended to diminish the citizen population. So too would
contraception, abortion, infant mortality and the exposure
of neonates; but only for the latter do we have any solid,
though again not quantifiable, evidence (Roussel 1943).
On the other hand, it seems certain that Spartan girls
married relatively late by Greek standards (Plut. 'Lyk.'

15.4), and this would perhaps have reduced total female
fertility. Such also would have been the effect, and was
perhaps the object, of the polyandry, especially adelphic
polyandry, attested by Polybius (12.6b.8): for the multiple
husbands were restricting the number of their legitimate
offspring to the childbearing potential of a single shared
wife.

However, no matter how great we suppose the effects of
these demographic factors to have been, they should have
been partly if not wholly offset by the measures to
encourage procreation discussed earlier. We must therefore look for an explanation of the drastic oliganthropy
to broader and deeper socio-economic conditions. This
after all is the general direction in which the ancient
sources pointed the finger.

We should not, however, follow Xenophon ('Lak. Pol.'
14.3) and Plutarch ('Lyk.' 30.1 etc.) in inflating the
significance of the wealth, especially coined wealth, that
flowed into Sparta following Lysander's successful imperialism (Xen. 'Hell.' 2.3.8f.; Diod. 13.106.8; 14.10.2;
Polyb. 6.49.10). For it was a commonplace from at least
Herodotus (9.122) onwards that military might was gained
through personal abstinence; and anyway wealth, even if in
less liquid forms, had been passing between the same kind
of few Spartan hands long before the end of the fifth century. Nor, I think, should we follow Phylarchos and Plutarch in attributing a decisive causal importance to the
probably inauthentic 'rhetra' of Epitadeus (Chapter 10),
even if the injection of foreign cash may have stimulated
the market in Lakonian land in the fourth century, as it
certainly affected Spartan lifestyles.

On the other hand, we are, I believe, bound to respect
the sources' unanimous association of Sparta's downfall
with materialistic greed. By this I suggest we should
understand not so much greed for cash and movables as
greed for land and the resultant anxiety of the ever fewer
rich Spartiates to keep their ever increasing property
intact. Aristotle tells us that most of the land in Lakonia in his day, the third quarter of the fourth century,
had fallen into a few hands ('Pol.' 1307a36) and that
almost two fifths of it were in the hands of women ('Pol.'
1270a23f.). This was but the culmination of a process
extending over at least a century and a half, in which the
rich had grown richer through bequests, adoptions and
marriage-alliances, while the impoverished majority found
themselves increasingly unable to maintain the stipulated
contribution to a common mess and so were degraded to the
status of 'Inferiors' (above).

There was of course nothing peculiarly Spartan about

this anxiety over the transmission of property, any more
than there was in the widening gulf between rich and poor
Spartans, in the fifth and fourth centuries. What seemed
to demand some exceptional explanation and so prompted the
misplaced recourse to the 'exogenous variable' was the
suddenness and distance of Sparta's fall, from the leadership of the Greek world to the status of a second-rate
power in less than a decade. In reality, though, the fall
exemplifies the rule enunciated by Montesquieu in 1734 in
his 'Considerations on the Causes of the Greatness of the
Romans and of their Decline': 'if the chance of a battle,
that is to say, a particular cause, has ruined a state,
there was a general cause ensuring that this state had to
perish by a single battle.' The battle was Leuktra, and
the 'general cause' was the acquisitiveness of the famous
'vaticinatio post eventum' (cited in Arist. fr. 544 and
Diod. 7.14.5) that 'acquisitiveness alone will destroy
Sparta'. For acquisitiveness in the matter of landed
property entailed the oliganthropy through which, as
Aristotle laconically put it, Sparta was destroyed and for
which, as Aristotle also saw, the remedy would have been
to keep landownership more evenly distributed, as was done
for example in the state in which he was himself resident,
Athens.

The destruction was not, however, a simple quantitative
process. The Spartiates had always been a minority in the
total Lakonian population and greatly outnumbered by their
allies in all major battles since the second half of the
sixth century. It was rather the effects of Sparta's
progressively shrinking citizen numbers first in Lakonia
and Messenia on the 'Inferiors', Perioikoi and Helots,
then in the Peloponnese on its Peloponnesian League
allies, and finally on its enemies, especially the Thebans, that brought the destruction about.

In short, if I were to single out any one group of
Spartans as chiefly responsible for Sparta's downfall,
that group would consist of the few rich Spartiates, per-
sonified precisely by those like Agesilaos for whom
Xenophon and Plutarch evinced such warm admiration. It
was perhaps fitting that Agesilaos should meet his end in
Libya at the age of about eighty-four, returning home from
fighting as a mercenary in Egypt.

NOTES ON FURTHER READING

The evidence for Spartiate oliganthropy is conveniently
brought together in Ste. Croix 1972, 331f.; it is well discussed in Toynbee 1969, 297ff., less convincingly in

Christien 1974 (in particular, I disagree with her interpretation of Epitadeus' 'rhetra' as a response to a debt-
crisis).

On social differentiation at Sparta in the fifth to
fourth centuries see Oliva 1971, 163-79. There is as yet
no wholly satisfactory account of the status of Spartan
citizen w˙ves in any period. I hope to publish shortly a
discussion dealing with among other things their property-
rights during the sixth to fourth centuries.

For Aristotle as an interpreter of Sparta see Ollier
1933, 164-88; Tigerstedt 1965, 155f.; Laix 1974.

15 Epilogue

The history of Lakonia in the late Classical, Hellenistic
and Roman periods deserves a book to itself. Here I shall
give only a chronological sketch of the years from 362 BC
to AD 78, in order to indicate how Sparta lost its remaining Helots and Perioikoi, how what we have for convenience
labelled 'Lakonia' shrank in size correspondingly, and how
the Spartans by the first century AD had become exhibits
in a museum of their past.

After the losses of manpower and territory in the wake
of Leuktra, Sparta next suffered such losses in 338 at the
hands of Philip II of Macedon. The Spartans had not
fought with the Greeks he defeated at Chaironeia, but
neither would they join his League of Corinth. In return,
perhaps after a fruitless attempt at negotiation, Philip
laid Lakonia waste as far south as Gytheion and formally
deprived Sparta of Dentheliatis (and apparently the territory on the Messenian Gulf as far as the Little Pamisos
river), Belminatis, the territory of Karyai and the east
Parnon foreland (Roebuck 1948, 86-9, 91f.). The principal
beneficiaries were respectively Messene, Megalopolis,
Tegea and Argos; but the latter at least seems to have
been unable to reap the full benefit of Philip's largesse,
since in the early third century Tyros and Zarax were
still in Spartan control (Charneux 1958, 9-12).

By the time Agis IV ascended the Eurypontid throne in
c.244, the number of Spartiates had further declined from
Aristotle's 'not even 1,000' (in the 360s?) to 'not more
than 700' (Plut. 'Agis ' 5.6). Of the latter, Plutarch
says, perhaps only 100 possessed a kleros as well as real
property. How Plutarch understood the distinction between
these two kinds of land is unclear, although I suspect
that he wrongly believed the kleros to have been inalienable and somehow publicly owned before the 'rhetra' of
Epitadeus (cf. Chapter 10). What is clear, however, is

that by the mid-third century the 'Lykourgan' system of
social organization, with its strict nexus between agoge,
kleros, common mess, army and citizenship, had completely
broken down. Most of the non-Perioikic land in Lakonia
was in the hands of women (Agis' mother and grandmother
were the two richest individuals in Sparta), while the
majority of those who were not either Perioikoi or Helots
were Hypomeiones or what Plutarch describes as 'an indig-
ent and disenfranchised mob'.

To remedy this drastic situation, Agis proposed to
realize the twin revolutionary slogan of all oppressed
Greek peasantries, cancellation of debts and redistribution of the land. He, however, was executed in 241, and
it was left for the Agiad king Kleomenes III to carry out
Agis' plans in a modified form in 227. The propaganda of
Agis and Kleomenes, preserved in Plutarch, and the
counter-propaganda of the recently established and hostile
Achaian League, preserved in Polybius, have made a sorry
mess of the evidence for the original 'Lykourgan' régime,
as we saw in Chapter 10. We are no more in a position to
say whether the programme of Agis and Kleomenes 'was
devised by them for the greater good of the world at
large, of Spartans, of Sparta, or of themselves' (Forrest
1968, 144). Clearly, however, the essence of the programme was an attempt to increase the numbers of the Spartiates, resubmit this enlarged body to the 'Lykourgan'
régime and so restore Sparta's military and political
status to what it had been before 371. The new Spartiates, making a total of about 4,000, were drawn from the
Hypomeiones, Perioikoi and foreigners. The Helots, on
the other hand, were to remain the economic basis of
Spartan power.

This revolution was certainly a step in the right
direction, but it is, I think, an exaggeration to say that
'now for the first time the Spartan State utilised to the
full the resources of the country and its population'
(Toynbee 1913, 274). For a few years, though, Kleomenes
did achieve remarkable success both at home and abroad,
until his unremitting hostility to the Achaian League
served as the occasion for a second Macedonian intervention in Lakonia in 223 or 222. Kleomenes' new army was
hastily reinforced by some 6,000 emancipated Helots, who
unlike the 6,000 or more enlisted in 370 were required to
purchase their freedom with cash (Plut. 'Kleom.' 23.1).
Even so the less than 20,000 men on Kleomenes' side were
no match for the 30,000 troops under king Antigonos Doson,
who won a crushing victory at Sellasia and then proceeded
to take Sparta itself, the first time the site had been
occupied by outsiders since the Dorian 'invasion' of the

tenth century (Chapter 7). Sparta was forcibly enrolled
in the Hellenic League and subjected to a Macedonian
governor. Moreover, as in 338, Macedonian intervention
had unfavourable implications for the size of Lakonia.
For Doson either confirmed or renewed the dispensations of
Philip II, as far as Denthéliatis and the east Parnon
foreland were concerned, and he seems also to have
deprived Sparta of (presumably Perioikic) Leukai, which is
perhaps to be associated with the Hyperteleaton sanctuary.
     The immediate aftermath of Sellasia was fifteen years
of political and social chaos in Lakonia, complicated
internationally by the intervention of Rome in Greece
against Macedon and the Achaian League. By 206 Sparta
naturally enough found itself on the Roman side, but in
that year the central direction of Spartan affairs was
assumed by a third revolutionary leader, Nabis, allegedly
a direct descendant of the deposed Damaratos. His overriding aim (savagely misrepresented of course by our uniformly hostile sources) was no doubt the same as that of
Agis and Kleomenes; but his methods were significantly
different in two crucial respects. First, whereas Kleomenes had freed Helots purely for military reasons, Nabis
emancipated them in order to prop up his rule. Logically,
therefore, he made them beneficiaries of his land redistribution and incorporated them in the Spartan citizen
body. (It is possible too that under Nabis the state, as
in Crete, was made responsible for financing the common
messes.) Second, whereas Kleomenes had put all his military eggs into one land-orientated basket, Nabis also built
up Sparta's first-ever navy of any value and used the
Perioikoi of the coastal towns of Lakonia as his elite
troops (though apparently without giving them citizenship).
     For about a decade Nabis (and Sparta) prospered remark-
ably, but in 197 he made the twofold mistake, in Roman
eyes, of accepting Argos from Philip V of Macedon (by then
deserted by the Achaian League) and extending his social
programme to that city. In 196 Philip was defeated by the
Romans, whose representative, T. Quinctius Flamininus,
then invaded Lakonia. Nabis was not in fact eradicated,
since, as Briscoe (1967, 9) has rightly pointed out, the
aim of Flamininus was 'a balance of power, not upper-class
constitutional government, and he preferred to tolerate
the continued existence of a revolutionary government in
Sparta rather than allow the Achaean League excessive
power in the Peloponnese'. The importance of Nabis and
Sparta, however, was irretrievably reduced by the liberation of the remaining Perioikic dependencies and their
transfer either to the direct control of Argos (in the
case of Prasiai to Zarax inclusive) or to the general

protection of the Achaian League. Perhaps it was between
195 and the death of Nabis in 192 that the liberated Perioikic towns went over to the Roman side and were formally
recognized as the 'Koinon (League) of the Lakedaimonians'.
Sparta, however, retained its 'Lykourgan' socio-economic
institutions, including the by now severely reduced Helot
base, until 188, when all apart from the agoge were viol-
ently abrogated by the Achaian League (of which Sparta had
been a member perforce since 192).

In 146, however, the Achaian League was itself disbanded, greatly to the benefit of Sparta, which had opposed the League's attempt to shake off the Roman yoke.
Under the aegis of Rome Sparta seems to have recovered
Belminatis and Aigytis from Megalopolis, but Denthieliatis
remained Messenian. It was perhaps now that the few
remaining Helots exchanged their anomalous status for
another. Thereafter the Spartan propertied class derived
its surplus from the exploitation of chattel slaves or
tenants.

The struggle for control of the Roman world between
Antony and Octavian/Augustus also redounded to the advantage of the Spartans, since they had taken the winning
side. According to the Augustan settlement, presumably of
27, Lakonia was divided into two separate political entit-
ies, Sparta (with enlarged territory: below) and the
'Koinon of the Free Lakonians' (the Eleutherolakonian
League). The League originally comprised twenty-four
members, but of these only eighteen remained by c.AD 150,
the time of Pausanias (3.21.7): Gytheion, Teuthrone, Las,
Pyrrhichos, Kainepolis (the successor to Tainaron, established at modern Kyparissi on the opposite, western, flank
of south Mani), Oitylos, Leuktra (in north-west Mani),
Thalamai, Alagonia, Gerenia, Asopos, Akriai, Boiai, Zarax,
Epidauros Limera, Prasiai, Geronthrai and Marios. The six
communities which had left the League or disappeared
between 27 BC and c.AD 150 may have been Kotyrta, Hippola,
Pharai, Kyphanta, Leukai and Pephnos. The original total
of twenty-four corresponds roughly to the thirty or so
'polichnai' referred to by the contemporary Strabo (8.4.
11, C362), and the decrease from the conventionally 100
(actually perhaps eighty) of the fourth century has been
plausibly explained as the result of political amalgam-
ations by the smaller communities after 195. The process
of amalgamation may have been furthered by an absolute
decline in the former Perioikic population from the mid-
second century.

The new, separate Sparta appears to have controlled the
Eurotas furrow as far south as Aigiai, together with
Skiritis and the territory of Karyai. In addition,

Augustus ceded to the Spartans Kardamyle, Thouria and
Kythera, the two former giving them respectively an outlet
to the sea and a foothold in the south-east Pamisos valley,
the latter becoming more or less the personal property of
the Spartan C. Julius Eurycles (Bowersock 1961). The
chief losers by the Augustan dispensation were of course
the Messenians, who had improvidently sided with Antony at
Actium. Their southern boundary with the Free Lakonians
was fixed at the Choireios Nape (modern Sandava gorge)
towards Alagonia and Gerenia, but to the north they lost
among other territory the psychologically important
Dentheliatis (in dispute since the eighth century).

Under Tiberius, however, in AD 25 the Dentheliatis was
returned to the Messenians by the Senate (Tac. 'Ann.' 4.
42), and in AD 78 a boundary commission under the auspices
of Vespasian confirmed the award. The official record of
the AD 78 boundary between Messenian and Spartan territory
has been found at ancient Messene (IG V.1.1431), and the
discovery of boundary-marks helps us to trace the frontier
from the sanctuary of Artemis Limnatis in the south (where
the whole trouble may have begun: Chapter 8) to a point
not far east of ancient Asea (Chrimes 1949, 60-70; Kahrstedt 1950, 232-42; Giannokopoulos 1953).

It is also with the Flavian period that there commences
in earnest the mass of epigraphical material bearing on
the Spartan social system. This material was first comprehensively studied by Chrimes (1949, 84-168) and, whatever errors of fact and interpretation she may have committed, her overall conclusion - that in their social
organization the Spartans were monumentally conservative -
is cogent and indeed unsurprising. It was, however, an
empty and fetishistic conservatism. 'The keeping up of
ancient appearances was no more than a colourful stage
setting for the benefit of visitors, particularly wealthy
Romans, who would come to Sparta as to one of the most
famous cities of Greek history' (Oliva 1971, 318) - partly,
we might add, to witness the floggings in the sanctuary of
Artemis Orthia (Appendix 5). Perhaps as good an indication as any of Lakonian decadence is conveyed by the suggestion of Rawson (1969, 107f.) that 'the ordinary Roman
... would seem to have thought, when he heard the word
Laconia, primarily of the hunting dogs, fine marble, and
purple dye that she exported, and perhaps also of the hot-
air chamber in the baths called the "laconicum".' Sic
transit gloria.

NOTES ON FURTHER READING

For the main outlines of the changes in Sparta's former
dominions I have mostly followed Toynbee 1969, 405-13;
other modern work has been cited in the text.
   Will 1966 covers thoroughly, and with helpful bibliographical notes, the political history of the Greek world
in the last three centuries BC; for Hellenistic Sparta as a
whole add now Oliva 1971, 201-318; and for the century
prior to the Roman conquest Shimron 1972.
   The revolutions of Agis, Kleomenes and Nabis are
considered from the standpoint of the treatment of the
Helots by Welwei (1974, 161-74). Tarn 1925 remains a
stimulating essay on the wider socio-economic situation in
Greece in the third century.

Appendix 1

Gazetteer of sites in Lakonia and Messenia

For the purposes of this gazetteer Lakonia is taken to
embrace the entire Mani, up to and including Kalamata.
Listed under Lakonia are all sites for which there is
archaeological evidence for any period from the Neolithic
(N) to the Classical (C), taking in on the way Early,
Middle and Late Helladic (EH, MH, LH), Protogeometric (PG),
Geometric (G) and Archaic (A). Under Messenia are listed
only those sites for which there is archaeological evidence for the G, A or C periods. Ancient names, where
certain or possible, are given in brackets.

A. Lakonia (numbers in brackets indicate the site-numbers
   in Hope Simpson 1965, of which a second edition is
   forthcoming)

ALEPOTRYPA: N EH
AAA 1971, 12ff., 149ff., 289ff.; AAA 1972, 199ff.; BCH
1972, 845ff.; AD 1972B, 251-5.
ALMYROS: C
MME, no. 543.
AMYKLAI
Amyklaion (97): EH MH LH II LH IIIA-C PG G A C
AE 1892, 1ff.; JdI 1918, 107ff.; AA 1922, 6ff.; AM 1927,
1ff.; BSA 1960, 74ff.
Ay. Paraskevi (sanctuary of Alexandra/Kassandra): G A C
BCH 1957, 548ff.; AD 1960B, 102f.; PAAH 1961, 177f.
Sklavochori (Amyklai?): C
BSA 1960, 82, no. 3.
ANALIPSIS (Iasos/Iasaia?) (135): EH LH I-IIIB G A C
PAAH 1950, 234f.; 1954, 270ff.; 1955, 241f.; 1956, 185f.;
1957, 110f.; 1958, 165f.; 1961, 167f.; BSA 1961, 131; BSA
1970, 95f., no. 36.
ANEMOMYLO (149): EH LH III

BSA 1961, 138.
ANGELONA (148): EH LH III? A C
BSA 1905, 81ff.; Kahrstedt 1954, 216 n. 1; BSA 1961, 138.
ANOYIA (Dereion?): A C
AM 1904, 13; BSA 1910, 65f., 70f.; Kahrstedt 1954, 199f.;
BSA 1960, 82, no. 5.
ANTHOCHORION (100): LH IIIB-C PG G A C
PAAH 1962, 113ff.
ANTIKYTHERA (Aigilia): C
Kahrstedt 1954, 214; BSA 1961, 160ff.; AR 1975, 42, no. 10.
APIDIA (Palaia/Pleiai?) (106): N EH MH LH II-IIIC PG C
BSA 1908, 162; BSA 1921, 146; Kahrstedt 1954, 215; BSA
1960, 86f.
ARACHOVA (Karyai): not certainly located
JHS 1895, 54ff., 61; RE s.v. Karyai; IG V.1, p.172; Pelop-
onnisiaka 1958-9, 376ff.
ARCHASADES: see XIROKAMBI (Spartan plain)
ARKINES (101): LH III C?
AE 1889, 132ff.; BSA 1910, 67; Philippson 1959, 434; BSA
1961, 128ff.
ARNA: C?
AE 1889, 132f.; BSA 1910, 67.
ARVANITO-KERASIA (Oion): C
JHS 1895, 61f.; Kahrstedt 1954, 202; A. Andrewes in Gomme
1970, 33.
ASTROS (137): MH LH PG? A C
Frazer 1898, 307; AA 1927, 365; RhM 1950, 227ff.; Kahr-
stedt 1954, 171; BSA 1961, 131; BCH 1974, 604.
AY. ANDREAS: C?
Frazer 1898, 307f.; AA 1927, 365; RhM 1950, 229; BCH 1963,
759.
AY. EFSTRATIOS (110): N EH MH LH II-IIIB C
BSA 1960, 87ff. ('Ay. Strategos' is a slip.)
AY. GEORGIOS (155): LH A C
BCH 1958, 714; BSA 1961, 145; AD 1971B, 122.
AY. GEORGIOS (Spartan plain): C
AM 1904, 6f.
AY. IOANNIS (147): EH LH III
BSA 1908, 179; BSA 1961, 137.
AY. IOANNIS (Bryseiai?): C
PAAH 1909, 295f.; Boelte 1929, 1330f.; Kahrstedt 1954,
199f.
AY. IOANNIS (lower Eurotas valley): LH III C
BSA 1960, 95.
AY. IOANNIS (west Parnon foreland): C
BCH 1961, 691.
AY. NIKOLAOS (116): MH LH IIIB
BSA 1960, 94f.
AY. PETROS: C

Appendix 1

Frazer 1898, 310; AM 1905, 415f.; AM 1908, 177ff.
AY. STEPHANOS (120): EH MH LH I-IIIC C
BSA 1960, 97ff.; BSA 1972, 205ff.; AR 1975, 15ff.
AY. TRIADA (Thyrea?): C?
Frazer 1898, 307. See also ASTROS.
AY. TRIADA (Malea peninsula): LH
BSA 1961, 145.
AY. VASILIOS (99): EH MH LH IIIB   C
AE 1936B, 1f.; BSA 1960, 79ff.

BRINDA: C
MME, no. 548.

CHAROUDA: not certainly occupied.
AM 1876, 162f.; AM 1904, 44ff.; Kahrstedt 1954, 209;
Fermor 1958, 71ff.; Giannokopoulos 1966, 45f.
CHASANAGA (Hyperteleaton sanctuary): PG? G? A C
PAAH 1885, 31ff.; BSA 1908, 165f.; IG V.1, pp.187ff.; BSA
1921, 147f.; Kahrstedt 1954, 211; AD 1969B, 138f.; BCH
1971, 888.
CHELMOS (Belmina): G A? C
JHS 1895, 36ff., 71ff.; Kahrstedt 1954, 201f.; BSA 1961,
125; BCH 1961, 686; BSA 1970, 101, no. 53; AD 1973B, 175.
CHERSONISI (138): EH MH LH III
AA 1927, 365; BCH 1963, 759.
CHOSIARO (Las) (127): LH? A C
BSA 1906, 274f.; BSA 1907, 232ff.; Kahrstedt 1954, 209f.;
BSA 1961, 118; Giannokopoulos 1966, 52ff.
CHRYSAPHA (102): EH LH? A C
BSA 1910, 65; BSA 1921, 144f.; BSA 1960, 82ff.

DAIMONIA (Kotyrta) (152): EH? MH LH I-IIIB PG A C
BSA 1908, 166; BSA 1921, 148f.; BSA 1961, 141.
DICHOVA: A
BSA 1907, 233f.; AD 1968B, 153.
DRAGATSOULA (111): EH MH LH III
BSA 1960, 89.

ELAPHONISOS (Onougnathos) (157-8): EH LH III
RE s.v. Onou gnathos (1); Kahrstedt 1954, 213; BSA 1961,
145ff.; Arvanitis 1971, 55-9.
ELEA (Biandina?) (150): EH MH? LH III C
BSA 1908, 162; BSA 1921, 149; BSA 1961, 139.
EPIDAUROS LIMERA (Epidauros Limera) (146): N? LH I-IIIC A C
RE s.v. Epidauros (2); BSA 1908, 176ff.; BSA 1961, 136f.;
AD 1968A, 145ff.

GANGANIA (107): EH MH LH IIIB
BSA 1961, 139.

GERAKI (Geronthrai) (105): N EH MH LH III (IIIC?) A C
BSA 1905, 91ff.; BSA 1910, 72ff.; BSA 1960, 85f.; Le Roy
1974, 220-2.
GIANNITSA (Kalamai?): C
MME, no. 537; Meyer 1978, 178, 180f.
GORITSA (103): N EH MH LH I-II LH IIIB
BSA 1960, 83.
GOULES: see PLYTRA
GOUVES: A? C
BSA 1909, 163; BSA 1921, 146; BSA 1960, 87 n. 101.
GYTHEION (Gytheion): A C
RE s.v. Gytheion; BSA 1907, 220ff.; Giannokopoulos 1966;
AAA 1972, 202ff.; IJNA 1975, 103ff.

HELLENIKO (Eua): G
Frazer 1898, 306; AA 1927, 365; RhM 1950, 230.

IERAKA (Zarax): C?
BSA 1909, 167ff.; RE s.v. Zarax; BSA 1961, 136 n. 147.

KALAMATA (Pharai) (166): EH? LH IIIA-B G A C
BSA 1957, 242f.; BCH 1961, 697; MME, nos 141-2, 540.
KALYVIA GEORGITSI (Pellana) (133): EH? LH IIIA-C C
AD 1926, Parart., 41ff.; RE s.v. Pellana (1); BSA 1961,
125ff.
KALYVIA TIS SOCHAS (Eleusinion sanctuary): A? C
BSA 1910, 12ff.; BSA 1950, 261ff.; BSA 1960, 82, no. 4.
KAMBOS (169): N? LH II-IIIA-B   C
MME, no. 146.
KARAOUSI (112): N EH MH LH I-IIIC PG? G? C
BSA 1960, 89ff.; AR 1960, 9; BSA 1972, 262f.
KARDAMYLI (Kardamyle) (170): N? EH? MH? LH A C
BSA 1904, 163; MME, no. 147; AD 1972B, 265; Meyer 1978,
176f.
KARYAI: see ARACHOVA
KASTRI (164): see KYTHERA
KIPOULA (Hippola) (130): LH? A C
BSA 1907, 244f.; IG V.1, p.237; BSA 1961, 123; Rogan 1973,
68f.
KOKKINIA (Akriai) (108): LH? C
BSA 1908, 162; BSA 1961, 138f.
KOKKINOCHOMATA: see PIGADIA
KOSMAS (Glympeis/Glyppia?) (144): LH? A C
BSA 1909, 165; PAAH 1911, 277f.; RE s.v. Glympeis,
Glyppia; BSA 1961, 135; BCH 1963, 759.
KOTRONAS (Teuthrone) (128): EH MH? LH? C
BSA 1907, 256f.; BSA 1961, 119; BCH 1961, 215ff.; BCH
1965, 358ff.
KOTRONI (141): LH IIIA-B

BSA 1961, 132f.
KOUPHOVOUNO (96): N EH LH IIIB
BSA 1960, 74.
KOUTIPHARI (Thalamai) (173): LH G? A C
BSA 1904, 161f.; MME, no. 150.
KRANAI (Kranae) (124): EH? LH IIIA-C
BSA 1907, 223; BSA 1961, 114; Giannokopoulos 1966, 25, 185.
KROKEAI (Krokeai) (121): MH? LH II-IIIC C
BSA 1910, 68f.; Kahrstedt 1954, 200f.; BSA 1960, 103ff.;
BCH 1961, 206ff.
KYPARISSI (Kyphanta): C
BSA 1909, 173f.; RE s.v. Kyphanta.
KYPRIANON (129): LH? C
BSA 1961, 119ff.; BSA 1968, 333ff.
KYTHERA (Kythera) (159-65): N EH EM MM I-LM IB LH II LH M
IIIA-B G A C
RE s.v. Kythera; Kahrstedt 1954, 213f.; BSA 1961, 148ff.;
Coldstream/Huxley 1972.

LAGIO (122): EH LH III
BSA 1960, 105; Giannokopoulos 1966, 26.
LEKAS (119): EH MH LH IIIB C
BSA 1960, 97.
LEONIDHION (Prasiai) (140): LH III A C
BSA 1908, 167, 174f.; PAAH 1911, 278f.; RE s.v. Prasiai;
BSA 1961, 131.
LEVTRO (Leuktra) (171): MH? LH III C
BSA 1904, 162; MME, no. 548; Meyer 1978, 176.
LIONI (161): see KYTHERA
LYMBIADA (Glyppia?) (143): EH LH III C?
BSA 1909, 165; BSA 1961, 135.

MARI (Marios) (145): LH? A C
BSA 1909, 166f.; RE s.v. Marios; BSA 1961, 136.
MAVROVOUNI (125): EH LH IIIB-C PG C
BSA 1961, 114ff.
MELATHRIA: LH IIIA-B C
BCH 1960, 693; AD 1967B, 197ff.; AAA 1968, 32ff.
MELIGOU (Anthana?): A
Frazer 1898, 308; RhM 1950, 230; AM 1968, 182f.
MENELAION (sanctuary of Menelaos and Helen) (95): MH III
LH II-IIIB G A C
PAAH 1900, 74ff.; BSA 1909, 108ff.; BSA 1910, 4ff.; BSA
1960, 72, 82; AR 1977, 24ff.
MEZAPOS (Messe?) (131): LH III?
BSA 1907, 243f.; BSA 1961, 122f.
MIKRA MANDINIA: LH? C
MME, no. 144.
MONEMVASIA: see EPIDAUROS LIMERA

NEAPOLIS (Boiai) (154): EH LH IIIA-B   A C
RE s.v. Boiai; BSA 1908, 168ff.; BSA 1961, 142ff.; Arvan-
itis 1971.
NEROTRIVI (Selinous?): C?
BSA 1909, 164f.; BSA 1921, 145.

OITYLON (Oitylos) (132): LH? C
BSA 1904, 160f.; BSA 1961, 121.

PAIZOULIA (123): EH MH LH II-IIIB   C
BSA 1960, 105; Giannokopoulos 1966, 26.
PALAIOCHORA (Abia): C?
BSA 1904, 164f.; MME, no. 545; Meyer 1978, 178.
PALAIOCHORA (Aigiai) (126): LH? A C
BSA 1907, 231f.; BSA 1961, 114, 173ff.
PALAIOCHORI (142): EH MH LH I-IIIB
BSA 1961, 132ff.
PALAIOGULAS (Sellasia): A C
RE s.v. Sellasia; PAAH 1910, 277f.; Pritchett 1965, ch. 4.
PALAIOPOLIS (164): see KYTHERA
PALAIOPYRGI: see VAPHEIO
PANAYIOTIS (118): EH MH LH IIIA-B   C
BSA 1960, 95ff.
PAPPAGENIES DAPHNI: C
BSA 1961, 141 n. 181.
PAVLOPETRI: EH MH? LH IIIB
BSA 1969, 113ff.; Archaeology 1970, 242ff.
PEPHNOS (Pephnos) (172): LH III
BSA 1904, 162; RE s.v. Pephnos; MME, no. 149.
PERIVOLAKIA (Kalamai?): LH III
MME, no. 140; Meyer 1978, 178, 180f.
PHARAI: A? C
MME, no. 542.
PHLOMOCHORI: A (but not certainly occupied)
BCH 1965, 366, 371ff.
PHONEMENOI (Hermai?): A C
BSA 1905, 137f.; Athena 1908, 383ff.; PAAH 1950, 235f.
PIGADIA (168): N? EH? MH? LH I-II-IIIA-C PG?
MME, no. 145.
PLYTRA (Asopos) (151): N EH MH LH III   C
Frazer 1898, 382f.; BSA 1908, 163ff.; BSA 1961, 139ff.;
Archeologia: trésors des âges, Nov.-Dec. 1968, 42f.
PORTO TON ASOMATON (Tainaron): C
BSA 1907, 249ff.; AM 1915, 100ff.; RE s.v. Tainaron; BSA
1961, 123f.; AAA 1975, 160ff.
POULITHRA (Polichna): C?
BSA 1909, 176; PAAH 1911, 276f.; RE s.v. Polichna.
PYRRHICHOS (Pyrrhichos): C?
BSA 1904, 160: BCH 1965, 378ff.

SKOUTARI (Asine): C?
BSA 1907, 235; CR 1909, 221f.; Kahrstedt 1954, 209.
SPARTA
Akropolis: LH III PG G A C
BSA 1907, 137ff.; BSA 1908, 142ff.; BSA 1925, 240ff.; BSA
1927, 37ff.
Limnai (Artemis Orthia sanctuary): PG G A C
AO; Boardman 1963.
Pitana (tile-stamps, Hellenistic): BSA 1907, 42.
Pitana (A settlement): BSA 1960, 82.
Mesoa (A graves): AD 1964A, 123ff.
Kynosoura? (A sanctuary at modern Kalogonia): PAAH 1962,
115ff.; BCH 1963, 759f.
City-wall (Hellenistic): BSA 1907, 5ff.
Thornax?: BSA 1960, 82, no. 1.
STENA (153): EH LH II-IIIB
BSA 1961, 141f.
STENA (near Gytheion): see MAVROVOUNI
STROTSA: A?
BSA 1907, 226f.; BSA 1910, 67f.

TRINASA (Trinasos): C?
Frazer 1898, 380; BSA 1907, 230f.; Kahrstedt 1954, 206.
TSASI (115): EH LH IIIA-B A? C
BSA 1960, 92ff.
TSERAMEIO (Alesiai?): C
BSA 1960, 82, no. 2.
TYROS (Tyros) (139): EH LH? A C
PAAH 1911, 253ff.; PAAH 1953, 251ff.; BSA 1961, 131.

VAPHEIO (98): EH MH LH II-IIIB
AE 1889, 132ff.; BSA 1960, 76ff.
VERGA: LH
BSA 1966, 116; MME, no. 143.
VEZANI (Helos) (109): MH LH? C
BSA 1909, 161f.; Kahrstedt 1954, 212; BSA 1960, 87ff.
VLACHIOTI (114): EH LH III C
BSA 1909, 162; BSA 1921, 150; BSA 1960, 92.
VRONDAMA (104): LH III C
BSA 1960, 83ff.

XERONISI (117): EH MH LH IIIA-C C
BSA 1960, 95.
XIROKAMBI (136): LH?
AA 1927, 365; BSA 1961, 131.
XIROKAMBI (Spartan plain): A? C?
BSA 1960, 81.

B. Messenia (spelling and site-numbers are those of MME,
    where references to earlier work may be found; see also
    Meyer 1978, 169-212)

AETOS: AY. DHIMITRIOS (226): C
AITHAIA: ELLINIKA (Thouria) (137): G? A? C
AKOVITIKA (151): G A C
ANO KOPANAKI: AKOURTHI (234): C
ANO KOPANAKI: STILARI (Polichne) (233): C
ARTEMISIA: VOLIMNOS (sanctuary of Artemis Limnatis) (138):
G A C
AY. FLOROS (temple of Pamisos) (530): A C
AY. ANDHREAS (temple of Apollo Korynthos) (504): A C

BALIRA (525): C?

CHANDRINOU: PLATANIA (33): A C
CHAROKOPIO: DEMOTIC SCHOOL (109): C
CHAROKOPIO: GARGAROU (509): C
CHATZI: BARBERI (26): C
CHORA: ANO ENGLIANOS (Mycenaean Pylos) (1): G
CHORA: VOLIMIDHIA (20): G
CHRISOKELLARIA: AY. ATHANASIOS (111): C?
CHRISTIANI (410): C?

DHIODHIA: AY. IOANNIS (518): C

EVA: NEKROTAFION (125): C

FINIKOUS: AYIANALIPSI (79): G C

GARGALIANI: KANALOS (15): C

HELLENIKA: see AITHAIA

ITHOME: see MAVROMATI

KAFIRIO: see LONGA
KAKALETRI: AY. ATHANASIOS (Hira?) (611): A C
KALOYERAKI: SAMARINA (522): C?
KASTELIA-VOUNARIA (Kolonides?) (507): C
KASTRO TOU MILA: CHAMOUZA (604): C
KATO KREMMIDHIA: FOURTZOVRISI (34): C
KATO MELPIA: KREBENI (216): A? C
KONSTANDINI: AY. ATHANASIOS (Andania?) (607): C
KORIFASION: PORTES (3): C
KORONI: BOURGO (Asine) (512): A C
KORONI: KAMINAKIA (514): C
KORONI: ZANGA (513): C

KOUKOUNARA (35): G
KYPARISSIA (Kyparissia) (70): A C

LAMBAINA: TOURKOKIVOURO (122): G
LAMBAINA (523): C?
LONGA: KAFIRIO (107): G? A? C
LOUTRO: KOKKALA (Ampheia?) (211): G?

MALTHI: GOUVES (Dorion?) (223):G A (AE 1972B, 12-20)
MAVROMATI (Messene, Ithome) (529): G A (BSA 1926, 138,
no. 9) C
RE Supp. XV, 136-55.
METHONI (Mothone) (412): A C
MILITSI: G A C
AD 1970B, 181f.
MIROU: PERISTERIA (200): C
MONI VOULKANOU (526): C?

NEDON VALLEY: A
Valmin 1930, 46, 48ff., 207ff.; RE s.v. Nedon; Jeffery
1961, 206, no. 5.
NEROMILOS: PANAYITSA (517): A
NICHORIA: see RIZOMILO

PALIO NERO: VOUNAKI (Aulon?) (601): C?
PAPOULIA (53): A
PERISTERIA: see MIROU
PETALIDHI (Korone) (502): C
PETROCHORI: CAVE OF NESTOR (10): C
PETROCHORI: PALIOKASTRO (Koryphasion/Pylos) (9): C
PIDHIMA: AY. IOANNIS (136): A? C
PILA (402): A
PLATI (524): C?
POLIANI: PALIOCHORA (535): C
POLICHNI: AY. TAXIARCHOS (Andania?) (212): C
PROTI (Prote, Prokonnesos) (407): A (Jeffery 1961, 206,
no. 2) C?

RIZOMILO: NICHORIA (Aipeia?) (100): G A C
Hesperia 1972, 218-73; 1975, 69-141.
ROMANOU: VIGLITSA (400): A C

SPERCHOYIA (533): C?
SPILIA: PRINDZIPA (69): C?

TRIKORFO: KAKO KATARACHI (121): C

VALTA: AY. PANDELEIMONAS (58): C?
VASILIKO: FILAKION (605): A C?

VELIKA: SKORDHAKIS (112): C?
VOLIMIDHIA: see CHORA
VOLIMNOS: see ARTEMISIA
VOURNAZI: BAROUTOSPILIA (127): C

YIALOVA: DHIVARI (401): A C

The Homeric poems as history

Concerning Homer everything, not excluding the name, has been the subject of immemorial debate. For my limited purposes, however, I shall accept without discussion that the Homeric poems, our 'Iliad' and 'Odyssey', are traditional oral formulaic poems, which reached approximately the form in which we have them, perhaps with the aid of writing, somewhere in the eighth or early seventh centuries. Their formulaic diction is characterized by the mixture of scope and economy diagnostic of the epic genre, and their language is an artificial amalgam of dialectal forms of diverse origin and date, never spoken outside the context of an epic recital.

The crucial period for the formation of the tradition was probably the early Dark Age (second half of the eleventh and tenth centuries) rather than the tail-end of the Mycenaean era, and the process took place among the Ionian and Aiolian Greeks of the Asiatic diaspora, although the precise nature of 'colonial' society and in particular the social milieu in which the Homeric poems were created and developed are still obscure. The great advance in our knowledge of the epic genre and the relevant archaeological data makes it necessary to pose the overall problem of historicity as follows: 'is the Homeric world Mycenaean with a few anachronisms, or eighth century with a few garbled survivals, or something intermediary, or a synthesis of them all, or a fictional world of the imagination?' (D.H.F. Gray in Myres 1958, 293). I shall concentrate on two facets of the problem, the historicity of the Trojan War as it is envisaged in the 'Iliad' and the historical status of the 'Catalogue of Ships' ('Il.' 2.484-760), with special reference to the 'Kingdom of Menelaos'.

In the absence of contemporary and directly relevant written documents, on either the Greek or Trojan side, the suggested solutions must depend on evaluation of Homer as

traditional oral poetry and interpretation of the archaeological evidence. It is generally agreed today that
there is a profound discontinuity between the world in
which the events described in the 'Iliad' could have
occurred, the thirteenth century, and the world in which
'Homer' lived and thought. 'The world of the (sc. Linear
B) tablets is one of which the Homeric poems retain only
the faintest conception' (Page 1959, 202). Thereafter,
however, scholars are divided between those who believe
that there is a historical basis to the poem, overlaid and
distorted no doubt in the course of transmission but none
the less still recoverable; those who believe that there
is a historical basis but one that is no longer recoverable, at least not with any certainty or precision; and
those who believe that there is no or only a very slight
historical basis. In relation to the two problems isolated for discussion in this Appendix I belong with the
intermediary group. Space forbids much more than a skel-
etal justification of this stance, and I would stress that
I am concerned only with the historical basis of the
essential plot, not with all the elaborations and incid-
entals, apart from those of the 'Kingdom of Menelaos'.
    Comparative studies of heroic poetry, of which the
'Iliad' is no doubt in several respects an exceptional
representative, indicate that such poetry takes its origin
in a historical event but that in the final version historical matter may be very scanty or even entirely absent.
To take an extreme case, a defeat may be transformed into
a victory, although this is of course by no means a prerogative of heroic poetry. The likeliest occasion for
the creation of oral epic poetry is an impoverished era
which stands self-consciously in the shadow of a more
expansive predecessor. To simplify, 'saga presupposes
ruins' (Lesky 1971, 27). Too much reliance should not
perhaps be placed on comparative evidence, which cannot
replace the direct evidence we lack. But it is not unreasonable to postulate that a Trojan War may have taken
place during LH IIIB and that the epic commemorating it
originated perhaps in the eleventh century.
    The evidence from the excavations at Hissarlik, if - as
it surely is - this is Homer's Troy, suggests that there
were two destructions around the LH IIIB period, the first
(c.1300) due to natural agency, probably an earthquake,
the second later in the thirteenth century due to man.
However, the dispute about the relative chronology of LH
IIIB pottery (Chapter 6) and a controversy over the stylistic identification of the sherds associated with the
second, man-made, destruction have led to confusion over
both its relative and its absolute dating. What is

undisputed, or should be, is that excavation has not disclosed the identity of the destroyers. If we suppose them
to have been Greeks, and Homer is the sole unambiguous
support for this hypothesis, it is still open to question
whether they fought and were organized in the manner described in the 'Iliad'. For many scholars the 'Catalogue
of Ships' has seemed to offer certain answers.

Any satisfactory explanation of the 'Catalogue', however, must account for at least the following four facts:
it contains elements which descend ultimately from the
Mycenaean period; it contains elements which could only
have been incorporated after the Mycenaean era; it was not
sung originally for the place in which we now – and ex
hypothesi the Greeks from the eighth century on – read it;
and finally there are discrepancies between it and the
rest of the 'Iliad'. In the light of these facts it is
perhaps understandable that the 'Catalogue' is still among
the most controversial passages of the entire 'Iliad'. My
own view in summary is that it is basically a composition
of either the latest (LH IIIC) phase of Mycenaean civilization or the immediate post-Mycenaean period, which has
subsequently undergone a process of amplification, omission and conflation; and, second, that it is in no sense a
documentary record of an actual warfleet muster.

Specifically, the kingdom ascribed to Menelaos ('Il.'
2.581-7, below) has resisted more successfully than most
of the others all attempts to prove on archaeological
grounds the hypothesis that it corresponds to the political geography of a particular historical epoch.

> those who held hollow Lakedaimon full of ravines,
> Pharis and Sparte and many-doved Messe,
> and dwelt in Bryseiai and lovely Augeiai,
> and held Amyklai and Helos a city on the sea,
> and who held Laas and dwelt around Oitylos,
> these his brother led, Menelaos of the loud warcry,
> sixty ships in all.

Of the ten place-names listed, the first, Lakedaimon, to
judge from its epithets probably applies to the kingdom as
a whole, just as it certainly applied to the whole Spartan
state in historical times, rather than to an individual
site (but see below). Of the remainder only four (Amyklai,
Laas, Oitylos and Messe) can be identified at all confidently with actual sites, and this only if two further
hypotheses are well grounded, namely that the names
remained unchanged from the time at which they were first
incorporated in the 'Catalogue' to the time of their first
use by a post-Homeric literary source; and, second, that
the sites identified on the ground have been correctly so
identified from the indications of the written sources.

Neither hypothesis is unassailable.

Of the four plausibly identified on this basis only
Amyklai has so far yielded material remains earlier than
the Archaic period. Of the rest Sparte (also mentioned in
the 'Odyssey': below) may refer either to classical Sparta
or to an earlier counterpart of that name, for which the
site on the Menelaion ridge is the only real candidate.
If it is the former, then in view of the dearth of Mycenaean remains here Sparte at least would be a post-Mycenaean insertion. If on the other hand there was a Mycenaean
Sparte on the Menelaion ridge, then what is to be done
with the 'well-towered Therapne' of Alkman (fr. 14b),
which was clearly a settlement rather than an area whatever Pausanias (3.19.9) may have thought when he described
the Menelaion sanctuary ambiguously as 'in Therapne'?
This difficulty might be resolved if Homer's Lakedaimon
could be equated with Alkman's Therapne, but I do not
think it would be justifiable to adopt the less likely
interpretation of Lakedaimon as an individual site in
order to effect this equation. So non liquet. Pharis,
however, may well be the Palaiopyrgi site, and Helos may
be Ay. Stephanos. But Bryseiai, whose historical homonym
is itself not surely located, is not identifiable with any
Mycenaean site, despite attempts to preserve the pristine
Mycenaean purity of the 'Catalogue' by identifying it
alternatively with Anthochorion or Ay. Vasilios in the
Spartan basin. Finally, Augeiai, if it is not simply a
doublet of the Lokrian Augeiai ('Il.' 2.532), could be a
forerunner of Perioikic Aigiai, but the latter, if correctly identified, has nothing to show for itself archaeologically before the sixth century. In short, it is
impossible to decide on archaeological grounds either when
this section of the 'Catalogue' was composed or to what
period if any it ostensibly refers. We may add in conclusion that the two post-Mycenaean linguistic forms used
here are not of course unambiguous proof that the whole
section was originally a post-Mycenaean composition.

This leaves the problems of the role and status of
Menelaos. In the first place, there seems to be nothing
in the 'Iliad' which could be due to a poet's desire to
flatter a Spartan audience. Second, the number of ships
attributed to him in the 'Catalogue' seems appropriate to
his status as brother of the overall commander, Agamemnon,
and in proportion to his relative importance in the rest
of the 'Iliad' by comparison to, say, Nestor, who brought
ninety ships. Whether these absolute figures bear any
relation to Mycenaean reality of any period is impossible
to say, but, if we interpret them along the lines of Thucydides (1.10), then perhaps they do roughly correspond to

our current archaeological pictures of thirteenth-century
Lakonia and Messenia.

On the other hand, I am not persuaded that Agamemnon's
overall command at Troy necessarily tells us anything
about the political organization of Mycenaean Greece under
less exceptional conditions, and I tend to see it as
mainly due to the exigencies of the plot. Moreover, no
palace fit for a Menelaos has yet been located in Lakonia
to match the 'Palace of Nestor' at Pylos and the other
known palatial establishments of the thirteenth century.
There is therefore nothing to disprove the suggestion that
the description of Menelaos' palace in the fourth book of
the 'Odyssey' is as fictional as the alleged chariot-route
over Taygetos taken there by Odysseus' son Telemachos
when he came to visit Menelaos at Sparte. Indeed, it is
even possible on present evidence to argue that Lakedaimon (or whatever the name of Menelaos' supposed realm
was) did not in fact exist as an independent kingdom in
the thirteenth century but was controlled from the Argolis
or even Messenia; the latter situation after all would
only be the converse of the historical relationship
between the two areas from c.700 to 362.

However that may be, I hope I have brought forward
sufficient arguments to show why I do not believe it to be
sound method to use the 'Iliad' as part of an explanation
of the last centuries of the Mycenaean era. Thus I cannot, for example, accept that an enterprise of this Homeric magnitude weakened Mycenaean Greece and acted as a
prelude to the destructions and desertions evident in the
material record for the latter part of the thirteenth and
for the twelfth centuries. Nor can I agree that it was
the prolonged absence of Mycenaean rulers which encouraged
factional strife and internecine war on their return from
Troy. In the present state of our evidence the only
respectable intellectual position is honest agnosticism.

NOTES ON FURTHER READING

The bibliography on Homer, following the 'Homeric question'
hare let loose by F.A. Wolf at the start of the nineteenth
century, is vast. The best brief guides are perhaps
Hainsworth 1969 and Lesky 1968. Of the longer treatments
Kirk 1962 is still useful.

The demonstration of the traditional formulaic nature
of the Homeric poems is due to Milman Parry, whose oeuvre
has been collected by his son as Parry 1971. That the
poems were also oral was a hypothesis Parry set out to
test in Yugoslavia; it is now generally accepted as

proved, with important doubts about the role of writing in
the closing stages of the living tradition. On the
'Parry-Lord thesis' see the bibliography Haymes 1973.
According to Hainsworth (1969, 9), 'the real question, as
yet unattempted, is whether the dramatic quality could
have been orally conceived'; but this is not wholly fair
to Thomson 1961, 433-582, where an attempt is made and the
possibility strongly indicated.

For the language of the epics see Meister 1921; Hiersche 1970, 80-106; Shipp 1972. The dispute over the existence and character of Mycenaean poetry is usefully
reviewed in Kirk 1960, esp. sections 18-25.

The archaeological background to Homer is considered in
Lorimer 1950 (now very outdated); in various contributions
to 'Archaeologia Homerica' (still in progress and uneven
in quality); and in Bouzek 1969.

Kirk 1975 is a helpful short discussion of the historical value of the poems. Of the longer treatments Page
1959 is still stimulating, but Adam Parry (in Parry 1971,
xliv) perhaps understates the case when he says that Page
'takes the argument for the historicity of the Homeric
epics as far as it can reasonably go'. On the question
whether there was a unified 'Homeric world' identifiable
in space and time I agree with the negative conclusion of
Snodgrass 1974.

For the 'Catalogue' see e.g. Burr 1944; Jachmann 1958;
and Hope Simpson and Lazenby 1970. All these have powerful axes to grind.

The archaeological aspect of the Trojan War controversy
is well summarized by Wiseman (1965). On the hegemony
allegedly exercised by Mycenae I agree with Thomas 1970
against the cautiously positive view of Desborough (1972,
18).

The Spartan king-lists

The purposes of this Appendix are twofold: to discuss the source and significance of the lists of Agiads and Eurypontids preserved in Herodotus (Table 1) and to illustrate briefly the cardinal role that the upper reaches of these and comparable lists appear to have played in the elaboration of a chronology for early Greek history.

TABLE 1

Agiads (7.204)		Eurypontids (8.131.2)
	Herakles	
	Hyllos	
	Kleodaios	
	Aristomachos	
	Aristodamos	
Eurysthenes		Prokles
Agis (I)		Euryp(h)on
Echestratos		Prytanis
Labotas		Polydektes
Doryssos		Eunomos
Agesilaos (I)		Charillos
Archelaos		Nikandros
Teleklos		Theopompos
Alkamenes		Anaxandridas (I)
Polydoros		Archidamos (I)
Eurykrates		Anaxilaos
Anaxandros		Latychidas (I)
Eurykratidas		Hippokratidas
Leon		Agesilaos*
Anaxandridas (II)		Menares*
Leonidas (I)		Latychidas (II)

* Did not reign

We must first decide what these lists represent. Are
they, as the ancients believed (although, as we shall see,
they differed in detail), king-lists? Or are they, as
Henige (1974, 207-13) has now argued in a fundamental
study of oral tradition, merely the pedigrees of Leonidas I
(reigned c.490-480) and Latychidas II (c.491-469)? The
way in which Herodotus introduces the lists suggests the
latter, and this view is apparently supported both by the
omission of otherwise recognized kings (from the Agiads
Kleomenes I; from the Eurypontids Agasikles, Ariston and
Damaratos) and by his cross-reference at 9.64.2, where he
points out that regent Pausanias had the same ascendants
('progonoi') as Leonidas. On the other hand, Herodotus
states explicitly (8.131.3) that 'all except the two named
immediately after Latychidas (viz. his father and grandfather) became kings of Sparta', and this may indeed imply
that he believed all Leonidas' ascendants had done so too.
At any rate, this was how he was understood by all later
writers.

Neither interpretation is entirely cogent, but on balance I think Herodotus did indeed mean the lists for king-
lists. The major obstacle in the way of this interpretation is the omission of recognized kings from both lists,
but this has been adroitly circumvented by Prakken (1940)
with the suggestion that Herodotus was adapting lists compiled, perhaps by Hekataios (below), in the joint reign of
Kleomenes I and Damaratos, neither of whom was succeeded
by a son. Whether or not Hekataios (or whoever) was the
first to produce and publish written king-lists we cannot
of course say.

A minor objection, that not even the Spartans believed
Leonidas' and Latychidas' ascendants before Aristodamos to
have been kings of Sparta, has been proven groundless by
Huxley (1975b), who rightly distinguishes between kings
'of' Sparta and kings 'in' Sparta; we may add that in 371
the Dioskouroi, 'the model and divine guarantee of the
Spartan dyarchy' (Carlier 1977, 76 n. 42), could be referred to as 'fellow citizens' of the Spartans (Xen. 'Hell.'
6.3.6). Moreover Herodotus' confusion over the name of
Latychidas II's grandfather - Agesilaos in Table 1, but
Agis at 6.65.1 - seems most easily explicable if, as
Herodotus himself states, Agesilaos/Agis did not in fact
reign. Thus, since Latychidas II and Damaratos were
coevals (they fell out over the girl they both wanted to
marry: 6.65.2), Latychidas' grandfather could have been a
younger brother of Damaratos' grandfather, Agasikles, the
co-king of Leon. This would make Latychidas and Damaratos
second cousins, closely enough related for Kleomenes I to
use the former as an acceptable replacement for the latter.

To these negative arguments in favour of the interpretation of the lists as king-lists we may add the evidence
of two papyri from Oxyrhynchos published after Prakken's
important paper. One of these (2390, with Harvey 1967)
proves that Latychidas I did indeed reign - probably
c.600, since Alkman sang of him. The other (2623.1, a
choral lyric fragment attributable to Simonides or Bacchy-
lides) mentions a Zeuxidamos (see Table 2, below) and
perhaps a Hippokratidas (cf. Table 1), apparently in a
royal context. We know that Stesichoros sang before a
Spartan prince in Sparta c.550 and that he lent his voice
to Heraklid propaganda (West 1969, 148). Perhaps the poet
of this fragment was doing the same for a Eurypontid
prince in the early fifth century.

Granted then that we have access to Spartan king-lists
in Herodotus, two further and related questions arise.
How far may we accept them as true records of the dyarchy?
Second, what role or roles might the lists have played in
forming the Spartans' view of their past and in determining
the way that past was presented to or used against
outsiders?

We may start with the connection of the eponyms Agis
(I) and Euryp(h)on through the twin sons of Aristodamos
to Herakles. The Heraklid connection is first explicitly
attested in Tyrtaios (fr. 2.12-15W), but it should go back
to the dissemination of the Homeric or similar poems in
Sparta and the foundation of the Menelaion sanctuary in
the late eighth century, if not to the incorporation of
'Achaean' Amyklai c.750. Indeed, it is likely enough to
have been forged at the same time as the dyarchy itself,
which perhaps began with Archelaos and Charillos (Chapter
8). From Tyrtaios the assertion of the connection can be
traced in an almost unbroken chain of poetical references
through the Lakonians Kinaithon and Alkman in the seventh
century, Stesichoros and the Delphic Oracle in the sixth
to Pindar, the contemporary of Leonidas I and Latychidas
II.

As far as the outside world was concerned, the function
of the Heraklid connection was to legitimate Spartan supremacy in Lakonia and indirectly, the Peloponnese. Within
Sparta itself, however, it had other functions. All
'Heraklids' were Spartans, but not all Spartans were
'Heraklids' (Hdt. 8.114.2). Moreover, within the Spartan
aristocracy there were other 'Heraklid' families besides
the Agiads and Eurypontids, and families like the
Aigeidai (Hdt. 4.149.1) who were not Heraklid at all. The
king-lists therefore were a very special kind of genealog-
ical charter (Malinowski's expression) or 'mnemonic of
social relationships' (Goody and Watt 1963, 309), serving

to affirm the superior blue-bloodedness of the Agiads and
Eurypontids against the claims of other aristocratic families and to distinguish the aristocracy from the commons.
   So much for the roles of the lists. Now for their
accuracy. We must at once admit the depth of our ignorance. We do not know when, if ever, after the introduction of writing the lists were committed to script at
Sparta; nor, if and when the transmission was purely oral,
how that transmission was effected; nor how much circumstantial detail was passed on in association with any
particular name. However, we do know that by the time of
Pausanias (3.2.1-7; 3.1-8; 7.1-10) Herodotus' lists were
regarded as king-lists and were taken to imply both that
each Agiad king had had his one Eurypontid counterpart and
that succession had been hereditary from father to son
over fifteen generations within each house. Why then do
the Eurypontid lists of the two authors differ (Table 2)?

TABLE 2   Eurypontids

Herodotus	Pausanias
Prokles	Prokles
Euryp(h)on	Soos
Prytanis	Eurypon
Polydektes	Prytanis
Eunomos	Eunomos
Charillos	Polydektes
Nikandros	Charillos
Theopompos	Nikandros
Anaxandridas (I)	Theopompos
Archidamos (I)	Zeuxidamos
Anaxilaos	Anaxidamos
Latychidas (I)	Archidamos (I)
Hippokratidas	Agasikles
Agesilaos*	Ariston
Menares*	Damaratos
Latychidas (II)	Latychidas (II)

* Did not reign

The introduction of Soos is easy to explain: the Eurypontid list in Herodotus was one shorter than the Agiad, and
he was probably inserted in the fourth century (Kiechle
1959, 90-101). The discrepancies after Theopompos are
more difficult. In effect Pausanias has Zeuxidamos and
Anaxidamos for Herodotus' Anaxandridas (I) and Anaxilaos,
and he has omitted Herodotus' Latychidas (I) and Hippokratidas. Of these Latychidas I was certainly a king

and Hippokratidas may have been referred to as such in the choral lyric fragment of the early fifth century (above). On the other hand, Pausanias' Zeuxidamos may be the man who appears in the same fragment and so may also have some claim to have ruled; alternatively, he could be the son of Latychidas II (Hdt. 6.71). Either way, it is possible that Pausanias had independent access to genuine Eurypontid tradition, perhaps ultimately through Charon of Lampsakos (262T1 Jacoby). If therefore we accept that both Herodotus and Pausanias may preserve the truth about the ruling members of the Eurypontid house, the most economical hypothesis to explain the discrepancies between their lists is that both lists are selective king-lists, the one confined to Latychidas II's direct ascendants, the other recording those of Damaratos.

This hypothesis has many merits, of which two may be singled out here. First, as we shall see in the second part of this Appendix, it helps to solve a puzzle in early Greek chronography. Second, it does away with the glaring contradiction between the allegedly unbroken father/son succession down to Kleomenes I and Damaratos and the situation thereafter. For between c.491 and 219 lineal succession broke down in no less than twelve out of the twenty-six instances; of the remaining fourteen successions the largest number, five, were consobrinal - brother succeeding brother. We must make some allowance for changed political conditions after c.491, which saw the first attested deposition of a Spartan king (Ste. Croix 1972, 350-3). But as Henige (1974, 210) rightly says, it 'beggars the imagination' to postulate two series of unbroken father/son succession in a single state over the same sixteen generations from Eurysthenes and Prokles. In other words, even if Herodotus' lists are adaptations of king-lists drawn up in the joint reign of Kleomenes I and Damaratos, we should make allowance for an unknowable number of collateral successions.

By a still more opaque process than those of their creation and transmission the Spartan king-lists transcended their local political significance to occupy a unique niche in the chronography of early Greek history. The first exponent of 'scientific' chronography, a byproduct of the shift in emphasis of Ionian 'historia' from nature to man (Chapter 5), was probably Hekataios. It could then have been he who drew up the king-lists which Herodotus adapted (Jacoby 1949, 306 n. 25, 323 n. 28, 357 n. 26). He too it may have been who interpreted the fifteen kings in each line from Agis and Eurypon to Kleomenes I and Damaratos as fifteen generations and, making allowance for the Heraklid connection, gave to each generation the notional value of forty years (Meyer 1892, 153-88, esp. 169ff., 179-82). However, since 'it is impossible to accept a generation average as high as forty years over a period of fifteen generations, no matter what contingencies are postulated' (Henige 1974, 208), the hypothesis about collateral, and especially perhaps consobrinal, succession may again be invoked to account for it, if indeed it is felt that the forty-year generation has any basis in fact.

However that may be, exact lengths were subsequently attached to the reigns at least down to those of Alkamenes and Theopompos. Various candidates for the role of first calculator have been proposed, of whom the third-century Lakonian Sosibios (595 Jacoby) has possibly the strongest claim. Eratosthenes of Cyrene, also in the third century, brought the lists into an acceptable relationship with the First Olympiad, which was for him the dividing line between 'mythical' and 'historical' Greece (Fraser 1970, esp. 190, 196f.). From Eratosthenes descends the 'vulgate' chronology of early Greek history through Apollodoros (c.100) and Diodorus to Eusebius (AD 263-339).

It goes without saying that the absolute dates arrived at by these erudite men have no truly scientific foundation, and that differences between their dating and ours are to be expected. On the other hand, to tamper with their relative chronology is hazardous. In general, their absolute dates are too high, a natural consequence of the Heraklid distortion. If we substitute the more plausible allowance of thirty years per generation for the 'Hekataian' forty, we achieve a satisfying congruence between potsherds and pedigrees, at least for the Agiads: Agis I could have been on the throne around the last third of the tenth century (Forrest 1968, 21). At the same time, however, we cannot pretend that in the present state of our knowledge this is much more than a happy coincidence.

NOTE

I was greatly helped in the preparation of the original version of this Appendix by my late friend Richard Ball, although the responsibility for any remaining errors is of course entirely mine. It is good to know that his Oxford doctoral thesis on Greek chronography is to be seen through the press by W.G. Forrest.

The Helots: Some ancient sources in translation

A. GENERAL

1 Thucydides (5c.)

(a) 4.80.2: Most Spartan institutions have always been
designed with a view to security against the Helots. (OR
As far as the Helots are concerned, most Spartan institutions have always been designed with a view to security.)
(b) 8.40.2: The Chians possessed many slaves (oiketai),
the most in fact of any one state apart from Sparta.

2 Plato (4c.)

(a) 'Laws' 776C (quoted, with minor verbal differences,
ap. Athen. 6.264DE): The Helot-system (OR The Helots) of
Sparta is (are) practically the most discussed and controversial subject in Greece, some approving the institution,
others criticizing it. (OR The condition of the Helots
among the Spartans is of all Greek forms of servitude the
most controversial and disputed about, some approving it
and some condemning it.)
(b) 'Laws' 777BC: (Man) is a troublesome piece of goods,
as has often been shown by the frequent revolts of the
Messenians, and the great mischiefs which happen in states
having many slaves (oiketai) who speak the same language.
... Two remedies alone remain to us, - not to have the
slaves of the same country, nor, if possible, speaking the
same language (Jowett).
(c) 'Alk.' I.122D: No one could doubt that their land in
Lakonia and Messenia is superior to our [Athenian] land,
both in extent and quality, not to mention the number of
their slaves (andrapoda) and especially the Helots.

3 Aristotle (4c.)

'Pol.' 1330a25-8: The very best thing of all would be that
the farmers should be slaves, not all of the same people
and not spirited; for if they have no spirit, they will be
better suited for their work and there will be no danger
of their making a revolution.

4 Strabo (1c. BC/1c. AD)

8.5.4: Helotage lasted right up to the Roman conquest.

B. ORIGINS

1 Hellanikos (5c.)

FGrHist 4F188: The Helots are those who were not by birth
the slaves (douloi) of the Spartans but those occupying
the city of Helos who were the first to be defeated.

2 Antiochos (5c.)

FGrHist 555F13: After the [First] Messenian War the Spartans who did not participate in the expedition were adjudged slaves (douloi) and called Helots, while all those who
had been born during the campaign were called Partheniai
and deprived of full citizen rights. (OR.... while all
those to whom children had been born during the campaign
(had to accept that their sons) were called Partheniai,
etc.)

3 Thucydides

1.101.2: The majority of the Helots were descended from
the Messenians who were enslaved (doulothenton) of old.
Hence all were called Messenians.

4 Ephorus (4c.)

FGrHist 70F117: Agis [I] son of Eurysthenes robbed (the
Perioikoi) of their equal political status and compelled
them to pay contributions to Sparta. They obeyed, but the
Heleioi, those who held Helos, revolted and were conquered
by force of arms and adjudged slaves (douloi) on fixed

conditions.

5 Theopompos (4c.) FGrHist 115

(a) F13: They are those who have been enslaved (katadedou-
lomenoi) for a very long time by the Spartiates, some of
them being from Messenia, while the Heleatai formerly inhabited Helos in Lakonike.
(b) F122: The Chians were the first Greeks after the
Thessalians and Spartans to make use of slaves (douloi),
but they did not acquire them in the same way as these.
For the Spartans and Thessalians ... recruited their slave
populations from the Greeks who previously inhabited the
country they now control, the Spartans from the Achaeans,
the Thessalians from the Perrhaiboi and Magnetes; and they
called those whom they had enslaved respectively Helots
and Penestai.

6 Plutarch (1-2c. AD)

'Lyk.' 2.1: Of these ancestors (of Lykourgos) the most
distinguished was Soos, in whose reign the Spartans made
the Helots their slaves (douloi).

7 Pausanias (2c. AD)

(a) 3.2.7: (In the reign of Alkamenes) the Achaeans of
Helos by the sea revolted too, and (the Spartans) defeated
the Argives who came to the aid of the Helots.
(b) 3.20.6: (The inhabitants of Helos) were the first to
become slaves of the community (douloi tou koinou) and the
first to be called Helots.

8 Anecdota Graeca

(ed. Bekker) I.246, s.v. 'Heilotes': The slaves (douloi)
of the Spartans ... so called because they were first
defeated in Helos and enslaved.

9 Stephanos of Byzantion (6c. AD)

s.v. 'Chioi': (The Chians) were the first to use servants
(therapontes), just as the Spartans used Helots, the
Argives Gymnesioi, the Sikyonians Korynephoroi, the

Italians Pelasgoi, and the Cretans Dmoitai (sic).

C. STATUS (see also A.1b, 2b-c, B)

1 Kritias (5c.)

88B37 D-K: In Lakedaimon are to be found those who are the most enslaved (douloi) and those who are the most free.

2 Thucydides

(a) 4.118.7 (armistice of 423): Neither side is to receive deserters during this period, whether free or slave (doulos).
(b) 5.23.3 (alliance between Sparta and Athens, 421): If the slave class (douleia) revolts, the Athenians are to come to the aid of the Spartans in full strength in accordance with their ability.

3 Xenophon (4c.)

(a) 'Hell.' 7.1.13: You [Athenians] become leaders merely of their slaves (douloi, i.e. Helot rowers) and men of least account.
(b) 'Lak. Pol.' 6.3: They are able to use even the slaves (oiketai) of another (Spartiate), if they so request.
(c) 'Lak. Pol.' 7.5: (Lykourgos made Spartan money value-less so that) a man should not be able to conceal it from his slaves (oiketai) if he dragged it home.
(d) 'Lak. Pol.' 12.4: They keep the slaves (douloi) away from the arms-dumps (in camp).

4 Isokrates (4c.)

12 ('Panath.') 178: The souls (of the Perioikoi) are reduced to slavery no less than those of (the Spartans') slaves (oiketai).

5 Ephorus

(continuation of B.4): Their master was permitted neither to manumit them nor to sell them beyond the frontier.

6   Theopompos

F40: The Ardiaioi (of Illyria) possess 30,000 dependent labourers (prospelatai) on the same conditions as (the Spartans) possess Helots.

7   Aristotle

(a) 'Pol.' 1264a32-6: Again (Sokrates) makes the Farmers the masters of the estates, for which they pay a rent (apophora). But in that case they are likely to be much more unmanageable and rebellious than the Helots, Penestai or slaves in general.
(b) fr. 586: (The Kallikyrioi at Syracuse) are like the Spartans' Helots, the Thessalians' Penestai and the Cretans' Klarotai.

8   Myron (3c.)

FGrHist 106F1: The Spartans often freed their slaves (douloi) calling some Aphetai (released?), some Adespotoi i (masterless?), some Erykteres (curbers?), others again Desposionautai (master-seamen?); the last they assigned to naval expeditions.

9   Kallistratos (3c.)

FGrHist 348F4: They called the Mariandynoi (of Herakleia Pontika) Dorophoroi (gift-bearers) to take away the sting in the word 'slaves' (oiketai), just as the Spartans did for the Helots, the Thessalians for the Penestai, and the Cretans for the Klarotai.

10 Phylarchos (3c.)

FGrHist 81F8: The Byzantines rule over the Bithynoi in the same way as the Spartans rule over the Helots.

11 Strabo

8.5.4: The Spartans held (the Helots) as slaves (douloi) as it were of the community (tropon tina demosious).

12   Livy (1c. BC/1c. AD)

(a) 34.27.9: Next some of the Helots - these had been
'castellani' (farm- or fort-dwellers) from remotest times,
a rural people - were accused of wishing to desert and
were lashed to death in all the villages (vici).
(b) 34.31.11: But the name of 'tyrant' and my actions are
held against me (Nabis), because I liberate slaves (servi).

13   Pollux (2c. AD)

3.83: Between free men and slaves (douloi) (are) the
Lakonian Helots, the Thessalian Penestai, the Mariandynian
Dorophoroi, the Argive Gymnetes and the Sikyonian Koryn-
ephoroi.

D. TREATMENT (see also C.1, 3b, 4, 8; F.i.2b)

1   Tyrtaios (7c.)

(a) fr. 6: Like asses exhausted under great loads: under
painful necessity to bring their masters full half the
fruit their ploughed land produced.
(b) fr. 7: They and their wives too must put on mourning
and bewail their lords whenever death should carry them
away.

2   Kritias

(following C.1): Through distrust of these Helots a
Spartiate at home removes the arm-band from his shield.
Since the frequent need for speed prevents him taking this
precaution on campaign, he always carries his spear with
him, in the belief that he will be stronger than the Helot
who tries to revolt with a shield alone. They have also
devised keys which they think are strong enough to resist
any Helot attempt on their lives.

3   Thucydides

(a) 1.128.1: The Spartans had once dragged some Helot suppliants from the sanctuary of Poseidon and led them away
to be killed, as a result of which, so they believed, the
great earthquake had hit Sparta.
(b) 4.80.3 (following A.1a): (The Spartans) made a proclamation that the Helots should choose from their number

as many as claimed to have done the best service in the war. They implied that these Helots would be freed, but in fact it was a test conducted in the belief that those who thought themselves best qualified for freedom would also be the most likely to revolt. About 2,000 were selected, who put garlands on their heads and did the rounds of the sanctuaries as if they had been freed. But not much later the Spartans did away with them, and no one knew how each of them was killed.

4 Isokrates

12.181: The Ephors have the right to choose as many (Perioikoi) as they wish and put them to death, and this when for all Greeks the murder of even the most nefarious slaves (oiketai) is considered impious.

5 Theopompos

F13: The Helot population is in an altogether cruel and bitter condition.

6 Aristotle

(a) 'Pol.' 1269b7-12: Apart from other drawbacks, the mere necessity of policing (the Helots) is a troublesome matter - the problem of how contact with them is to be managed. If allowed freedom, they grow insolent and think themselves as good as their masters; if made to live a hard life, they plot against and hate them. It is clear therefore that those whose Helot-system works out like this have not discovered the best way of managing it.
(b) fr. 538 (ap. Plut. 'Lyk.' 28): The so-called 'Krypteia' of the Spartans, if this really is one of Lykourgos' institutions, as Aristotle says, may have given Plato ('Laws' 630D) too this idea of (Lykourgos) and his polity. The Krypteia was like this. The magistrates from time to time sent out into the country those who appeared the most resourceful of the youth, equipped only with daggers and minimum provisions. In the daytime they dispersed into obscure places, where they hid and lay low. By night they came down into the highways and despatched any Helot they caught. Often too they went into the fields and did away with the sturdiest and most powerful Helots. (Here Plutarch retails D.3b.) And Aristotle specifically says also that the Ephors upon entering office declared war on

the Helots, so that their murder might not bring with it ritual pollution.

(c) 'Lak. Pol.' (excerpted by Herakleides Lembos 373.10 Dilts): It is said that (Lykourgos) also introduced the Krypteia. In accordance with this institution even now they go out by day and conceal themselves, but by night they use weapons to kill as many of the Helots as is expedient.

7   Myron

F2: They assign to the Helots every shameful task leading to disgrace. For they ordained that each one of them must wear a dogskin cap and wrap himself in skins and receive a stipulated number of beatings every year regardless of any wrongdoing, so that they would never forget they were slaves (douleuein). Moreover, if any exceeded the vigour proper to a slave's condition, they made death the penalty; and they allotted a punishment to those controlling them if they failed to rebuke those who were growing fat. And in giving the land over to them they set them a portion (of produce) which they were constantly to hand over.

8   Plutarch

(a) (following D.6b): And in other ways too they treated the Helots harshly and cruelly. For example, they would compel them to drink a lot of unmixed wine and then bring them into the common messes to show the young men what drunkenness was like. They would also order them to sing songs and perform dances that were ignoble and ridiculous but to refrain from those appropriate to free men. However, such cruelties were, I believe, inflicted by the Spartans only relatively late, especially after the great earthquake....

(b) 'Comp. Lyk. et Num.' 1.5: (Helotage was) the cruellest and most lawless system.

E. ATTITUDE OF HELOTS (see also D.2, 6a)

1   Xenophon

'Hell.' 3.3.6: The secret (of the Helots, Neodamodeis, Hypomeiones and Perioikoi) (was that), whenever among these mention was made of Spartiates, none was able to conceal that he would gladly eat them - even raw.

2   Aristotle

(a) 'Pol.' 1269a37-b5: The Penestai of the Thessalians
repeatedly revolted, as did the Helots - who are like an
enemy constantly sitting in wait for the disasters of the
Spartans.   Nothing of this kind has yet happened in Crete,
the reason perhaps being that the neighbouring cities,
even when at war with one another, never ally themselves
with the (servile) rebels.   For since they themselves
possess a subject population (perioikoi), this would not
be in their interest.   The Spartans, on the other hand,
were surrounded by hostile neighbours, Argives, Messenians
and Arkadians.
(b) 'Pol.' 1272b17-20: (Crete) is saved by its geographical situation; for distance has had the same effect as
the expulsion of aliens (from Sparta).   A result of this
is that, whereas the Cretan perioikoi stay loyal, the
Helots frequently revolt.

F.   FUNCTIONS

i.   Agriculture (see also D.7)

1   Aristotle

'Pol.' 1271b40-72a2: The Cretan institutions resemble the
Spartan.   The Helots are the farmers of the latter, the
perioikoi of the former.

2   Plutarch

(a) 'Lyk.' 8.7: The kleros was large enough to yield
seventy medimnoi of barley for a man and twelve for a
woman, and the corresponding amount of fresh fruits.
(b) 'Mor.' 239DE: A curse was decreed to fall upon (the
Spartan) who exacted more than the long-established rent
(apophora), so that (the Helots) might serve gladly
because gainfully, and (the Spartans) might not exceed the
fixed amount.
(c) 'Mor.' 223A: Kleomenes [I] son of Anaxandridas said
that Homer was the poet of the Spartans, Hesiod of the
Helots; for Homer had given the necessary directions for
warfare, Hesiod for agriculture.

ii Warfare

Hdt. 6.80f. (batmen, etc.); 9.28f., 80.1, 85 (auxiliary
personnel); Thuc. 4.80 (hoplites); Xen. 'Hell.' 3.1.27
(batmen), 6.5.28f. (hoplites), 7.1.12f. (rowers).

iii Miscellaneous

Hdt. 6.52.5-7, 63.1; Xen. 'Hell.' 5.4.28; 'Lak. Pol.' 7.5;
Plut. 'Agis' 3.2 (all household servants); Hdt. 6.68.2
(groom); 6.75.2 (armed guard); Kritias 88B33 D-K (cup-
bearer at mess).

Appendix 5

The sanctuary of (Artemis) Orthia

By the beginning of the present century the British School
of Archaeology at Athens could look back on striking successes in the excavation of prehistoric sites but lacked
for a classical counterpart to Delphi and Olympia, secured
respectively by the French and German Schools. Somewhat
boldly, in view of the weight of ancient literary evidence suggesting artefactual sterility, the School selected Sparta for its operations. Sensibly, however, they
spread the risks by simultaneously conducting smaller
excavations in other parts of Lakonia, on both prehistoric
and classical sites, and by undertaking invaluable and
unrepeatable topographical surveys of the southern portion of the region. The groundwork was laid by M.N. Tod
and A.J.B. Wace in their still serviceable 'Catalogue of
the Sparta Museum', which was published in the same year,
1906, as the School began excavations in Sparta itself.

The most significant ancient landmark at that time, in
a landscape undistinguished for its ancient remains, was a
Roman theatre on the right (west) bank of the Eurotas.
Even this, though, had been extensively looted and largely
denuded since the foundation of the modern town in 1834
and was being slowly encroached upon by the river. It
was, however, precisely the Greek remains dislocated by
the ingress of the Eurotas which gave hope of important
early finds - a hope that was to be fulfilled far beyond
the expectations even of those responsible for the decision to concentrate the digging here. As the main director
of excavations, R.M. Dawkins, later wrote (AO 50): 'The
Roman theatre had done its work thoroughly in preserving
untouched ... the great wealth of archaic objects which by
their fresh light on early Sparta have given this excavation its chief importance.'

The stone theatre, it emerged, had been constructed in
the third century AD. Its function was to enable blood-

357

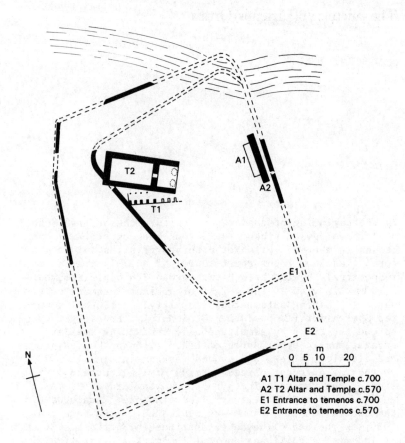

FIGURE 19   The sanctuary of Orthia at Sparta

thirsty spectators to watch Spartan youths being flogged,
preferably to death, in a painful simulacrum of what had
once been an initiation-rite integral to the Spartan
social system. The deity in whose honour this gory per-
formance was staged was then known as Artemis Orthia, but
her original title, attested by inscriptions from the late
seventh century onwards, had been simply Orthia. (I retain
this conventional spelling for convenience; in fact,
several variants are recorded epigraphically.) The literary evidence for her cult was such that it was 'one of the
most puzzling and vehemently discussed in the Greek world'
(Rose in AO 399), but it appeared to have been more intim-
ately linked to the routine of Spartan life than that of
the state's patron deity Athena Poliachos (later known
also as Chalkioikos). The excavation of Orthia's sanctuary

was therefore thought the more likely to illuminate the
nature and development of Spartan taste and religio-
political observance.

So indeed it proved, and such was the richness and complexity of the deposits that the School initially devoted
five seasons to unearthing and reconstructing them.
Dawkins, reporting in 1910 that no further excavation was
contemplated, stitched together the results into a
'History of the Sanctuary', which was reprinted almost
unchanged in the supposedly definitive publication of the
site nineteen years later (AO ch. 1). Yet in the interim
the School had spent another five seasons on Sparta (1924-
8), including a cleaning operation at Orthia in 1928 which
yielded important new results. Since these results made
no impression on the 'final' 1929 publication, they have
been largely neglected hitherto. But this neglect has
been more than made up for by the attention lavished since
1919 on the reports of the main series of excavations.

To some extent the participants in this dig were pioneers in their attempt to apply consistently the stratigraphical method to a classical Greek site, and like all
pioneers they quickly excited over-warm approval - or
acrimonious disparagement. Now that the dust has settled,
there is still the need for a full discussion both of the
excavators' view of their objectives, methods and achieve-
ments and of the course of subsequent revaluations (the
most important to date being Boardman 1963). Here, however, there is space only to attempt answers to the two
major questions arising from a study of the Orthia stratigraphy. First, what is the most likely reconstruction of
the history of the sanctuary before the laying of the
sand? Second, in what way and to what extent may we use
the stratigraphical evidence to establish the sequence and
absolute dates of Lakonian artefacts of the Geometric and
Archaic periods (c.750-500)? (After c.500 the archaeological evidence from Lakonia as a whole declines markedly in
quantity and quality, and the stratigraphy of Orthia
becomes correspondingly less significant.)

Taking the history of the sanctuary first, we find that
the construction of a cobble pavement c.700 provides the
stratigraphical terminus ante quem for the beginnings of
cult in this natural hollow by the Eurotas. Since this
was a new Dorian cult on an uninhabited and not previously
used site, topography offers a major clue to the nature of
the deity - vegetational and chthonic. The earliest portion of the deposit contained PG pottery, which cannot be
more closely dated than between c.950-900 and 750. As the
depth of the deposit is no guide to the length of time
required for its formation, the origin of the cult may be

placed on grounds of general probability alone in the
ninth century, perhaps in its first half.

Worship, consisting of animal-sacrifice and presumably
also the pouring of libations, took place on and around an
earthen altar in what later became the eastern rectangle
of the delimited sacred area. For c.700 the sanctuary was
enclosed by a wall and paved with river-cobbles, upon
which were set a part-stone altar and temple, the former
close to the circuit wall, the latter at an angle of about
90° on the west and also hard by the wall. The sanctuary
retained this format until the second quarter of the sixth
century, when the whole area was raised and levelled with
a layer of river sand, perhaps in response to a devastating Eurotas flood. Upon the sand were erected an all-
limestone altar and temple, with the same general orient-
ations as their predecessors, and a new enlarged enclosure
wall. This second temple was rebuilt in the second century BC, but the altar remained substantially unchanged
until the third century AD, when its Roman successor was
built to accompany the new stone theatre.

The second question posed above is considerably more
problematic, the answer more tentative. In the first
place, the excavators' chronology, both relative and absolute, must be scrapped, since it was based on an untest-
able assumption of regular deposition (involving an un-
reasonably mechanical translation of depth of deposit into
period of years) and a now superseded dating of PC pottery.
Second, although four pre-sand Lakonian pottery styles
were distinguished, only two pre-sand strata were eventually recognized. Third, the earlier ('Geometric') stratum
was not sealed by a floor or pit: the cobble pavement was
built actually in it, towards its close. Since, therefore,
there is no clearcut stratigraphical evidence to help date
the pottery styles, and since the pottery cannot be used
to date the cobble pavement precisely, there must be an
element of subjectivity in interpreting the pottery associations and/or findspots of particular artefacts. Fourth,
as Dawkins rightly stressed, the strata were thin and
partly disturbed by subsequent building or natural agen-
cies, so objects could easily have been displaced from
their original place in the earth. Finally, in a votive
deposit the original position of an artefact can anyway
never indicate more than the relative date at which it was
discarded.

Extreme caution is therefore obligatory when using the
Orthia stratigraphy. However, as long as it is treated
just as a general guide, there seems to be no compelling
reason not to place some faith in it. As for the pottery,
not only is its sub-division into styles somewhat

arbitrary but its dating by reference to its association
with PC and to the development of other Greek fabrics is
also uncertain. None the less, a workable chronological
framework can be and has been devised, subjective though
it inevitably is. The extent to which the results obtained for the Orthia sanctuary hold good for other sites in
Sparta and Lakonia is problematic, not least because of
the absolute dearth of excavated and stratified settlement
deposits. However, in Sparta and Amyklai at least, where
the evidence is fullest, there seems to be scarcely any
aspect of the material record which does not have its
correlate on one or other of the sites. For most purposes,
therefore, Orthia may be taken as a typical, if generally
more informative, sample.

NOTES ON FURTHER READING

Preliminary reports of the Orthia excavations: BSA 1906-10
(with the Annual Reports); JHS 1907-10 ('Archaeology in
Greece', by Dawkins). Cleaning dig of May 1928: BSA 1928,
1, 306 (with the Annual Report); JHS 1928, 185. Process
of digging: BSA 1907, 71; 1908, 14.
    The most important discussions of the excavators'
methods and conclusions are: Rodenwalt 1919, 182; V. Wade-
Gery 1930; Droop 1932; Hartley 1932; Kunze 1933; Yavis
1949, 108-10; Benton 1950, 17f.; Kirsten 1958; Boardman
1963; Bergquist 1967, esp. 47-9.
    For the cult of Orthia see Rose in AO ch. 12; a new
study is promised by G. Kipp. The temple of c.700 is discussed by Drerup (1969, 19-21); the Archaic temple of
c.570-560 was not distinguished and has attracted little
art-historical attention.

Abbreviations

AA	Archaeologischer Anzeiger (until 1961 with JdI, thereafter published separately)
AAA	Athens Annals of Archaeology
AC	L'Antiquité Classique
AD	Archaiologikon Deltion
AE	Archaiologiki Ephemeris (earlier Ephemeris Archaiologiki)
AHR	American Historical Review
AJA	American Journal of Archaeology
AJP	American Journal of Philology
AK	Antike Kunst
AM	Mitteilungen des Deutschen Archaeologischen Instituts (Athenische Abteilung)
Annales (ESC)	Annales (Economies, Sociétés, Civilisations)
AO	Artemis Orthia, JHS Supp.5, ed. R.M. Dawkins, London, 1929
AR	Archaeological Reports (supplement to JHS)
AS	Ancient Society
ASAA	Annuario della Scuola Archeologica di Atene
BAMA	Bronze Age Migrations in the Aegean. Archaeological and Linguistic Problems in Greek Prehistory, ed. R.A. Crossland and A. Birchall, London, 1973
BCH	Bulletin de Correspondance Hellénique
BICS	Bulletin of the Institute of Classical Studies
BJ	Bonner Jahrbuecher des Rheinischen Landesmuseums in Bonn und des Vereins von Altertumsfreunden im Rheinlande
BRL	Bulletin of the John Rylands Library
BSA	Annual of the British School at Athens
CAH	The Cambridge Ancient History
CP	Classical Philology
CQ	Classical Quarterly

362

Abbreviations

CR	Classical Review
CSSH	Comparative Studies in Society and History
EHR	Economic History Review
ESAG	Economic and Social Atlas of Greece, ed. B. Kayser et al., Athens, 1964
GR	Greece and Rome
HT	History and Theory
IG	Inscriptiones Graecae
IJNA	International Journal of Nautical Archaeology and Underwater Exploration
JdI	Jahrbuch des Deutschen Archaeologischen Instituts
JHS	Journal of Hellenic Studies
JRS	Journal of Roman Studies
JWG	Jahrbuch fuer Wirtschaftsgeschichte
LCM	Liverpool Classical Monthly
MH	Museum Helveticum
M/L	A Selection of Greek Historical Inscriptions to the End of the Fifth Century B.C., ed. R. Meiggs and D.M. Lewis, Oxford, 1969
MME	The Minnesota Messenia Expedition: Reconstructing a Bronze Age Regional Environment, ed. W.A. McDonald and G.R. Rapp, Jr, Minneapolis, 1972
OA	Opuscula Atheniensia
PAAH	Praktika tis en Athenais Archaiologikis Hetaireias
PBA	Proceedings of the British Academy
PCPhS	Proceedings of the Cambridge Philological Society
PP	La Parola del Passato
RD	Revue Historique de Droit français et étranger
RE	Paulys Real-Encyclopaedie der classischen Altertumswissenschaft
REA	Revue des Etudes Anciennes
REG	Revue des Etudes Grecques
RhM	Rheinisches Museum
RSA	Rivista Storica dell'Antichita
SEG	Supplementum Epigraphicum Graecum
SMEA	Studi Micenei ed Egeo-Anatolici
TAPA	Transactions and Proceedings of the American Philological Association
TLS	The Times Literary Supplement
WA	World Archaeology
YCS	Yale Classical Studies
ZPE	Zeitschrift fuer Papyrologie und Epigraphik

Bibliography

This bibliography is consciously selective and biased towards recent works in English, especially those which provide full references to the ancient and modern literature.

AALDERS, G.J.D. (1968), Die Theorie der gemischten Verfas-
sung im Altertum, Amsterdam.
AALIN, P. (1962), Das Ende der mykenischen Fundstaetten
auf dem griechischen Festland, Lund.
AMIT, M. (1973), Great and Small Poleis. A Study in the
Relations between the Great Powers and the Small Cities in
Ancient Greece, Brussels.
AMOURETTI, M.-C. (1976), 'Les instruments aratoires dans
la Grèce archaïque', Dialogues d'Histoire Ancienne, Annales
Littéraires de l'Université de Besançon 188, 25-52.
ANDERSON, J.K. (1970), Military Theory and Practice in the
Age of Xenophon, Berkeley and Los Angeles.
ANDERSON, J.K. (1974), Xenophon, London.
ANDRESKI, S. (1972), Social Sciences as Sorcery, Harmonds-
worth.
ANDREWES, A. (1938), 'Eunomia', CQ 32, 89-102.
ANDREWES, A. (1952), 'Sparta and Arcadia in the early
fifth century', Phoenix 6, 1-5.
ANDREWES, A. (1956), The Greek Tyrants, London.
ANDREWES, A. (1961), 'Thucydides and the Persians', His-
toria 10, 1-18.
ANDREWES, A. (1971), 'Two notes on Lysander', Phoenix 25,
206-26.
See also GOMME, A.W. (1970) and HILL, G.F. (1951).
ANGEL, J.L. (1972), 'Ecology and population in the eastern
Mediterranean', WA 4, 88-105.
ARVANITIS, T. (1971), Vatika through the Centuries, Athens
(in Greek).
ASTOUR, M.C. (1967), Helleno-Semitica. An Ethnic and Cul-
tural Study in West Semitic Impact in Mycenaean Greece,

2nd edn, Leiden.

AUJAC, G. (1975), La Géographie dans le monde antique, Paris.

AUSTIN, M.M. and VIDAL-NAQUET, P. (1977), Economic and Social History of Ancient Greece. An Introduction, London.

BADEN, H. (1966), 'Untersuchungen zur Einheit der Hellenika Xenophons', dissertation, Hamburg.

BAKHUIZEN, S.C. (1975), 'Social ecology of the ancient Greek world', AC 44, 211-18.

BARTONEK, A. (1973), 'The place of the Dorians in the Late Helladic world', BAMA 305-11.

BASS, G.F. (1967), Cape Gelidonya: a Bronze Age Shipwreck, Philadelphia.

BAYER, E. and HEIDEKING, J. (1975), Die Chronologie des Perikleischen Zeitalters, Darmstadt.

BELOCH, K.J. (1913), Griechische Geschichte I, 2nd edn, Strassburg, Berlin and Leipzig.

BENGTSON, H. (1975), Die Vertraege der griechischroemischen Welt von 700 bis 338 v. Chr., 2nd edn, Munich.

BENGTSON, H. (1977), Griechische Geschichte von den Anfaengen bis in die roemische Kaiserzeit, 5th edn, Munich.

BENTON, S. (1950), 'The dating of horses on stands and spectacle fibulae in Greece', JHS 70, 16-22.

BERGQUIST, B. (1967), The Archaic Greek Temenos, Lund.

BERLIN, I. (1960), 'History and theory: the concept of scientific history', HT 1, 1-31.

BERNHEIM, E. (1894), Lehrbuch der historischen Methode und Geschichtsphilosophie. Mit Nachweis der wichtigsten Quellen und Huelfsmittel zum Studium der Geschichte, Altenburg.

BERVE, H. (1967), Die Tyrannis bei den Griechen, 2, Munich.

BIEBER, A.M. et al. (1976), 'Application of multivariate techniques to analytical data on Aegean ceramics', Archaeometry 18, 59-74.

BINFORD, L.R. (1972), An Archeological Perspective, New York.

BINTLIFF, J. (1977), Environment and Settlement in Prehistoric Greece, 2, British Archaeological Reports Supp. 28, Oxford.

BLINKENBERG, C. (1926), Fibules grecques et orientales, Copenhagen.

BOARDMAN, J. (1963), 'Artemis Orthia and chronology', BSA 58, 1-7.

BOARDMAN, J. (1973), The Greeks Overseas, 2nd edn, Harmondsworth.

BOCKISCH, G. (1965), 'Harmostai', Klio 46, 129-239.

BOCKISCH, G. (1974), 'Die Sozial-oekonomische und politische Krise der Lakedaemonier und ihrer Symmachoi im 4. Jahrhundert v. u. Z.', in Hellenische Poleis. Krise-

Wandlung-Wirkung, 4, ed. E.C. Welskopf, Berlin, 199-230.

BOELTE, F. (1929), 'Sparta', RE IIIA, 1265-373.

BOEMER, F. (1960), Untersuchungen ueber die Religion der Sklaven in Griechenland und Rom II. Die sogenannte Freilassung in Griechenland und die (douloi) hieroi, Wiesbaden.

BOURGUET, E. (1927), Le Dialecte laconien, Paris.

BOUZEK, J. (1969), Homerisches Griechenland im Lichte der archaeologischen Quellen, Prague.

BOWERSOCK, G.W. (1961), 'Eurycles of Sparta', JRS 51, 112-18.

BRANIGAN, K. (1970), The Foundations of Palatial Crete. A Survey of Crete in the Early Bronze Age, London.

BRANIGAN, K. (1974), Aegean Metalwork of the Early and Middle Bronze Age, Oxford.

BRAUDEL, F. (1972), The Mediterranean and the Mediterranean World in the Age of Philip II, 2, 2nd edn, London.

BRISCOE, J. (1967), 'Rome and the class struggle in the Greek states 200-146 B.C.', Past & Present 36, 3-20.

BRUCE, I.A.F. (1967), An Historical Commentary on the Hellenica Oxyrhynchia, Cambridge.

BRUNT, P.A. (1953/4), 'The Hellenic League against Persia', Historia 2, 135-63.

BRUNT, P.A. (1965), 'Spartan policy and strategy in the Archidamian War', Phoenix 19, 255-80.

BUCHHOLZ, H.-G. (1973), Jagd und Fischfang, Archaeologia Homerica IIJ, Goettingen.

BUCHHOLZ, H.-G. and KARAGEORGHIS, V. (1973), Prehistoric Greece and Cyprus, London.

BUCK, R.J. (1969), 'The Mycenaean time of troubles', Historia 18, 276-98.

BURKERT, W. (1965), 'Demaratos, Astrabakos und Herakles. Koenigsmythos und Politik zur Zeit der Perserkriege (Herodot VI, 67-69)', MH 22, 166-77.

BURKERT, W. (1977), Griechische Religion der archaischen und klassischen Epoche, Stuttgart.

BURN, A.R. (1960), The Lyric Age of Greece, London.

BURR, V. (1944), Neon Katalogos. Untersuchungen zum homerischen Schiffskatalog, Leipzig.

BUSCHOR, E. and von MASSOW, W. (1927), 'Vom Amyklaion', AM 52, 1-64.

BUSOLT, G. (1893), Griechische Geschichte I, 2nd edn, Gotha.

CALAME, C. (1977), Les Choeurs de jeunes filles en Grèce archaïque, 2, Rome.

CARLIER, P. (1977), 'La vie politique à Sparte sous le règne de Cléomène 1er: essai d'interprétation', Ktema 2, 65-84.

CARPENTER, R. (1966), Discontinuity in Greek Civilization,

367 Bibliography

Cambridge.
CARTER, J.C. (1975), The Sculpture of Taras, Philadelphia.
CARTLEDGE, P.A. (1975), 'Early Sparta c.950-650 B.C.: an
archaeological and historical study' (unpublished Oxford
doctoral thesis).
CARTLEDGE, P.A. (1976a), 'A new 5th-century Spartan
treaty', LCM 1, 87-92.
CARTLEDGE, P.A. (1976b), 'Did Spartan citizens ever prac-
tise a manual tekhne?', LCM 1, 115-19.
CARTLEDGE, P.A. (1977), 'Hoplites and heroes. Sparta's
contribution to the technique of ancient warfare', JHS 97,
11-27.
CARTLEDGE, P.A. (1978), 'Literacy in the Spartan olig-
archy', JHS 98, 25-37.
CASKEY, J.L. (1971), 'Greece, Crete, and the Aegean is-
lands in the Early Bronze Age', in CAH I.2, 3rd edn, 771-
807.
CASKEY, J.L. (1973), 'Greece and the Aegean islands in the
Middle Bronze Age', in CAH II.1, 3rd edn, 117-40.
CATLING, H.W. (1977), 'Excavations at the Menelaion,
Sparta, 1973-76', AR, 24-42.
CATLING, H.W. and CAVANAGH, H. (1976), 'Two inscribed
bronzes from the Menelaion, Sparta', Kadmos 15, 145-57.
CAWKWELL, G.L. (1963), 'The SYN coins again', JHS 83, 152-
4.
CAWKWELL, G.L. (1968), 'The power of Persia', Arepo 1, 1-5.
CAWKWELL, G.L. (1970), 'The fall of Themistocles', in
Auckland Classical Essays Presented to E.M. Blaiklock, ed.
B.F. Harris, Auckland and Oxford, 39-58.
CAWKWELL, G.L. (1975), 'Thucydides' judgment of Periclean
strategy', YCS 24, 53-70.
CAWKWELL, G.L. (1976), 'Agesilaus and Sparta', CQ 26, 62-
84.
CHADWICK, J. (1976a), The Mycenaean World, Cambridge.
CHADWICK, J. (1976b), 'Who were the Dorians?', PP 31, 103-
17.
CHADWICK, J. (1976c), 'Der Beitrag der Sprachwissenschaft
zur Rekonstruktion der griechischen Fruehgeschichte', Anz.
d. Oesterreichischen Akad. d. Wiss., phil-hist. kl. 113,
183-98.
See also VENTRIS, M.G.F.
CHARNEUX, P. (1953), 'Inscriptions d'Argos', BCH 77, 387-403.
CHARNEUX, P. (1958), 'Inscriptions d'Argos', BCH 82, 1-15.
CHRIMES, K.M.T. (1949), Ancient Sparta. A Re-examination
of the Evidence, Manchester.
CHRISTIEN, J. (1974), 'La loi d'Epitadeus. Un aspect de l'
histoire économique et sociale à Sparte', RD 52, 197-221.
CHRISTOU, C. (1964), 'Archaic graves in Sparta and a Lac-
onian funeral figured relief amphora', AD 19A, 123-63

(Greek), 283-5 (English summary).
CLOCHÉ, P. (1915), La Restauration démocratique à Athènes en 403 avant J.-C., Paris.
COHEN, P.S. (1969), 'Theories of myth', Man 4, 337-53.
COLDSTREAM, J.N. (1968), Greek Geometric Pottery. A Survey of Ten Local Styles and their Chronology, London.
COLDSTREAM, J.N. (1973), 'Kythera: the change from Early Helladic to Early Minoan', in BAMA 33-6.
COLDSTREAM, J.N. (1976), 'Hero-cults in the age of Homer', JHS 96, 8-17.
COLDSTREAM, J.N. (1977), Geometric Greece, London.
COLDSTREAM, J.N. and HUXLEY, G.L. (1972), Kythera. Excavations and Studies, London.
COLE, S. (1970), The Neolithic Revolution, 5th edn, London (British Museum).
COLEMAN-NORTON, P.R. (1941), 'Socialism at Sparta', in The Greek Political Experience. Studies in Honor of W.K. Prentice, Princeton, 61-77.
COLLINGWOOD, R.G. (1946), The Idea of History, Oxford.
COOK, R.M. (1962), 'Spartan history and archaeology', CQ 12, 156-8.
COOK, R.M. (1972), Greek Painted Pottery, 2nd edn, London.
COX, P.R. (1970), Demography, 4th edn, Cambridge.
DALY, L.W. (1939), 'An inscribed Doric capital from the Argive Heraion', Hesperia 8, 165-9.
DAUBE, D. (1977), The Duty of Procreation, Edinburgh.
DAVIES, J.K. (1971), Athenian Propertied Families 600-300 B.C., Oxford.
DAVIS, E.N. (1973), 'The Vapheio cups and Aegean gold and silver ware', dissertation, New York University.
DEANE, P. (1972), Thucydides' Dates 465-431 B.C., Don Mills (Ontario).
DEGLER, C.N. (1970), 'Slavery in Brazil and the United States: an essay in comparative history', AHR 75, 1004-28.
DEMACOPOULOU, K. (1968), 'Mycenaean vases from chamber tombs of the region of Ay. Ioannis, Monemvasia', AD 23A, 145-94 (Greek with English summary).
DEMACOPOULOU, K. (1971), 'A Mycenaean pictorial vase of the fifteenth century B.C. from Laconia', BSA 66, 95-100.
DESBOROUGH, V.R.d'A. (1952), Protogeometric Pottery, Oxford.
DESBOROUGH, V.R.d'A. (1964), The Last Mycenaeans and Their Successors, Oxford.
DESBOROUGH, V.R.d'A. (1972), The Greek Dark Ages, London.
DIAKONOFF, I.M. (1974), 'Slaves, Helots and serfs in early antiquity', Acta Antiqua 22, 45-78.
DICKINSON, O.T.P.K. (1974), 'The definition of Late Helladic I', BSA 69, 109-20.
DICKINSON, O.T.P.K. (1977), The Origins of Mycenaean

Civilisation, Goeteborg.
DIEHL, E. (1964), Die Hydria: Formgeschichte und Verwen-
dung im Kult des Altertums, Mainz.
DIETRICH, B.C. (1974), The Origins of Greek Religion,
Berlin and New York.
DIETRICH, B.C. (1975), 'The Dorian Hyacinthia: a survival
from the Bronze Age', Kadmos 14, 133-42.
DOVER, K.J. (1973), Thucydides, Oxford.
See also GOMME, A.W. (1970).
DOW, S. (1968), 'Literacy: the palace bureaucracies, the
Dark Age, Homer', in A Land called Crete. A Symposium in
Memory of Harriet Boyd Hawes, Smith College Studies in
History 45, Northampton (Mass.), 109-47.
DRERUP, H. (1969), Griechische Baukunst in geometrischer
Zeit, Archaeologia Homerica IIO, Goettingen.
DROOP, J.P. (1932), 'Facts or fancies?', BSA 32, 247-50.
DUCAT, J. (1974), 'Le mépris des Hilotes', Annales (ESC)
29, 1451-64.
EDGERTON, H. and SCOUFOPOULOS, N.C. (1972), 'Sonar search
at Gythion harbor', AAA 5, 202-6.
EDMUNDS, L. (1975), Chance and Intelligence in Thucydides,
Cambridge (Mass.).
EHRENBERG, V. (1924), 'Spartiaten und Lakedaimonier',
Hermes 59, 22-72 (=Ehrenberg 1965, 161-201).
EHRENBERG, V. (1962), The People of Aristophanes. A Soci-
ology of Old Attic Comedy, 3rd edn, New York.
EHRENBERG, V. (1965), Polis und Imperium. Beitraege zur
alten Geschichte, ed. K.F. Stroheker and A.J. Graham,
Zurich.
EHRENBERG, V. (1973), From Solon to Socrates. Greek His-
tory and Civilization in the Sixth and Fifth Centuries
B.C., 2nd edn, London.
FEBVRE, L. (1925), A Geographical Introduction to History,
London.
FERMOR, P.L. (1958), Mani, London.
FINLEY, M.I. (1957), 'The Mycenaean tablets and economic
history', EHR 10, 128-41.
FINLEY, M.I. (1964), 'Between slavery and freedom', CSSH
6, 233-49.
FINLEY, M.I. (1968a), Ancient Sicily to the Arab Conquest,
London.
FINLEY, M.I. (1968b), ed., Slavery in Classical Antiquity,
2nd edn, Cambridge.
FINLEY, M.I. (1973), The Ancient Economy, London.
FINLEY, M.I. (1975), The Use and Abuse of History, London.
FINLEY, M.I. (1976), 'A peculiar institution?', TLS 2 July,
819-21.
FORNARA, C.W. (1971), 'Evidence for the date of Herodotus'
publication', JHS 91, 25-34.

FORNARA, C.W. (1977), ed. and trans., Archaic Times to the End of the Peloponnesian War, Baltimore and London.

FORREST, W.G. (1960), 'Themistokles and Argos', CQ 10, 221-40.

FORREST, W.G. (1968), A History of Sparta 950-192 B.C., London.

FORSTER, E.S. (1904), 'South-western Laconia', BSA 10, 158-89.

FORSTER, E.S. (1907), 'Gythium and N.W. coast of the Laconian Gulf', BSA 13, 219-37.

FORSTER, E.S. (1909), 'A geographical note on Thucydides IV.54', CR 23, 221f.

FOSS, C. (1975), 'Greek sling bullets in Oxford', AR, 40-4.

FRANKFORT, H. et al. (1946), The Intellectual Adventure of Ancient Man, Chicago.

FRASER, P.M. (1970), 'Eratosthenes of Cyrene', PBA 56, 175-207.

FRASER, P.M. (1972), Ptolemaic Alexandria, 3, Oxford.

FRAZER, J.G. (1898), Pausanias' Description of Greece III, London and New York.

FRENCH, E. (1971), 'The development of Mycenaean terracotta figurines', BSA 66, 102-87.

FREYER-SCHAUENBERG, B. (1970), 'Kuon Lakonos Kuon Lakaina', AK 14, 95-100.

FUKS, A. (1972), 'Isocrates and the social-economic situation in Greece', AS 3, 17-44.

FURUMARK, A. (1941), The Mycenaean Pottery I. Analysis and Classification. II. The Chronology of Mycenaean Pottery, Stockholm.

GALANOPOULOS, A.G. (1964), 'Seismic geography of the Peloponnese', Peloponnisiaki Protochronia, 49-53 (in Greek).

GEORGOUDI, S. (1974), 'Quelques problèmes de la transhumance dans la Grèce ancienne', REG 87, 155-85.

GIANNOKOPOULOS, N.A. (1953), 'Three new boundary-marks of the boundary between ancient Messenia and Lakonia', Platon 5, 147-58 (in Greek).

GIANNOKOPOULOS, P.E. (1966), Gytheion, Athens (in Greek).

GOMME, A.W. (1951), 'Four passages in Thucydides', JHS 71, 70-80.

GOMME, A.W. (1945, 1956, 1970), A Historical Commentary on Thucydides I, II-III, IV (with A. ANDREWES and K.J. DOVER), Oxford.

GOODY, J. and WATT, I. (1963), 'The consequences of literacy', CSSH 5, 304-45.

GOUROU, P. (1973), Pour une Géographie humaine, Paris.

GREIFENHAGEN, A. (1970), Staatlichen Museen Berlin, Schmuckarbeiten in Edelmetall I. Fundgruppen, Berlin.

GRIERSON, P. (1959), 'Commerce in the Dark Ages: a

critique of the evidence', Transactions of the Royal Historical Society 9, 123-40.

CRIFFITHS, A. (1976), 'What Syagrus said: Herodotus 7.159', LCM 1, 23f.

GROTE, G. (1873), 'Grecian legends and early Greek history', in Minor Works, ed. A. Bain, London, 73-134.

GROTE, G. (1888), History of Greece, new edn in 10 vols, London.

GSCHNITZER, F. (1958), Abhaengige Orte im griechischen Altertum, Munich.

GSCHNITZER, F. (1962), 'Zum Namen Poseidon', Serta Philologica Aenipontana 7-8, 13-18.

HABICHT, C. (1970), Gottmenschtum und griechische Staedte, 2nd edn, Munich.

HAEGG, R. (1968), 'Mykenische Kultstaetten im archaeologischen Material', OA 8, 39-60.

HAINSWORTH, J.B. (1969), Homer, Oxford.

HAMILTON, C.D. (1970), 'Spartan politics and policy, 405-401 B.C.', AJP 91, 294-314.

HAMPL, F. (1937), 'Die lakedaemonischen Perioeken', Hermes 72, 1-37.

HAMPL, F. (1962), 'Die Ilias ist kein Geschichtsbuch', Serta Philologica Aenipontana 7-8, 37-63.

HARLEY, T.R. (1942), '"A greater than Leonidas"', GR 11, 68-83.

HARTLEY, M. (1932), 'Facts', BSA 32, 251-4.

HARVEY, F.D. (1967), 'Oxyrhynchus Papyrus 2390 and early Spartan history', JHS 87, 62-73.

HAUPTMANN, H. (1971), 'Forschungsbericht zur aegaeischen Fruehzeit. Das Festland und die kleineren Inseln. Steinzeit, besonders Neolithikum', AA, 348-87.

HAYMES, E.R. (1973), A Bibliography of Studies relating to Parry's and Lord's Oral Theory, Cambridge (Mass.).

HENIGE, D.P. (1974), The Chronology of Oral Tradition. Quest for a Chimera, Oxford.

HEXTER, J.H. (1971), Doing History, London.

HIERSCHE, R. (1970), Grundzuege der griechischen Sprachwissenschaft bis zur klassischen Zeit, Wiesbaden.

HIGGINS, W.E. (1977), Xenophon the Athenian. The Problem of the Individual and the Society of the Polis, Albany.

HIGNETT, C. (1963), Xerxes' Invasion of Greece, Oxford.

HILL, G.F. (1951), Sources for Greek History between the Persian and Peloponnesian Wars, ed. R. Meiggs and A. Andrewes, Oxford.

HILLER, S. and PANAGL, O. (1976), Die fruehgriechischen Texte aus mykenischer Zeit: zur Erforschung der Linear B-Tafeln, Darmstadt.

HOLLADAY, A.J. (1977a), 'Spartan austerity', CQ 27, 111-26.

HOLLADAY, A.J. (1977b), 'Sparta's role in the First Pelop-
onnesian War', JHS 97, 54-63.
HOOD, M.S.F. (1971), The Minoans, London.
HOOKER, J.T. (1976), 'The coming of the Greeks', Historia
25, 129-45.
HOOKER, J.T. (1977), Mycenaean Greece, London.
HOPE SIMPSON, R. (1965), A Gazetteer and Atlas of Mycen-
aean Sites, London.
HOPE SIMPSON, R. (1972), 'Leonidas' decision', Phoenix 26,
1-11.
HOPE SIMPSON, R. and LAZENBY, J.F. (1970), The Catalogue
of the Ships in Homer's Iliad, Oxford.
HOPE SIMPSON, R. and WATERHOUSE, H.E. (1960), 'Prehistoric
Laconia. Part I', BSA 55, 67-107.
HOPE SIMPSON, R. and WATERHOUSE, H.E. (1961), 'Prehistoric
Laconia, Part II', BSA 56, 114-75.
HOWE, T.P. (1958), 'Linear B and Hesiod's breadwinners',
TAPA 89, 44-65.
HOWELL, R.J. (1970), 'A survey of Eastern Arcadia in pre-
history', BSA 65, 79-127.
HULL, D.B. (1964), Hounds and Hunting in Ancient Greece,
Chicago.
HUNTER, V.J. (1973), Thucydides: the Artful Reporter,
Toronto.
HUTCHINSON, J.S. (1977), 'Mycenaean kingdoms and mediaeval
estates (an analogical approach to the history of LH III)',
Historia 26, 1-23.
HUXLEY, G.L. (1962), Early Sparta, London.
HUXLEY, G.L. (1969), Greek Epic Poetry from Eumelos to
Panyassis, London.
HUXLEY, G.L. (1975a), Pindar's Vision of the Past, Belfast.
HUXLEY, G.L. (1975b), 'A Problem in a Spartan king-list',
Lakonikai Spoudai 2, 110-14.
See also COLDSTREAM, J.N.
JACHMANN, G. (1958), Der homerische Schiffskatalog und die
Ilias, Cologne.
JACOBY, F. (1902), Apollodors Chronik: einer Sammlung der
Fragmente, Berlin.
JACOBY, F. (1944), 'Chrestous poiein (Aristotle fr. 592R)',
CQ 38, 15f.
JACOBY, F. (1949), Atthis: the Local Chronicles of Ancient
Athens, Oxford.
JARDÉ, A. (1925), Les Céréales dans l'antiquité grecque I.
La production, Paris (Part II never appeared).
JEANMAIRE, H. (1913), 'La cryptie lacédémonienne', REG 26,
121-50.
JEFFERY, L.H. (1961), The Local Scripts of Archaic Greece:
a Study of the Origin of the Greek Alphabet and its Devel-
opment from the Eighth to the Fifth Centuries B.C., Oxford.

JEFFERY, L.H. (1976), Archaic Greece. The City-states
c.700-500 B.C., London.
JONES, A.H.M. (1966), 'The Lycurgan Rhetra', in Ancient
Society and Institutions. Studies Presented to V. Ehren-
berg on his 75th Birthday, ed. E. Badian, Oxford, 165-75.
JONES, A.H.M. (1967), Sparta, Oxford.
JOST, M. (1975), 'Statuettes de bronze provenant de
Lykosoura', BCH 99, 339-64.
KAGAN, D. (1969), The Outbreak of the Peloponnesian War,
Ithaca (New York).
KAGAN, D. (1974), The Archidamian War, Ithaca (New York).
KAHRSTEDT, U. (1922), Griechisches Staatsrecht I. Sparta
under seine Symmachie, Goettingen.
KAHRSTEDT, U. (1950), 'Zwei Geographica im Peloponnes',
RhM 93, 227-42.
KAHRSTEDT, U. (1954), Das wirtschaftliche Gesicht Griech-
enlands in der Kaiserzeit. Kleinstadt, Villa und Domaene,
Bern.
KANTOR, H. (1947), 'The Aegean and the Orient in the
second millennium B.C.', AJA 51, 1-103.
KAYSER, B. (1965), 'La carte de la distribution de la
population grecque en 1961', Annales (ESC) 20, 301-8.
KELLY, T. (1966), 'The Calaurian Amphictiony', AJA 70,
113-21.
KELLY, T. (1976), A History of Argos to 500 B.C., Minne-
apolis.
KIECHLE, F. (1959), Messenische Studien. Untersuchungen
zur Geschichte der Messenischen Kriege und der Auswanderung
der Messenier, Kallmuenz.
KIECHLE, F. (1963), Lakonien und Sparta. Untersuchungen
zur ethnischen Struktur und zur politischen Entwicklung
Lakoniens und Spartas bis zum Ende der archaischen Zeit,
Munich.
KIECHLE, F. (1966), 'Die Auspraegung der Sage von der
Rueckkehr der Herakliden', Helikon 6, 493-517.
KIRK, G.S. (1960), 'Objective dating criteria in Homer',
MH 17, 189-205.
KIRK, G.S. (1962), The Songs of omer, Cambridge.
KIRK, G.S. (1975), 'The Homeric poems as history', in CAH
II.2, 3rd edn, 820-50.
KIRSTEN, E. (1956), Die griechische Polis als historisch-
geographisches Problem des Mittelmeerraumes, Bonn.
KIRSTEN, E. (1958), 'Heiligtum und Tempel der Artemis
Orthia zu Sparta in ihrer aeltesten Entwicklungsphase',
BJ 158, 170-6.
See also PHILIPPSON, A. (1959).
KOENEN, L. (1976), 'Fieldwork of the International Photo-
graphic Archive in Cairo', Studia Papyrologica 15, 55-76.
KOTHE, H. (1975), 'Der Hesiodpflug', Philologus 119, 1-26.

KRAAY, C.M. (1976), Archaic and Classical Greek Coins, London.

KRAFT, J.C. et al. (1975), 'Late Holocene palaeography of the coastal plain of the Gulf of Messenia, Greece, and its relationship to archaeological settings and coastal change', Bulletin of the Geological Society of America 86, 1191-208.

KUNZE, E. (1933), Gnomon 9. 1-14 (review of AO).

LAIX, R.A. de (1974). 'Aristotle's conception of the Spartan constitution'. Journal of the History of Philosophy 12, 21-30.

LAMB, H.H. (1974), 'Climate, vegetation and forest limits in early civilized times', in The Place of Astronomy in the Ancient World, a joint symposium of the Royal Society and the British Academy, ed. F.R. Hodson, Oxford, 195-230.

LAMB, W. (1926), 'Arcadian bronze statuettes', BSA 27, 133-48.

LAMBERT, N. (1972), 'Grotte d'Alépotrypa (Magne)', BCH 96, 845-71.

LANE, E.A. (1934), 'Lakonian vasepainting', BSA 34, 99-189.

LARSEN, J.A.O. (1938), 'Perioikoi', RE XIX, 816-33.

LAUFFER, S. (1950), Gnomon 22, 107-11 (review of Philippson 1948).

LAUTER-BUFÉ, H. (1974), 'Entstehung und Entwicklung des kombinierten lakonischen Akroters', AM 89, 205-30.

LAZENBY, J.F. (1975), 'Pausanias, son of Kleombrotos', Hermes 103, 235-51.
See also HOPE SIMPSON, R. (1970).

LEAHY, D.M. (1955), 'The bones of Tisamenus', Historia 4, 26-38.

LEAHY, D.M. (1956), 'Chilon and Aeschines', BRL 38, 406-35.

LEAHY, D.M. (1957), 'The Spartan embassy to Lygdamis', JHS 77, 272-5.

LEAHY, D.M. (1958), 'The Spartan defeat at Orchomenus', Phoenix 12, 141-65.

LEAHY, D.M. (1959), 'Chilon and Aeschines again', Phoenix 13, 31-7.

LEAKE, W.M. (1830), Travels in the Morea I, London.

LEGON, R.P. (1967), 'Phliasian politics and policy in the early fourth century B.C.', Historia 16, 324-37.

LEHMANN, G.A. (1978), 'Spartas arche und die Vorphase des Korinthischen Krieges in den Hellenica Oxyrhynchia. 1', ZPE 28, 109-26.

LEHMANN, H. (1937), Argolis. Landeskunde der Ebene von Argos under ihrer Randgebiete, Athens.

LEON, C. (1968), 'Statuette eines Kuros aus Messenien', AM 83, 175-85.

LE ROY, C. (1974), 'Inscriptions de Laconie inédites ou revues', in Mélanges helléniques offerts à G. Daux, Paris, 219-38.

LESKY, A. (1968), 'Homeros', RE Supp. XI, 687-846.

LESKY, A. (1971), Geschichte der griechischen Literatur, 3rd edn, Bern.

LÉVY, E. (1977), 'La Grande Rhètra', Ktema 2, 85-103.

LEWIS, D.M. (1977), Sparta and Persia, Leiden.

LIVATHINOS, A.N. and MARIOLOPOULOS, E.G. (1935), Atlas climatique de la Grèce, Athens.

LO PORTO, F.G. (1971), 'Topografia antica di Taranto', Atti del 10° Convegno di Studi sulla Magna Grecia, Taranto 1970, 343-83.

LORIMER, H.L. (1950), Homer and the Monuments, London.

LORING, W. (1895), 'Some ancient routes in the Peloponnese', JHS 15, 25-89.

LOTZE, D. (1959), Metaxy Eleutheron kai Doulon. Studien zur Rechtsstellung unfreier Landbevoelkerung bis zum 4. Jahrhundert v. Chr., Berlin.

LOTZE, D. (1964), Lysander und der Peloponnesische Krieg, Berlin.

LOTZE, D. (1971), 'Zu einigen Aspekten des spartanischen Agrarsystems', JWG/II (Fest. E.C. Welskopf), 63-76.

LOTZE, D. (1974), 'War Xenophon selbst der Interpolator seiner Hellenika I-II?', Philologus 118, 215-17.

LOY, W.G. (1970), The Land of Nestor. A Physical Geography of the Southwest Peloponnese, Washington (DC).

MARANGOU, E.-L.I. (1969), Lakonische Elfenbein- und Beinschnitzereien, Tuebingen.

MASON, B.J. (1977), 'Man's influence on weather and climate', Journal of the Royal Society of Arts 125, 150-65.

MEIGGS, R. (1972), The Athenian Empire, Oxford.

MEISTER, K. (1921), Die homerische Kunstsprache, Leipzig.

MERITT, B.D. (1944), 'Excavations in the Athenian Agora. Greek inscriptions', Hesperia 13, 210-65.

MEYER, C. (1970), Die Urkunden im Geschichtswerk des Thukydides, 2nd edn, Munich.

MEYER, E. (1892), Forschungen zur alten Geschichte, Halle.

MEYER, Ernst (1969), 'Kynuria', Der kleine Pauly III, 402.

MEYER, Ernst (1978), 'Messenien', RE Supp. XV, 155-289.

MITSOS, M. (1974), 'Damaratos II king of Sparta', Peloponnisiaka 10, 81-116 (in Greek).

MOGGI, M. (1976), I sinecismi interstatali greci I. Dalle origini al 338 a.c., Pisa.

MOMIGLIANO, A.D. (1966), Studies in Historiography, London.

MOORE, W.G. (1976), Dictionary of Geography, 5th edn, London.

MORETTI, L. (1971), 'Problemi di storia tarantina', Atti

del 10° Convegno di Studi sulla Magna Grecia, Taranto 1970, 21-65.

MORITZ, L.A. (1955), 'Husked and "naked" grain', CQ 5, 129-34.

MORITZ, L.A. (1958), Grain-mills and Flour in Classical Antiquity, Oxford.

MOSCHOU, L. (1975), 'Topographical studies of the Mani', AAA 8, 160-77 (in Greek).

MUELLER, K.O. (1839), The History and Antiquities of the Doric Race, 2nd edn, 2, London.

MUHLY, J.D. (1970), 'Homer and the Phoenicians. The relations between Greece and the Near East in the Late Bronze and Early Iron Ages', Berytus 19, 19-64.

MUHLY, J.D. (1973), Copper and Tin: the Distribution of Mineral Resources and the Nature of the Metals Trade in the Bronze Age, New Haven (Conn.).

MYLONAS, G.E. (1964), 'Priam's Troy and the date of its fall', Hesperia 33, 352-80.

MYRES, J.L. (1943), Mediterranean Culture, Cambridge.

MYRES, J.L. (1958), Homer and his Critics, ed. D.H.F. Gray, London.

NICHOLLS, R.V. (1970), 'Greek votive statuettes and religious continuity c.1200-700 B.C.', in Auckland Classical Essays Presented to E.M. Blaiklock, ed. B.F. Harris, Auckland and Oxford, 1-37.

NICKLIN, K. (1971), 'Stability and innovation in pottery manufacture', WA 3, 13-48.

NIEBUHR, B.G. (1847), Historische und philologische Vortraege II.1, Berlin.

NIESE, B. (1906), 'Neue Beitraege zur Geschichte und Landeskunde Lakedaemons. Die Lakedaemonischen Perioeken', Goettingische Gelehrte Nachrichten, 101-42.

OBERG, K. (1940), 'The kingdom of Ankole in Uganda', in African Political Systems, ed. M. Fortes and E. Evans-Pritchard, Oxford, 121-62.

OLIVA, P. (1971), Sparta and her Social Problems, Amsterdam and Prague.

OLLIER, F. (1933, 1943), Le Mirage spartiate: étude sur l'idéalisation de Sparte dans l'antiquité grecque, 2, Paris.

ORMEROD, H.A. (1910), 'Bardounia and north-eastern Maina', BSA 16, 62-71.

PAGE, D.L. (1951), Alcman. The Partheneion, Oxford.

PAGE, D.L. (1959), History and the Homeric Iliad, Berkeley and Los Angeles.

PAPADAKIS, J. (1966), The Climates of the World and their Agricultural Potentialities, Buenos Aires.

PARETI, L. (1917), Storia di Sparta arcaica I, Florence (Part II never appeared).

PARKE, H.W. (1930), 'The development of the second Spartan

empire (405-371)', JHS 50, 37-79.
PARKE, H.W. (1931), 'The evidence for harmosts in Laconia',
Hermathena 46, 31-8.
PARKE, H.W. (1933), Greek Mercenary Soldiers from the
Earliest Times to the Battle of Ipsus, Oxford.
PARKE, H.W. and WORMELL, D.E.W. (1956), The Delphic
Oracle, 2, Oxford.
PARRY, M. (1971), The Making of Homeric Verse, ed.
A. Parry, Oxford.
PEARSON, L. (1939), Early Ionian Historians, Oxford.
PEARSON, L. (1962), 'The pseudo-history of Messenia and
its authors', Historia 11, 397-426.
PÉDECH, P. (1976), La Géographie des Grecs, Paris.
PELAGATTI, P. (1957), 'La ceramica laconica del Museo di
Taranto', ASAA 17-18 (1955-6), 7-44.
PEMBROKE, S. (1970), 'Locres et Tarente. Le rôle des
femmes dans la fondation de deux colonies grecques',
Annales (ESC) 25, 1240-70.
PERLMAN, S. (1964), 'The causes and the outbreak of the
Corinthian War', CQ 14, 64-81.
PERLMAN, S. (1976), 'Panhellenism, the polis and imperial-
ism', Historia 25, 1-30.
PHELPS, W.W. (1975), 'The Neolithic Pottery Sequence in
Southern Greece' (unpublished London Ph.D. thesis).
PHILIPPSON, A. (1892), Der Peloponnes: Versuch einer
Landeskunde, Berlin.
PHILIPPSON, A. (1948), Das Klima Griechenlands, Bonn.
PHILIPPSON, A. (1959), Die griechischen Landschaften IV,
ed. E. Kirsten, Frankfurt am Main.
PICCIRILLI, L. (1973), Gli arbitrati interstatali greci,
Pisa.
PIGGOTT, S. (1959), Approach to Archaeology, London.
PLEINER, R. (1969), Iron Working in Ancient Greece,
Prague.
POUNDS, N.J.G. (1973), An Historical Geography of Europe,
450 B.C.-A.D. 1330, Cambridge.
PRAKKEN, D.W. (1940), 'Herodotus and the Spartan king
lists', TAPA 71, 460-72.
PRENTICE, W.K. (1934), 'The character of Lysander', AJA
38, 37-42.
PRITCHETT, W.K. (1953), 'The Attic Stelai, Part I',
Hesperia 22, 225-99.
PRITCHETT, W.K. (1956), 'The Attic Stelai, Part II',
Hesperia 25, 178-317.
PRITCHETT, W.K. (1965), Studies in Ancient Greek Topo-
graphy I, Berkeley and Los Angeles.
PRITCHETT, W.K. (1974), The Greek State at War, 2, Ber-
keley and Los Angeles.
PUGLIESE CARRATELLI, G. (1971), 'Per la storia dei culti

di Taranto', Atti del 10° Convegno di Studi sulla Magna
Grecia, Taranto 1970, 133-46.
RAMOU-CHAPSIADI, A. (1978), Archidamos Son of Zeuxidamos
and the Foreign Policy of Sparta during his Reign, Athens
(in Greek).
RAPP, G.R., Jr and COOK, S.R.B. (1973), 'Thera pumice
recovered from LH IIA stratum at Nichoria', AAA 6, 136f.
RAWSON, E. (1969), The Spartan Tradition in European
Thought, Oxford.
REINHOLD, M. (1970), History of Purple as a Status Symbol
in Antiquity, Brussels.
RENFREW, A.C. (1972), The Emergence of Civilisation: the
Cyclades and the Aegean in the Third Millennium B.C.,
London.
RENFREW, A.C. (1973), Social Archaeology, Southampton
(inaugural lecture).
RHOMAIOS, K.A. (1905), 'Laconia. The Hermai on the N.E.
Frontier', BSA 11, 137f.
RHOMAIOS, K.A. (1951), 'Exploratory journey in Kynouria',
PAAH 1950, 234-41 (in Greek).
RHOMAIOS, K.A. (1960), 'Karyatides', Peloponnisiaka 3-4,
376-95 (in Greek).
RICE, D.G. (1974), 'Agesilaus, Agesipolis, and Spartan
politics, 386-379 B.C.', Historia 23, 164-82.
RICE, D.G. (1975), 'Xenophon, Diodorus and the year 379-
378 B.C.: reconstruction and reappraisal', YCS 24, 95-130.
RICHTER, W. (1968), Die Landwirtschaft im homerischen
Zeitalter, Archaeologia Homerica IIH, Goettingen.
RIDGWAY, B.S. (1977), The Archaic Style in Greek Sculp-
ture, Princeton.
RIDLEY, R.T. (1974), 'The economic activities of the Peri-
oikoi', Mnemosyne 27, 281-92.
RISCH, E. (1954), 'Die Sprache Alkmans', MH 11, 20-37.
RISCH, E. (1955), 'Die Gliederung der griechischen Dial-
ekte in neuer Sicht', MH 12, 61-76.
RODENWALT, G. (1919), 'Zur Entstehung der monumentalen
Architektur in Griechenland', AM 44, 175-84.
ROEBUCK, C.A. (1941), A History of Messenia from 369 to
146 B.C., Chicago.
ROEBUCK, C.A. (1945), 'A note on Messenian economy and
population', CP 40, 149-65.
ROEBUCK, C.A. (1948), 'The settlements of Philip II in 338
B.C.', CP 43, 73-92.
ROGAN, D.E. (1973), Mani, Athens (in English).
ROLLEY, C. (1977), 'Le problème de l'art laconien', Ktema
2, 125-40.
ROUSSEL, P. (1943), 'L'exposition des enfants à Sparte',
REA 45, 5-17.
ROUSSEL, P. (1960), Sparte, 2nd edn, Paris.
ROWTON, M.B. (1970), 'Ancient Western Asia', in CAH I.1,

3rd edn, 193-239.

ROY, J. (1967), 'The mercenaries of Cyrus', Historia 16, 287-323.

ROY, J. (1971), 'Arcadia and Boeotia in Peloponnesian affairs, 370-362 B.C.', Historia 20, 569-99.

ROY, J. (1973), 'Diodorus Siculus XV.40 - the Peloponnesian revolutions of 374 B.C.', Klio 55, 135-9.

RUBINSOHN, Z. (1975), 'The Dorian invasion again', PP 30, 105-31.

RUTTER, J.B. and RUTTER, S.H. (1976), The Transition to Mycenaean: a Stratified Middle Helladic II to Late Helladic IIA Pottery Sequence from Ayios Stephanos in Lakonia, Los Angeles.

RYDER, T.T.B. (1965), Koine Eirene. General Peace and Local Independence in Ancient Greece, Oxford.

SACCONI, A. (1974), Corpus delle iscrizioni vascolari in Lineare B, Rome.

STE. CROIX, G.E.M. de (1972), The Origins of the Peloponnesian War, London.

SALMON, J.B. (1977), 'Political hoplites?', JHS 97, 84-101.

SAMUEL, A.E. (1972), Greek and Roman Chronology: Calendars and Years in Classical Antiquity, Munich.

SANDARS, N.K. (1978), The Sea Peoples: Warriors of the Ancient Mediterranean, London.

SARKADY, J. (1975), 'Outlines of the development of Greek society in the period between the 12th and 8th centuries B.C.', Acta Antiqua 23, 107-25.

SCHACHERMEYR, F. (1976), Die aegaeische Fruehzeit: Forschungsbericht ... I. Die vormykenischen Perioden des griechischen Festlandes und der Kykladen, Vienna.

SCHAMP, J. (1976), 'Sous le signe d'Arion', AC 45, 95-120.

SCHWARTZ, G.S. (1976), 'IG V^1 213: the Damonon stele - a new restoration for line 39', ZPE 22, 177f.

SCOUFOPOULOS, N.C. and McKERNAN, J.G. (1975), 'Underwater survey of ancient Gythion, 1972', IJNA 4, 103-16.

SEAGER, R.J. (1967), 'Thrasybulus, Conon and Athenian imperialism, 396-386 B.C.', JHS 87, 95-115.

SEAGER, R.J. (1974), 'The King's Peace and the balance of power in Greece 386-362 B.C.', Athenaeum 52, 36-63.

SEAGER, R.J. (1976), 'After the Peace of Nicias: diplomacy and policy, 421-416 B.C.', CQ 26, 249-69.

SEALEY, B.R. (1975), 'The causes of the Peloponnesian War', CP 70, 89-109.

SEALEY, B.R. (1976), 'Die spartanische Nauarchie', Klio 58, 335-58.

SERGENT, B. (1977), 'La liste de KOM EL-HETAN et le Péloponnèse', Minos 16, 126-73.

SHERO, L.R. (1938), 'Aristomenes the Messenian', TAPA 69,

500-31.

SHIMRON, B. (1972), Late Sparta: the Spartan Revolution 243-146 B.C., Buffalo.

SHIPP, G.P. (1972), Studies in the Language of Homer, 2nd edn, Cambridge.

SKEAT, T.C. (1934), The Dorians in Archaeology, London.

SMITH, R.E. (1953/4), 'The opposition to Agesilaus' foreign policy 394-371 B.C.', Historia 2, 274-88.

SMITH, W.S. (1965), Interconnections in the Ancient Near East: a Study of the Relationships between the Arts of Egypt, the Aegean, and Western Asia, New Haven.

SNODGRASS, A.M. (1964), Early Greek Armour and Weapons from the End of the Bronze Age to 600 B.C., Edinburgh.

SNODGRASS, A.M. (1971), The Dark Age of Greece: an Archaeological Survey of the Eleventh to the Eighth Centuries B.C., Edinburgh.

SNODGRASS, A.M. (1974), 'An historical Homeric society?', JHS 94, 114-25.

SNODGRASS, A.M. (1977), Archaeology and the Rise of the Greek State, Cambridge (inaugural lecture).

SOLMSEN, F. (1907), 'Vordorisches in Lakonien', RhM 62, 329-38.

STARR, C.G. (1961), The Origins of Greek Civilization, 1100-650 B.C., New York.

STARR, C.G. (1965), 'The credibility of early Spartan history', Historia 14, 257-72.

STARR, C.G. (1968), The Awakening of the Greek Historical Spirit, New York.

STARR, C.G. (1977), The Economic and Social Growth of Early Greece 800-500 B.C., New York.

STIBBE, C.M. (1972), Lakonische Vasenmaler des sechsten Jahrhunderts v. Chr., 2, Amsterdam.

STRONG, D.E. (1966), Catalogue of the Carved Amber in the Department of Greek and Roman Antiquities, British Museum, London.

STUBBINGS, F.H. (1970), 'The Aegean Bronze Age', in CAH I. 1, 3rd edn, 239-47.

STYRENIUS, C.-G. (1975), 'Some notes on the new excavations at Asine', OA 11, 177-83.

TARN, W.W. (1925), 'The social question in the third century', in J.B. Bury et al., The Hellenistic Age, Cambridge, 108-40.

TAYLOUR, W.D. (1972), 'Excavations at Ayios Stephanos', BSA 67, 205-70.

TAYLOUR, W.D. (1975), AR, 15-17 (Ay. Stephanos).

THEMELIS, P.G. (1970), 'Archaic inscriptions from the sanctuary of Poseidon at Akovitika', AD 25A, 109-25 (Greek), 260f. (English summary).

THEOCHARIS, D.R. (1973), ed., Neolithic Greece, Athens.

THOMAS, C.G. (1970), 'A Mycenaean hegemony? A reconsideration', JHS 90, 184-92.

THOMAS, H.L. (1967), Near Eastern, Mediterranean and European Chronology: the Historical, Archaeological, Radiocarbon, Pollen-analytical and Geochronological Evidence, 2, Lund.

THOMPSON, M. et al. (1973), An Inventory of Greek Coin Hoards, New York.

THOMPSON, W.E. (1973), 'Observations on Spartan politics', RSA 3, 47-58.

THOMSON, G.D. (1961), Studies in Ancient Greek Society I. The Prehistoric Aegean, 3rd edn, London.

TIGERSTEDT, E.N. (1965, 1973), The Legend of Sparta in Classical Antiquity, 2, Stockholm.

TOD, M.N. (1948), A Selection of Greek Historical Inscriptions II. 403-323 B.C., Oxford.

TOD, M.N. and WACE, A.J.B. (1906), A Catalogue of the Sparta Museum, Oxford.

TOMLINSON, R.A. (1972), Argos and the Argolid, London.

TOYNBEE, A.J. (1913), 'The growth of Sparta', JHS 33, 246-75.

TOYNBEE, A.J. (1969), Some Problems of Greek History, Oxford.

TREU, M. (1968), 'Alkman', RE Supp. XI, 19-29.

TREVES, P. (1944), 'The problem of a history of Messenia', JHS 64, 102-6.

UNDERHILL, G.E. (1900), A Commentary on the Hellenica of Xenophon, Oxford.

VALMIN, M.N. (1930), Etudes topographiques sur la Messénie ancienne, Lund.

VANSINA, J. (1973), Oral Tradition. A Study in Historical Methodology, 2nd edn, Harmondsworth.

VENTRIS, M.G.F. and CHADWICK, J. (1973), Documents in Mycenaean Greek, 2nd edn, Cambridge.

VERMEULE, E.T. (1964), Greece in the Bronze Age, Chicago and London (reprinted with supplementary bibliography in 1972).

VERNANT, J.-P. (1971), Mythe et pensée chez les Grecs: études de psychologie historique, 2, Paris.

VERNANT, J.-P. (1974), Mythe et société en Grèce ancienne, Paris.

VICKERY, K.F. (1936), Food in Early Greece, Urbana.

VIDAL DE LA BLACHE, P. (1926), Principles of Human Geography, ed. E. Martonne, London.

VIDAL-NAQUET, P. (1968), 'The black hunter and the origin of the Athenian ephebeia', PCPhS 14, 49-64. See also AUSTIN, M.M. (1977).

VITA-FINZI, C. (1969), The Mediterranean Valleys. Geological Changes in Historical Times, Cambridge.

VITALIS, G. (1930), Die Entwicklung der Sage von der
Rueckkehr der Herakliden, untersucht im Zusammenhang mit
der politischen Geschichte des Peloponnes bis auf den
ersten Messenischen Krieg, dissertation, Greifswald.
VOGT, J. (1975), Ancient Slavery and the Ideal of Man,
Oxford.
WACE, A.J.B. (1957), 'Mycenae 1939-1956. The chronology of
Late Helladic IIIB', BSA 52, 220-3.
WACE, A.J.B. and BLEGEN, C.W. (1939), 'Pottery as evidence
for trade and colonisation in the Aegean Bronze Age', Klio
32, 131-47.
WACE, A.J.B. and HASLUCK, F.W. (1908), 'South-eastern
Laconia', BSA 14, 161-82.
WACE, A.J.B. and HASLUCK, F.W. (1909), 'East-central Lac-
onia', BSA 15, 158-76.
See also TOD, M.N. (1906).
WADE-GERY, H.T. (1949), 'A note on the origin of the Spar-
tan Gymnopaidiai', CQ 43, 79-81.
WADE-GERY, H.T. (1958), Essays in Greek History, Oxford.
WADE-GERY, H.T. (1966),'The "Rhianos-hypothesis"', in
Ancient Society and Institutions. Studies Presented to V.
Ehrenberg on his 75th Birthday, ed. E. Badian, Oxford,
289-302.
WADE-GERY, V. (1930), JHS 50, 146-50 (review of AO).
WAGSTAFF, J.M. (1975), 'A note on settlement numbers in
ancient Greece', JHS 95, 163-8.
WALBANK, F.W. (1957, 1967), A Historical Commentary on
Polybius, 2, Oxford.
WALLACE, W.P. (1954), 'Kleomenes, Marathon, the Helots and
Arcadia', JHS 74, 32-5.
WARREN, P.M. (1969), Minoan Stone Vases, Cambridge.
WEINSTEIN, A. and GATELL, F.O. (1973), American Negro
Slavery. A Modern Reader, 2nd edn, New York.
WELWEI, K.-W. (1974, 1977), Unfreie im antiken Kriegs-
dienst I. Athen und Sparta. II. Die kleineren und mitt-
leren griechischen Staaten und die hellenistischen Reiche,
Wiesbaden.
WEST, M.L. (1965), 'Alcmanica I. The date of Alcman', CQ
15, 188-202.
WEST, M.L. (1969), 'Stesichorus redivivus', ZPE 4, 135-49.
WESTLAKE, H.D. (1968), Individuals in Thucydides, Man-
chester.
WESTLAKE, H.D. (1969), Essays on the Greek Historians and
Greek History, Manchester.
WESTLAKE, H.D. (1974), 'The naval battle at Pylos and its
consequences', CQ 24, 211-26.
WESTLAKE, H.D. (1977), 'Thucydides on Pausanias and Them-
istocles - a written source?', CQ 27, 95-110.
WHITE, K.D. (1967), 'Latifundia', BICS 14, 62-79.

WHITE, K.D. (1970), Roman Farming, London.
WHITE, M.E. (1964), 'Some Agiad dates: Pausanias and his sons', JHS 84, 140-52.
WHITTEN, D.G.A. and BROOKS, J.R.V. (1972), The Penguin Dictionary of Geology, Harmondsworth.
WHORF, B.L. (1956), Language, Thought and Reality, ed. J.B. Carroll, New York and London.
WIDE, S. (1893), Lakonische Kulte, Leipzig.
WILL, E. (1956), Doriens et Ioniens. Essai sur la valeur du critère ethnique appliqué à l'étude de l'histoire et de la civilisation grecque, Paris.
WILL, E. (1966-7), Histoire politique du monde hellénistique, 2, Nancy.
WILL, E. (1972), Le Monde grec et l'orient I. Le Ve siècle (510-403), Paris.
WILL, E. (1975), Le Monde grec et l'orient II. Le IVe siècle et l'époque hellénistique (with C. Mossé and P. Goukowsky), Paris.
WILLEMSEN, F. (1977), 'Zu den Lakedaemoniergraebern im Kerameikos', AM 92, 117-57.
WILLETTS, R.F. (1967), The Law Code of Gortyn, Berlin.
WILLETTS, R.F. (1977), The Civilization of Ancient Crete, London.
WILLIAMS, R.T. (1965), The Confederate Coinage of the Arcadians in the Fifth Century B.C., New York.
WISEMAN, J. (1965), 'Greece and early Greeks', Arion 4, 700-20.
WISEMAN, J. (1969), 'Epaminondas and the Theban invasion', Klio 51, 177-99.
WOODWARD, A.M. (1907), 'Taenarum and S. Maina', BSA 13, 238-67.
WOODWARD, A.M. (1950), Historia 1, 616-34 (review of Chrimes 1949).
WREDE, W. (1927), 'Archaeologische Funde in den Jahren 1926-1927', AA, 365.
WRIGHT, H.E., Jr. (1968), 'Climatic change in Mycenaean Greece', Antiquity 42, 123-7.
WRIGHT, H.E., Jr. (1972), 'Vegetation history', in MME 188-99.
YAVIS, C.G. (1949), Greek Altars: Origins and Typology. An Archaeological Study in the History of Religion, St Louis.
ZIEHEN, L. (1933), 'Das spartanische Bevoelkerungs-problem', Hermes 68, 218-37.

Index

Toponyms are listed under their ancient form, where this is known, with the modern name in brackets where the identification is secure. For an alphabetical listing of the modern names of archaeological sites in Lakonia and Messenia readers are referred to Appendix 1.

of (c.465), 214, 216
dogs, hunting (Lakonian
hounds), see Sparta/
Spartans
Dorians, 99, 106, 111, 114,
121, 126, 139, 204, 230,
359; character, 77, 100;
dialect, 23, 77-9, 96,
102, 239, 240, 243;
migration, 56, 75, 77-88,
93-4, 94-5, 100, 101,
104, 118, 133, 152, 168,
320-1; tribes, 93; see
also Doris; Herakleidai;
Karneia
Dorieus (Agiad prince), 143,
144, 145-6, 207, 309
Doris, supposed Dorian homeland, 93, 227
drought, annual summer, 25,
26
'dual hegemony' thesis, 220,
221, 226, 230, 236, 242,
292
Dymanes, see Dorians, tribes

earthquakes, 17, 336; see
also Lakonia
Egypt, 60-1, 71, 120, 137,
244, 260, 317
Einstein, Albert, 256
Eleians/Elis: democracy,
215; and Sparta: ally,
127, 138, 139, 258, 301;
hostile to, 201, 205,
249, 250, 252, 271, 275,
277, 295-6, 297; see also
Triphylia
Eleusinion (Kalyvia tis
Sochas), 191, 233
Eleusis (in Attika), 49, 270
Eleutherolakonian League,
see Leagues
environment, possibilities
of, 11, 22, 24
Epameinondas (Theban):
invasions of Lakonia,
149, 152, 296-8, 302;

liberation of Messenians,
128, 298-9; victories,
294, 302
Ephesos, 277
Ephors, at Thera, 108; see
also Sparta/Spartans,
Ephorate/Ephors
Ephorus of Kyme, 56, 76,
113, 129, 140, 166; and
Helots, 348-9, 350; see
also Diodorus Siculus, as
historian
Epic Cycle, 52-3
Epidauros (in Argolis),
Spartan ally, 238, 243,
252, 253, 258, 298
Epidauros Limera (Epidauros
Limera): historical, 15,
86, 141, 181, 189, 190,
245, 259, 322; prehistor-
ic, 41, 44, 45, 66, 68,
70
Epirus, 62, 93
Epitadeus (Spartiate),
alleged rhetra of, 167-8,
316, 318, 319
epiteichismos, 229, 239,
243, 249, 258, 259;
Kythera, 243-5, 248, 249,
258, 263, 283-4, 285,
303; near Onougnathos,
259; Pylos, 240-3, 263;
see also Dekeleia
Erasinos, river (in Argolis),
149, 192
Eratosthenes of Cyrene, 54,
56, 59, 102, 346
Eretria, 151, 210
Erythrai, 283
Eua (Helleniko), 112, 189
Euagoras (Spartiate), 233
Euaiphnos (Spartan), 115
Eualkes (Perioikos), 257,
313
Euboia/Euboians, 191, 238;
and Athens, 147, 229,
263; and western coloniz-
ation, 102, 103, 114
Eunomos (alleged Eurypontid